Law of Defamation in Commonwealth Africa

JILL COTTRELL
Faculty of Law
University of Hong Kong

Routledge
Taylor & Francis Group
LONDON AND NEW YORK

First published 1998 by Dartmouth and Ashgate Publishing

Reissued 2018 by Routledge
2 Park Square, Milton Park, Abingdon, Oxon OX14 4RN
711 Third Avenue, New York, NY 10017, USA

Routledge is an imprint of the Taylor & Francis Group, an informa business

A Library of Congress record exists under LC control number: 97038535

ISBN 13: 978-1-138-32304-9 (hbk)
ISBN 13: 978-0-429-45162-1 (ebk)

Contents

Preface

Defamation is an area of the law in which there is, in most Commonwealth African countries, quite vigorous activity. Indeed, this was true of many traditional societies, too. This book deals mainly with the common law, that is the English system imported as part of the colonial baggage into most of these countries. It discusses cases from almost all the countries suggested by its title. There are however, none from Mozambique, which is a civil law country recently admitted to the Commonwealth, few from South Africa and only one from Cameroon.

Nigeria is more prominently represented than the other countries simply because of its own size and of the number of reported cases. This began as a Nigerian book, but I have expanded it because I believe that lawyers, and students, and the media, may find the experience of other African countries useful or at least interesting, and because there is all too little literature which encourages South-South cross-fertilisation.

African courts refer very often to English precedent, and to the "bible" of the law of defamation *Gatley on Libel and Slander*. I too owe that book a great debt; many of the cases I cite I have learned of from the pages of that book and cite it so often that I simply refer to "Gatley" and the paragraph number in the current, eighth edition (London: Sweet and Maxwell, 1981). I have tried to refer to almost all of the cases of which I am aware, in the jurisdictions which are my main focus; though many of them serve simply as illustrations, in the absence of comprehensive reference materials it may be useful for readers to be aware of their existence.

I hope that this book may be of use to legal practitioners in the common law African countries and to teachers, students and even the media. It is mainly a "black-letter" analysis of the law. However, this topic is intensely sociological and also political, so the ways in which the law of defamation is used in Africa may be of interest to scholars in other disciplines.

The book is in a sense an expression of my gratitude for 10 happy years in Nigeria, now many years ago; I should like to feel that at least some of the friends, colleagues and students of those days might find some interest in this book which has taken so long to appear.

Other debts include to the Bodleian Law Library in Oxford which now houses unreported cases originally collected by Dr Alan Milner for the

African Law Reports, and the libraries of the School of Oriental and African Studies and the Institute of Advanced Legal Studies in London (virtually all the cases were found in one of these three libraries). I am grateful to my current institution, the University of Hong Kong, for its facilities, especially the computers. And, although I have done most of the typing myself on that equipment, I am grateful to the staff of the Faculty of Law, especially Miss Rita Wai Wai-min and Ms Veronica Yiu Mau-ping for shouldering some of the most boring secretarial tasks involved. For encouragement, and helpful suggestions, I thank Abdul Paliwala of the University of Warwick, and, particularly, Yash Ghai, who has constantly urged "finish your book".

Jill Cottrell
Hong Kong
August 1997

A note on Nigeria

Nigeria presents a terminological problem due to its federal structure and the periodic creation of additional states. The law of torts is a matter for state legislative power. Some of the old regions adopted a piece of legislation modelled on the English Defamation Act of 1952. The Northern Region did not. That region has been progressively split up since 1967 and there are now 16 states where the Northern monolith used to be: Adamawa, Bauchi, Benue, Borno, Jigawa, Kaduna, Kano, Katsina, Kebbi, Kogi, Kwara, Niger, Plateau, Sokoto, Taraba and Yobe. The former Western Region adopted its own Defamation Law; that Law was inherited by the Mid-Western Region created in 1964, later known as Bendel. There are now six states where once there were the Western and Mid-Western States: Delta, Edo, Ogun, Ondo, Osun, Oyo. The former Eastern Region also had a Law: now that of Abia, Anambra, Awka-lbom, Cross River, Enugu, Imo, and Rivers. That leaves Lagos, which also had its own law, originally as the Federal Capital Territory and then as a state. The new Federal Capital Territory, Abuja, applies the law applying there before the creation of the FCT - Decree No. 6 of 1976, s. 13. One can refer to the Northern states, Western states and so on. But this is to perpetuate the very divisions which the creation of states was to eliminate. Unfortunately, it is not possible to refer to the Nigerian Law in an omnibus fashion because they are not identical; I have therefore referred to Abia etc., when referring to the former Eastern Region and Delta etc. when referring to the former Western/Mid-Western Regions.

Table of Cases

Note: the cases are arranged by country: Africa first then others. African cases are arranged under current names of the countries. West African or East African Court of Appeal cases come under the country of origin of the case. Privy Council cases from jurisdictions not otherwise listed are included under United Kingdom. European institutions come under that heading. Law report abbreviations which may be obscure appear after the name of the country.

Mauritius

Note: "Mauritius Digest"refers to G. Laloutte, *Mauritus Digest* (Mauritus Publishing Co., Port-Louis, nd)

Reports; HCNLR=*High Court of Nigeria Law Reports*; Imo *SLR*=*Imo State Law Reports*; LLR=*Lagos Law Reports*; LRN=*Law Reports of Nigeria*; MNCyclLR(Begho's Judgments)= *Mid-Western State Law Reports (Begho J's decisions)* (published by himself); MWSNLR=*Mid-Western State of Nigeria Law Reports*; NCLR=*North Central State Law Reports*; NNLR=*Northern Nigeria Law Reports*; NSNLR=*Northern States of Nigeria Law Reports; NMLR*=*Nigerian Monthly Law Reports*; NWLR=*Nigerian Weekly Law Reports*; PLR=*Plateau Law Reports*, *QLRN*=*Quarterly Law Reports of Nigeria*; Ogun SLR=*Ogun State Law Reports*; Ondo SLR=*Ondo State Law Reports*; OySHC=*Oyo State High Court*; SC=*Supreme Court (cyclostyled)*; *SCNJ*=*Supreme Court of Nigeria Judgments*; SelJ Ondo SHC=*Selected Judgments of Ondo State High Courts*; TWLR= *The Weekly Law Reports*; WRNLR=*Western Region of Nigeria Law Reports*; *WNLR*=*Western Nigeria Law Reports*; WSCA=*Western State Court of Appeal*; *UILR*=*University of Ife Law Reports*

Note: "Fawehinmi" refers to Fawehinmi, G., *Nigerian Law of Libel and the Press* (Lagos: Nigerian Law Publishers, 1987); "Chukura, 1974" refers to Chukura, Olisa, *Digest of Nigerian Case Law 1991-1968* (Ibadan: Gillford); "Chukura, 1981" refers to the same author's *Privy Council Judgments: Opinions of the Judicial Committee of the Privy Council in Appeals from West Africa 1841-1973* (Ibadan: Gillford)

South Africa

Abbreviations: AD=*Appellate Division*; EDL=*Eastern District Local Division*; NAC=*Native Appeal Court*; NLR=*Natal Law Reports*; OPD=*Orange Free State Provincial Division*; TH=*Reports of Witwatersrand High Court*; TPD=*Transvaal Provincial Division*; WLD=*Witwatersrand Local Division*

Tanzania (contd.)

Uganda

Abbreviations CLB=EA or EALR=*East African Court of Appeal Reports*; HCB=*High Court Bulletin*; KA Commonwealth Law Bulletin; LR=*Kampala Law Reports*; Ug Prot LR=*Uganda Protectorate Law Reports*

Note: Veitch refers to Veitch, E., *East African Cases on the Law of Tort*, (London: Sweet & Maxwell, 1972)

United Kingdom (contd.)

United Kingdom (contd.)

United Kingdom (contd.)

United Kingdom (contd.)

United Kingdom (contd.)

Table of Statutes and Subsidiary Legislation

[Note: page number in italics indicates extended quotation; * indicates reproduced in Appendix]

1 Introduction

> An effective way of punishing a person guilty of slander of serious consequences, is to make him walk through the town or village carrying a heavy stone in front of an officer of the court, who, at convenient halting-places, beats a gong: the guilty slanderer is compelled to recant his base falsehoods, and to confess his disgraceful behaviour, amid the sneers and jeers of the multitude.
> Sarbah (1904a), quoted in *Kwaku v Addo* (Ghana 1957) p. 310.

Against this vivid picture of liability for defamation in one African society we can place the cases which form the main focus of this book. These are civil cases under the imposed law, especially the common law imported from England, and the defamer will be required to pay a sum of money supposed to reflect the damage to the defamed; the affair is treated as a matter between the parties, not a community concern as in Fanti society; most strikingly, the civil law of defamation does little to require the recantation of defamatory statements.

Neither judges nor commentators feel as much satisfaction with the common law as Sarbah seemed to feel about customary law. In 1987 the Nigerian Law Reform Commission recommended that states should enact legislation incorporating the major changes in the English statutes, with one or two further changes, and that in the long run the law ought to be codified. The Ghanaian Law Reform Commission produced a report, and the Zambian Commission a working paper, but none of these has resulted in legislation.[1]

The Essential Nature of Defamation Law

The law of defamation is, of course, about words (though gestures, symbols and images may equally convey meaning; as may drumming "to the Akan, the drum can and does speak" - Nketia (1963) quoted by Kanyoke, 1973). In Africa the word retains much power, whether in the form of witchcraft, or divination, oral history, or praise-singing, or singing as a form of social control (see Roberts, 1979, p. 60 citing Bohannan, 1957, pp. 142-4).[2] Among the Dinka, indeed, what looks like defamation in the form of song may be almost a compliment,

> Nobody wastes time or trouble on criticising a poor man or a person of low status in a song. You look very important or noble when many people tend to criticise you, whether rightly or wrongly (Makec, 1988, p. 213).

West African chiefs spoke through "linguists", rather than directly to their subjects - as though their words were so precious that they were not to be wasted on ordinary people. In some Ghanaian societies public announcements, and accusations, were made by the "gong beater", and sometimes this itself gives rise to litigation. In 1845 and as recently as 1981 plaintiffs complained that gong-gong beaters accused them of stealing the defendant's sheep (*Mensah v Quamina Attopi* (1845), *Bogya v Baokye* (1981))! In *Ackah Essah of Bomuapelly v Anuah Sofo of Tandan* (1974) the plaintiff was a chief's linguist, and sued the defendant wanting to know why he had "so recklessly and frivolously" sworn the oath "Ehanu" against the plaintiff.

Words may have three types of (injurious) impacts on the person about whom they are spoken. They may have measurable financial consequences, they may injure his or her reputation, and they may be hurtful to the feelings of that person. Concepts of society, and of the individual's place in society - of the nature of "self" - will have profound effects upon how words are viewed. The common law has carved out from the universe of words and their impact on individuals those which injure reputation and labelled them "defamation". It excludes statements about ancestors, certain sorts of insults, remarks in the absence of anyone except the two actors. Most systems of customary law would find this demarcation quite incomprehensible.

What is reputation? Is it something which is of intrinsic value, so that any loss or risk of loss should be actionable? Or is it valuable because of the benefits it brings - or more likely because of the detriment its loss may cause - more like a piece of property? Does its value lie in one's own sense of satisfaction in having it? Even the concept of being thought well of, or in the case of defamation being thought less of, leaves room for doubt. Will you be esteemed less only because of what you yourself are responsible for, or will things beyond your control, such as illness or background, damage your reputation? The common law, as we shall see, has no very clear answer to these questions.[3]

One writer (Post, 1986) has related different conceptions of reputation to different types of society:

> The concept of reputation as dignity...presupposes a particular kind of society, a social world that I shall call a "communitarian society".

> Communitarian societies and market societies have in common the concept of equality. Just as in market societies all persons are equally subordinated to the market, so in communitarian societies all persons are equally eligible for inclusion within the community. In most other respects, however, market and communitarian societies are radically different. In market societies individuals create their reputation; in communitarian societies individuals are in a very important sense created by their reputation. In market societies reputation is a private good; in communitarian societies it is both a private and public good....

One might broadly equate traditional African societies with the "communitarian" and modern European society (and modern African society) with "market" societies - though one must be careful not to exaggerate the differences.

In England, this area of the law may reflect popular views more readily than any other, for it is the one civil field in which jury trial is still common. But until recently the jury could not really reflect the community, being, in Devlin's famous words, "predominately male, middle-aged, middle-minded and middle-class" (1956, p. 20). The potential effect of jury trial is to impose upon minorities the value-judgments of the majority, as is the effect of the rule that there is no defamation if only a section of society would think less of a person of whom the statement in issue was made (see Chapter 6). And the judges have the power to take away from the jury the decision if they hold that the words *cannot* be defamatory - which may tend to impose upon the majority the value judgments of the minority to which judges belong. How does that work in African jurisdictions, which do not have jury trials and which are generally heterogenous in ethnic and often in religious terms?[4] What is "the community" for the purposes of the law of defamation?

Who Sues and Why?

This book does not attempt an empirical study of who brings defamation actions and for what in Commonwealth Africa.[5] The analysis of why people might sue in defamation needs to be rather different from that which is appropriate in, for example, personal injury litigation. There can be no possible way of assessing the value of a reputation (unless damages are restricted to compensation for financially measurable things like loss of employment). In England, it sometimes seems, a defamation action can be the occasion not so much for compensation as for a windfall (see e.g. Littleton, 1991). The heavy damages awarded by juries in certain cases against the popular press would seem to have a denunciatory function, and possibly reflect condemnation not of the specific litigated statement, but of press practices more generally. This is less true in African jurisdictions where there is no jury, although certain judicial dicta reflect similar concerns.

Deterrence is obviously one of the major supposed functions of defamation. Indeed, the assumption of freedom of speech attacks on defamation is that it deters rather more than simply defamatory statements. Exemplary damages, if awardable, will increase the deterrent effect (see Chapter 19). To the limited extent that it is possible to obtain an injunction to restrain the impending publication of something on the basis that it is defamatory, the law is also preventive (Chapter 20).

Can the law achieve correction, that is to undo what was done? In the common law system this has not been a traditional possibility, but there are some incentives to publishing apologies and corrections by statutory provisions that reduce damages or even provide a defence to the press if a correction has been published, and there has been something of a modern trend in favour of such relief. Psychological satisfaction for the plaintiff looms larger in defamation than most other torts (Tunc, nd, p. 96, citing Williams, 1951, pp. 138-40). An interesting finding of empirical research in the US is that plaintiffs care more about vindication than about money (Bezanson, 1985). Perhaps, therefore, an observation of Dr Danquah in Ghana is overstated:

> The delicate feelings of the average African are not half so blunted and atrophied as those of the average European (1928p. xxiii).

Litigants may have other, less obvious, agenda (as we are reminded by Brown (1992)): plaintiffs may hope to discredit their political opponents, or put publications of which they disapprove out of business, or stop investigative journalism. In some instances it is hard to believe that "show-business" personalities have any motive other than to put themselves further in the public eye. Even less public figures may be driven by a wish to hurt a long-standing adversary, rather than to vindicate, or receive compensation for, a wounded reputation. One writer, observing that in Uganda in the early years of independence plaintiffs in defamation cases were overwhelmingly politicians and other public figures - and defendants were usually newspapers, suggested:

> the practice of using the more recent English cases, arising from different political and social conditions and based on the role of law as merely protecting

the reputations of private individuals, may not be suitable to Uganda where the law of defamation may be required to do more. That is to say, it is clear that politicians and holders of public office feel that any aspersions cast against them must be vindicated by legal action and that rumour, having the unsettling power it does in Africa, must be combatted by the use of the law of civil defamation (Veitch, 1971).

A Social Importance?

Is it entirely true, even in England, that the role of law is merely that of protecting individual reputations, as assumed by Veitch? It can be argued that society has an interest in encouraging high standards of journalism; if the press has little incentive to report accurately, will it not be discredited in the eyes of the public and unable to perform a valuable role in holding institutions accountable? It is sometimes said that removal of protection of reputation would be a disincentive to people to enter public or political life (e.g. Bellah, 1986, p. 744). A judge in Mauritius once said,

> Men do not lightly add political duties to their daily avocations, already sufficiently arduous. There will be fewer still if they are made the subject of ridicule, invective and abuse by those who do not agree with them (Piggott Ag. CJ in *Ritter v Newton* (1896) p. 93).

On the other hand, a Singapore writer observed,

> One would have thought that they would be made of sterner stuff. Moreover, the picture is not complete. It fails to show that if less than honourable men gain public office, the public may never know their true colours without a firm protection of speech concerning public affairs (Hor, 1992, p. 555).[6]

The last chapter returns briefly to this question of the tension between competing social interests.

The African Context

Because most of the material in this book is imposed law - and mostly the English-derived law - it is necessarily skewed: towards urban, English-speaking (or in a few instances French-speaking) segments of society, and the disputes which they generate. But Africa is not African only when it is traditional; nor is this solely because the influence of village and traditional community is still felt in the city - true as this may be. Society, identity, language, reputation, disputes are all affected by social context. Ethnicity is a real factor in African politics and African senses of identity. That English (or French) is the language of a minority, that illiteracy is common and poverty endemic, corruption and dependency are all part of most African realities. In many countries there has been at least a rhetoric of specifically African ideologies - African socialism in Tanzania, humanism in Zambia. In almost all Commonwealth African countries there has been the reality of the one-party state, whether *de jure* or not, and in many the experience of military rule - with the correlative absence of democracy in both. The ownership of the press by government or party in most countries, the absence of non-government radio and television - these are important political contexts of speech and therefore of defamation. Socially there is a tradition of polygamy (usually polygyny); the reality of the extended family; and respect for elders. A widespread characteristic of traditional African societies was a belief in sorcery and witchcraft: "In Malaŵi, witchcraft is not an obsession, but merely a daily danger that must be faced, like the possibility of an automobile accident" (Brietzke, 1972, p. 17). The position of women is not by any means identical in all African societies, but is generally not strong: though there are powerful women traders especially in West Africa and generally in the continent women do most of the farming, they have few property rights, they have little political power (there has been no woman African head of government, for example); there are very few women parties to the cases in this book. The existence in many countries of written constitutions and guarantees of fundamental rights including freedom of speech forms an element in the legal context (see Chapter 22), as also do the tensions created by the relationship between the judiciary and the state (a matter of especial relevance if defamation has political dimensions[7]).

Law in Africa

The principal focus of this book is upon common law systems - which means upon the Commonwealth countries of sub-Saharan Africa. However, there are a few cases from Sudan, which is not Commonwealth and only partially sub-Saharan, from Seychelles and Mauritius which, while Commonwealth countries, are not part of continental Africa, and which generally apply French law as much as English[8] (and just one case from Cameroon - sub-Saharan and only partly ex-British colony[9]). And there are some cases from the Roman-Dutch countries of Southern Africa - though few from South Africa which has a substantial legal literature of its own, and which was not part of the Commonwealth when most of the writing of this book was done.

The Table shows the applicable laws of the various countries, so far as defamation is concerned.

The Systems of Law in African Countries

Country	"European" system	Others
Botswana	Roman-Dutch/English	Customary
Gambia	English	Customary/Islamic
Ghana	English	Customary
Kenya	English	Customary (Islamic)
Lesotho	Roman-Dutch/English	Customary
Malaŵi	English	Customary/Islamic
Mauritius	French (English)	
Namibia	Roman-Dutch/English	Customary
Nigeria	English	Customary
Seychelles	English	
Sierra Leone	English	Customary/Islamic
Sudan	English	Islamic/Customary
Swaziland	Roman-Dutch/English	Customary
Tanzania	English	Customary/Islamic
Uganda	English	Customary
Zambia	English	Customary
Zimbabwe	Roman-Dutch/English	Customary
[South Africa	Roman-Dutch	Customary]

Of course to say that "English law" applies in most of these countries is not to say that the law is identical, but, to anticipate remarks in the final chapter, it is not markedly different. One hypothesis would be that the rules suit African society just as they presumably suit English society - or at least suit the litigating elite. Another hypothesis would be that the law discussed in this book represents only part of the entire legal scene - and a small part at that - and that a great mass of law activity goes on somewhere else, whether in an alternative system of courts provided by the state, or in a non-state legal system. Thirdly, it is possible that the law is not inevitably a reflection of economic and other reality, but that it does have some autonomy from economy and society. If that is true, and when the origin of law is the same for a number of countries, then one might expect that law to be similar across countries, even though their economic and political systems may differ considerably.

From this perspective, any departure from English rules on the part of the African courts becomes a matter of some significance. Such departures may represent a deliberate attempt by the legal profession and the judiciary to shape rules appropriate to society as they view it; or an attempt by the judiciary to legitimate the law - and therefore themselves - in the eyes of a government and a society which would otherwise be somewhat suspicious of them; they may represent errors - in other words the lawyers and the judges just get the rules wrong, a risk which is particularly real with a very technical body of rules such as that with which this book deals.

The Media in Africa[10]

The importance of the press for the functioning of democracy - in the provision of information and the holding of government up to scrutiny - means that the potential impact upon the press is the most significant aspect of the law of defamation.[11] General Babangida, then military ruler of Nigeria, observed

> [A]n informed public opinion coupled with an enlightened citizenry constitute an essential prerequisite for the attainment of a progressive and stable state. Such an informed and enlightened populace could evolve more quickly through media unhindered in the performance of their duties (*West Africa* Feb. 9 1987, quoted by Maja-Pearce, 1991, pp. 85-6)

Unfortunately such a positive view of the media has not characterised most African governments (including that of General Babangida[12]).

Colonial governments viewed newspapers with suspicion, and hardly laid a firm foundation for a free press in independent Africa. The laws of sedition were both stricter than those in England (see the famous case of *Wallace-Johnson v R* (Ghana 1945)) and more frequently invoked.[13]

But the history of the press in independent Africa has been no happier, for both political and economic reasons. In many African countries there have been few newspapers, in some no daily paper at all (Maja-Pearce, 1990; Article 19, 1991; Ziegler & Asante, 1992). The parlous economic condition of Africa over the last decade or so has also had its impact upon the press; newsprint is a precious commodity, requiring foreign exchange, and it is often extremely expensive (Konde, 1984, p. 84 gives some figures). African newspapers are often small, as well as few, in consequence of these problems.

Literacy rates are low (ranging from 30% to 75%). Moreover, most of the major newspapers are English (or French) language publications. There are vernacular papers, but on the whole they are not where the elite looks for its news - reflected in the fact that few of the cases in this book are against such papers. A far higher proportion of the population listens to the radio and much more of this is in the vernacular languages, typically. But there are very few cases against these other media.

Government and the Media

The press has been very often government owned, with consequences hardly to be wondered at.[14] In 1965 the *Ghanaian Times* (quoted in Furinger, 1991, p. 47) said,

> Our socialist society cannot, and would not, tolerate any publication of any newspaper in Ghana which departs from the ideology and loyalties demanded from the press and society of Nkrumahist Ghana. Under these circumstances, there cannot be any real difference in fundamental views between the *Graphic*, the *Times* and the *Evening News*.

(Evidently times had changed: during colonial times Nkrumah had spent considerable time and money on libel suits against the *Evening News* (*ibid.*, p. 18).)

In Zambia in 1981 the Minister of State for Information and Broadcasting apparently encouraged a graduating class of journalists in these terms:

> Don't bite the hand that feeds you in the name of a free press. You may end up without a job...there is no such thing as a free press, it is an illusion, a creation of journalists (Article 19, above, p. 59).

The Tanzanian government took over the *Standard* newspapers in 1970. The President gave the newspapers a "Charter":

> The new "Standard" will be free to criticize any particular acts of individuals in TANU [the ruling party] and Government leaders, and publicize any failures in the [East African] Community by whomsoever they are committed. It will be free to criticize the implementation of agreed policies, either on its own initiative or following complaints or suggestions from its readers.
>
> The New Standard will aim at supplying its readers with all the domestic and world news as quickly and fully as possible. It will be run on the basis that a newspaper only keeps the trust of its readers, and only deserves their trust, if it

reports the truth to the best of its ability and without distortion, whether that truth is pleasant or unpleasant (quoted from *Eyakuze v Editor of Sunday News* (1974) p. 217).

The newspaper tried to rely on this Charter in a defamation action, and it was held that it gave them no protection if what they published was untrue (*ibid*). Interestingly, however, the judge did say that he assumed that as a publicly owned newspaper the defendants were not motivated by the desire for profit (which would presumably have incurred the risk of exemplary damages).

Colonial traditions have suited independent governments only too well, including the tradition of requiring licences to publish (e.g. Lagos State Newspapers Law, Kenyan Books and Newspapers Act Cap. 111). (In one Nigerian defamation case the ingenious argument was raised that the plaintiff must fail because he had not proved that the registration requirements of the law had been complied with. The argument was given short shrift (*Asiodu v Abodunde* (1979).) In some countries, there is a provision, ostensibly in the interests of potential libel plaintiffs, and employees, requiring a deposit to be placed with the authorities (e.g. Mauritius Newspaper and Periodical (Amendment) Act No. 13 of 1984, s. 5, Nigerian Newspapers Act 1964, s. 3, Kenyan Books and Newspapers Act Cap. 111 s. 11).

The press may be harassed by prosecution, (see e.g. Africa Watch, 1990, p. 80; Mukale, 1986, p. 26); some journalists have been physically assaulted or even killed by government agents (to take just one example, a human rights lawyer brought a private prosecution against two army officers for killing a Nigerian journalist (Fawehinmi, 1988).[15]

In the case of radio and television there is censorship of reports unfavourable to government (e.g. Agbaje, 1992, p. 103), aided by universal government ownership. In 1965 Tanzania turned Radio Dar es Salaam from a statutory corporation into a department of government, and its staff became civil servants, to strengthen government (and party) control (Mytton, 1983, p. 102).

Democratic revival brings, however, new papers, and fresh hopes of independence of the press. In the Ghanaian Constitution, passed in 1992, there is a whole Chapter devoted to Freedom and Independence of the Media. For example, "there shall be no law requiring any person to obtain a licence as a prerequisite to the establishment or operation of a newspaper" (Art. 162 (3)). It provides that editors and publishers are to be free from government control, that the media shall be free to uphold the "responsibility and accountability of the Government to the people of Ghana", and interestingly, a right of reply for those against whom statements are published (art. 162 (4), (5), (6)). There is a National Media Commission to promote the freedom of the media and to insulate even state-owned media from government control (art. 176). Registration of newspapers is to continue under regulations made by the Commission.

Governments and Defamation

After the first coup in Ghana in 1966 the military government took over the national press. But fearing the financial commitment which might follow libel actions from the Nkrumah period it passed a decree barring such actions, and abating any then pending. It followed this up with another decree equally barring litigation for post-coup statements (*Mercer v Guinea Press Ltd.* (1967)). The latter, the Newspapers Decree, (NLCD 107) provided:

> 1. Until such time as the National Liberation Council may determine, no action for defamation shall be brought against the owners, publishers or editors of the newspapers specified in paragraph 2 of this Decree without the *fiat* of the Attorney-General.
> 2. The newspapers referred to in the foregoing paragraph are newspapers owned or published by a corporation established under the Statutory Corporations Act 1964 (Act 232) or newspapers wholly or partially subsidised from public funds or newspapers which are managed by a board or other body appointed by the National Liberation Council.

That provision came before the court in *Mercer v Guinea Press*, brought against the defendants as printers of the *Evening News*. The plaintiffs pointed out that the *printers* were not mentioned, and here the publishers were also the printers. The judge explained the purpose of the legislation as being "to give the Attorney-General a chance of investigating such defamatory publications and if possible to settle such actions out of court thereby saving public funds" (p. 645), and construed the decree as barring the action, the only concession being that he declined to order the plaintiff to pay the defendants' costs, since the government was responsible for the obscure drafting in the first place.

One interesting African case comes from Rhodesia: after UDI but long before independence proper. The press sued the government for defamation: for alleging what the judge described as a fairly high degree of irresponsibility, namely slanted reporting, and deliberately publishing news calculated to undermine confidence in Rhodesia. The main thrust of the statements complained of was to justify censorship. The judge, Fieldsend J, held that the statements were defamatory, and that there was no defence of fair comment, since the government could not have believed that censorship was necessary to balance an unfair picture which the press would otherwise have painted (*Rhodesian Printing and Publishing Corpn. v Howman* (1967)); the judge did decline to award punitive damages.

Judicial Attitudes to the Press

It is difficult to extract any coherent attitude towards the role of the press from the cases, even in one country. But the most persistent theme has perhaps been that of the responsibilities of the press. On the whole judges have not stood up for a free press, despite constitutional guarantees of free speech and media.

> The courts...have been very strict against the newspapers and seem to have been willing to protect the public officers and the politicians regardless of the consequences this has had (Muburimusoke, 1978, p. 172).

The judges tend to say how important a free press is, and then go on to talk about the necessity for it to be "responsible", and hold it liable. To take an example from a case of sedition rather than defamation, but the sentiments are very much the same:

> Warning barks are always necessary to help maintain a free and healthy society...if a party or an individual would publish a paper or any matter, and it would contain no more than a dispassionate, calm and quiet discussion, allowing something for a little feeling in men's minds, that will certainly be no libel, but if the publication goes beyond that limit and be calculated to excite tumult, strife, hatred, contempt or ridicule then it is libel. The discussion in the press of political matters, measures and policies of Government cannot lawfully be made a cloak for an attack on private character (*IGP v Tarawally* (Gambia 1971)).

A court in Mauritius was rather cynical about the press:

> The expression "*liberté de la presse*" which is lavishly used appears to have given rise to a misconception. It means only this, that the press, which in the days of the old monarchy in France, had been so cleverly gagged, has in fact regained the unfettered right to use any language which is not prohibited by law, and especially to print and publish it (*Daurat v Le Cernéen* (1933) p. 18.)

> I am afraid that Buganda editors have hardly realized how difficult and responsible is the task of editing a newspaper (*Giles & Geeson v "The Ugandan News"* (1929) p. 247).

Also in Uganda,

> One naturally wishes to encourage such a laudable enterprise as a native newspaper and not cripple it, but it is essential to teach the lesson that while a newspaper's privileges are very great, so also are its responsibilities (Guthrie Smith J in *"Munyonyozi" (Publishers) v The Lukkiko of Buganda* (1923)).

Some judges have expressed concern about the potential for harm on the part of the press in a developing country:

> Zambian society is in a state of development of much less sophistication than that of England. Its two daily newspapers are in a very powerful position by reason of the fact that many persons are ignorant of their rights and many others are afraid to assert them (*Cobbett-Tribe v Zambia Publishing Co. Ltd.* (1973) p. 21)).

While in Nigeria a judge said

> Freedom of expression, a slogan that has become part of our armour and culture in this country, especially in journalistic circles, is not without its duty. If that freedom is to have any meaning the media practitioners must accept as its essential corollation [*sic*] a judicious exercise of that freedom in line with the tenets of other professions (*Omolowo v Punch Nigeria Ltd.* (1985) p. 1259).

And in another case Obi-Okoye CJ said

> Many articulate and uncommitted members of Nigerian society nowadays view with serious concern, the professional behaviours and ethical values of a number of media organs in this country...In the circumstances traditional or liberal journalism has become a thing of the past. In its place is substituted and enthroned partisan journalism in all its facets, so that many a practitioner or his organ of information is either adversary in one extreme or sycophantic in the other extreme (*Bulus v Suleiman* (1972)).

On the other hand, there have been some instances of the judiciary standing up to government in defence of the media[16] and of courts emphasising the role of the press in the unmasking of injustice and corruption - Ademola JCA in Nigeria said,

> The spectacle of the nosy journalist out to make his newspapers sell by scooping scandals that have crept into documents files in the Registry may be an ugly one, but in the light of a duty cast upon the press to inform the public about what is going on in public institutions, it qualifies in my view not for censure but for commendation (*Daily Times v Williams* (1986) p. 540).

Notes

1. Australia has agonised more than any other common law jurisdiction recently. New Zealand amended its law in 1992 while Ireland has also proposed significant changes - Law Reform Commission (1991). England has introduced recent changes including the Defamation Act 1996.
2. It would be interesting to understand the full context of the case in which the plaintiff complained that in the market the defendants "by a concerted action in unison falsely and maliciously published, by singing, of and concerning the plaintiff the following song in Ibo language...'Mgbafor Igḅa killed the Chief; she killed the Chief and should not live'" (*Nwankwo v Okeke)* (Nigeria 1980)).
3. Post (1986) explored three different meanings of "reputation", all of which have some reflection in the modern common law of defamation.
4. In Tanzania, where the case concerns libel in a newspaper, trial is supposed to be by judge sitting with three assessors, whose decision, unlike that of the jury in England, is not binding - Newspapers Act 1976 ss. 56-7.
5. However, there have been such studies elsewhere. An Australian study showed that elected office-holders and candidates, while being the largest single group, brought only 15% of the actions brought by individuals. Politicians were also the largest groups of non-media defendants. Politician-plaintiffs settled their actions more often than anyone else - suggesting that their threats to sue are "more likely to be bluster". When they settled or succeeded in their actions they did not do any better than, if as well as, other plaintiffs in financial terms. And non-politician plaintiffs are more likely to succeed at trial (Edgeworth & Newcity, 1992).
   In England, at national level at least, politicans rarely sue for statements about their conduct as such (Barendt, 1997, p. 69).
6. Fleming described arguments about discouraging people of honour as a "quaint survival of Victorian ethos" (1991, p. 348).
7. On the independence - or lack of independence - of the judiciary see Scotton (1970).
8. Though not in defamation in the case of Seychelles as we shall see. Mauritius, indeed, might be expected to have Hindu law as well but it is unusual to see

any reference to this in the literature, and I have come across none in connection with defamation.

9. Part of which was a French colony and part of which British - administered as part of Nigeria - after the first World War. The case is from West Cameroon - the Anglo-phone part: *Wilson v Ntoko* (1972).
10. See generally, as well as the items cited later, Wilcox (1982). There is a bibliography in Mytton (1983). Many issues of *Index on Censorship* contain information about the treatment of the press and other news media, and also the theatre in Africa.
11. The point is well, and concisely made by Feltoe (1993, p. 44).
12. The same year a government appointed body recommended against the privatisation of government owned media because this would mean passing them "to private, wealthy and powerful individuals..[whose].. interests are not synonymous [sc. with], and indeed are usually diametrically opposed to those of the people" *Report of the Political Bureau*, quoted by Karikari (1993, p. 59) himself quoting from Agbaje (1990).
13. Furinger (1991, p. 59) says that between 1945 and 1952 the sedition law was used in Kenya only 9 times; I should have thought that the use of "only" here was at best a matter of opinion!
14. Though see Ochieng (1992), not for a defence of Government but for an indictment of the press also.
15. The case was *Fawehinmi v Akilu* (1987). The publicity he gave to his prosecution gave the accused army officers the opportunity to sue him for libel! - see *Akilu v Fawehinmi* (1989). This report is limited to an interlocutory application, however, apparently ₦5,000,000 damages were awarded against Fawehinmi! See Chap. 19 below.
16. See *New Patriotic Party v Ghana Broadcasting Corporation* (1993) (unrep.): the Supreme Court declared it was unconstitutional for the Corporation to refuse to cover an opposition meeting (Ghartey (1994)). More remarkably, the same year in Nigeria, under a military regime, a judge ordered the police to leave the premises of a newspaper, and another declared the Decree under which onerous conditions were imposed on the press unconstitutional (Arogundade, 1994, p. 24).

2 Customary and Islamic Law

Introduction

Many studies of African customary law say little about anything except land and family law. This is partly because of perceptions about the economic importance of land, and of emphasis in the literature on the position of women which naturally leads to concentration on land and family matters. The limited attention paid to the law of words is regrettable: how people react to what is said about them surely offers an insight into the whole question of social identity. Where literature - and cases - do exist we come up against another problem: the extent to which what is now written of as "customary law" is a construct of the colonial period, even of the colonial state (among the considerable literature see Snyder, 1981; Charnock, 1985; Woodman, 1988)). This book offers limited insight into the customary law of statements, being based mainly upon reported cases, and not at all upon the limited records which may be kept of the proceedings of customary courts.[1]

The Law

Most societies did recognise injury to reputation as a wrong for which a remedy could be sought. Abel (1970, p. 28) indicated substantial rates of litigating about defamation in some societies: about 20% of "tort" cases among the Luyia and Luo. Among the Luo in Kenya and the Ashanti in Ghana, shame arising from defamation may even lead to suicide (Wilson 1967, p. 197, cited by McCullough, 1971, p. 227; Rattray, 1929, p. 326). Liability for defamatory statements was traditionally recognised in most of the societies of Tanzania (see e.g. *Tumanieli v Aisa d/o Issai*, (1969); *Herman v Ndava* (1971)), and of West Africa (for Ghana see *Kwaku v Addo* (1957), *Quacoe v Dadson* (1958) and Danquah, 1928, p. 253, including a number of cases which he describes as "defamation" involving allegations of improper sexual relations, witchcraft, and one that the plaintiff, a pastor, hated certain children). The same is true of the societies of Zimbabwe (Storry, 1979, pp. 76-6) and Zambia (*R v Hachoko* (1938-1942)). Some southern African societies did not consider protection of reputation to be a concern of the law (e.g. the Shangani, but contrast the Zulu and Xhosa: Burchell (1985) citing Code of Zulu Law s. 132(2) (Natal)); some other groups (like the Tswana, Venda, Pedi and Sotho) give a remedy in only limited circumstances (Burchell, p. 22; Becker, 1989, pp. 343-4).

Many societies penalised not only injury to reputation, but even injury to feelings. A judge in Ghana said,

> The society of England is different from the society of Ghana. In this country, where words of abuse are taken seriously, it would, in my opinion, be socially intolerable if customary law provided no sanctions against a man who finds pleasure in injuring the feelings of his neighbour by vituperation (Apaloo J in *Wankyiwaa v Wereduwaa* (1963) p. 335).

In the many societies where injury to feeling is sufficient, a statement to the plaintiff without any third party being present may be actionable. Words which the common law would dismiss as "mere abuse", having taken place in a quarrel and not to be taken as a serious attack on reputation, may give rise to liability. Abel (1970, p. 49) comments,

> In a small-scale society the man who is subjected to abuse may well suffer a greater loss of self-respect and of standing in the community than the man who is defamed

and points to the "vast number" of complaints about abuse in Kenyan courts as evidence.

The significance of community runs throughout African "defamation" law. Community perhaps explains why, among the Akan and the Nyamwezi, at least, telling tales was punishable, regardless of the truth of what was said (Rattray, 1929, pp. 327-8; Kwikima, 1966, p. 44). The penalty for defaming, as for other wrongs, may itself be exclusion from or ostracism by the community (Kwikima, p. 44), and the object of proceedings may be to restore harmony, or the integrity of the community, and involve cleansing ceremonies as much as compensation (e.g. *ibid.*). The structure of society would naturally be reflected in defamation laws: whether it was that defaming superiors was more serious than defaming one's equals, or that one could not bring an action against people or societies with whom one had a "joking relationship".[2] This importance of family and community means that a person may be able to sue for an attack on members of his or her family, especially on ancestors, even if they are dead, unlike the common law position. Dr J.B. Danquah (1938, p. xxiv, quoted in *Nkrumah v Manu* (Ghana 1971) p. 183) wrote,

> [A]n Akan man would receive full redress at law if anyone dared cast a slur on his ancestry or said of him that he was not a true member of the ancient Akan clan.

It may be that descendants who failed to defend their ancestors feared being the victims of those ancestors' anger, as suggested by Rattray (p. 326), or that desecrating an ancestor's grave defamed the living, because it suggested that the living came from a family of evil doers, as the Nyamwezi in Tanzania believed (Kwikima, 1966, p. 43); the sharp division between the living and dead which western thought assumes is not part of African tradition.

Finally, though there may be some doubt as to whether allegations which expose one to exclusion from society but imply no fault are actionable at common law (Chapter 6), there would be no such doubt under customary law. Exposure to exclusion would be the very core of the wrong.

The objective of litigation may also differ between common and customary law. The common law is weak when it comes to rectifying allegations, although there are some, largely statutory, incentives to apology and rectification. Many African systems share one of the characteristics of Fanti law identified by a court in Ghana, namely that the main purpose of customary law is not to seek compensation but to obtain a recantation (*Kwaku v Addo* (1957)). In Southern Sudan, too, "The action is brought primarily to vindicate the plaintiff's reputation rather than to obtain damages" (Makec, 1988, p. 210, quoting with approval Ashton (1967); and see *Uwejeyan v Onabeje* (Nigeria 1970).

It has been suggested that the points of tension in Luo society, at least in the mid-1960s, which gave rise to defamation, were pressure on land resources, politics and education (McCullough, 1971). Disputes over land, whether themselves litigated or not, might lead to the exchange of insults; defamation might be used to discredit an opponent in local politics; defamatory allegations might figure in disputes between parents and school authorities. The allegations themselves were predominantly of four types: of witchcraft, of sexual misbehaviour, of theft or of being a *jadak* (a squatter, or stranger in the community with limited land rights). The author suggests that defamation, and litigation over defamation, are so important among the Luo for a number of reasons. Firstly there is the general importance of gossip and scandal for the cohesion of society.[3] Secondly was a Luo tradition of competitiveness, and thirdly jealousy of success. The use of litigation he attributes to a social attitude which decries violence,[4] as well as to the indignity inflicted on the defendant by litigation (referring to Wilson (1967)).

Allegations of witchcraft show up in many other African societies. Some of the South African courts took the view that this was the only form of defamation recognised by indigenous peoples in that country (for example, *Nopanjwa v Mhlambiso* (1954)). Danquah (1938, p. xxiii, quoted in *Nkrumah v Manu* p. 180). said of Akan law,

> A suit of this nature (slander)...covers such serious assertions as that a person as an *Odonkoba*, 'son of a slave', and *obayifo*, 'a witch', an *odutufo*, 'one who has killed another by sympathetic magic, a poisoner'..

Especially noteworthy is the prominence of women litigants in some East African communities. Among the Gusii 61% of plaintiffs in defamation cases (and in assault cases) were women, and 29% of defamation defendants were women. Among the Kikuyu 37% of defamation plaintiffs and 23% of defamation defendants were women (Abel, 1970, p. 25). The judges have a sense that women are prone to quarrelsome, verbal behaviour:

> ...a quarrel in the Ghanaian sense whatever it may connote in other climes, is in my experience, if between women, nothing but angry exchanges of insults (*Nkrumah v Manu* (1971) p. 179 (Taylor J).

(See also *Ajala v Adelagun* (Nigeria 1979), quoted in Chapter 5.)

The Status of Customary Law

What is the place of this customary law in the modern legal systems of Africa? One important factor must be how far a system of separate customary courts has been retained, and to what extent those courts, whatever they are called, are customary in any real sense. All states in Nigeria now have separate courts, though there have been vacillations in policy in the southern states (Fawehinmi (1992, pp. 96-7) lists all 30 states as having customary or area courts). These courts may have unlimited jurisdiction in financial terms over customary disputes, and they do dispose of large numbers of cases (for some relatively recent figures see Narebor (1993) on Edo and Delta States). How far the law these courts apply is customary will depend on their personnel, as well as on the choice of law provisions.

Countries have legislated upon the latter question in different ways, and what actually goes on in the courts may not accurately reflect the statutory position. Nigerian law, for example, tends to provide that customary law is to apply to disputes between indigenous inhabitants (defined variously as indigenous to Nigeria and to Africa) unless that law is "repugnant to natural justice, equity and good conscience" or is inapplicable to the particular *transaction*. In *Ada v Fasola* (1981) Obi-Okoye CJ of Plateau State held that the Area Courts Edict providing that if parties opted or are deemed to have opted that the transaction should be governed by common law principles the court should apply that law could "hardly be applicable to a tort suit" (p. 237). This left customary law, or "principles of natural justice equity and good conscience" to apply. This ought to mean that customary law should apply to most disputes between Nigerians, unless perhaps they come from different ethnic groups and it is difficult to decide which system of law should apply. The reality is that rural residents and the poorer or less well-educated citizens tend to make use of the customary courts, in many of which lawyers have not been permitted (though it has been held that the Constitution precludes such exclusion of practitioners *Yakubu v Paiko* (1985)) or are less necessary; there they will usually argue and be judged in terms of customary law. (But not always: in *Okoro v Adogwu* (Nigeria 1982) - a case which even involved a "customary allegation", namely of witchcraft - Idoko J had "no doubt" that the common law of slander had been applied and that the Area Courts had the power to do so!) Other people will go to the more English style of courts and the more English type of law will be applied. In fact the tendency is probably for traditional types of disputes to go to more traditional courts and be judged according to traditional law, and more "modern" types of dispute - arising in the press, out of politics, in relation to employment, and so on - to go to the imported type of court.

But the boundary between "traditional" and "modern" disputes is often impossible to discern. In a Nigerian case where the statement was made at a village meeting, and seems to have involved an allegation of killing by "juju" by the plaintiff, but there were party political undertones, too, no suggestion was made that customary law should apply (*Olola v Alabi* (1984)). And in *Osuji v Agulanna* (Nigeria 1980) the dispute in question occurred at a village meeting, the words were spoken in Igbo, the plaintiff sued for what might be called traditional motives - because a thief (as the defendant had called him) could not take a title or be on any village committee - and the amount claimed in damages was small, only ₦5,000. However, the suit was brought in the High Court (possibly there were then no customary courts in Imo state), and it does not seem that anyone suggested that customary law was appropriate. In *Ikuenobe v Ogbeide* (Nigeria 1980) the case originated in the customary court, but the defendant appealed. The High Court (Aluyi J) held that the plaintiff had not shown that Ishan customary law made abuse of the type complained of - namely calling her an ugly woman - actionable. This seems unfortunate; this looks like a case which should never have left the customary court level.

The countries of East Africa have not preserved a separate system of customary courts, and there seems some doubt over how far customary law of wrongs survives. Sir John Spry (1976, p. 2) suggested it did not, pointing out that Defamation is not included in the definition of a "claim under customary law" in the Magistrate's Courts Act of Kenya. The elements enumerated in the Act are basically those concerned with land and family matters. E. Cotran has suggested that exclusion of customary torts and contacts could not have been intended (though the Act says "means" not "includes"). However, in 1970 a Kenyan case held that negligence fell outside "claims under customary law" - *Chiwaya v Tsuma*, cited, as Cotran is quoted, by Ojwang (1992, p. 28).

There seems no reason why the Judicature and Application of Laws Ordinance of (then) Tanganyika does not provide for the application of the customary law of defamation,[5] and the Interpretation and General Clauses Ordinance says now, "'Customary law' means any rule or body of rules whereby rights and duties are acquired or imposed, established by usage in any Tanganyika African community and accepted by such community in general as having the force of law". One might make a similar observation about the Uganda provision.

In the Ghanaian courts there have been a number of cases in which it is impossible to tell which law was being applied. In one case (*Chuku v Nkrumah* (1958)) the court both quoted from Sarbah (1904b), and cited English cases; on the other hand, those courts are unusual in having addressed explicitly in several reported cases whether the common law or customary law ought to apply. Under the Courts Act 1971 s. 49 there are a number of rules intended to guide the courts in the choice of law issue.

> Rule 1. An issue arising out of a transaction shall be determined according to the system of law intended by the parties to govern the issue or the system of law which the parties, from the nature or form of the transaction, may be taken to have intended to govern the issue.
> Rule 5. Subject to the foregoing Rules, the law applicable to any issue arising between two or more persons, shall, where they are subject to the same personal law, be that law; and where they are not subject to the same personal law, the Court shall apply the relevant rules of their different systems of personal law to achieve a result conformable to natural justice, equity and good conscience.

Rule 6. In determining any issue to which the foregoing Rules do not apply, the Court shall apply such principles of the common law, or customary law, or both as will do substantial justice between the parties, having regard to equity and good conscience.

This seems to have shifted the balance in favour of customary law,[6] at least where both parties are subject to customary law. Such law has been apparently applied even at first instance in the High Court: it seems that *Serwah v Sefa* (1986) was at first instance and the summary says "Held: the parties in the instant case were Ghanaians and customary law as distinct from English common law was to govern the case". A Ghanaian commentator has suggested that where the personal law of the defendant is the common law the court should apply in effect both systems in order to achieve the result "conformable to natural justice, equity and good conscience required by the Courts Act s. 49 (1) rule 5" (Date-Bah, 1977, p. 102).

In Lesotho the customary courts administer a statute copied from the Natal Code of Native Law (Laws of Lerotholi, Rule 36 Part II, issued under the Native Administration Proclamation of 1938; see Poulter (1970) pp. 142-145, from which this paragraph is derived).[7] The statute provides that "Every *malicious* statement whether spoken or written, alleging *evil conduct* on the part of any person constitutes defamation". Though the Sotho recognized defamation as well as insult (Poulter, citing Ashton, 1967), the current law cannot be considered as truly "customary". Indeed, one court thought that "The law on the question of defamation is something new to the Basotho...The court is therefore bound to invoke European law and principles..." (*Ramakabane v Ramusi*, quoted in Poulter, p. 145; this statement is very similar to one in Stafford & Franklin (1950, p. 221, quoted in *Biyela v Shamase* (1975-77) p. 259). The restrictions created by the italicised words means the law is narrower than the common law or Roman-Dutch law (see *Biyela v Shamase*). However, there is an additional provision specifically protecting unmarried women from allegations of unchastity, with no requirement of imputation of evil conduct.[8] Poulter suggests that the general approach of the relevant court was to fill in any gaps in the statute by resort to Roman-Dutch law.

Customary law is changing. Even institutions called "customary courts" are often far from customary even if those who staff them are not lawyers in the "English" sense (Singer, 1985, p 109); in some jurisdictions there are no customary courts. These factors, and the fact that an appeal system sometimes leads to cases from the customary courts coming into the English-type courts, leads to interpenetration of the systems - or more accurately to erosion of the customary law. Judges have hardly ever modified common law principles in the light of notions derived from customary law, whereas the converse is by no means true. Abel pointed out (1970, p. 47, n. 249), even before the abolition of courts administering specifically customary law, that "One of the most fascinating aspects of the evolution of customary law in Kenya is the gradual introduction of common law actions, for which there is no legal basis whatsoever".

One Nigerian judge observed, "...in my opinion it is regrettable, though perhaps unavoidable, that common law defences should be imported into arguments upon proceedings in Customary Courts in defamation matters." (*Uwejeyan v Onabedje* (1970) p. 241; it is not clear what, if any, common law defences were imported in this case). An example of inevitability is when, as in some Tanzanian cases, the complaint made is to the police (e.g. *Tumanieli v Aisa* above).

The judge in *Nkrumah v Manu* took a somewhat negative view of certain aspects of customary law, observing that,

> When village communities were small and the written word was unknown to customary law the only means of communication was the spoken word. It was therefore essential for the preservation of the peace of those small communities that idle insults which ridicule and may therefore ruin a person be discouraged in the body politic. With the very drastic changes which modern civilization has imposed on community and rural life throughout the country it seems to me that the law has more serious problems to tackle than silly vituperation.... When two persons are engaged in insulting each other freely, surely the law cannot be serious if it undertakes the invidious task of weighing...the quantum of insults on each side and penalising the side that tipped the scale by the preponderance of its vituperation.

And he said he was surprised that the customary rules had not been held contrary to "natural justice, equity and good conscience" (Ghana 1971) pp. 181-2; contrast the view of Enoch Edusei J in *Tsinagyah v Kyeiwaah* (1974) quoting Danquah (1938), "Introduction": "Our native custom is more in accordance with natural justice, equity and good conscience than the English law of slander", and *Wankyiwaa v Wereduwaa* (1963) p. 335). If people do feel that, in the context of their own village community perhaps, a statement diminishes their self-respect to the point that they feel driven to litigate relying on customary principles, that is possibly evidence that changes have not in fact affected rural society as greatly as Taylor J seemed to believe. Abel (1970, p. 25) pointed out that both parties to abuse and assault cases tended to come from the same small geographical area.

A Ghanaian judge took the view that libel could not be a customary law wrong, because customary society was pre-literate (Wiredu J in *Anthony v University College of Cape Coast* (1973), and *Oppon v Advance Press Co. Ltd*. (1980)). This view, criticised by Ghanaian scholars (e.g. Date-Bah, 1977, p. 103), denies to customary law one of its most significant features, its flexibility, and not all judges have found difficulty in accepting that customary law might apply to statements in writing: as in *Kivu v Lukiko* (Uganda 1942, pp. 112-3 - quoted in Morris & Read (1972, p. 208)) - where it was held, in the context of criminal libel, that if the "native court" punished a person, the appellate court could accept that this constituted an offence under customary law: "native customary law is capable of growth". To take another example of customary law changing with society: among the Kamba in Kenya, in the past, it was actionable for a young person to insult an older, but not *vice versa,* but as the age-grade system has broken down, the courts began to give compensation regardless of the age status of the parties (Penwill, 1951, p. 110). In *Herman v Ndava* (above) the court observed that since the institution of chief had become an anachronism it was no longer appropriate to award chiefs with fattened goats by way of compensation while ordinary mortals received unfattened ones.

As mentioned earlier, statements reflecting on status in other senses have given rise to litigation, whether for abuse or for injury to reputation: statements imputing slave ancestry, or not being a full member of the community in some other respect, for example. Taylor J in *Nkrumah v Manu* (p. 183) looked forward to a time when some of these statements might no longer assume such significance:

> Dr Danquah explained further (at p. xxiv)[see above] that an assertion that an Akan man is not a member of the ancient Akan clans "is tantamount to saying that the person referred to has no connection with any royal house or that he is a descendant of a slave or a slave tribe". One can only hope that with the inevitable future break-up of our heterogenous tribal groups implicit in the present efforts at a unitary state, and with the gradual process of inter-tribal marriage that these pompous tribal sentiments will eventually disappear.

Customary law was once the law of a community. While there may be something offensive about the notion of people having become so "educated" and "de-tribalised" that they should no longer be governed by community law, the co-existence of different systems of law may offer opportunities for "system-shopping" - a total departure from the notion of law as an aspect of community. In Ghana a judge said it was unnecessary for a party to elect which system of law he was suing under when the law was the same, but, "the plaintiff might decide to go by either the common law or customary law depending on the size of the damages and the jurisdiction of the court in which he wished to commence the action" (*Boagya v Boakye* (1981) p. 232). How far could this be allowed to go? On the other hand, there is nothing inherently objectionable about the idea that one might have more than one, intersecting, community; one might have one "traditional" reputation in one's community of origin, and another, "non-traditional" reputation in relation to one's political, or professional or marital life. Each reputation might be protected by the corresponding legal system (see Chapter 6).

Islamic Law

Islamic law has the status of "customary law"[9] in those countries which recognise systems of personal law, most particularly Nigeria and Sierra Leone. In Zanzibar before the Revolution Islamic law was the fundamental law in civil matters and otherwise the common law and English statutes of general application in force on July 7 1897 applied; this position had not changed by 1970 (Cotran, 1970). In Sudan at independence Islamic law applied to certain types of dispute between Muslims, but not in the case of defamation (Civil Justice Ordinance s. 5); currently, among the countries which inherited the common law Islamic law is strongest in Sudan, but I have no cases from the Islamic revival period. Other countries with significant numbers of Muslims include Uganda and Kenya, Gambia, Ghana, Mauritius, Nigeria and Tanzania. While Islam may influence what statements are perceived to be injurious to reputation in these countries (an allegation of alcohol drinking is an obvious example) there seem to be virtually no reported cases in which Islamic values are an issue, even if Islamic law may in theory be applied to torts or delicts.

Indeed, it seems that Islamic law does not recognise a civil wrong of defamation. One source gives as the closest equivalent to the civil law of defamation an *offence* under Islamic law namely "False accusation of illicit intercourse or of illegitimate birth of a woman's child" for which the remedy was 80 lashes, or divorce if it was a case of a husband defaming his wife (Lippman et al., 1988, pp. 41, 46.) Another source suggests that other types of defamatory statement are also punishable, and would embrace imputations, written or spoken, of acts forbidden by Islam (or while not specifically forbidden, are undesirable from the perspective of what one might term the "reasonable Muslim") (Majzoub, 1985, p. 3). Moral damages - as for damage to reputation - are unknown to Islamic law (Liebesny, 1975).

Being a Muslim may not preclude reliance upon customary law also, and in the absence of any provision in Muslim law for defamation it would not be surprising to find Muslims suing at customary law. Certainly it has happened in Nigeria, for example *(Alhaji Umaru) Ada v (Alhaji Garba) Fasola* (1981) - two Muslims are the parties; one seems to be a Yoruba (Fasola) but the other does not. What law is actually applied is unclear, except that the Chief Judge says it cannot be the common law. No-one mentions Muslim law.

Notes

1. Save for a very small number of references either to material collected by the Customary Law Research project of the Institute of Administration of Ahmadu Bello University, Nigeria, or to articles such as those by Abel and McCullough cited in this chapter.
2. As among the Nyamwezi - Kwikima, p. 45. A joking relationship has been defined as "a relationship between two persons in which one is by custom permitted, and in some situations required, to tease or make fun of the other, who in turn is required to take no offence" - Radcliffe-Brown (1952, p. 90ff). The Nyamwezi had such relationships (known as *utani* of which "joking" was but one aspect) with a number of other peoples. Examples of "jokes" include "Yours is a rotten tribe", and "Baboon yourself" - see Moreau (1944).
3. Something which has been underlined in Welsh valleys and American native peoples as well as in Africa- see Gluckman (1963).
4. However, Abel, *op. cit,* p. 28, says of the Luo "[they] do feel that the obligatory response to abuse, if honour is to be protected, is counter-abuse or physical violence"! Who is right? If these writers, with specialised knowledge, can disagree, I can do no better than record their observations.
   Of the Gusii, also in Kenya, Abel observes (p. 30) that they have a high rate of litigation for assault and abuse because they dislike physical and verbal hostility and would opt for litigation.
5. "Customary Law shall be applicable to, and courts shall exercise jurisdiction in accordance therewith in matters of a civil nature - (a) between members of a community in which rules of customary law relevant to the matter are established and accepted, or between a member of one community and a member of another community if the rules of customary law of both communities make similar provisions for the matter".
6. In comparison with the Courts Decree 1966 s. 64 (1) (originally s. 66 of the Courts Act 1960):

> Rule 6. Subject to the foregoing rules, an issue should be determined according to the common law unless the plaintiff is subject to any system of customary law and claims to have the issue determined according to the system, when it should be so determined.

For a case in which this provision was applied to hold that customary law could not apply - and that the common law rules on "mere abuse" defeated the plaintiff, see *Nkrumah v Manu* (1971).

For a discussion of s. 64 see *Kyei v Donkor* (1974). One post-1971 case is *Afriyie v Dansowah* (1976) which holds that customary law was applicable, but does not have a very satisfactory discussion of the statutory provisions.

7. Cases on the Code as applied in South Africa are to be found in that country's Native Appeal Commissioner's reports e.g. *Mkize v Conco* (1953), *Mvubu v Chilza* (1972), *Nsele v Mncube* (1974).

8. *Biyase v Shamale*, above. This case is not easy to understand. The Appeal Court seems to be saying that a reference to "rotten vagina" could be taken as an allegation of unchastity but not of evil conduct. Is an allegation of unchastity anything but an allegation of wrongful conduct?

9. By this I mean that the legislation often assimilates Islamic law to customary for the purpose of internal conflicts of laws issues. In fact Muslims often find this rather offensive. Islamic law is, after all, believed to represent largely divine revelation, and is therefore thought to be on a different plane from customary law which depends on earthly authority. The implicit assumption that Islamic, with customary, law is inferior to the common law is also resented.

3 The Colonial Systems

Although the common law is the only system which this book purports to discuss in a comprehensive fashion, this chapter provides an introduction to the various non-indigenous systems, and their place in African legal systems.

The "Common Law": An Introduction

To this day the common law bears the scars of the complex nature of its origins, especially in the distinctions between libel and slander. Defamation was originally dealt with by local courts and church courts. Later the notorious Star Chamber developed the criminal law of defamation, which was originally highly political. After its abolition the common law courts created the tort of libel, which was restricted to words in writing, leaving older rules to apply to defamation in spoken form (for the full history see Veeder (1903-4) and, especially, Helmholz (1985)).

The Ingredients of the Modern Torts

In order to succeed in an action for either libel or slander (the distinction is discussed in Chapter 4) the plaintiff must prove (i) that the statement would have been understood in a defamatory sense, (see Chapters 5-7) (ii) that the statement would have been taken by the reader to refer to the plaintiff (Chapter 5) and (iii) that the statement was published (Chapter 8). Only in a few circumstances must the plaintiff prove that he has suffered special damage. Establishing a *prima facie* case requires proof neither that the statement was untrue, nor that the defendant intended to defame.

In civil (as opposed to criminal) law, at least, it is a defence to show that the statements complained of were true (Chapter 11). More frequently, defendants rely upon one of a number of defences which do not confront the question of truth but plead that the statements were made on occasions or in circumstances to which the law gives special protection, whether an occasion of absolute privilege when no action can be brought even if the statement was maliciously made (Chapter 12), or an occasion of qualified privilege - when malice is relevant - (Chapters 13 and 14), or that the statement was one of comment not of fact and was on a matter of public interest and therefore given the protection of the law, provided it is fair and not malicious (Chapter 15).

Relationship with Other Torts[1]

Defamation affects the reputation, and may extend to business as well as personal reputations. However, a business may be injured by statements that are disparaging without being defamatory - for example that a product is bad, or that the plaintiff has gone out of business. If they are untrue and cause damage such statements may be actionable as "slander of goods" or "slander of title", or even as a more general "malicious falsehood" - as in a Kenyan case in which the statement was to the effect that the plaintiff, who was Chairman of the ruling party, KANU, had made a mistake in electing the President, and that the plaintif should step down for the defendant. This was held not to be defamatory, but to constitute malicious falsehood (*Nzomo v Kasoa* (1989)). However, it is not entirely clear that this is right, because this tort requires proof of special damage, and this would not include distress - *White v Mellin* (England 1895)). Other torts concerned with words are negligent misstatement, deceit and the "innominate torts" (*Wilkinson v Downton* (England 1897)).

The torts of malicious prosecution and defamation have remained distinct; Fleming (1992, p. 579) suggests because of the overriding interest of society in the efficient functioning of the prosecution process. Thus someone who initiates a criminal proceeding cannot be sued unless the plaintiff can prove both untruth (in the sense of failure of the prosecution) and malice, whereas in defamation the latter is assumed, and only becomes a real issue if certain defences are raised. There is a Tanzanian case in which the court spoke as though prosecution can be something for which compensation can be sought in defamation, but this is clearly wrong (*Hamiei v Akilimali* (1971)). In *Japhet Mwangwa v Mtemi Senge* (1969), the editor observes "the court does not make it clear which publication [to the court officials or to others] is being relied on, but since a formal complaint to a court is absolutely privileged...it appears that the communication of the allegation to persons in the community was the actionable publication".

Finally, there is interference with privacy: only in the US has a fully fledged tort of infringement of privacy been developed. Roman-Dutch law also recognises a right to privacy, which has been held to be subject to the same sorts of privileges as laid down in the American *Restatement of Torts* (see *Rhodesia Printing and Publishing Ltd. v Duggan* (1975); and Feltoe, 1976).

The Application of English Law in Africa

There are few instances of true departure from English precedent in these jurisdictions; it is unnecessary here to discuss the extent to which they are technically binding on the African courts (see, e.g. Allott, 1970, Chapter 2). Hodgin (1973 - citing Holdsworth, 1941) points out that the rule that no intention to defame need to be proved was decided in *Hulton v Jones* (1910). This piece of judicial legislation came after the reception dates (see below), but seems to have been universally accepted in African cases.

Ademola JCA said (*Daily Times Nigeria Ltd. v Williams* (1986), p. 540),

> We cannot talk meaningfully of the development of a common law of defamation in Nigeria unless the statutory umbilical cord which tied our law to the Law of England is severed. Any self-respecting profession cannot forever accept an inferior position in the development of its laws and mores.

The obstacle in the particular case, however, was not the common law, but a Lagos state statute, admittedly copied from England (Defamation Law cap. 34 s. 10, Lagos), which prevented the Court of Appeal from doing what it wished, namely giving the benefit of privilege to a newspaper report of a writ of summons.

The main pieces of English legislation relevant to defamation are:

Libel Act 1843
Libel Act 1845
Law of Libel (Amendment) Act 1888
Slander of Women Act 1891
Defamation Act 1952.

These apply in an African jurisdiction if it has "received" English statutes, and they were passed before the relevant "reception date" under local legislation. These dates are:

Tanzania	22 July 1920
Kenya	12 August 1897
Uganda	11 August 1902
Malaŵi	11 August 1902[2]
Zambia	17 August 1911
Nigeria	1 January 1900
Gambia	1 November 1888
Sierra Leone	1 January 1880
Ghana	24 July 1874

The reception statutes provide that only English statutes of "general application" apply; all the above statutes have in fact been applied under that rubric.

In the former Western Region of Nigeria, however, a decision was made with respect to every piece of legislation whether it should be adopted. In the defamation context most of the features of the English law were reproduced (Torts Law, cap. 32 of the former Western Region, now Cap. 34 Laws of Ondo State 1978 and Laws of Oyo State 1978, cap. 33 Laws of Ogun State 1978, Defamation Law cap. 52 Laws of Bendel State 1976 (now Edo and Delta)). In Sudan the law to be applied was "natural justice, equity and good conscience", a provision which resulted in the application of English common law in most circumstances (Mustapha, 1971, p. 152). Statutes have also been applied, on the basis that it made no sense to apply out-dated English law, but I am not aware of any case in which defamation legislation was applied.

In 1979 the Ghana Law Reform Commission recommended that customary and common law of defamation should be unified into one body of rules which should abolish the distinction between libel and slander and give protection to freedom from insult as well as to reputation; this has not been implemented by 1989 (see 7th Annual Report, reporting the presentation of the *Report on Defamation* on August 31 1979, and the 14th report in 1989).[3]

The result of the cut-off date is that the changes embodied in the English 1952 Act do not apply. However, a number of countries have passed legislation based on that Act. This is true of the "southern states" of Nigeria (Defamation Act 1961, Lagos, now cap. 34 Laws of Lagos State 1973, Defamation Law of former Eastern Region applicable in Anambra, Imo, Rivers, Cross River and Awka Ibom and the "Western" Laws cited above), Sierra Leone (Defamation Act cap. 32 of 1961), Kenya (Defamation Act No. 10 of 1970, now cap. 36 of Laws of Kenya 1972) and Zambia (Defamation Act cap. 70). That legislation does not apply in the "northern states" of Nigeria, nor to Uganda, Gambia, Mauritius or the Roman-Dutch jurisdictions.

Seychelles applies the common law of defamation but not, in general, the rest of the common law of tort. The French Code Civil applied generally, but the Defamation Ordinance 1948 provided that the "Civil Law of Defamation shall mutatis mutandis be the English law of slander and libel for the time being" (cap. 78 s. 2). It was held that this had the effect of applying the law of England as at May 3 1948, thus of excluding the Defamation Act 1952 (*Moulinié v De Comarmond* (1972) p. 86). In the event this has become of academic interest since the passing of the Seychelles' own Civil Code, which, however, in article 1383 (3) provides that the general article (1382) establishing liability does not apply to the civil law of defamation "which shall be governed by English law". (Chloros (1977, p. 135 n. 246) comments "The existence of a 'tort' of defamation side by side with the civilian approach to delict is a curious mixture typical of a mixed legal system.") The new provision was intended to make it clear that *current* English law was to apply (*ibid.*, p. 123 - Prof Chloros was the draftman of the Code). This seems to have passed by at least one Seychelles Judge who said, *obiter*, "after the 1st January 1976 the civil law of defamation is governed by English law as at the 31st October 1975 which is the date when the Bill of the Civil Code of Seychelles Ordinance, 1975 was passed by the House of Assembly" (*Kim Koon v Wirtz* (1976) p. 103). The effect of the civil code is on any interpretation to apply the English Act of 1952 to Seychelles. Recent English changes in the law, including the Act of 1996, would apply to Seychelles on Chloros' interpretation of the Code.

Roman-Dutch Law

The countries of southern Africa apply Roman-Dutch law as their "common law". The two main roots of the Roman-Dutch law of delict (the equivalent of tort in the common law system) are the *lex Aquilia* and the *actio iniuriarum*. The former derives from a Roman statute of 287 BC, which provides for compensation for injury to the person, or to property, including measurable financial loss, inflicted deliberately or negligently (Spiller, 1989, p. 336). It would not, however, cover injury to the intangible interests of reputation. In fact, defamation generally falls under the broad head of *actio injuriarum* which includes also malicious prosecution, interference with marital relations, and invasion of privacy (Feltoe, 1976). This action protects *dignitas*: "self-respect, mental tranquillity and privacy" (Hunt, 1970, p. 495ff., quoted in Lee and Honoré, 1978, p. 310). Thus an action may be brought for words which are insulting though not defamatory (*Brenner v Botha* (South Africa 1956, p. 260) cited Lee & Honoré), or which are defamatory but not published (*Whittington v Bowles* (1934, p. 151ff.) cited *ibid.*).

The courts of South Africa itself - and of Botswana, Lesotho, Swaziland, Zimbabwe and Namibia - apply English authorities as well as the authoritative texts of Roman-Dutch law (such as Voet - see, e.g. Kleyn & Viljoen, 1995)) and the cases based on them. Defamation "has long served as the focal point of the purist-pragmatist controversy - the unremitting debate between those who wanted to exorcise the English influence from our law and those who wanted to retain it" (Boberg, 1989, p. 35). A judge in Rhodesia observed (*Smith v Wonesayi* (1972) pp. 297-8),

This influence may not always have been to the benefit of our system and many writers on the Roman-Dutch law have regretted it, notably Mr. Justice van den Heever in his work, *Aquilian Damages in South African Law*, where he equates the effect of English law in South Africa to "a cuckoo in the nest"...
To foil the cuckoo and prevent her laying more eggs in the nest, however, is one thing, but to destroy the fledglings that have already hatched and flown away is quite another. The courts cannot put the clock back.

And since independence another judge in Zimbabwe said (*Boka Enterprises (Pvt) Ltd. v Manatse* (1989) pp. 133-4),

Although we are bound by the Constitution to follow Roman-Dutch law, that is not necessarily the same as South African law. South African precedent is followed in this country as a matter of convenience for historical reasons, because of the volume of precedent flowing from the superior courts of that country, and certainly not least because of the consistently high standards in jurisprudence which have been upheld over many years by the members of the various Benches. However, this country has for many years been independent of binding South African precedent and our courts have been influenced by English common law to a greater extent than has the South Africa judiciary. There appears no reason why, if we find the South African system wanting in a particular respect, we should not supplement that deficiency from English practice and precedent...

French Law in Africa

French law applies in the former French colonies, but there is French influence in Mauritius and Seychelles (by virtue of the fact that the French were the original colonialists, although both were ceded to the British in 1814) (see Bogdan, 1989).[4] In Mauritius the French Civil Code (Code Napoléon) has been applicable since 1808 (Arrêté du 21 .4. 1808). André Tunc has written, "We [the French] have no specific torts. We have a general law of tort, based upon the general principles of Articles 1382 and 1385" (1965, p. 1091; see also Carter-Ruck (1992) pp. 325-330)). The main article (1382) simply provides:

Every act whatever of man that causes damage to another obliges him by whose fault it occurs to repair it (*Tout fait quelconque de l'honneur, qui cause à autrui un dommage, oblige celui par la faute duquel il est arrivé, à le réparer*)

which must be read with article 1383, which explains that liability extends to injury caused by negligence or imprudence, as well as by acts (*Chacun est responsable du domage qu'il a causé non seulement par son fait, mais encore par sa négligence ou par son imprudence*).

Over the years the courts have not been very consistent in their approach, sometimes using the Code and sometimes ignoring it.[5] In some cases, one judge seems to be relying on the common law tradition and another on the French! This uncertainty, not to say confusion, may be traceable to the English oriented training of many of the judiciary,[6] and perhaps to a relative paucity of French material in this field. In France "defamation is regarded primarily as a breach of the civil law" (Lawson, Amos & Walton, 1967, p. 202). This does not seem to be so in Mauritius where there is a vigorous tradition of defamation litigation - perhaps under the common law influence. In *Legrand v Thatcher* (1896) p. 42, Piggott CJ said,

> As actions for libel are frequent in this Colony and as there seems to be very little jurisprudence in French law on the subject, I cannot but regret that the English law of libel has not been introduced into Mauritius. But as the law stands we must do our best with such few French principles as we can find.

Recent cases have emphasised the central role of the Civil Code. In *Lesage v Mason* (1976) the court reviewed the law of defamation, and the existing Mauritian authorities, at some length. It observed:

> In trying an action the cause of which is an allegation or imputation of fact prejudicial to the plaintiff, principles of the French law of tort should be resorted to.
>
> The English law of libel is not the law of Mauritius, but guidance may be sought from English authorities and case-law on the subject where the principles applicable to any question arising in the action are the same in the French and English systems (e.g. with respect to the defence of fair comment).

Mauritian courts still cite both French and English authority; in this very case the court cited a classic French work, Dalloz, *Nouveau Répertoire* on *Diffamation* and the English case of *Campbell v Spottiswood* (1863).

When applying the Civil Code, from where is further guidance to be found as to what is actionable? The Mauritian courts have looked to French authority, in the form of leading writers (often Savatier e.g. *Boodhoo v Sun Printing Ltd.* (1992)) and, less often, cases (*Boodhoo* cites, as do a number of other cases, the case of *Drappier v Creuzot* (1881) in the Cour de Cassation).

The basic principle is that there must be fault (*faute*). As Leconte J explained (*Lesage* p. 24),

> a *faute* under article 1382 includes not only all *délits civils* that is to say: illicit acts causing prejudice and done with malice (*avec intention de nuire*) but also *quasi délits* [quasi-delicts] which are illicit acts causing prejudice but done through negligence or imprudence without any malice.

Negligence and imprudence as types of fault are specified in art. 1383, as we have seen. (Leconte J is here using the French expression *avec intention de nuire* meaning with intention to injure and translating it by the English expression "malice", which is perhaps unfortunate in view of the rather peculiar usage of this word in the context of defamation. In fact, as we shall see later, in Mauritius and in common law systems, words which have the tendency to injure are treated as being with "fault" unless the defendant can show otherwise.)

But,

> The principle is that if the Penal Code punishes an act as a criminal delict, that act is necessarily a civil delict, and this applies not to defamation alone but to all acts - there cannot be a criminal act without a fault, and if there is fault then, there is liability under art. 1382

(*Loumeau v D'Unienville* (1909) p. 169 (Brown J); see also *Lesage v Mason* p. 178; for French authority, see, e.g. Planiol & Ripert, 1952, para. 485: "All acts forbidden by the criminal law, all criminal faults, constitute equally civil faults"). Older cases which treated the criminal and civil law as quite independent are therefore no longer to be treated as good law (examples are *Legrand v Thatcher* above and *Ritter v Newton* (1896)). Article 288 of the Criminal Code creates an offence consisting in "any allegation or imputation *of a fact* prejudicial to the honour, character or reputation of the person or of the body to whom such fact is imputed" (according to *Lesage v Mason* at 179, this is taken from the French Law of the Press of July 29 1881). This offence is defined quite narrowly in terms of how the publication took place, and requires a genuinely public element.[7] Another offence - "*injure*" (insult) - consists in "any injurious expression or any term of contempt or invective, or other abusive language, not carrying with it the imputation of a fact" (art. 296); this is sometimes, confusingly (and quite wrongly), referred to in English as "slander".

However, although a criminal act is necessarily a fault, and therefore a civil wrong, the converse is not true: what is not criminal may still be a civil delict or quasi-delict. So words not publicly uttered, even though published to a third party, could be actionable as a civil delict or quasi-delict (*Le Cernéen v Laurent* (1901) p. 56).

Insult is a criminal offence whether in public or not; the penalty is heavier for public insult, and heavier still for insult in visible form (art. 296 itself). But a private statement *of fact* would not be criminal. Other ways in which a statement might fall outside the criminal law but still be civilly actionable would include one which did not attack a person's honour, character or reputation but was still calculated to injure his trade.

A common lawyer, looking at the Civil Code would ask two questions about what constitutes a *prima facie* case: does the "*dommage*" requirement mean that there is no action unless there is proven damage? And does the plaintiff have to prove the intention to injure, or the negligence or imprudence? As we shall see, the law in Mauritius in these respects actually comes very close to the English law.

Another question relates to defences: especially whether an act which is actionable because it is an offence under the Criminal Code ceases to be so if, and only if, a defence under that code can be raised? Article 290[8] provides a specific defence, analogous to absolute privilege, expressed to be for both civil and criminal actions. There are a number of provisos to the main article creating criminal liability - art. 288 - which amount to what in the common law system would be considered defences. The history of the defences under art. 288 is intriguing. Although the "offence-creating" aspect of the article is derived from French law, the defences come, directly or indirectly, from English law. So the "justification" defence in art. 288 proviso (a[9]) is based on section 6 of the English 1843 Libel Act, and originally came into Mauritian law in 1852 as art. 79 of the Criminal Procedure Code, replacing an earlier provision to the effect that truth was a defence only when the allegation was in support of a denunciation to the Ministère Public (*Cordouan v Jardin* (1883)). Most of the other defences in the proviso to section 288 are said to have been derived from the Indian Penal Code (*Daurat v Le Cernéen* (1933) p. 24).

In *Lesage* the court said that the art. 288 defences could not be relied upon unless either they *expressly* applied to civil cases, or if the statement in question amounts to a civil wrong *only* by virtue of its being a criminal offence, or if the defence is also open in civil proceedings. The last exception somewhat begs the question: when *does* a defence avail a defendant in a civil case. The Civil Code says nothing explicit on this, other than to make it clear that there is to be liability for *faute*. A recent case emphasises that although under French law good faith is a defence, it must arise from certain "justifying" circumstances (*Boodhoo v Sun* above, and see p. 137 below).

The defences are discussed with their closest common law equivalent. The most substantial difference, in practical terms, is that there is no clear equivalent in French and Mauritian law of the defence of qualified privilege.

Notes

1. Generally it would be to the law of tort that one looked to to protect reputation. However, the House of Lords has recently decided that loss shown to flow from damage to reputation which itself is caused by breach of contract may be actionable (*Malik v Bank of Credit and Commerce International SA* (1997)).
2. It has been argued that statutes of general application no longer apply to Malaŵi, as a consequence of the Constitution Act 1966 s. 3 with First Schedule having revoked the Independence Order in Council provision (s. 83 (1), Nyasaland (Constitution) Order in Council 1961 (Nzunda, 1981).
3. Under the previous military constitution PNDC Law 42 of 1982 - existing law was to remain in force but "...especially where they are derived from foreign sources shall only be in operation to the extent compatible with national aspirations". This does not seem to have survived the the 1993 Constitution
4. Also in Cameroon, formed of an amalgam of French and British colonies, but it joined the Commonwealth after most of this book was written.
5. *Merven v Millien* (1945) was an example of a case ignoring the Code. However, the court in *Bouffé v Lemaire* (1886) held that the English libel/slander distinction should not be applied. See also *Cordouan v Jardin* (1883) - liability based on art. 1382, and resort must be had to Penal Code to identify what is "fault". The latter was repudiated by the common law nationalist Piggott Ag. CJ in *Ritter v Newton* (1896) p. 92.
6. Bogdan, *op. cit.* p. 40 says even now their education must leave traces on the law, but "it is surprising how well they master French legal techniques and French legal thinking".

   This may be changing. Apparently in the law course at the University of Mauritius, tort is treated as being an area of the law which is French in its basis and is taught by French teachers (this information supplied by Dr S. Offei who used to teach in that Faculty). It is interesting that there seem to be relatively few defamation cases reported these days (fewer litigated or fewer reported?) A rare example is *Boodhoo v Sun* (1992), which is more French in its approach than has been traditional.
7. By reference to section 206, which refers to statements in a public place or meeting, writing, or printed matter, or pictures or images sold distributed or exhibited in a public place or meeting, placards or handbills exhibited for public inspection. It also refers to hawking for sale, circulating and exhibiting

(sub-s. 2). S. 206 actually creates the offence of outrage against public and religious morality by these means, while s. 288 makes defamation by the same means an offence. Sub-s. 2 would seem intended to expand sub-s. 1 by including hawking for sale (offering or inviting to treat a common lawyer would presumably say), and also to include the circulator/exhibitor as well as the author. To argue that exhibit in sub-s. 2 does not require any public element would seem to go too far, though the wording is, to the mind of a common lawyer, far from precise.

8. "Said to have been borrowed from a French law of the year 1919" Tracey Watts J in *Decotter v Winson* (1936) p. 77, and originally entering Mauritian law, in a form restricted to criminal law, in the Penal Code 1838, (*ibid.*), although the modern article "bears no relation" to the original - *ibid.* 78. LeConte J, *ibid.* gives the text of the original art. 299, and a detailed history of the law - pp. 90-93.

9. Older version of the Criminal Code (or Penal Code) called the exceptions (i) etc. rather than (a) etc.

4 Form

Introduction

The most important distinction drawn in the common law in connection with the form of defamation is between words spoken and those written. Most African cases have not involved difficult issues of form - except for a few instances of broadcasts. Several African cases have involved cartoons, whether associated with written words or not (e.g. *Williams v West African Pilot* (Nigeria 1961), *Ajala v Are* (Nigeria 1985), and photographs (*University College, Cape Coast v Anthony* (Ghana 1977), *Omotayo v African Newspapers of Nigeria Ltd.* (1986), *Daily Times v Emokpae* (Nigeria 1979), *Rwabugabya v East African Newspapers Ltd.* (Uganda 1964)).

Libel or Slander?

In the common law - and peculiar to the common law - there is a distinction between two torts: libel and slander. Customary law developed in largely illiterate societies, often without a written language at all. Roman-Dutch law does not recognise the slander/libel distinction (*Channing v South African Financial Gazette* (1966)), nor does the French Civil Code - and therefore not the law of Mauritius[1] (see *Bouffé v Lemaire* (1886)). Islamic law recognises no distinction (Majzoub, 1985, p. 4).

The Nigerian Law Reform Commission recommended that the distinction between the two torts should be abolished (1987, p. 77), and similar proposals have been made in Zambia (Molotsi, 1984), and in Ghana (Law Reform Commission, 1979).[2] In New Zealand (Defamation Act 1954 s. 4) and parts of Australia (e.g. New South Wales 1974 Defamation Act) the distinction has been abolished.

The existence of the two torts today serves mainly to cause confusion and possibly injustice.[3] The courts themselves were compelled to elaborate the distinction: libel is defamation in permanent form and slander in transient form; so a defamatory gesture would be slander and a statue libel - a rare example of this last was a wax model of the plaintiff placed in close proximity to the "Chamber of Horrors" section of Madame Tussaud's waxworks show, suggesting that he shared with the models in that part of the show the characteristic of being a notorious murderer (*Monson v Tussaud's* (England 1894)). (Apparently there is a Sudanese case to the effect that conduct is slander not libel: *Muckle v Sudan Light and Power Co* (1953-54).)

The law dates from a period before the invention of typewriters and shorthand, let alone the fax machine or machines which can electronically represent speech in writing, or writing in synthesized speech.

The Spoken Word Reduced to Writing

Common sense would suggest that dictating a document is slander - though in at least one English Court of Appeal decision the dictation seems to have been treated as libel (*Pullman v Hill & Co.* (1891); see also *Boxius v Goblet Frères* (1894)). Courts in Uganda and Nigeria have followed later English and New Zealand authority in holding that the publication is indeed slander (*Gidando v Chief Imam of Odo-Ado* (Nigeria 1962) p. 126, citing *Angelini v Antico* (New Zealand 1912) and *Osborn v Boulter* (England 1930) and *Senteza v Shell & BP Uganda Ltd.* (1973), also citing *Osborne*). In the Nigerian case of *Echo v Interbeton BV* (1980 p. 567), it was assumed without argument that dictation to a secretary was slander, while English writers are almost unanimous in assuming the same - "almost" because Hudson (1987) is of the opposite view, pointing out that all the textbooks disagree. Once the dictated matter is typed and published to a third party - but not if only to the dictator: *Eglantine Inn Ltd. v Smith* (Northern Ireland 1948), *Osborn v Boulter* - the written version is libel for which the original dictator will be liable, on the basis of simple agency.

A Document Expressed in Speech

It has been held that it is libel if a written document is read out, at any rate if the hearers knew that there was a written version (*Forrester v Tyrrell* (England 1893)), but others have taken the view that the determining factor is the type of communication complained of, in this case oral (Fleming, 1992, p. 546, citing *Meldrum v ABC* (Australia 1932) p. 435 and *Hebditch v McIlwaine* (England 1894) p. 58). However, a New York case held that it was libel regardless of whether the audience knew that there was a written version (*Hartmann v Winchell* (1947)). One could easily imagine ever more complex problems: suppose the defamatory remark was interpolated into a written script by the reader, in such a way that the audience would have assumed it was written. Modern law is unclear about the basis for the distinction between these torts. Is the issue the permanence of the record, or the size of the audience? (In England everything that takes place on a theatrical stage, including gestures and unscripted remarks, is treated for the purposes of the law of defamation in the same way as libel - Theatres Act 1968 s. 4).

Films and Recordings

Events visible on a film are libel (*Youssoupoff v Metro-Goldwyn-Mayer* (England 1934)). There seems to be some doubt about the status of a sound recording, whether on a record, an audio-tape or a film soundtrack - although it is clear that the last is libel if it is linked with what is visible (*ibid.*). An East African court held that the broadcast of a tape-recording was libel (*Olowo v AG* (Uganda 1972)), as did one in Seychelles (*Kim Koon v Wirtz* (1976)). This should apply to any playback of a recording, whether over the air or not; by analogy with the existence of a script, the existence of the recording provides the element of permanence.

Broadcasting

Broadcasting raises a particularly interesting problem: radio is addressed only to the ears yet reaches a far wider audience than most pieces of written material. Relying on the old cases about reading aloud from documents, some common law courts held that a broadcast read from a script was libel, but an extemporary one was slander. In Nigeria it was held that a broadcast not proved to have been read from a script was slander, leaving us to infer that where there was a script it would be libel (or would it matter that the audience knew there was a script?) (*Mukete v Nigerian Broadcasting Corporation* (1961)). Somewhere in the common law world it would be possible to find authority for any proposition: that all radio broadcasts were libel, that they were libel only if read from a script (Fuld J in *Hartmann v Winchell* (above); *Kim Koon v Wirtz*, p. 103); that they were libel if *known* to be read from a script (Lowe & Cussen JJ in *Meldrum v ABC* (above)) or that they were slander because addressed only to the ear (Mann & McArthur JJ, *ibid.*). The advent of television only added to this confusion.

Under modern legislation broadcast defamation is to be treated as "publication in permanent form"; this is a way - albeit a clumsy way (Gatley, para.76 n. 35) - of saying it is to be treated as libel. The expression used is "publication for general reception by means of wireless telegraphy" (in some jurisdictions television is expressly mentioned[4]). This leaves two problems: first of all what is general reception? It clearly covers state as well as national networks in a federation like Nigeria; would it also cover local broadcasting? (Gatley, para. 147 n. 36 suggests "tentatively" that it does). "Wireless" telegraphy would seem not to cover cable television.

Modern technology will continue to raise problems; ultimately the only solution will be to abolish the distinction between libel and slander.

The Consequences of the Distinction

> A plaintiff in an action for libel need not allege or prove that he has suffered damage. If he has been libelled without lawful justification or excuse, the law presumes that the publication of the libel has of itself a natural tendency to injure the plaintiff.

This statement by Sankey LJ (from *Hobbs v Tinling* (England 1929) p. 17, quoted by (among others) Somolu J in *Williams v West African Pilot* (Nigeria 1961) p. 884) represents the law of libel, but not that of slander. At common law the plaintiff must prove special damage in all instances of slander, save in the case of three specific allegations: that of having committed a criminal offence, that of having certain diseases and that of being unfit for one's profession. Statute added an imputation of unchastity concerning a woman (in England the Slander of Women Act) (for a Nigerian case setting out the four situations see *Stephen v Atuegbehunu* (1971) p.102). The former Eastern Region of Nigeria added an imputation of being an *osu* (see below). The legislation makes no mention of the three common law situations; this does not mean that they are no longer actionable *per se*, simply that the legislation adds new situations. This point was made in *Nweze v Ugwu* (Nigeria 1976). However, a few years later another Nigerian judge thought that the legislation (specifically s. 4 of the Anambra State Defamation Law, see below) had repealed the common law rules - (*Nwankwo v Okeke* 1980). The latter is clearly wrong.

The essence of the liability in customary law is as much the injury to the feelings of the plaintiff as to his reputation - indeed in some systems abuse is as actionable as injury to reputation. Also important is the damage to the community (e.g. Goldin & Gelfand, 1975, p. 201). So we find:

> Held: Words imputing witchcraft, adultery, immoral conduct, crime and all words which sounded to the disrepute of a person of whom they were spoken were actionable. Slander as known and recognised by customary law was actionable per se without the English requirement of proof of actual or legally presumed pecuniary damage.(*Serwah v Sefa* (Ghana 1984-5) p. 279).

And

> The essence of an action for defamation in a Customary Court is to vindicate the character or reputation of the injured party, redeem his good name and thus avoid any likelihood of a breach of the peace. It is not an element of the claim that the party defamed should suffer any pecuniary or special damage (*Uwejeyan v Onabedje* (Nigeria 1970) p. 241).

Imputation of Commission of a Crime

At common law, an allegation that the plaintiff was guilty of a criminal offence is actionable *per se*. However, this only applies if the offence alleged was punishable physically, by imprisonment or caning, for example. The original notion was that the statement put the plaintiff in jeopardy of punishment. However, in modern law a statement that the plaintiff has been convicted and served his sentence is equally actionable (*Gray v Jones* (England 1939), citing a number of authorities going back as far as *Gainford v Tuke* (1620)). And it is actionable *per se* to say that a person is guilty of an offence for which he has just been acquitted, even though the plea of *autrefois acquit* would mean that he is in no jeopardy of punishment (e.g. *Oziwo v Aghegba* (Nigeria 1977)). A statement of mere suspicion, however, is not enough (*Simmons v Mitchell*, Privy Council (1880) - though the Judicial Committee observed that they had "nothing to do" with the policy - p. 162; this case was followed in *Dewhirst v Larkins* (Uganda 1911).

Among the African cases are allegations of having attempted to pervert the course of justice (*Abasi v Williams* (Nigeria 1942)), of being a thief (*Agoaka v Ejiofor* (Nigeria 1972), *Akolade v Julius Berger (Nig.) Ltd.* (Nigeria 1977) esp. p. 2445, *Williams v Fey* (Sierra Leone 1964-66), *Tufuor v Beng* (Ghana 1963), *Renaud v Arnefy* (Seychelles 1974)), or hiring a gang to commit theft (*Mavromatis v Douglas* (Rhodesia 1971)). It was held actionable *per se* to say to a legal practitioner "You are posing as a lawyer when you are not. You were a taxi driver in England. You bought your certificate". The judge observed that this satisfied the "unfit for profession" test as well (*Iwowo v Emelezie* (Nigeria 1977)).

The statement need not be precise; it is enough to accuse the plaintiff of having done something for which he ought to go to prison (e.g. *Webb v Beavan* (England 1883) - "I know enough to put you in gaol"), or of conduct which would amount to a corporally punishable offence - as in an East African case in which the allegation was that the plaintiff had attended a meeting the purpose of which was to cause confusion and overthrow the government. The court took this to be an allegation of treason (the alleged meeting being the overt act) (*Odongkara v Astles* (1970)). And in *Giwa v Laogun* (Nigeria 1957) the statement "You threw your child into a well on account of your greed for money" was held to impute a criminal offence - at least, as Abbott Ag. CJ observed, cruelty to the child. On the other hand, there are a number of cases in which the courts have held that an allegation did not clearly suggest that the plaintiff had committed a crime. One of the judges suggested in *Egbe v Adefarasin* that to say that the plaintiff had "dealt irregularly with 4 million naira" was insufficiently precise to be an imputation of crime (Nigeria 1987) p. 25 *per* Oputa JSC), and in an old Ghanaian case it was held that "misused the books" would not be understood to mean "defrauded" (*Callerholm v Esilfie* (1896)). Also in Gold Coast (now Ghana) a court said *Cheetham v Bannerman* (1881),

> To call a man in the heat of discussion a thief, without more, is no accusation of the commission of an indictable offence, unless the defendant goes on to specify, at the same time, some particular act of theft which the plaintiff has committed.[5]

It is not enough that the offence alleged is one for which arrest without warrant is possible, if the only possible punishment is pecuniary (England *Hellwig v Mitchell* (1910)). In one Nigerian case the defendant alleged that the plaintiff had committed adultery (*Farashi v Yakubu* (1970)). Under the Penal Code (s. 387) adultery is a criminal offence if it is an offence under the plaintiff's personal law.[6] The plaintiff's personal law was stated to be Ngizin, under which only compensation would be awarded (with any corporal penalty only being applicable if the offender failed to pay compensation awarded); thus the court held that under the plaintiff's personal law adultery was not punishable as a crime. Had the plaintiff maintained successfully that his personal law was the Sharia, under which ritual haddi lashing is awardable, the outcome would presumably have been different. But too late the plaintiff's lawyer raised the Sharia question, and the court held that he ought to have proved that it applied to the plaintiff. On the other hand, under which system of law was he suing? Had he relied on Islamic law it seems he would have been unable to claim compensation at all! (see Chapter 2).

Alleging a breach of trust (e.g. *Thompson v Bernard* (England 1807)) or a tort (as in *Chavula v Athumani* (Tanzania 1982), where the defendant had accused the plaintiff of enticing away his wife) also falls short of alleging a corporally punishable offence; so special damage would have to be shown.

Allegations of witchcraft are commonly at issue in customary "defamation" cases, and may still be taken very seriously. In Sierra Leone a judge held that an allegation of "killing by fetish" was not actionable *per se* since there was no such offence known to the law (*Marke v Johnson* (1950-56)). And a Nigerian judge held that it was not actionable *per se* to say, orally, that someone was a witch - although he did observe that the law was "rather restrictive" (*William v Chinda* (1977), Okara J). In the former the court could perhaps have held that the allegation was in effect one of homicide, as in *Olola v Alabi* (Nigeria 1984) where it seems that the plaintiff was accused in a village meeting of killing by juju, but it was treated as an allegation of killing. But simply being a witch is not necessarily a criminal offence; as one judge said, "I find that the accusation of calling some other person a witch puts in danger of prosecution the person who accuses the other of witchcraft and not the person so accused" (*Otto v Amabeoku* (Nigeria 1975) (Inko Tariah J)). However, Idoko J observed in another Nigerian case that under s. 216 Penal Code it is an offence to *represent oneself* as being a witch (*Okoro v Adogwu* (1982)). He concluded that to accuse someone of being a witch was therefore to accuse them of a criminal offence. These cases show very clearly the problems of applying such culturally derived rules in a totally different context.

Imputation of Disease

Older cases asked whether the disease was "lingering", but antibiotics have made this a far less relevant concept. It has been suggested that venereal disease is the only example of a disease the imputation of which is actionable *per se* (*Milner v Reeves* (England 1617)); the Jamaican courts took the view that only venereal diseases were covered, thus excluding tuberculosis, despite its being lingering (*Murray v Williams* (1936), *Hinds v Lee* (1952) (see Kodilinye, 1982, p. 138)). If the test is the risk of social ostracism, leprosy ought to be included; there is some authority to this effect (e.g. *Taylor v Perkins* (England 1607) - "Thou art a leprous knave"). Authorities were divided on smallpox (Gatley, p. 84 n. 17); since it has been eliminated from the world, should it anyway now be considered as not covered? AIDS presents the best known modern example of a dreaded disease. Clearly it is lingering, indeed incurable; there is no reason for sufferers to be excluded from social (as opposed to sexual) contact, but experience shows that they often are, and certainly many people would associate the disease with irregular sexual behaviour. The cases reflect the dreaded diseases of the English past, and it is to be hoped that African courts will relate the law to African realities.

Imputation in Connection with Business or Calling

The courts assumed that it was so obvious that a statement suggesting unfitness for one's business or calling would cause loss that it was not necessary to prove it; the rule applies to offices as well as to trades and professions. It applies to any occupation, but it must be one carried on when the words were uttered (*Riddick v Thames Board Mills* (England 1977) p. 909, *Bull v Vazquez* (England 1947)). African examples have included a Nigerian lawyer of whom the defendant had said he had never employed him because he did not trust him (*Lambrou v Thomopoulos* (1935) - see the English case *Baker v Morfue* (1668): Lawyer "hath no more law than Mr C's bull"), the Sudanese doctor of whom it was said "he administered to me such medicine which will poison me" (*Saadani v Sassoun* (1917)), and a Tanzanian insurance broker accused of quoting a higher premium than permitted (*Sawe v Nyakyi* (1976)).

At common law there was a rather restrictive rule - which still applies in jurisdictions without legislation similar to the 1952 English Act: that a statement was only actionable *per se* if it related *directly* to the plaintiff's occupation or office. The best known English example is a headmaster alleged to have committed adultery with the school cleaner (*Jones v Jones* (1916); it is interesting to contrast a case from a customary court in Nigeria in which a teacher recovered damages for a statement that he committed adultery with another teacher's wife (*Inakwu v Ojeden* (1963)). The rule also defeated a solicitor who had written the reference complained of in his private capacity (*Hopwood v Muirson* (England 1945)). In Nigeria it was held that to say of a building contractor that he is a rogue and "he has run away with my money" did not relate directly to his business, although if the plaintiff had been able to prove additional words alleged, namely that "he cannot pay his workers" the plaintiff would have succeeded (*Onojioghofia v Okitipai* (1974)). At common law, in the case of a trader an allegation of even personal insolvency was actionable *per se* - the rationale being that solvency is so vital to a trader that such an allegation must necessarily affect his business (*Jones v Jones* at p. 507; *Stanton v Smith* (England 1727)). This explains why the Nigerian building contractor would have been able to sue if he had been able to prove the second statement. Non-traders - such as lawyers - were in a different position (see *Dauncey v Holloway* (England 1901) p. 444).

This rule - so far as it concerned non-traders - was obviously unsatisfactory; an allegation may well have a tendency to dissuade people from patronising a business or person even though it does not directly attack his competence or fitness in this sense. The English 1952 Act, copied in African jurisdictions, therefore makes actionable *per se* any remark which "is calculated" to affect adversely the plaintiff's business or profession. "Calculated" - means "likely" and not "intended" (*Customglass Boats v Salthouse Boats* (1976) p. 602 on the New Zealand legislation). Even since the legislation it has been held in Nigeria that it was not calculated to hurt a school messenger or clerk in his occupation that he was accused of adultery with the wife of another staff member living in the same compound; it might be different, the court said, if the plaintiff had been dealing directly with students (*Adah v Nwafor* (1961)).

Under the common law an allegation of corrupt or dishonest behaviour in carrying out the functions of an honorary, as opposed to remunerated, office was actionable *per se*. But if the allegation was of general incompetence or misconduct not in the performance of those functions, it was only actionable *per se* if the incompetence or conduct would be grounds for removal from the office (*Alexander v Jenkinson* (England 1892) - town councillor "drunk"). It has been suggested that the legislation has not changed this (Gatley, para. 174 citing *Robinson v Ward* (England 1958)). In one Nigerian case the court held that "office" referred to in the Defamation Law included one "of pure honour and dignity"- in this instance a chief (*Ezejiofor v Ogu* (1981)). It is not entirely clear why this was in issue here since the allegation was one of crime - having killed his colleagues in order to rule alone.

Imputation of Unchastity to Woman

During the late Victorian period the British Parliament passed the Slander of Women Act 1891 making it actionable *per se* to accuse a woman of acts of unchastity. The Act refers to words, and it has been suggested that this would exclude gestures to the same effect (Gatley, p. 92 n. 97). It has been suggested, *obiter*, that unchastity includes rape (*Youssoupoff v M-G-M* (England 1934)), and homosexual as well as heterosexual acts are included (*Kerr v Kennedy* (England 1942); the word complained of was "lesbian" - could one argue that this word suggests sexual preference rather than activity and implies unchastity to no greater extent than to say a woman is heterosexual?).

The Ghanaian reception date is earlier than the English Act which does not therefore apply. Other jurisdictions have applied the English Act without hesitation. A court in Malaŵi (*Hampton v Herkes* (1961-63) p. 378) said of the Act

> It relates to women generally, to whom it gives an important right. There is nothing in this brief enactment to imply that it was passed to meet conditions to be encountered only in England. It has a universal effect by altering the law before it was applied here in 1902. The Act would seem, therefore, a likely candidate for acceptance as a statute of general application. There is no person here to whom it is repugnant or inapplicable or unsuitable by race religion or custom.

There was a similar approach in *Cornelius v Martinaglia* (Tanzania). (This was criticised by Muburimusoke (1978) - though he criticises the process of reasoning rather than the outcome.) The same rule has been applied in Seychelles, in *Bouchereau v Guichard* (1970) (though there is no mention of the Act). (See also Daniels, 1973, p. 18.)

Although there is little doubt that the Act reflects the hypocrisy of a society which still tends to regard adultery or fornication by a woman as more serious than by a man, the same is true of other societies, including those of Africa. The provision has in fact been copied in a number of jurisdictions, including the southern states of Nigeria, Zambia and Kenya (see Appendix), so its applicability is beyond question there.[7] The suggestion was made to the Nigerian Law Reform Commission that allegations against married men should also be actionable *per se* (1987, p. 7); however, this was overtaken by the recommendation to abolish the distinction between libel and slander entirely, and the Commission expressed no views on the proposal.

The legislation has a proviso to the effect that the plaintiff is not to recover more costs than damages unless the court certifies that there was reasonable ground for bringing the action. In the Malaŵian case mentioned earlier, the court refused such a certificate because of what it described as the plaintiff's own misconduct and provocation, the partial colour of veracity of some of the allegations and her own lack of sensitivity.

Imputation of Being an Osu

In some Igbo communities certain people (known as *osu*, or *oru*, *ohu*, *ume* or *omani*) were dedicated to the gods and they and their descendants were treated as a separate caste, subject to disabilities including being unable to inter-marry with freeborn people (see Green, 1964, pp. 23-4; Uchendu, 1965, pp. 89-90, and for a novelist's account Achebe, 1963). In theory this status was abolished by the Abolition of the Osu System Law 1956,[8] which also provides that "Words spoken and published which impute that a person is Osu shall not require special damage to render them actionable" (s. 4). (I say "in theory" because the *Customary Law Manual* - for Anambra and Imo - (Obi, 1977, para. 285), still specifies disabilities for *osu*; and *No Longer at Ease* was set in the 1960s; and see Okafor, 1992, p. 87.) The legislation merely relieves the plaintiff of the necessity to prove special damage (for a successful case see *Okorogu v Odunze* (1967)); it is still necessary for the plaintiff to prove that in the context in which the statement was uttered it was defamatory - it must not be "mere abuse" and the hearers must consider an *osu* to be inferior. The latter point was held in *Nwachukwu v Nnoremele* (1957) (on the question of whether "right thinking members of society" would take that view, see Chapter 6 below). This case arose in Owerri, and according to the *Manual of Customary Law* the *osu* system does exist in that Division.

Other Differences

At common law, libel, but not slander, could be a criminal offence. In some countries, however, both are offences. (see for Nigeria s. 391 of the Penal Code and s. 373 of the Criminal Code.) In Swaziland spoken words can be a crime (for example, *R v Mathebula* (1977-78)). However, in Tanzania slander is not a criminal offence (Newspapers Act No. 3 of 1976 s. 38 replacing s. 187 Penal Code, and *Japhet s/o Mangwa v R* (1967) quashing a conviction for oral defamation, and *Cosmas v Faustini* (1971) p. 265).

Finally, historical anomaly also means that the limitation periods may be different - a topic discussed later (Chapter 18).

Notes

1. At one point the word slander was used in art. 290 of the Penal Code, but was later replaced with insult/*injure*.
2. Outside Africa, the Irish Law Reform Commission has made a similar recommendation (1991) para. 3.3), as have a number of Commonwealth

bodies (e.g. the English Committee on Defamation (Cmnd 4509, 1975); the Australian Law Reform Commission, 1975)

3. Just to take a small example: in *Akin-Olugbade v Iro* (Nigeria 1980) p. 286, Bada J quotes from Gatley on necessity to prove special damage in the case of the imputation of a criminal offence, apparently not understanding that this relates to slander, while the litigation before him was for libel.
4. E.g. legislation applying in Abia State etc. in Nigeria. In Zambia it is defined as "radiotelephonic emissions" and in Kenya as "radio communication within the meaning of the East African Posts and Telecommunications Act" - now the Kenyan Post and Telegraph Corporation Act Cap. 411.
5. This is perhaps better explained on the basis, emphasised later in the judgment, that the words were spoken in anger, what is often called the "mere abuse" principle (see Chap. 5), rather than on the basis of the absence of precision in the allegation. Nor do the English authorities require that the crime charged be punishable *on indictment*.
6. The Penal Code applies only in the former Northern States (Adamawa etc.); in the rest of the country the Criminal Code does not recognise "personal law" offences like adultery at all. In Uganda also the Penal Code made adultery an offence punishable with imprisonment - s. 150A, but this was not true in Tanzania, see *Mwaipopo v Simithy* (Tanzania 1968). However, as Spry (1976, p. 17) points out, the Slander of Women Act applies in Tanzania, but this will not help the defamed man.
7. Ordinances identical in effect to the Slander of Women Act were introduced into the colonies of Lagos and Southern Nigeria in 1900 (Ordinance 12 in each case), and repealed in 1917. I would hypothesise that the reason for the repeal was that when the reception date was changed to January 1 1900 (from an earlier date) it was realised that the local legislation was unnecessary as the English Act would now apply as a statute of general application.
8. For a case on the application of the Law to land see *Ebiriukwu v Ohonyerenwa* (1950).

5 Meaning

Introduction

In this and the next two chapters, I shall discuss two questions, the first of which can be divided:

(i) What do the words mean?
  (a) does the statement refer to the plaintiff; and
  (b) what is it that is being said about the plaintiff?
(ii) Is the meaning of the words defamatory?

In this chapter I discuss (i); in the next, I turn to the "defamatory or not?" question. Very often question (i) (b) and (ii) are conflated. The court will say something like: "did the statement convey a defamatory meaning to those to whom they were published?" (Gatley, para. 31 n. 2). One can illustrate the fact that there are really two questions by reference to the famous English case of *Liberace v Daily Mirror* (1959; quoted from Markesinis and Deakin, 1994, p. 571): the paper described the glittering pianist as

> the summit of sex - the pinnacle of masculine, feminine and neuter. Everything that he, she or it can ever want to be...a deadly, winking, sniggering, snuggling, chromium-plated, scent impregnated, luminous, quivering, giggling, fruit flavoured, mincing, ice-covered heap of mother-love.

The jury had to decide whether those words conveyed the meaning that Liberace was a homosexual; then they had to decide whether such an imputation was defamatory.[1]

At common law it is unnecessary for the plaintiff to prove intention, and bootless for the defendant to disprove it:

> The meaning is not what the defendant (i.e. the speaker) attributed to the words, but what meaning the hearers would on the occasion in question have reasonably given to the words (*Callerholm v Esilfie* (Ghana 1896) (Brandford Griffith CJ)).

Aguda CJ in Botswana said "where two or more interpretations are possible in regard to an alleged defamatory statement then the court must take that which is innocent in the absence of proof that that interpretation was not meant" (*Karim v Wetterings* (1974) citing Voet 47.10.20). This does not represent the common law.

The court is not obliged to find the words non-defamatory just because some such meaning is possible (*Dumbo v Idigboe* (Nigeria 1983) p. 55, citing *Morris v Sandess Universal Products Ltd.* (England 1954); English authorities include *Roberts v Camden* (1807), quoted by Gatley, para. 93 n. 71). Nor must it strain to find some defamatory sense, however improbable. "The test is not what a man avid of scandal or a jester, or an opponent of the person allegedly defamed would read into the words complained of..." (*Okafor v Ikeanyi* (Nigeria 1979) p. 113; *Ekanem-Ita v Fetuga* (Nigeria 1991) p. 474). And Lord Halsbury observed, "It is unreasonable that when there are a number of good interpretations, the only bad one should be seized upon to give a defamatory sense to the document" (in *Nevill v Fine Art & General Insurance Co.* (1897) p. 77, quoted in *Caltex (Africa) Ltd. v Oddie*) (Kenya 1955) p. 342). According to the Supreme Court of Nigeria:

> In determining whether the words are capable of a defamatory meaning, the Judge will construe the words according to the fair and natural meaning which would be given to them by reasonable persons of ordinary intelligence and will not consider what persons setting themselves to work to deduce some unusual meaning might extract from them (*Dumbo v Idugboe* at p. 48).

The fact that the words will not bear one defamatory meaning does not mean they cannot bear another; in a Rhodesian case the court accepted that when the defendant said that the plaintiff had stolen some money that would not have been taken, in the circumstances, as being meant to suggest theft: the words being uttered in the heat of the moment, and in "intemperate and exaggerated language". But they still imputed impropriety and were defamatory (*Mahomed v Kassim* (1972)).

Although common experience teaches that few, if any, words have one fixed meaning, for the purposes of the law of defamation the court must find *the* meaning of the words in question, as the House of Lords reiterated in *Charleston and Another v News Group Newspapers Limited* (1995).

The Judge Without a Jury

A good deal of the law is bedevilled by the fact that English defamation cases are still usually tried by jury. The jury must decide whether the words had a defamatory meaning, and whether they referred to the plaintiff. Fox's Libel

Act (1792) declared that defamation or not was a matter for the jury; Although restricted in terms to criminal libel, it has always been applied to civil cases as well. If the judge considers that no reasonable jury could decide that the words were defamatory, he must withdraw the case from the jury (*Sim v Stretch* (England 1936)). Similarly, the judge should withdraw the case if he considers that there is no evidence on which the jury could find that the words would be reasonably understood to refer to the plaintiff (*Knupffer v London Express* (England 1944), *Morgan v Odhams Press Ltd.* (England 1971); see Gatley para. 296).

Sometimes judges will distinguish their judge and jury capacities - for example, *Okolo v Midwest Newspapers Corporation*, where the Nigerian Supreme Court (1977) said that the trial judge "was saying in effect that the publication, when read as a whole, was incapable of conveying to a reasonable jury any defamatory meaning", and *Williams v West African* ((Nigeria 1961) p. 868). Remarkably, one Nigerian judge held that the words were incapable of a defamatory meaning (his "judge" function) and then went on to decide (as jury) whether they did have a defamatory meaning (*Nigerian Textile Mills Ltd. v Punch Nig. Ltd.* (1986 Onalaja J.) p. 901). Had he been sitting with a jury he would not have sent the latter question to the jury. In *Eyo v Eastern Nigeria Information Service* (1963), the judge held that the words were capable of defamatory meaning, but in his "jury capacity" held that they did not have that meaning, although he conceded that it was not impossible for a reasonable jury to come to the opposite conclusion! Is such frankness wise? Nigerian judges still seem attached to the distinction (see *Nigerian Television Authority v Babatope* (1996)).

With respect, Spry Ag. P was correct when he said that reference to juries should be avoided in countries in which the judge sits alone (*Patel v Dhanji* (Kenya 1975) p. 11). He went on to say, *obiter*,

> In my opinion, it serves no useful purpose for a judge sitting alone to take the dual approach and consider first whether the words complained of are capable of a defamatory meaning and then whether they were in fact defamatory. A judge sitting with a jury has "to put an accurate interpretation on the words used" (*per* Lord Porter in *Turner v M-G-M Pictures* [1950] 1 All ER 449 at p. 456) and if he thinks a reasonable jury likely to find the words defamatory, he leaves the question of fact to them. For a judge sitting alone to undertake this exercise seems to me futile. He is hardly likely to take one view of the words in one capacity and a different view in the other. I think he need do no more than decide if the words were defamatory; obviously, if he thinks the words were incapable of a defamatory meaning, he will hold that they were not defamatory (pp. 12-13).

Diplock LJ in *Slim v Daily Telegraph Ltd.* (England 1968) said:

> ...with the concentration of functions in a single adjudicator, the need for his distinguishing between meanings which words are capable of meaning and the choice of one 'right' meaning which they do bear disappears.

The function of the jury is to operate as the voice of the community, for it is in the eyes of the community that the plaintiff alleges he has been defamed. As a judge in Australia (*Dawes v News Ltd.* (1935) p. 318) said,

> ...a judge, who has to discharge the functions of a jury, is not at liberty to affect ignorance of the colloquialisms and vulgarisms, which are familiar to every reader of popular fiction and every habitué of 'the pictures'.

The Audience

Society is not a homogeneous mass of people with the same vocabulary, analytical abilities and social experiences. If there is special knowledge, language or vocabulary which can be proved to have given the words a special meaning in the eyes or ears of the audience, this can be relied upon (the "innuendo" - see below). But what about ordinary people's reactions to ordinary words? Lord Reid said, "The ordinary man does not live in an ivory tower and is not inhibited by a knowledge of the rules of construction" (*Lewis v Daily Telegraph* (1964) AC at 258).

The English Court of Appeal in a recent case observed of the television programme which was the subject of the case before them,

> Its audience would not have given it the analytical attention of a lawyer to the meaning of a document, an auditor to the interpretation of accounts, or an academic to the content of a learned article (*Skuse v Granada Independent* (1993) quoting Lord Diplock in *Slim v Daily Telegraph* (1968) p. 157).

And Lord Devlin observed in *Lewis v Daily Telegraph*,

> The proposition that ordinary words are the same for the lawyers as for the layman is as a matter of pure construction undoubtedly true. But it is very difficult to draw the line between pure construction and implication and the layman's capacity for implication is much greater than the lawyer's. The lawyer's rule is that the implication must be necessary as well as reasonable. The layman reads in an implication much more freely; and unfortunately, *as the law of defamation has to take into account*, is especially prone to do so when it is derogatory (p. 277 - emphasis supplied).

The ordinary man is to be assumed "possessed of such degree of knowledge of the current circumstances of the industry as it may be proper to infer in the circumstances of the case" (*Holdsworth v Associated Newspapers Ltd.* (England 1937) p. 880, quoted in *ACCOR v Brooks* (Rhodesia 1972) p. 4), with "general knowledge and experience of world affairs" in the light of which he will interpret what he hears or reads (Lord Reid in *Lewis v Daily Telegraph* quoted by Onalaja J in *Nigerian Textile Mills v Punch Nig. Ltd.* (1986)).

Some members of the Nigerian Supreme Court seem, with respect, to have erred, when construing words in a newspaper to the effect that the Panel chaired by the plaintiff sought to destroy the institutions in Idoma land "but also *in the prevalent misguided view of the political, administrative and judicial upstarts,...*": they held that the emphasised words did not refer to the Panel but to "upstarts" outside the Panel. Irikefe JSC referred to this as a "tedious parsing exercise" - an unkind but justified judgment, one would think (*Onu v Agbese* (1985)). As the English Court of Appeal recently said, "the court should be cautious of an over-elaborate analysis of the material in issue...[and]...should not be too literal in its approach" (*Gillick v BBC* (1996)). The ordinary reader in *Onu* would surely have associated the misguided view with the plaintiff. Perhaps things should be different if the material was directed at a highly educated readership. The Harare High Court took into account the fact that the publication appeared in a financial newspaper, with a readership "of a generally higher standard of education and intelligence who have a particular interest in political, financial and business affairs" (*Auridiam Zimbabwe (Pvt) Ltd. v Modus Publications (Pvt) Ltd.* (Zimbabwe 1993) p. 370), a case with an extended discussion of the "audience" issue.

If the circumstances giving the statement a particular meaning would be general knowledge, it would seem desirable for the court to take account of them. The Nigerian Supreme Court took "judicial notice" of the fact that when the statement was made - to the effect that the plaintiff had been removed as director of a company "with immediate effect" - the military government was in the process of purging large numbers of public servants for various types of misconduct, and that such removals were always said to be "with immediate effect" (*Dumbo v Idigboe* at 49).

Is the court to decide what would have been the meaning of the words to the *actual* audience - the people who heard or read the words when they were published? Or how the *ordinary* member of the public would have understood the words? Or how the *reasonable* member of the public would have understood them? The courts rarely articulate the question, and tend to talk about "ordinary" and "reasonable" person interchangeably. The House of Lords recently reiterated the principle that the test is what the *reasonable and fair-minded reader* would have understood. There was a conflict between the message conveyed by a headline and that by the text of the article which followed. Lord Bridge (*Charleston and Another v News Group Newspapers Limited* (1995) p. 73) said,

> I have no doubt that [Counsel for the plaintiff] is right in his assertion that many "News of the World" readers who saw the offending publication would have looked at the headlines and photographs and nothing more. But if these readers, without taking the trouble to discover what the article was all about, carried away the impression that two well known actors in legitimate television were also involved in making pornographic films, they could hardly be described as ordinary, reasonable, fair-minded readers.

Not all members of the House were totally at ease with this approach; precedent weighed heavily with them. If the court is sure that substantial numbers of readers/viewers might leap to the wrong conclusion, through a reluctance to do more than glance at headlines and pictures, as may well be the case with readers of some tabloid newspapers, is it right that it should be required to hold that there was no defamation because this was an unreasonable reaction?

One possible view is that the issue is how would the *generality* of the *actual* audience have understood the words - reasonable or not. But an insuperable obstacle to any such approach, in the absence of jury trial, is - how are judges to make any such decision, especially since, as we shall see, no evidence may be called?[2]

Culture, as well as education, occupation and class may lead to different interpretations. Obi-Okoye J in Nigeria observed that "As an Igbo, I know as a fact that exaggeration is the Igbo man's way of emphasis" (*Oforka v Anisiuba* (1979) p. 141). (This was ano doubt ppropriate where both parties were Igbo, but had the hearer been someone whose cultural mores tended towards understatement or irony, what should the judge have presumed?).

Not Admitting Evidence

It has been said many times that the parties ought not to bring witnesses to testify as to how they understood the words complained of, and it was reiterated by the House of Lords in *Charleston*. Kolawole J in Nigeria said

> In the case of words defamatory in their ordinary sense the plaintiff has to prove no more than that they were published; he cannot call witnesses to prove what they understood by the words, nor will it avail the defendant to call any number of witnesses to say that they did not believe the imputation (*Onabanjo v Concord Press of Nigeria Ltd.* (1982) p. 78 actually quoting Goddard LJ in *Hough v London Express* (England 1940) p. 515).

And Jibowu FJ said

> Where the words are ordinary English ones and are plain and unambiguous in their meaning the jury, where there is one, and the judge, where he sits alone, is the judge without further evidence whether the words would reasonably be understood in a defamatory sense and it would be usurping the province of the jury or of the judge, as the case may be, to call a witness to say what he understood the words to mean (*Economides v S. Thomopoulos & Co. Ltd.* (Nigeria 1956)).

In *Ohanbamu v Midwest Newspapers Corporation* (Nigeria 1974), Adefarasin J refused to permit a question asking how a witness understood the words, in the absence of any plea of innuendo (citing the English cases *Tolley v Fry* (1930), *Lewis v Daily Telegraph*, *Grubb v Bristol United Press* (1963) ; see also, to similar effect, Nnaemeka-Agu, JCA in *Abdullahi v Ashadele* (Nigeria 1984) and *Eyo v Eastern Nigeria Information Services* (1963) citing *Daines v Hartley* (England 1848)). As another judge in Nigeria said, "It is settled law that where an action for libel is tried by a Judge sitting alone it is he who has to arrive at a single 'right' meaning of the words complained of" (Adefarasin CJ, in *Adewusi v Sketch* (No. 2) (1978) p. 303). And the Supreme Court of Zambia said, "it is neither for the plaintiff or any witness to give evidence as to, or to interpret, the meaning of the allegedly defamatory statement" (*Zulu v Times Newspapers (Zambia) Ltd.* (1985) pp. 32-3; see also *Zambia Publishing Co. v Zaloumis* (1978), and *Banda v Zambia Publishing Co.* (1982)). And it has been said that the ordinary meaning should not be pleaded (*Onu v Agbese* (Nigeria 1985) citing Gatley). In *Abdullahi v Ashadele* (Nigeria 1984), the words were that the plaintiff had been "arrested in connection with a foreign exchange scandal"; Nnaemeka-Agu J held this to be defamatory in its natural and ordinary meaning, and that evidence was unnecessary and to plead meaning surplusage. However, if the meaning is not very clear, the plaintiff should plead the meaning which he maintains the words have.

Is that law reasonable? It was criticised by Lord Diplock in *Slim v Daily Telegraph* (England 1968 p. 171). However, the Faulks Committee observed

> ...the defects so trenchantly described seem to us inherent in a system which prescribes the criterion as the interpretation of the ordinary reader...To allow the introduction of evidence as to the natural and ordinary meaning which various actual readers or classes of actual readers in fact placed on the words would add heavily to the length and expense of trial, and would we think only cause confusion in the mind of the tribunal of fact (Cmnd 5909, p. 26).

The latter point carries less weight in African jurisdictions for there the judge is the finder of fact as well. But one wonders how useful such evidence would be. The fact that the plaintiff is able to produce a few friends who say they understood the words in a particular way may give no better idea of how widespread (or even how genuine) a reaction this was than the judge would have from his own general knowledge and experience. In *Benson v West African Pilot* (Nigeria 1965), the judge ridiculed the evidence of the plaintiff's witnesses for this reason.

Levels of Meaning and Innuendos

The law now recognises essentially three levels of meaning for the purposes of the law of defamation. There is firstly what is termed the "ordinary and natural meaning" of the words. Secondly there may be an extended meaning which is not immediately apparent to the reader or hearer, but does not depend upon any particularly esoteric knowledge. And thirdly there is sometimes some meaning which would appear only to someone in possession of special knowledge. A statement may have only one of these type of meaning, or it may have two or all three - not necessarily all defamatory. If the plaintiff fails to show that the words can reasonably bear one of the meanings, he can still rely on another or other meanings (provided he has pleaded them if required) (see *Patel v Dhanji* (Kenya 1975) p.10, citing Gatley to the effect that though the plaintiff had failed to prove an innuendo he could still rely on the natural meaning of the words as defamatory).[3]

The leading English judicial exposition of the question of meaning is *Lewis v Daily Telegraph* (1964). The effect of this case is that in addition to setting out the actual words complained of in the pleadings (without which the plaintiff cannot succeed at all), he should also plead any other distinct meanings. Any meaning which is simply an extended meaning should be pleaded separately from any meaning which depends upon extrinsic facts (Gatley, notes to paras. 1075-8).

The three types of meaning are not in practice always easy to distinguish; and lawyers are best advised to err on the side of pleading rather than running the risks that something they thought of as part of the ordinary meaning is thought of by the court to be an extended meaning, or that an expression they thought of as having entered the language is viewed by the court as being an extrinsic fact which ought to be proved.

The third level of meaning is known as an innuendo: to someone with additional knowledge an otherwise innocent statement may take on a defamatory connotation, or a statement which is defamatory on its face may have a further, defamatory meaning, or the additional information may lead the reader to associate the statement with the plaintiff, although it does not identify the plaintiff on its face. (It would also be open to the defendant to argue that an innuendo rendered the meaning *non*-defamatory.)

The second, or extended, level of meaning is often called by the courts a "false" or "popular" innuendo, and the hidden fact type of innuendo a "true" or a "legal" innuendo (see *Lewis v Daily Telegraph*). In South Africa and Zimbabwe the former is sometimes known as a "quasi-innuendo"; one judge described this as "special or local overtones which give [the words] an extended or particularly pointed significance" (*Zvogbo v Kingston's Ltd.* (Zimbabwe 1986) p. 315). In *Auridiam Zimbabwe (Pvt) Ltd. v Modus Publications (Pvt) Ltd.* ((1993) p. 366) the judge expressed his dislike for this "inelegant term". Counsel used the expression "sting-pointing imputation" which the judge characterised as "just as inelegant" though possibly more apposite. He also quoted *Moyse v Mujuru* (Zimbabwe 1992): the quasi-innuendo "draws from [the words] and accentuates what are supposed to be the libellous implications already lurking there".

Some cases may involve both types of innuendo. A newspaper report of a road accident involving a prisoner said that a bottle of brandy was found in the car. The judge observed that this carried an "imputation of bibulousness and breach of prison discipline" (*Thakers v Chipunguhelo* (Tanzania 1965)). The former is a popular innuendo, the latter a legal one since it depended on knowing the prison rules. In the Nigerian case of *Johnson v Daily Times* (1966) the offending article asked "who got the [National] Stadium contract?" The answer given in the article was - the plaintiff. The extrinsic fact was that the plaintiff had been a Minister; the false innuendo was that the plaintiff used his former position improperly to obtain the contract. The judge refused to accept the latter saying "I am firmly of the view that no reasonable fair-minded person can read a defamatory meaning to it" (p. 120). In *Anthony v University College* (Ghana 1973), a number of innuendoes were pleaded, only one of which - based on the fact that the plaintiff was a married woman - was a true one, as pointed out by Date-Bah (1973c, p. 19).

There are many examples of "popular" innuendoes. In *Adewunmi v Oshinowo* (Nigeria 1977), the defendant had said that the plaintiff "brought strange people into the house day and night smoking nauseating substances that is a threat to peace and good health". Adefarasin CJ said "Words written like this would conjure up in the mind of the reasonable reader a person such as a hemp smoker" (p. 196). In *Bello (Haroun) v Oyebola* (Nigeria 1977) the *Daily Times* had published a report that the plaintiff was ordered by a Chief Magistrate to be detained for questioning; the plaintiff complained particularly of the headline "Detention Order...". The Judge held that by inference - an "extended meaning" - this could be taken to mean that the plaintiff had committed a criminal offence. This seems to be taking the inference too far; it might be possible to infer that he was suspected, but not, surely, that he was guilty (see *Lewis v Daily Telegraph*).

A Nigerian court refused to accept there was a popular innuendo in *Sorenson v Paterson* (1957). The school principal wrote to the plaintiff teacher, copy to the Director of Education, advising the plaintiff that she must not be accompanied after dark by any African man, and that the principal was acting especially to "protect the good name and respect which is due to all women in this country". The Supreme Court held that this could not be considered to cast any aspersion on the character of the plaintiff. I find this slightly surprising, and wonder whether the case ought not to have been dealt with as one of qualified privilege. A Malaŵian court refused to accept that a description of the plaintiff lawyer and his wife as "South African preachers" meant they had renounced their citizenship, or owed allegiance to South Africa, or were not proud of being Malaŵian, or were pretending to be preachers from South Africa (*Chiume v Blantyre Print & Packaging Co. Ltd.* (1981)). In *K.E. Poku Ltd. v National Investment Bank* (Ghana 1989-90) the court held that an announcement that the plaintiff's property was to be publicly auctioned did not necessarily mean that it was "broke".

It is approved practice to plead extended meaning; may the plaintiff call evidence as to how the words were understood? A Zimbabwean court observed,

> There is authority for the view that [the plaintiff] may call relevant evidence where the witness would be in a better position than the court in understanding how the words would probably be understood by the reasonable reader (*Zvogbo v Kingston's Ltd.* (1986) p. 315).

The authority cited for this was South African, rather than from common law jurisdictions (e.g. *Ngcobo v Shembe* (1983); *HRH King Zwelithini of*

KwaZulu v Mervis (1978)). Where the judge sits alone, there might seem to be some sense in this type of approach, although it does not seem to correspond to the main stream of English authority (Gatley is clear that it is only when extrinsic facts are also pleaded in support of the meaning that witnesses may be asked whether they in fact understood the words in this sense - para. 1316.). And permitting evidence to be called in the case of extended meaning simply invites counsel to plead such meanings in order to be able to call such witnesses, and would lead to the abrogation of the basic rule.

If the meaning depends upon some extrinsic fact, the facts which give the words a further meaning must be both pleaded and proved (see e.g. *Adedoyin v Nigerian National Press* (1964) which has an extended discussion of the legal innuendo, relying upon *Lewis v Daily Telegraph*).[4] To take a simple example: there is nothing apparently defamatory in saying that Chief S.L. Akintola was "the son of Chief Sawe of Ilesha and Alice" - unless you know that he was the Member of the legislatures for Ogbomosho and was always known as a son of Ogbomosho. Someone who knew the latter might think that he had been falsely representing himself as a son of Ogbomosho (*Akintola v Anyiam* (Nigeria 1961)). In *Awolowo v Zik Enterprises Ltd.* (Nigeria 1952) the Privy Council held the judge had been right in accepting a long list of true innuendoes, things which were not actually stated in the document complained of but which covered both identification of the plaintiff and the subject matter of the libel, which depended on the following extrinsic facts:

> ...that the appellant was the leader of the Action Group party; that he was a Minister; that he was a member of the delegation referred to in Exhibits B., B.1 and B.3, that the civil case known as Iga Idunganran was pending before the West African Court of Appeal; that Oba Adeniji Adele in whose favour judgement had been given was a prominent member and supporter of the Action Group party; that Sadiku Salami was a first cousin of the appellant's wife and had been convicted of murder and that an appeal was pending to the West African Court of Appeal.

It is necessary to prove that the words were published to someone in possession of the further facts which, it is alleged, made the statement defamatory, but it is not necessary to produce anyone who said they did understand the words in their "hidden" meaning (*Hough v London Express* (England 1940), cited without dissent in *Awolowo v Zik Enterprises*).

Statements not in Standard English

Where the statement complained of was made not in standard English but either in another language or in slang, the plaintiff must prove the meaning of which he complains. In *Ogbah v Akpede* the statement was "You Wayo chief" which the plaintiff alleged meant "you fraudulent and unreliable chief"; however, he failed to prove this - indeed the court pointed out that he did not even make clear whether the word was pidgin or Isoko (Nigeria 1975). The Court seems to have understood it sufficiently well to hold that it was mere abuse (pp. 120-1). A Seychelles court held that since the official language of the court is English, words in French and Creole must be proved (*Bouchereau v Rassool* (1975)). In Mauritius, although the judges use English for their own observations, they switch with ease between English and French, and do not insist on the proof of words in French.

However, in a few cases judges have declined to hold that it necessary to produce an interpreter when all the parties speak the language in which the defamatory remark was made. (All the cases of which I am aware concern Igbo.)

> How foreign is Ibo language in Ogwashi-Uku High Court? In the result I find that the host of authors relied on in art. 1207 [now para. 1297 of Gatley] are as to languages foreign to England and the English courts. In that sense Ibo cannot be said to be a foreign language in a Nigerian court where nearly all the parties involved are Ibos and any grave mistake can easily be detected and corrected (*Iwowo v Emelezie* (1977)).

And in *Osuji v Agulana* (1980) the court held it superfluous and a waste of time and money for the parties to call an independent interpreter to give evidence. If the court wished it could use the regular court interpreter to confirm the English translation. There is something somewhat ludicrous about the notion that a judge whose native tongue is Igbo, should be obliged in theory to take the meaning of words proved in English by an interpreter whose English is almost certainly less competent than that of the judge. In reality, of course, the judge will do no such thing; but his hands are tied if the plaintiff's lawyers fail to realise the necessity to plead, and to go through the ritual of proving, the meaning; the result may be, as another judge said in the same court, "She has been shut out from a proper determination of her case on the merits by a legal technicality which is not within her competence to understand or appreciate" (*Ejionfobiri v Anejemba* (1977), holding that Igbo must be proved in the same way as Yoruba or Russian).

The meaning of slang must be proved: plaintiffs have had to prove the meaning of "pansy" (homosexual) (*Thaarup v Hulton Press* (England 1943)), or that *pilon*, which literally means "pestle" also means homosexual in Seychelles Creole (*Wyatt v Corgat* (1964) - the court actually held the meaning not to have been established) or that "jumper" in Malaŵi means a woman who goes from one man to another (*Hampton v Herkes* 1961-63). The special meaning may be proved by evidence, or by the use of reference works such as a dictionary. But if the word has really entered everyday speech in the community it will be unnecessary to prove it - though it would be unwise for a pleader to assume that a word had sufficiently entered the language until a court had held it to be so. If the court takes the view that it has entered common speech evidence would be inadmissible (*Barnett v Allen* (England 1858), 157 ER at p. 517).[5]

Aids to Interpretation

Looking at the Context

The judge must strive to decide on the basis of the overall picture; he must not just select a word or two, or even a few sentences. "If in one part of the publication something disreputable to the plaintiff is stated, but that is removed by the conclusion, the bane and the antidote must be taken together" said Baron Alderson famously (*Chalmers v Payne* (England 1835) 150 ER at 68, quoted by Olagunju J in *Omolowo v Punch Ltd.* (Nigeria 1985) p. 1252). One Nigerian judgment reprints two lengthy newspaper articles in order properly to elucidate the defamatory content of one (*Ohanbamu v Midwest Newspaper Corporation* (1974)).

In *Okolo v Midwest Newspaper Corporation* (Nigeria 1977) the article had used the words "embezzlement", which on the face of it refers to a criminal offence (in English law, although the expression does not appear in the criminal law of Nigeria). However, the courts held that taking into account the full context, including the phrase "₦2,000 embezzlement suit" it was clear that the case which the paper was reporting was a civil one. The Court stressed the importance of not taking words out of their context and of deciding on the basis of the broad impression created. Another Nigerian judge, Akpata J, said, "the ordinary, reasonable man is not the man who bases his impression on an ambiguous headline of a publication without reading the body of the news item" (*Akpojaro v Bendel Newspapers Corporation* (1981)). While this approach has the merit of working against liability in libel, which is perhaps to the good, it does play into the hands of the popular press which sets out to create a shocking image in the minds of its readers, or attract the passer-by into buying the paper. This might particularly be so in countries in which significant proportions of the population have limited literacy and might well understand a headline but be reluctant to tackle the body of the text, especially in a foreign language.

The Nigerian Court of Appeal was surely wrong in *Benue Printing and Publishing Corporation v Gwagwada* ((1989) to hold defamatory this headline: "Contractor absconds with ₦1.46 million mobilisation fee"; only at the end of the article would it become clear who the contractor was, by which time it would also have become clear that the body of the article alleged nothing of the kind. And in *Sobayo v Daily Times of Nigeria Ltd.* (1977) where the headline said "Lawyer sued for negligence", the reader would not have known which lawyer was involved until two words before it became clear that it was *neglect* not negligence he was being sued for.

Using a Dictionary?

In *Omolowo v Punch* (Nigeria 1985) the judge looked up, or was referred to, *Webster's New Twentieth Century Dictionary* for the meaning of "debauchery". The same word was looked up in *Denloye v Solarin* (Nigeria 1974), and in *Okwuwe v Onifade* (Nigeria 1981) Yinka Ayoola J looked up "dead wood" in Webster's. Is this right? The judge is required to give his judgment of the reaction of the ordinary reader (except where there is an innuendo pleaded). Most of us do not do our ordinary reading with a dictionary in hand. Furthermore if one looks up a word in an *English* dictionary one will find the use of the word in England (or the American usage in Webster's). English as spoken in other countries may be very different. The dictionary will not tell one the meaning in these versions of English; and its use may divert attention from the real issue. In *Kamanyire v New Vision Newspaper* (1992) the judge held that "deal" did not carry a defamatory meaning, saying that Uganda does not have its own dictionary. Maybe it does not have its own dictionary - but it might have its own usages! The dictionary approach departs from the looking at the whole impression which is supposed to take place. There are Mauritian examples, too, such as *Gilchrist v Le Mauricien Co. Ltd.* (1927), on the meaning of "*palper*", in French: it means to touch but may specifically mean to touch money (quoting two dictionaries); but in the context of the language used as a whole was held to mean taking bribes. In fact judges seem to look up the meaning of words they must know already, and the exercise seems somewhat pointless.

Punctuation

In one Nigerian case the court held that putting the word "lawyer" into inverted commas carried a meaning which was defamatory - a suggestion that the plaintiff was not a proper lawyer (*Ogbuatu v Daily Times of Nigeria Ltd.* (1976); see also *Onu v Agbese* (Nigeria 1985)).

Abuse and Mere Rhetoric

The common law, emphasising reputation rather than dignity, does not give a remedy for abuse. It may be the words themselves which are abusive rather than defamatory, such as saying that the plaintiff was a fool like a cow (*Mandala v Mwamtobe* (Tanzania 1973)); but very often it is the circumstances in which they were uttered that are significant. Thus in *Bakare v Ishola* (1959) the defendant said (in Yoruba) "You are a thief. Ex-convict, you have just come out of prison", but since this was said during a heated argument it was held it was not actionable (1959).[6] In the Ghanaian case of *Bonsu v Forson* the words were "You are a hopeless lawyer" ((1964; see the comments of Date-Bah (1973a, p. 131)), and in *Ajala v Adelagun*, "You are an ex-convict" and "You are not the legal wife of Mr Oyeniyi Ajala" (Nigeria 1979). The judge in *Okunowo v Adebanjo* (Nigeria 1977) said (in a slightly sexist way, one might think)

> It is a matter of common knowledge of which I take judicial notice, that people in this country, particularly women, call each other 'ex-convict, prostitute' in their heated arguments, quarrels and/or altercations, which often lead to blows or fights and which no-one takes seriously as they were words of anger.

But in another case the words (in Igbo), "you brought the thieves with whom you stole my goat..." were held to be actionable because there was no quarrel between the parties (one might also observe that the words were rather more specific than a simple accusation of general knavery, and might therefore have been taken more seriously) (*Ibeanu v Uba* (Nigeria 1972); see also *Chuku v Nkrumah* (Ghana 1959)). And counsel in Nigeria, again, argued that "in our rural communities, one often gets the impression that vulgar abuse is a way of life, because on a trifle, they call themselves [sc. call each other names] and malign each other without anyone present taking them seriously" (*Ezejiofor v Ogu* (1981) p. 424). But the judge said that in the circumstances, where the plaintiff had been appealing for village unity, and received for his pains "an atrocious attack on his integrity" there was no room for the application of *Bakare v Ishola*. It seems that the "mere abuse" point was not argued in the Nigerian case of *Rashid v Adesuwa* (1974), where the statement was "You armed robber, where did you get the signboard which you are placing in front of your store? You are only 12 months at Lokoja, but you have acquired so much wealth with the stores full up". Was the defendant really saying the plaintiff was an armed robber?

However, courts assume that more reflection precedes writing. As Somolu J said in *Awolowo v West African Pilot* (Nigeria 1962, p. 29)

> Indeed, the very words 'vulgar abuse' imply verbal exchanges of words face to face, uttered in the heat of a quarrel and passion. I cannot see how there can be heat in a man who sits down to compose a libel, with his supposed opponent many miles away. Vulgar abuse arises out of a situation where a man answers back or abuses the other with no opportunity to cool off, but can that be said of a man who sits down to write a long article and reads it over before sending it over to the publishers? I say no. The heat in him, if any there is, must have time to cool down in the long process of thinking, writing and reading.

But suppose the words were spoken, but then reported in writing? In *Benson v West Africa Pilot* (Nigeria 1965) the judge felt compelled by this supposed rule about written abuse to hold that the words in question were actionable. The plaintiff and Mr B had been having a "squabble", and, in an interview with the newspaper, Mr B retaliated to an attack by the plaintiff by saying he had "no time for an idiot and a simpleton". The judge said (p.169),

> I am not at all satisfied that a reasonable reader of the article under reference will reasonably construe the words 'idiot or simpleton' as meaning that the plaintiff is mentally unsound or deficient in sense and intelligence or unfit to be a minister or practice his profession or hold any position of responsibility. It is obvious to me that before any such reader got to the concluding passage which contains the words idiot or simpleton, such reader would have discovered or understood from the article that Mr. B as a politician was refuting accusation levelled against him by the plaintiff and was challenging the latter to substantiate the accusation if he was serious. With this impression on the mind of the reader, the reference to the plaintiff in the concluding sentence as idiot or simpleton will obviously be understood by him as amounting to no more than a vulgar abuse. To hold otherwise is to my mind to abdicate one's common sense.

However, the Judge went on to hold that defamation in written form could not be dismissed as mere abuse. A rational distinction could surely be drawn between the defendant who sits down to write, and therefore, as Somolu J observed, will have cooled down somewhat, and writing which reports someone else's, perhaps heated, words. Furthermore, the cases elsewhere are to the effect that the judge may not decline to send a case to the jury on the basis that written words were mere abuse; the jury may still decide that they were not to be taken seriously as damaging the plaintiff's reputation. Since the judge in this case combined the functions of judge and jury, he was still at liberty to say that in all the circumstances he did not consider the words defamatory. (Perhaps in this case the judge would have done well to distinguish between his judge and jury functions!)

However, in another Nigerian case one Supreme Court justice dismissed words as "vulgar statement and mere abuse" when they were in fact written (*Sketch v Ajagbemokeferi* (1989) p. 698 (Wali JSC); see also the remarks of Sulu-Gambari and Akpabio JJCA in *Ekanem-Ita v Fetuga* (Nigeria 1991)). He was not using the expression to suggest the heat of a quarrel or a response to attack, but simply to signify loose language which would not be taken seriously. This seems quite appropriate.

Cases on the heat of political debate, as opposed to the heat of quarrel, are somewhat similar. In *Velempini v Engineering Services Department Workers' Committee for the City of Bulawayo* the judge pointed out that in discussion about the grievances of workers "the parties sometimes make wild allegations against each other and in my view these ought not to be the subject of defamation actions" ((Zimbabwe 1988) p. 184). Another Zimbabwean judge quoted a South African judge:

> How soon the audiences of political speakers would dwindle if the speakers were to use the tones, terms and expressions that one could expect from a lecturer at a meeting of the ladies' agricultural union on the subject of growing roses! (*Zvogbo v Kingston's Ltd.* (1986) p. 318, quoting Ludorf J in *Pienaar v Argus* (1956)).

In Zambia a newspaper published an item to which the plaintiff objected in which it said, *inter alia*, "Who really cares if some fool decides to quit one political party to join another one?" Of this, and other phrases including "cheap politician" the court said "the words constitute meaningless abuse, almost an occupational hazard of the cut and thrust of political life" (*Musonda v Zambia Publishing Co. Ltd.* (1976)). Some Mauritian courts too have expected some robustness of politicians: one suggested that politicians ought to be thick-skinned enough to tolerate some measure of invective (see *Lesage v Mason* (1976); *Chong Leung v Selvon* (1978)), while another said that allegations of racism were hurled about so much in Mauritian politics that they had lost much of their edge, and refused to hold an allegation of racism actionable (*Walter v Jugdami* (1976)).[7]

However, also in Mauritius compensation may be given for words which were viewed as abusive and insulting rather than damaging to reputation, even where they were only spoken (Mauritius law not recognising a distinction between libel and slander anyway) (see *Desbleds v Hugnin* (1942)). Such a statement may be an "*injure*" under the Penal Code, translatable as "abuse", although sometimes as "slander" by Mauritian courts (e.g. *Galéa v Rousell* (1891) p. 84). This is "any insulting expression, term of contempt or invective which does not include any imputation of fact", and is actionable. One court, however, held that the words "*Baise votre maman*" literally "Kiss your mother" did not convey the meaning that the plaintiff had improper relations with his mother, but were simply "an abusive expression". It may perhaps be accounted for on the basis of the influence of the English approach to abuse. This is speculation since neither the Civil Code nor any English case is mentioned (*De Vilaine v Montocchio* (1909)).

In many systems of customary law, with their concern about feelings, abuse is actionable (for example, Goldin & Gelfand, 1975, pp. 202-3; see also Chapter 2 above). In a Nigerian case, *Ayinuola v Olayimide* (1985), the High Court held that an action under customary law (on appeal from a customary court) should not succeed because in the circumstances of a quarrel the statement (that the plaintiff was a harlot) was mere abuse. Unfortunately the court seemed to be following *Bakare v Ishola* (above), which was not a case on customary law. Some have argued that the common law ought to be brought into line with customary law in this respect (e.g. Date-Bah, 1973a). It has also been suggested that in some systems of customary law the rationale for including abuse was at least partly the risk of breach of the peace (Goldin & Gelfand, 1975); the common law would these days consider the prevention of breaches of the peace to be the function of the criminal rather than the civil law, a distinction not so marked in customary law.

In Roman-Dutch law, too, statements which are abusive rather than defamatory are actionable, as infringements of *dignitas* - as in the case in which a black South African successfully sued for being called a "kaffir" by a policeman (*Ciliza v Minister of Police* (South Africa 1976)).

Identifying the Plaintiff

The mere fact that the plaintiff recognises himself, or thinks he does so, in the statement is not enough. In a Mauritius case the words (a supposed report of a trial for poaching) referred only to a "resident of Rose Hill" - apparently a "thickly populated township"). But the appeal court said that the reasonable reader could not have made the connection with the plaintiff (who had been actually prosecuted for the lesser offence of being found in possession of venison) and therefore the magistrate should have found for the defendant (*Maurice Press Ltd. v Grizell* (1964), citing *Knupffer v London Express* (England 1944)).

Newspapers sometimes run into trouble by illustrating news items with library pictures; which presumably happened in *Omotayo v African Newspapers of Nigeria Ltd.* (1986)): a press article about extravagant Igbo wedding customs was illustrated by a photograph of the wedding of the plaintiffs (judging by their name, a Yoruba couple). The court rejected the suggestion that the reader would link the plaintiffs with the content of the article; they would realise that the picture was just a picture of a wedding and no more. Somewhat similar was *Daily Times v Emokpae* (Nigeria 1979) where a picture of the plaintiff adorned an article on the immorality of youth. The Court of Appeal said that Savage J had erred in holding that the remarks were defamatory of the plaintiff.

It did not help a journalist sued in Sierra Leone that he had said "actual names have been altered" but used the plaintiff's real name, and a photograph (*Princess James v Charteris* (1962)). In one remarkable Nigerian case, the judge held that the plaintiffs were not referred to even though their names *were* used! A newspaper stated that prominent personalities were gripped with fear due to having received anonymous letters. One such was reproduced, having been supplied, the paper said, by the police, and it ended with the names of the signatories, which the plaintiffs said were read as being themselves. Obi-Okoye J held that a reasonable person would not have believed the plaintiffs were the signatories: the news item said that the letters were anonymous, and no addresses were mentioned (save for one street number and name but no town). All in all, the judge said (also influenced by the fact that two of the plaintiff's witnesses who purported to interpret the letter were illiterate!) the reasonable person would not have understood the publication to refer to the plaintiffs (*Ilonuba v Star Printing & Publishing Co. Ltd.* (1979), citing the *Newstead* and *Hulton* cases below). There should have been *no* evidence from the plaintiff's witnesses "interpreting" the letters, since this is a matter for the trier of fact. And is it not possible that the ordinary (and even reasonable) reader might not have engaged in the same textual analysis as the judge?

Generally if the plaintiff's actual name is used his task will be easier. It is irrelevant that the defendant did not intend to refer to him, even if, for example, the defendant thought he had invented the name. The test remains what the reasonable reader would have thought. Where a newspaper reported the conviction for bigamy of Harold Newstead of Peckham (in London) it was successfully sued by another Harold Newstead who lived in the same area (*Newstead v London Express* (England 1940)); *a fortiori*, a newspaper which reported that Mustapha Bello had been charged, when it was true of Bello Mustapha (*Bello (Mustapha) v Oyebola* (Nigeria 1974)). An example of a name believed to be fictitious was Artemus Jones - the actual possessor of this very unusual name was held able to sue (*Hulton v Jones* (England 1910)). Perhaps John Smith, to take the archetypical common English name, would find it difficult to satisfy the court that he was understood to be referred to in the absence of any other identifying factor. Indeed, in *Hulton* there was such another factor: "churchwarden".

And even if the plaintiff is convinced he was intended he must prove the link between himself and the statement, for example if the name used is not his own, but is, for example, a nickname. As a matter of pleading and proof the plaintiff must show he is the person who would have been understood: Nnamdi Azikiwe failed to show that he was meant by "Ben Azikiwe" (*Service Press v Azikiwe* (Nigeria 1951)). Counsel would have to have shown that readers of the paper would have known (as was the fact) that Azikiwe was christened Benjamin.[8] And in another Nigerian case the plaintiff failed because the statement of which he complained referred to Christian Emez*oum* but his name was Christian Emez*uom*! (*Daily Times of Nigeria Ltd. v Emezuom* (1990)). The Court of Appeal said he ought to have called a member of the public to testify that he understood the plaintiff to be referred to, notwithstanding the spelling difference - which goes counter to the usual approach of leaving interpretation to the courts. Does the name Emezoum even exist, one wonders. In *Etchie v Ozurumba* (Nigeria 1964-69) the plaintiff succeeded although the name used was slightly different from the official version of his name.

In *Williams v West African Pilot* (Nigeria 1961) three leading lights of the Action Group - Chiefs Rotimi Williams, Akintola and Awolowo - persuaded the court that they would be identified by nicknames (The Brain, the Propagandist and the Fuehrer respectively) coupled with cartoon portraits (stressing their large size, tribal marks and spectacles respectively.) A cartoon - including Ondo "tribal marks" - was also involved in *Ajala v Are* (Nigeria 1985).

In *Rwabugabya v East African Newspapers* (Uganda 1968) the plaintiff claimed that he resembled the person pictured in an advertisement - and that was defamatory because to permit his picture to be used would be contrary to the ethics of his profession. The court seemed to think that evidence of the true identity of the person pictured disposed of the case, but the criterion ought to have been what the reasonable reader would have thought - though obviously courts should be cautious about leaping to the conclusion that a newspaper photograph would be reasonably thought to resemble someone different from the true subject.

In many cases phrases without names have served to identify plaintiffs, especially where only one person fits the description: a "Minister from Aboh" in the state government (*Dafe v Tswinor* (Nigeria 1967), the "President of a Customary Court in Ipetumodu" (*Oloyede v Sketch Publishing Co. Ltd.* (Nigeria 1977) or the "first President of the Kenya National Union of Teachers" (*Ayany v Ogot* (1968)) and even "this bloody Greek" when the plaintiff was the only Greek shopkeeper in town (*Mavromatis v Douglas* (Zimbabwe 1971)). In an old case a Mauritian train driver succeeded for an allegation that he was drunk; his name was not mentioned, but the details of the train and time were (*Wright v L'Homme* (1868)). In *Shomade v Concord Press of Nigeria Ltd.* (1983) (decided by Onalaja J and referred to by the same judge in *Kuti v Vanguard Media Ltd.* (1991) p. 201), the paper referred to a UPN legislator, a legal practitioner, hailing from a popular and politically active indigenous Lagos family; the plaintiff was the only member of the State House of Assembly who was a lawyer hailing from a political, indigenous family. For other "close fits" see *Ukpomah v Daily Times of Nigeria Ltd.* (1979) and *New Nigerian Newspapers Ltd. v Adewusi* (1983) - "one-time senior police detective and now one of the most high-ranking police officers in the country", a description the plaintiff clearly fitted; indeed, he was one of the best-known police officers in Nigeria. More recently seven plaintiffs in Zimbabwe succeeded when the newspaper article had referred to seven members of an interim committee who had suspended Mr Tekere from ZUM the previous week, though none of them was named (*Mushonga v Bango* (1992)).

Reference to the Plaintiff and Innuendoes

Many of the cases mentioned above involved an identificatory innuendo. It is not clear in all these cases whether in fact the plaintiff had pleaded and proved the innuendo, or whether the facts seemed so obvious that the court accepted the reference to the plaintiff, although the strict position is that the facts ought to be pleaded, and proved. In *Mavromatis v Douglas* the judge says that the plaintiff pleaded an innuendo unnecessarily as the words were plainly defamatory, which seems to miss the point. It should be shown that the facts were known to some people who would have read or heard the publication, and evidence is admissible from those who read it as to whether they did in fact make the connection with the plaintiff (*Cassidy v Daily Mirror* (England 1929), *Hough v London Express* (England 1940)). It is not necessary for these witnesses to say that they thought the words defamatory (*The Nation v Chesire* (Kenya 1984)).

A particularly oblique form of innuendo is where there was no mention of the plaintiff as such at all. In *Cassidy v Daily Mirror* the statement complained of referred to a man and "his fiancée"; this was held to be defamatory of the plaintiff who was the man's wife: others would, she said, think she was living in sin with him. She had to prove that she was known to others as his wife. This was applied in Kenya (*The Nation v Cheshire*, above): the plaintiff had been separated from her husband for a number of years (and had started divorce proceedings by the time the libel suit came to trial). But she objected that a photograph in the press captioned to the effect that "Mrs Chesire, the wife of Mr Reuben Chesire" (not the plaintiff) had presented the prizes at a golf tournament would suggest to those who knew the plaintiff that she had lived in sin with him. Had it not been for English cases like *Cassidy* it seems that the court might well have decided that readers would not have reached any such conclusion. The Court was influenced also by the fact that the *Cassidy* line of cases (more specifically *Hough v London Express*) had been followed by the East African Court of Appeal: in *East African Standard v Gitau* (Kenya 1970) the plaintiff claimed he had been defamed because the newspaper had printed a photograph of his car after an accident, and said that no-one had reported the accident. Although he was not named, the plaintiff showed that the car was his and that some people knew that and identified him by his car. He was therefore able to establish the innuendo that he had not reported an accident in which his car was involved.[9]

The Court of Appeal in *Chesire* could have distinguished both *Cassidy* and *Gitau*, and held that where the plaintiff had been separated from her husband for so long the words were not capable of carrying any implication about her, or that they could have held that they did so only if she established knowledge of a monogamous marriage - which she had not done. And if the statement did refer to her it was more likely to imply that she was now divorced, which would not have been the assumption on the facts of *Cassidy*, and in the England of the 1920s. The holding that words are capable of a defamatory meaning is not a decision of law in the sense that a decision forms a binding precedent (Gatley, para. 49). There is authority for the fact that "the finding of fact as to the meaning of words may be reversed on appeal" (Gatley para. 1492, citing *Slim v Daily Telegraph* (England 1968) p. 186-7). However, the Court of Appeal felt unable to interfere with this finding by the trial judge - but did reduce the damages very much.

In *Oppon v Advance Press* (Ghana 1980), the statement on the face of it defamed a long dead woman; two of her descendants claimed they were defamed. The judge said, citing *Hulton v Jones* (above), that it was enough if people who knew the plaintiff would know he was the person defamed, and apparently accepted that this was the situation here.

More Than One Potential Plaintiff

If there are many people of the same name it may be difficult to convince the court that anyone was in fact defamed. But in *Wacha v Zambia Printing Co. Ltd.* (1975) the statement referred to a "black expatriate gynaecologist". There were only two people in the country who fitted this description, of whom the plaintiff was one; it was held that he could sue - as no doubt could the other one. In *Bolokor v Alade*, in which the plaintiff had been named with two other women students in an article which said a lecturer had had an affair with one of them, the plaintiff succeeded (Nigeria 1982).

It is sometimes suggested that there is a rule about "class libel": that if a class of people is defamed no individual member of the class can sue; in *Daily Times v Emokpae* (Nigeria 1977) it was observed, *obiter*, that the remarks were critical not of the plaintiff but of "youth" generally, who could not sue because they constituted a class. This is similar to the observation: "If a man wrote that all lawyers were thieves, no particular lawyer could sue him unless there was something to point to the particular individual" (*Eastwood v Holmes* (England 1858)). However, if the defendant said "All the lawyers in X town are thieves" and there were only three lawyers in town there is little doubt that all three could sue. This is not because one is a class defamation and the other is not - three lawyers can be a class as much as 4000 - but because the reasonable person in the first instance would not point the finger at any individual and say he had been described as a thief. In other words, the supposed class libel rule is only an application of the general question of whether the reasonable listener or reader would identify the plaintiff (*Knupffer v London Express* (England 1944), cited in various African cases including the Judicial Committee in *Awolowo v Zik Enterprises* (Nigeria 1955), also in *Oppon v Advance Press* above).

Lord Porter said,

> ...the first question is: Are the words in conjunction with the relevant circumstances reasonably capable of being understood to refer to the plaintiff? (*Hough v London Express* (England 1940) p. 510).

This is the way the courts approach the question, but it is some way from reality. Experience teaches that the public may indeed think less of an individual member of a class if it has been attacked by a source which it takes seriously, or the language of which is sufficiently inflammatory. The criminal law has long taken account of this, in the law of sedition which includes stirring up discord among classes of the population, and in more recent creations like the offence of incitement to racial hatred. But the civil law does not take the same approach. Fleming (1992, p. 535) suggests,

> The common law sets its face against civil sanctions for vilification, not of individuals, but of a whole class of persons distinguishable by race, colour, creed or calling, in part because of concern over multiplicity of claims, in part for fear of unduly inhibiting political discussion and criticism.

He does ask, however, "Why not a class action for an injunction?".

Incidentally, in a Tanzanian case the judge refused to accept a suggestion that Arabs generally were associated with homosexuality. The plaintiff was not himself an Arab, but complained that the defendant had referred to him "moving with Arabs in guest-houses". The judge said,

> It was impressed upon me, but I think without verve, that any informed person reading about movements with an Arab in a guest house would infer immorality of a perverted kind...An inference of immorality may probably be available [sc. applicable?] to a section of society but not generally...The plaintiff brought no evidence in this respect. And the court cannot assume that Arabs are as a rule disposed to perverted behaviour.

With respect the point is not whether Arabs are inclined to such behaviour, but what the ordinary Tanzanian would infer from the statement. It is a usage of language issue rather than one about the behaviour of Arabs (*Jonathan v Athuman Khalfan* (1980) pp. 179-80). Anyway the plaintiff won, without any need for the judge to rely on a tasteless ethnic stereotype.

To return to the way the courts actually approach this question: how likely they are to hold that a reader or listener would have understood the remark to relate to the plaintiff will depend on factors like the size of the class, and the plaintiff's place in that class.[10] However, in *Ortenburg v Plamoudon* (Canada 1914) the plaintiff who was Jewish successfully sued for an attack on Jews in Quebec, there being 75 families in a population of 80,000. It is unlikely that this would be the approach in most courts. In *Shellam v Leal* (Mauritius 1873) the court held that the plaintiff could sue when "Senior Officers" of police were defamed; it is not clear how many there were in this class, although the plaintiff clearly fitted the description. It is also obvious that had the description been much wider there would have been no liability.

Only two or three people fitted the description: "top officials of Nigeria Airways" who it was said had taken oaths to conceal corruption, and the Secretary of the Corporation could sue (*Dalumo v Sketch Publishing Co.* (1972)). This was distinguished in *Nzenwa v Kwara State Printing & Publishing Corpn.* (Nigeria 1980) (Araka CJ) - "several officials" of the Rangers International Football Club were being "indicted"; the plaintiff was Chairman, but there were 3 other officers, the coach and 4 other executive members, so the plaintiff was held unable to show the statement referred to him. In *Ebizie v Midwest Mass Communication Corporation* (decided originally 1977, Chukwuani J) a publication alleged fraud on the part of "Four top executives of the East Central State Ministry of Works Nsukka"; the plaintiff was the Principal Executive Engineer in the Nsukka area. Indeed, the judge said only two people fitted the description, so the plaintiff succeeded. Each of the barmaids in the Lords Bar could sue for the allegation that they had VD (*Lords Bar v The People Newspapers Ltd.* (Uganda 1972)); it is not apparent how many barmaids there were. The offending publication referred to "all", but only two sued. The Chairman and all the members of the Lint Marketing Board could sue for a statement which referred to that Board by name and to "those of the Board" (*Dasani v Uganda African Newspapers* (1971). In *Maskini v Mbugus* (Tanzania 1975) there was an allegation of tribalism favouring Chagga people on the part of the Tanzania Zambia Road Services; the plaintiff identified himself because he was a personnel officer, was himself a Mchagga, and other issues of the newspaper mentioned him by name. In *Cobbett-Tribe v Zambia Publishing Co. Ltd.* (1973) a newspaper had criticised the Zambian Law Society for a statement that the rule of law requires that people should not be detained without being taken to court. It said lawyers only wanted to get custom, were ignorant and a bunch of fortune-seekers. It was held that any member of the 7-strong Council of the Law Society could sue since the circumstances pointed at the

Council rather than the individual members of the society (the actual plaintiff was the Vice-President). In *Ajuang v Magak* (Kenya 1973) "Luos sack Nairobi Officials" was held to refer to the 6 officials of the Nairobi Branch of the Luo Union.

An interesting example is *Awolowo v Zik Enterprises* (Nigeria 1952) where the defendants argued that the allegations referred to a whole political party - the Action Group - and not to any individual. However, the Privy Council accepted the arguments of the plaintiff, based on innuendoes which it held proved, that a reasonable reader would link the allegations to a delegation of Ministers (of which the plaintiff, who was Minister for Local Government in the Western Region and Leader of the Action Group, formed part).

A reference to all the delegates to the Nigerian constitutional conference in London in 1957 could not be taken to be defamatory of any one delegate - but could be taken to refer to delegates actually named in one paragraph of the article (*Edukugho v Sunday Times* (1958)). A less convincing case is *Zulu v Times Newspapers (Zambia) Ltd.* (1985), where the statement was about "a good number of the leaders" - and elsewhere referred to leaders of the party and Government. There were surely too many such leaders in Zambia for the reasonable reader to be able to identify a particular individual. However, the court did hold that the reference to the plaintiff requirement was satisfied, though they went on to hold that the particular statement was not defamatory. Another Zambian case is *Musonda v Zambia Publishing Co. Ltd.* (1976) where a paragraph which said "some of the people now organising press conferences have never been heard of except perhaps by their unfortunate wives, girl friends..." was held not to be able to be construed as referring to the plaintiff for the purposes of defamation as it seemed that there were a number of people to whom the paragraph was referring.

A relevant factor ought to be whether the statement suggests that all, or only some, of the members of the class to which the plaintiff belongs have the alleged characteristic or defect. Even if the class is small it ought to make a difference whether the defect is attributed to "a few", or "some" or "all" of them. This is articulated in a Zanzibar case, where the statement said the members of the Ismailia Council were "mostly" illiterate and inexperienced (*Emperor v Fazal Jan Mohamed* (1907)). This was a criminal case under section 499 Indian Penal Code. The court said (p. 247), "There is an old English case in which it was held that a person who had said 'One of you three is perjured' was not guilty of slander in an action by the three persons referred to as no one of them could prove he was the person referred to (Sir

John Bourne's case, cited Cro. Eliz. 497, and see also Jones and Reddich [actually *James v Rutlech*] (1599) 4 Rep. 17)", also referring to *Giraud v Beach* (New York).

Language which is in the plural may be taken as referring to only one individual. In one Kenyan case the allegations were contained in letters published in a newspaper and written by people from Athi River; they referred to clinical assistants in the plural (and in the case of the headline to "Quacks at Athi River"). The plaintiff was the only clinical assistant at Athi River and succeeded in his action (*Kajima v East African Newspapers (Nation Series) Ltd.* (1972)). In *Bakare v Oluwide* (Nigeria 1969) language in the plural was coupled with a caricature which the court accepted could be taken to depict the plaintiff; he was held able to sue. The statement read in part:

> Not all Nigerians are poor, hungry, naked, unemployed and fatigued by toil. There are quite a few where tables are decked with venison and choice wine, whose palaces are built to face the ocean breeze, who lounge in luxury in their luxury clubs built with public funds in workers residential areas, who attire themselves in gold chains and beadly HATS [*sic*], who are opulent enough to sleep at traffic lights in their Rolls Royces...

The plaintiff lived in Queen's Drive, Ikoyi, Lagos (which looks across the lagoon), ran the Surulere Night Club, wore gold chains and beaded hats, and owned a Rolls Royce!

Extraneous circumstances may also point to a particular plaintiff even if on the face of it the statement is unclear as to which members of a class are referred to. In an East African case a newspaper story stated that "Ten Uganda Asians have been arrested in connection with an alleged passport and immigration racket". Clearly the entire Ugandan Asian community could not have sued. But the plaintiff had in fact been arrested two days before - under emergency regulations, not in connection with a passport racket. He was held able to sue (*Shah v Uganda Argus* (1972), see also *Maskini v Mbugus* above).

Other Publications

If there was a news item elsewhere in a newspaper, or in an earlier issue which, when read with the item actually complained of, would identify the plaintiff, this would call for the pleading of extrinsic facts. Thus the court read a statement in a newspaper referring to seven members of a committee who had done something the previous week, with an article published the previous week stating that they had done that thing (*Mushonga v Bango*

(Zimbabwe 1992)). And in Mauritius the court had no difficulty in identifying "Jimmy Boom" a member of the Legislative Council of the British Colony "Fortuna Juvat" with the plaintiff, who had been accused by name in earlier issues of the same paper of the same sins as "Mr Boom" (*Forget v La Press Mauricienne Ltée* (1958)). In *Onama v Uganda Argus* (1969) the court held that it did not matter that the earlier publication was privileged (as a report of proceedings in Parliament) (see to similar effect *Cushing v Peters* (New Zealand 1996), though also the doubts of Harris (1996)).

But if the defendant published something which enables the reader to connect the plaintiff with another, defamatory, publication for which the defendant is not responsible, the defendant will not be liable (*Astaire v Campling* (England 1966)). Adefarasin CJ said in Nigeria (*Adewusi v Sketch Publishing Co.*) (1978) [No. 1] p. 60 citing *Astaire* and *Bruce v Odhams Press Ltd.* (England 1936)),

> A false and defamatory statement made by a third party about an unidentified person cannot be the means of proving that a publication subsequently made by another to readers who might have read the previous defamatory statement actually refers to the plaintiff.

Notes

1. They answered Yes to both questions, though the judge was, as he admitted after the verdict, less sure. Years later Liberace died of AIDS, "after", as Adam Raphael (1993, p. 8) puts it, "being sued for palimony by one of his many male lovers."
2. In *Kuti v Vanguard Media Ltd.* Nigeria (1991), Onalaja J went to town on the meaning of "reasonable person" in Nigeria, searching for the equivalent of the Clapham omnibus! To what avail? In the end, in Nigeria, it is the judge who decides what the words mean, and it is, with respect, laughable to imagine that he will react in the same way as "the man who commutes between Agege, Ipapa, Iju in *molue* bus or Agege *danfo* bus to Apapa or Central Lagos and relish [*sic*] his *boli* (roasted plaintain) with ground nut …" (p. 204).
3. Apparently the judge ignored this when the case was remitted to him, and held that all he had to decide was whether the (popular) innuendo was established. He was again reversed on this by the Court of Appeal (1977).
4. Pleading of the innuendo was simplified by the English Common Law Procedure Act 1852 s. 61, cited in *Bosah v Onunuju* (Nigeria 1973). On

pleading of extrinsic facts see also the English RSC Order 82 r.3(1) introduced in 1949, and referred to (under its original number of Order 19r. 6(2) in *Bosah* and *Adedoyin v Nigerian National Press* (1964).

5. The word here was "blackleg" which was obviously used in a very different sense then from now. Deciding that slang words have entered the language in a particular sense should be approached with caution! Still less should it be assumed that because a word is used in one country it will be understood in the same sense in another.

6. Gatley cites in this connection *Thorley v Lord Kerry* (England 1812) 128 ER at 371; in fact Lord Mansfield was really concerned here with the whole question of whether there was, and should be, a difference between words spoken and those written, and his statement about abuse seems to have been really just a statement to the effect that in the absence of certain types of allegation (see Chap. 4) words spoken were not actionable.

7. The Indian Penal Code provided (s. 95) "Nothing is an offence by reason that it causes...any harm, if that harm is so slight that no person of ordinary sense would complain of such harm"; however, in *Emp. v Chatterbhuj Jog Jivan Bhut* (Zanzibar 1906), the court refused to hold that the words "senseless" and "illiterate" were rendered non-criminal either as abuse or under this section.

8. A name he renounced in 1936 in favour of Nnamdi, as a protest against that fact that his colour precluded him from competing as a member of the British team at the Berlin Olympics (Driver, 1996).

9. A commentator suggests that the decision ought to have been different in *Gitau* because there was no question of personal relationships (unlike *Cassidy*) and the decision required a double innuendo: that the car was the plaintiff's and that he was driving it (Anon, 1971) citing particularly *Morgan v Odhams Press* ((England 1970) p. 831), in which it was said, "there must be something in the article which pointed at the plaintiff" (Phillimore LJ agreeing with Lord Denning MR). However, this case was reversed by the House of Lords (1971)! I find this reasoning very unsatisfactory. *Gitau* is surely a stronger case than *Cassidy*: in the latter the paper had no reason to suppose the plaintiff even existed; in *Gitau* they knew *someone* in the position of the plaintiff existed.

10. However, in criminal libel the size of the class does not matter because the law is concerned with the possible outrage and breach of the peace of the victims of the attack; see *Adjei v R* (1951), *Gyimah v Republic* (1971), both Ghanaian cases.

6 Defamatory Meaning

Introduction

As a Ghanaian court said it is not enough for the plaintiff to say that the words conveyed some "obnoxious meaning" in his own estimation (*Amoako v Takoradi Timbers Ltd.* (1982)). But what does the estimation of others mean? There are statements which, while they impute no blame, may lead to a degree of exclusion from society, or from the full benefit of membership of society - such as that a person has some repellent disease. In a divided society a statement about a person's race or religion might lead to some hostility or to ostracism. Then there are statements which lead more to embarassment than to blame or ostracism. One would expect the common law to have some concept of which of these constitute damage to reputation, for no amount of concrete, even financial, consequences will make a statement actionable if it is not injurious to reputation, but in reality the common law has no very clear and generally accepted conception of reputation (see *Berkoff v Burchill* (England 1996)).

Then there is the question - whose estimation; whose standards are being applied - who is the community? The African cases, without juries, have thrown up some more interesting and difficult problems.

Definitions

The plethora of attempts to reach an adequate definition reflect the difficulty of the enterprise. The traditional phrase referred to exposing the plaintiff to "hatred, ridicule or contempt" (*Parmiter v Coupland* (England 1840) 151 ER at p. 342). This is at once too narrow and possibly too wide. Hatred and contempt are too strong: a person's reputation can be severely injured even though others do not react to him with the violence these words indicate. On the other hand, ridicule may not be strong enough.

"A false statement to his discredit" has occasionally been used (*Scott v Sampson* (England 1882) p. 503); it was preferred by Scrutton LJ in *Youssoupoff v MGM* (England 1934) p. 584, and referred to in *Nekyon v Tanganyika Standard Ltd.* (Uganda 1964)). The Faulks Committee objected that "discredit" was very vague, and suggested that Lord Atkin in *Sim v*

Stretch had found this formulation inadequate and had deliberately adapted it (Cmnd 5909, para. 62). Lord Atkin's formulation is very often cited: "a statement that would tend to lower the plaintiff in the estimation of right-thinking members of society generally" (*Sim v Stretch* (England 1926); used in Nigeria in, for example, *Enahoro v Associated Newspapers* (1960) p. 225). Winfield objected that this did not embrace the possibility that the effect of the words was "to make [members of society] shun or avoid [the plaintiff]", for example, if the allegation was of having a serious contagious disease, even though this need be in no way discreditable (see now 1994, pp. 312-3).

Halsbury's Laws of England's editors hedge their bets by including almost everything: "calculated to lower him in the estimation of right-thinking men or cause him to be shunned or avoided or to expose him to hatred, contempt or ridicule, or to convey an imputation on him injurious to him in his office, profession, calling, trade or business" (quoted, from *Words and Phrases Legally Defined* in *Sketch v Ajagbemokeferi* (Nigeria 1989) p. 695 (Wali JSC)). And many definitions add statements tending to the plaintiff's financial discredit (e.g. Gatley, para. 31). It is not clear that this adds anything to the Atkin approach.

The imputation must be, as the *Halsbury's* quotation says, "on him": if it casts a slur upon the plaintiff's goods but not upon him it may be the tort of slander of goods, but it is not defamation. A Nigerian court held that a statement that the plaintiff's security vehicles had been the subject of attacks was not defamatory (*Imianvan v American International Insurance Co. (Nigeria) Ltd.* (1977)).[1] The plaintiff also sued in malicious falsehood - but failed because the statements were true, which would equally have been a defence to the libel action. Similarly a statement that he is dead or has retired may be injurious but cannot be defamatory (Cmnd 5909, para. 60).

Ridicule

Although hallowed by usage, this word is somewhat unhelpful. It is not defamatory to say something which simply evokes mirth, but ridicule may be one way in which to injure another's reputation. A sober businessman failed in his action when an advertiser used his name in describing fascination exerted by a toy: he said he had been sent away to a quiet place in the country. It was held that although this might have made people laugh at the plaintiff it was not capable of defamatory meaning (*Blennerhassett v Novelty Sales Service Ltd.* (England 1933); Gatley refers to this as "debateable" - at para. 34 n. 22). But the line is not easy to draw. In the United States a plaintiff recovered damages for the publication by the defendant of a picture of the plaintiff, opposite one of a gorilla, with the caption "Stanislaus Zbysko, the Wrestler, not Fundamentally different from the Gorilla in physique" (*Zbysko v New York American* (1930)). Some would consider this goes too far in one direction; others would think that the plaintiff in *Blennerhasset* ought to have succeeded; there is authority, in Australia and England, which holds that ridicule, provided it is not trivial, may be sufficient, even though it does not involve disparagement (Watterson, 1993; *Boyd v Mirror Newspapers Ltd.* (Australia 1980) and *Berkoff v Burchill*, above).

A Nigerian case arguably went too far by holding that it was defamatory to ridicule the plaintiff by portraying him in a cartoon as a beggar (*Ajala v Are* (1985)), but clearly others would feel this was so demeaning that it was right to treat it as defamatory. A Seychelles court held that it was defamatory to describe the plaintiff (a popular singer) as having a face as flat as a bar of soap. Evidently he was ridiculed - and youths called him "*bar savon local*" (bar of local soap) several times (*Kim Koon v Wirtz* (1976)). Yet the court said the plaintiff had not been lowered in the estimation of anyone - and immediately went on to award him damages. This court therefore seems to have treated ridicule as something different from lowering of reputation, but still as defamatory.

Shunning and Avoiding

This is one of the more controversial elements of the definitions (and one which might be expected to receive different responses in England and Africa). It seems to explain why the allegation of having been raped was held to be defamatory in the case of *Youssoupoff v Metro-Goldwyn-Mayer* (England 1934).

In the context of slander it is defamatory and actionable *per se* to say that someone has a serious disease - presumably because this would lead to their being shunned. There are surprisingly few English *libel* cases about diseases, and certainly the cases are hard to reconcile (for one see *Villers v Monsley* (1769) a case in which leprosy, the plague and the itch [a contagious disease caused by a mite] were all mentioned). (This case refers to the plaintiff being cut off from society.) There are few African cases too; in *"Munyonyozi" (Publishers of) v The Lukkiko of Buganda* (Uganda 1923) it was held to be defamatory to say that a person was suffering from an infectious heart disease and should be removed from his office; the gist of the case seems to have been the unfitness for office, however. In the case of venereal disease the element of fault - indeed of immorality - is also involved, and it is difficult to isolate the true nature of the plaintiff's complaint. In a Ugandan case the proprietor of a bar and his barmaids sued for the allegation that the latter had venereal disease (*Lords Bar v The People Newspapers* (1972)). (Unfortunately the court did not really elucidate in what way this was defamatory of the proprietor.) Imputations of insanity as well as of physical illness may be actionable (*Onwuchekwa v Onowo* (Nigeria 1974); see also *Youssoupoff* at p. 587).

The English Committee on Defamation proposed a statutory definition: "matter which in all the circumstances would be likely to affect a person adversely in the estimation of reasonable people generally" (Cmnd 5909 p. 15), which was *intended* to exclude the shunning and avoiding test.[2] They put emphasis on the allegation casting aspersions upon the *character* of the plaintiff; they did not think the law ought to cover "the case of a person being shunned or avoided by society as a result of an allegation which imputes no moral blame" (Appendix V para. 7). However, more recently an English court held that it could be defamatory to say that someone "started from the gutter" - since it could mean his origins were "sordid and disreputable", relying on the *Youssoupoff* case (*Warren v Mirror Group (Newspapers) Ltd.* (1991)), and the Court of Appeal seems to have accepted that "shunning and avoiding" is one form of defamation (*Berkoff v Burchill* above).

It may be that the Faulks Committee was taking a somewhat unrealistic view of human reactions. They seemed to believe that reasonable people would not avoid someone unless they thought less of him or her. But people suffering from certain diseases are liable to be excluded from certain sections of society; AIDS would be the clearest example,[3] and leprosy another. True, as the Faulks Committee point out, an allegation of leprosy might be actionable if malicious, as injurious falsehood (Appendix V para. 9), but why should such a victim (or these days someone who is said to have AIDS) be denied the benefits of suing in defamation which are enjoyed by so many, frankly, undeserving plaintiffs? The Committee seemed opposed to liability for statements tending to lead to *social* exclusion though involving no imputation of fault. But they seemed to think that an allegation of insanity might be actionable by a professional person (*ibid.* para. 4), even under their proposed definition. Gatley, on the other hand, treats tendency to lead to exclusion from society as being one form of defamation (para. 37).[4]

A Zimbabwean court (*Velempini v Engineering Services Workers' Committee for City of Bulawayo* (1988) Muchechetere J) quoted with approval a South African writer (Burchell, 1985) on rather similar lines to the Faulks Committee:

> It is submitted that to elevate "shunning and avoiding" to the status of a test is both unhelpful and unnecessary. As was pointed out by Steyn CJ in *South African Associated Newspapers v Schoeman* [1962 (2) SA 613 (A)], it is not on its own defamatory to say that children have measles or chicken pox, or say of a Catholic that he has become a Protestant, even though his friends will tend to shun him. While loss of association may be cogent evidence of defamation it is not a primary "test" to be adopted to find the defamatory quality of matter. Loss of association is not in itself indicative of, but merely a pointer to what might be, defamation as Boberg puts it (1962) 79 SALJ 261 at 262): "That enjoyment of this association (with one's fellows) might be detrimentally affected by an impairment of reputation cannot be doubted, but it is the impairment of reputation which constitutes the delict, not the deprivation of association".

So far as minor diseases are concerned this must be right; in such cases the exclusion from society will be of a different nature from the reaction of fear and disgust which a suspicion of leprosy or AIDS might attract.

There is a curious East African case in which the statement of which the plaintiff complained was to the effect that he *ought* to be ostracised - from the Shree Cutch Leva Patel Samaj, a society of East African Indians. The Court of Appeal held that this was calculated to expose the plaintiff to hatred or ridicule, or lower him in the estimation of the community, and rejected the judge's view that there was no defamation since nothing dishonourable was alleged (*Patel v Dhanji* (Kenya 1977)). Mustapha JA said the words "were defamatory of the appellant, since they could result in his fellow community members shunning him". One wonders whether *reasonable* members of society would shun someone just because they were told to do so.

One other African case merits a brief mention: in Seychelles it was held defamatory to say that a woman had an abnormally narrow vagina leading to an inability to have sexual intercourse (*Dookun v Ramtohul* (1971)). This is one of the very few cases in Africa in which statements which cast no slur upon the character of the plaintiff have been treated as defamatory. Restricting defamation to slurs on character would, however, go directly contrary to one well-established feature of Nigerian law: that it is defamatory in some Igbo societies to say that someone is *osu* (see below).

The Society

> There is of course no agreed definition of what is defamatory, a definition which can fit every case that may come before the courts, this is because the tort of defamation cannot be divorced from the social context in which it is operating and there are as many social contexts as there are legal jurisdictions. But I think that within a legal jurisdiction at least, it should be possible to formulate a basic legal norm within which to protect the right of individuals to have their reputation unaffected. This norm will inevitably take into account the social context, so that where communalism received more emphasis than individualism the norm will vary accordingly and take note of this sociological factor (*Eyakuze v Editor of Sunday News* (Tanzania 1974, p. 195, Mfalila J)).

What is defamatory must depend upon the context of time and society. There are examples of statements which would be viewed differently in some societies than in others.

> The variable import of words such as "homosexual" or "gay", "communist", "coloured", "miscegenation" are but a few that spring to mind that may carry a defamatory meaning or not depending upon the contemporary understanding in the country concerned

said a Zimbabwean judge (*Zvogbo v Kingston's Ltd.* (1986) p. 316). A judge decided that the statement by a bank which "bounced" the plaintiff's cheque that there were "effects not yet cleared" was defamatory in Nigeria although it has been held not to be in England (*Adamolekun v Akanbi* (1978) p. 78, see next Chapter). Another Tanzanian judge said (*Heri Idd Ngungu v Editor of Uhuru* (1979),

> ...giving it the natural meaning of the words and in the context of the sociological setup of our society epitomised in the embodiment of Socialism and self-reliance, the charge that a reactionary leader has been exposed is most revolting and defamatory.

The Tanzania example is perhaps a little unusual, but in most instances it is hard to accept courts' insistence that in *their* society certain allegations are taken especially seriously. So,

> Since customary law permits of polygamy, Ghanaian society takes the view that every decent and respectable woman can properly settle down in marriage if she so desires, and that there is no justification whatsoever for a woman to indulge in prostitution except the most depraved; Ghanaian society therefore

> detests a prostitute, regards her with the greatest contempt, as unfit for association of decent and honourable citizens, a social outcast

said Ollenu JA (*Atiase v Abbobtey* (1969). This assertion of a peculiarly Ghanaian view of prostitution seems uncalled for; this is without taking issue with the learned judge over his social analysis! Allegations of witchcraft possibly offer a genuine example of an allegation which would be taken more seriously in African societies than those of Europe, at least (see Chapter 7).

"Right Thinking Members of Society Generally"

But it is not the standard of every member of society that is taken as the touchstone of what is defamatory. Iguh JSC in *AMORC v Awoniyi* (Nigeria 1994, at p. 428) referred to "average right-thinking members of the public generally", and a variety of expressions appear in the cases: "right-thinking reader of normal intelligence" (*Association of Rhodesian Industries v Brooks* (1972) p. 4), "ordinary" people (*Lilford v Rhodesian Printing and Publishing Co. Ltd.* (1967) p. 281), "reasonable persons" (*Sketch v Ajagbemokeferi* (Nigeria 1989) p. 696 (Wali JSC)). Reynolds J in *Zvogbo v Kingston's Ltd.* (1986) p. 317 preferred "ordinary" (and reasonable) to "right-thinking"). One judge referred to "ordinary, just and reasonable men" (*Odongkara v Astles* (Uganda 1970)). Fleming (1992, p. 502) prefers "ordinary" to "reasonable" saying the former more accurately reflects cases like *Youssoupoff*, and the Australian courts favour "ordinary, decent folk in the community, taken in general" (*Gardiner v John Fairfax & Sons Pty. Ltd.* (1942)). As we have seen, the English Defamation Committee favoured "reasonable".

Minority Standards

It would clearly be wrong for a plaintiff to be able to claim damages just because a few people of eccentric views would think less of him. It was held not defamatory to suggest that the plaintiff had reported a breach of the law to the police; whatever members of the club might think right-thinking members of society would not think less of him (*Byrne v Deane* (England 1937)). In Mauritius it was held not to be defamatory to accuse someone of being "an informer". However, the court does not articulate very clearly whether it thought that the behaviour of which the plaintiff argued he was accused, including informing to the police in return for money, would lower him in the estimation of society; its main ground of decision was truth (*Oliver v Rochecouste* (1940)). The Supreme Court in Nigeria said: "A particular section...means a body of persons who subscribe to standards of conduct which are not those of society generally" (*Egbuna v Amalgamated Press* (1967)).

The real problems arise where there may be a variety of quite respectable views. It is particularly hard to imagine that African countries, with great differences between religions and ethnic groups, rural and urban lifestyles and levels of education, have a single "right" view on all issues. *Kiwanuka v Obote* (Uganda 1965) quoted *Letham v Rank* (England 1912) "It is not enough to prove that the words spoken rendered the plaintiff obnoxious to a limited class; it should be proved that the words are such as would produce a bad impression on the minds of average reasonable men". The Prime Minister of Uganda was held guilty only of disrespect - not of defamation - for saying that if the Kabaka had anything he wished to discuss with the PM he should drive to Entebbe to see him. The judge based his decision at least in part on the basis that the Baganda people, in whose eyes this remark would be disparaging of their King, formed only part of Ugandan society (and indeed that only uneducated Baganda would have taken this view - though Hodgin, 1973, p. 70n, said that this was not borne out in his discussions with his colleagues). With respect one can only agree that this is a regrettable application of this supposed principle of English law (Muburimusoke,1978, p. 167). On the other hand, it seems to this reader at least that the plaintiff in this particular case was seeking redress not so much for defamation as for disrespect, which is not usually considered to be within the scope of the common law.

Perhaps more difficult was a Ghanaian case in which the plaintiff complained that her photograph had been used without her consent on a postcard illustrating a traditional hairstyle. She said that among her people this would damage her reputation as a married woman. The appeal court, reversing the Judge of first instance, applied the "right-thinking person" principle and said that as the Fante are only part of the population of Ghana she could not recover (*University College, Cape Coast v Anthony* (1977). The first instance decision had produced an interesting divergence of views (Date-Bah, 1973c; and Bimpong-Buta, Daniels and (on the choice of law aspect) Kanyoke, 1973). One Ghanaian commentator said that he could see nothing wrong in a wife having her photograph taken and used for commercial purposes (Date-Bah, 1973c, p. 22). But it does seem that the evidence that the Fante would take a different view was strong. Another alleged "ethnic group difference" was *HRH King Zwelithini of KwaZulu v Mervis* (South Africa 1978) where it was held that standards of Zulu people alone were not enough. This case actually arose in Johannesburg. But if it had arisen within KwaZulu, then a notionally independent "homeland", presumably the standards of the Zulu people ought to have been enough. And now that the homelands are reintegrated into South Africa does the community change - an odd result?

In *Harding v Sierra Leone Daily Mail* (1946-7) it was held that a statement that a "no case submission" made by the plaintiff had been overruled was not defamatory because it would demean him in the eyes of the legal profession only. On the face of it the statement ought not to be defamatory at all. If the allegation conveyed incompetence then he ought to have succeeded. In *Akomolafe v African Newspapers of Nigeria Ltd.* (1990) it was held that it was not defamatory to say that a lawyer had lost a case, even one brought on his own behalf.

Sometimes the principle is overlooked or downplayed. A Cherubim and Seraphim preacher in Nigeria recovered damages when he was defamed in the eyes of his flock by being accused of "paganic practices" (*Bandele v Daily Times* (1974)). The judge said he was "entitled to be protected against any imputation which may cause them to be hated or despised or shunned by other people, even members of their own sect"; he also said that the statements would tend to lower the plaintiff in the eyes of the "Community as a whole". And in an old Zanzibar case the defendants were the managers of the Hindu caste to which the plaintiff belonged. The defendants communicated to the members of the caste that they had excommunicated the plaintiff from the caste because he had attended a feast given by a member of another caste (*Velji v Hirachand* (1901)). This was held to be defamatory - without discussion as to "whole community" values; no doubt the Arab and African members of Zanzibar society would not have shared the values of the caste in question, nor indeed Indian Muslims or even the members of the other Hindu caste! Years later the East African Court of Appeal seems to have ignored the generality requirement when it held that it was enough that the plaintiff would be shunned by "his community" (*Patel v Dhanji* (Kenya 1977)).

Sometimes what matters seems to be not really the "average", still less the "reasonable", view, but what might be called the "dominant" view"; it has been held defamatory to call a white person "black" in the Southern United States (*Natchez Times v Dunigan* (1954))[5] and even more remarkably in South Africa (*Pitout v Rosenstein* (1930)). Of the latter case, however, it has been said "it is submitted that the better view is that such a statement is not defamatory unless there is some imputation of criminal, or immoral conduct" (Lee and Honoré, 1979, p. 320). (In Botswana it was held that it did not necessarily give rise to hatred, ridicule or contempt to call someone a "kaffir"; this was a criminal case: *State v Arnold* (1975); contrast *Ciliza v Minister of Police* (South Africa) 1976).

In many cases the decisions are at heart policy ones, and the court is upholding what might be called "correct" attitudes. Some allegations of sexual impropriety perhaps fall into this category - such as that it is defamatory to say that a monogamously married man has a girl friend (*Musonda v Zambia Publishing Co. Ltd.* (1976). In *Byrne v Deane* (above), the court as upholder of the law could hardly have held it to be defamatory to say that a person had reported an offence to the police, regardless of popular. The same was true in a Nigerian case which arose in the then Mid-Western State during the civil war. The plaintiff, who worked in an area recently liberated from rebel control and where there were large numbers of federal troops, complained that the defendant had reported to her employer a conversation in which a third party had told a federal officer that she (the plaintiff) was an Igbo, and the officer had said that her place of work would be blown up. The plaintiff had been dismissed. The judge held that to say that someone belonged to a particular ethnic group could not be defamatory. He admitted that some ordinary people would not draw a distinction between an "Igbo" and a "rebel" - but that still could not make the statement defamatory (*Mowoe v Aghoba* (1968)). (The situation might be different in an international rather than a civil war - *Slazengers Ltd. v Gibbs* (England 1916) holding it defamatory to call a person German during the First World War.) A similar reluctance to give judicial recognition to unacceptable social attitudes very likely underlay the refusal of a Tanzanian judge to accept that in East Africa Arabs are associated with homosexuality (*Jonathan v Athuman Khalfan* (1980)). In a 1955 case from South-West Africa (Namibia) the allegation was to the effect that the plaintiff had sold land to a non-European. The court said, "What is wrong with a 'decent and upright person' doing what the law permits him to do?" (*Swart v Thirion* (1955) p. 117). The court did not point out that in the eyes of the non-European majority of the population of the country the statement would not be defamatory - any more than the South African courts made the same point when discussing whether it was defamatory to say that someone was black. Now it would be defamatory to say of someone that he *refused* to sell land to a non-European in Namibia. Such behaviour, as well as being morally unacceptable, would be contrary to the Constitution, which not only prohibits racial discrimination but singles out apartheid practices for special condemnation (art. 23). Similarly one might say that the Nigerian Constitution has decreed that no right-thinking person would think less of someone because they belong to a particular ethnic group - and therefore the courts could not hold it to be defamatory to make a statement of the sort made in the *Mowoe* case.

Describing Someone as "Osu"

Nigerian law - in the shape of the Abolition of the Osu System Law - has said that no one should discriminate against another on the grounds of their being *osu*. One might say that no reasonable person would therefore think less of one for being *osu*. But far from that, the same Law (see Chapter 4) not only assumes such a statement may be actionable but makes it actionable *per se*. One must conclude that in this context at any rate the test of defamatory meaning is that of the ordinary member of certain communities despite being unreasonable! It is also clear that evidence will have to called to show that such an allegation was indeed defamatory in the particular community.

The Wider Issue Approach

In some cases plaintiffs have succeeded because they have been able to argue that there is a further meaning (a popular innuendo) which would damage them in the eyes of the wider community. Thus one can be defamed by an accusation of breach of a standard of conduct which is peculiar to a group of which one is a member; obedience or loyalty to a group of which one is a member is a generally accepted social value. This may explain why it was defamatory to suggest that an amateur sportsman had taken money to permit his photograph to be used in an advertisement, this being inconsistent with his amateur status (*Tolley v Fry* (England 1931)). It is clearly defamatory to say that someone has broken the ethical standards of his profession (e.g. *Drummond-Jackson v British Medical Association* England (1970)). An English trade unionist recovered damages for the statement that he tried to work during a strike (*Myroft v Sleight* (1921)). A British Muslim was accused of making satirical remarks about the Prophet. The Court of Appeal held that although the ordinary member of the community would have no views on the Prophet, he or she would disapprove of one who attacked another's religion (*Shah v Akram* (1981)). By such devices these situations could all be said to fit into the mainstream views of British society, and the judge could leave the issue to the jury. It is much more difficult where one section of the community may be unaware of the norms of another, or may even disapprove of them. It seems to me that this is a device, and often little more, for circumventing the "right-thinking members" principle, and leaves many problems. To take the *Shah* case: does English society generally really disapprove of those who attack religion? The fact that he was awarded damages does not really help, since we have no way of knowing why juries award them (he was awarded £10!). Judges have to be more explicit.

A "Sectional" Approach?

It has sometimes been suggested that the test of what is defamatory should not be based on the views of society at large but on views and attitudes in the section of society to which the plaintiff belongs (e.g. Burchell, 1974, pp. 182-6). This is in effect what the Abolition of the Osu System Law endorses. What is meant by a "sectional view"? In the African context it has been argued that the views of particular ethnic groups, even if not shared by others, ought to be recognised. This is the view accepted by Wiredu J in *Anthony v University College Cape Coast*, and rejected by the Court of Appeal (above). One commentator said

> The application of Lord Atkin's test within the Ghanaian context logically leads to the ridiculous conclusion that if an Akan in the South of Ghana, living in a predominantly Akan area of society, finds himself allegedly defamed in that society then the trial judge...should not merely decide the issue in the light of the customs and estimation of the Akan people and of the locality, but he must also consider whether in the estimation of the Dagomba people in the north that person has in fact been defamed (Bimpong-Buta, 1973, p. 25).

With respect, Date-Bah has a more accurate understanding of the situation when he said of the Atkin test, "The test of what is defamatory is not the community's actual attitudes and beliefs but what the courts *believe those opinions ought to be*" (1973c, p. 22; emphasis supplied).

In *Peck v Tribune* (1909) in the United States Holmes J said, "If the advertisement obviously would hurt the plaintiff in the estimation of an important and respectable part of the community, liability is not a question of a majority vote". Muchechetere J in the Zimbabwean case of *Velempini* said he would be prepared to adopt the "substantial and respectable portion of the community" test (above). (He quoted Burchell (1985, p. 101-2) who had pointed out that the South African courts had in some circumstances adopted a sectional test - e.g. *Brill v Medely* (1937), *Pillsay v Irvins* (1919), *Naidu v Naidu* (1915)).

It is not normally proper to call witnesses to the effect that the words were defamatory. But how else would one show that a sub-group of society took such a view? In the *Anthony* case such evidence was accepted by the trial judge. If this were to become permissible, does it seem right to exclude evidence of defamatory quality in the ordinary case? In *Elechi v Daily Times* (Nigeria 1980) the plaintiff called a witness who testified as to his reaction to the statement. The judge observed that he was from the plaintiff's community but said "it is my considered view that one's reputation must not be treated in isolation but must *inter alia* be related to one's Community" an observation which has merit as common sense, but, as we have seen, does not represent the law. Secondly, in the US the case would still presumably go to the jury, which might well reject the evidence of the views of the section of society. In African jurisdictions the judge alone would have to decide this - and explain why. Thirdly, how does one decide what is a sufficient substantial and respectable portion of society? What does "portion" mean? Must it be a sub-section of society definable in some other way, as by membership of a religious or ethnic or professional group? Or would it be enough that the "portion" shared only its view of certain behaviour or attributes, for example, that they would think less of someone who was homosexual?

Such a rule would also increase the risk of a defendant being found liable for a statement which she did not intend to be defamatory - indeed which she did not know could be defamatory. The risk is clearly shown in the *Anthony* case; one might take the view that the University bookshop ought not to have made money out of the plaintiff's likeness, but that is not as such defamation - and how could it have known that the Fante people would so regard its postcard? So long as the plaintiff is required to prove neither intention nor falsity, the abolition of the present rule is extremely difficult. For this reason the Australian Law Reform Commission rejected a change in the law, even with the added refinement that such cases should be actionable only on proof of intention or negligence (1979, p. 47).

In effect a defamation suit under customary law is based upon a lowering in the estimation of a section of society (relative to the modern nation state). A Ghanaian judge observed in an appeal involving customary law, "It is in his town or country that he is probably well-known rather than in a strange place and it is the former locality that any defamatory words spoken against him will be widely known and this will tarnish his reputation" (*Tsinagyah v Kyeiwaah* (1974) (Enoch Edusei J)). In many countries this option is still open; maybe that should be the answer in the case of ethnic differences: if in the eyes of your own community you have been defamed it is under the law of that community that you should sue. This was in fact suggested by Janet Daniels as the better course of action for a case like *Anthony* (1973, p. 31). But that would be impossible if the community in question were an immigrant one in a large city where no customary tribunal was available. Nor does it cope with the possibility that the parties are from different ethnic groups. Nor respond to the possibility that the relevant section of the community is not to be defined in ethnic terms but is, for example, of a particular religious persuasion.

A court in the Philippines took a constitutional approach to the whole issue. The allegation was that a certain person (not the plaintiff: the "maligned" person was dead and his heirs were suing) had had an advantage in local politics because he had lived with an American family. It was claimed that this "had a repugnant connotation" in the local society. The Supreme Court observed (*Bulletin Publishing Corp. v Noel (*1988) (quoted from Mendoza, 1987) that Philippines are "both republican in character and egalitarian in inspiration" (referring to the Constitution):

> It is to the standards of the national community, not to those of the region, that a court must refer especially where a newspaper is national in reach and coverage [to determine whether a remark is defamatory]. Any other rule in a national community with many diverse cultural, social, religious and other groupings is likely to produce an unwholesome "chilling effect" upon the constitutionally-protected operation of the press and other instruments of information and education.

There is a good deal in this. But it does hint at a different rule for the press and possibly for the national, as opposed to local, press.

The Use of Evidence

Earlier it was stated that the parties ought not to call evidence as to the meaning of the words unless a true innuendo was pleaded (Chaper 5). Is evidence permissible to show that the words were defamatory? On the whole the view is the same: it is the function of the judge (as it would be the function of the jury in some countries) to decide what the community view would be.

The plaintiff is not required to prove that any person actually thought less of him as a result of the statement complained of (indeed (see Chapter 8) it is unnecessary even to prove that any *actually* read or heard the statement). As Somolu J said in *Williams v West African Pilot* (Nigeria 1961), citing *Ratcliffe v Evans* (England 1892) p. 529, *South Hetton Coal Co. v North Eastern News Association* (England 1894) p. 144, *Hobbs v Tinling* (England 1929) p. 17),

> It was argued on behalf of the defendants that Jakande [witness for plaintiffs] did not say that the plaintiffs lost a jot of his respect for them as a result of the cartoons complained of, that there is no evidence before the court to show that the plaintiffs were pointed to, or shunned because of the said publications. With great respect, I do not think that such evidence is necessary at all. Once any publication has been found to be a defamatory libel, the law presumes damage.

Indeed, the statement does not cease to be actionable just because it seems that no-one believed it - provided that a reasonable person could have done.

> If words are used which impute discreditable conduct to my friend, he has been defamed to me, although I do not believe the imputation, and may even know it is untrue

observed Goddard LJ (*Hough v London Express Newspapers Ltd.* (England 1940)); this was quoted in *Maskini v Mbugus* (Tanzania 1975) and in *Bendzel v Katar Singh* (Kenya 1952) where the defendant tried to argue that there was no defamation because the plaintiff's employer, to whom he made the statement, would have known the truth. The argument was given short shrift. The position seems to be true of Roman-Dutch as well as the common law: in Southern Rhodesia it was held that absence of belief would affect damages, but not the actionability of the statement (*Vaughan v Ford* (1953)). However, it was held in Mauritius that if the hearers utterly disbelieved the statement there was no "moral damage" or *dommage* under the Civil Code, and no liability (*Mahraz v Jenkins* (1899)).

In this respect the common law and at least some systems of customary law seem to be at one. Francis Deng has written of Sudan, "The name does not have to be actually spoiled; so long as it is "spoilable" an action will lie. In other words it is not a condition precedent that people should believe the imputation or alter their attitude in any way towards the defamed" (1965, p. 560).

It is in fact not uncommon for plaintiffs to call witnesses as to this sort of fact. I would suggest that Fakayode CJ showed, albeit inadvertently, precisely why evidence ought not to be permitted when he said evidence of the plaintiff's colleagues was of no value but "There must be evidence coming from the ordinary members of society" (*Ijeh v Daily Times* (Nigeria 1977)). Is that not precisely what the judge is there to decide? In at least one case this unnecessary evidence backfired on the plaintiff: his witness said that he believed the statement because he was the sort of person to do such a thing! The judge said that the plaintiff's reputation was evidently not good, and the damages should take that into account (*Adedoyin v Nigerian National Press* (1964)).

It is not entirely easy to square with the general principle the famous case of *Tolley v Fry* (England 1931). Evidence was given that if an amateur allowed his picture to be use for advertising that would damage his reputation as an amateur, and Viscount Haldane said that if the jury accepted this they would have to find the publication defamatory (p. 338). Lord Buckmaster said this accorded with common experience (p. 343). If it was a matter of common experience it is hard to see why evidence was needed or permitted, and if it did not would right-thinking people really have thought less of the plaintiff? The latter point is not discussed, and was perhaps not argued.

It is no doubt difficult for a jury to serve as the voice of the community in a plural society, but it is surely much more difficult for the judge to do so. Judges are in no way representative of the society. It has not been uncommon for a judge to be a foreigner, especially in African countries. Aguda CJ, a Nigerian sitting in Botswana (*Karim v Wetterings* (1974)), refused to hold that it was defamatory in that country to say that someone had been declared a prohibited immigrant; there had been no evidence to this effect (and evidence would have been admissible (citing *Sutter v Brown* (South Africa 1926)).

We noted earlier that defamatory meaning may actually reflect the "dominant" or "correct" view in society; judges as part of the dominant class find little difficulty in equating their views with those of society. Maybe their Lordships in *Tolley v Fry* readily assumed that the views of golfers were the views of society because golf is a sport of the elite. Would sociological evidence be permissible to show what society's views really are? If one could hear the evidence of golfing experts why not those of sociologists? But the general approach of the courts is that this question is not a matter for evidence; and Lidsky (1966, p. 18) states that US courts do not expect social surveys or even witnesses to establish the attitudes of the section of society before which the plaintiff claims to have been defamed. The only possible exception to this which comes to mind is that it might be permissible to use sociological evidence to show that in a particular Nigerian community it is defamatory to say that someone is *osu*.

Notes

1. Contrast *Sungravure Pty. Ltd. v Middle East Airlines* (Australia 1975) in which it was held that it could be defamatory to suggest that travelling with the plaintiff airline involved a risk of being hijacked.
2. There is a strong dissenting note, to the effect that no statutory definition should be attempted: p. 189.
3. Otieno-Abuodha (1992) raises the various issues: whether the issue is that an imputation of infection with AIDS suggests sexual impropriety (clearly not though many people think so); whether such a person would be ostracised (he suggests they would be though this is undesirable, and unnecessary). His conclusion is that for the law to treat such an imputation as defamatory would be wrong because it would serve to reinforce an irrational and socially undesirable attitude. I wonder how much consolation these considerations would be to someone who was alleged, wrongly, to be HIV positive?
4. Concrete disadvantages may flow from statements which impute no blame; for example if the candidate for a stool, or traditional kingship, was excluded because he was alleged to have a physical infirmity (see Mair (1977, p. 122) on Dahomey: heirs must have no physical defect, and being left-handed was such a defect. It is improbable that a court would hold it defamatory to say that someone was left-handed!) If the statement was deliberate with a view to depriving the candidate of the kingship, an action for malicious falsehood would lie in common law countries).
5. Not however recently, see Lidsky (1996, p. 30), citing Crabb (1956, p. 1287).

7 Examples of Defamatory Statements

The cases here give some indication of how the law of defamation is being used, though they have no formal precedent value.

Criminal Offences

It will be defamatory to say that someone has been convicted or is guilty of a criminal offence (e.g. *Okotcha v Olumese* (Nigeria 1967)); or being a member of an illegal organisation, such as the Communist Party when the Suppression of Communism Act was in force in South Africa *(Dube v Buthelezi* (1975-77)). The offence need not be specified, so it was defamatory to say that the plaintiff was always telephoning to insult the defendant in "dirty language", since this would constitute common nuisance (*Moulinié v de Comarmond* (Seychelles 1972)). Among the more common allegations are those of theft (e.g. *Ibeanu v Uba* (Nigeria 1972), *Akolade v Julius Berger (Nig.) Ltd.* (Nigeria 1977), *Oredein v Laseinde* Nigeria (1975)); in the Ghanaian case of *Benneh v New Times Corporation* (1982) the allegation was that the plaintiff had "diverted" a consignment of 12 barrels of pigsfeet. Corruption is also commonly alleged (*Pedro v Orafidiya* (Nigeria 1974) (customary court judge), *Tharia v Morrison* (1910) (public works dept. supervisor in Zanzibar), *Ibe v Azubirike* (Nigeria 1977) employee of railways took bribe to allocate wagons); less often, naturally, murder (*Mutual Aids Society v Akerele* (Nigeria 1966), *Olola v Alabi* (Nigeria 1984); *Gunigina v Wakabala* (Uganda 1975)). An allegation of a minor offence to which no moral blame attaches, such as pulling the communication cord in a train (*Berry v British Transport Commission* (England 1962)) is not defamatory.

It is defamatory to say that someone has been charged with an offence (*Omo Bare v Odukomaiya* (Nigeria 1973) *Bello (Mustapha) v Oyebola* (Nigeria 1974)), or even being investigated (*Bello (Haroun) v Oyebola* (Nigeria 1977)); in *Ukpomah v Daily Times of Nigeria Ltd.* (1979), the defendants did not dispute that it was defamatory to say that the plaintiff was being investigated by the Corrupt Practices Bureau for alleged bribery and in *Wusu v African Newspapers Nig. Ltd.* (Nigeria 1977) it was held defamatory to say that the plaintiff was arrested and detained for questioning, and in *Prakash v Wilson* (Zimbabwe 1992) to say that someone is being sought by Interpol. In Rhodesia, Fieldsend J said "to hold a man up as an accused person, against whom suspicion has arisen, even though it is made clear that the court acquitted him, may be regarded as lowering his esteem in the eyes of ordinary, right-thinking people" (*Lilford v Rhodesian Printing and Publishing Co. Ltd.* (1967) p. 218). A court in Calabar was wrong to say "To suspect another of having committed a criminal offence is not actionable" - at least where the suspicion has been conveyed to another (*Ita v Ene* (Nigeria 1973)). The court would usually not hold that it was right to infer from a statement about investigation or allegation that the plaintiff was actually guilty (see *Lewis v Daily Telegraph* (England 1964) and *Eda v Bendel Newspaper Corpn.* (Nigeria 1982)). On the other hand, it is clearly defamatory to say that someone has been pardoned, with the implication that he has previously been found guilty (e.g. *Gbajabiamila v Commercial Amalgamated Press* (Nigeria 1972)). (In some systems the power to grant "pardon" may be used where no-one has yet been convicted (for example, under the Nigerian Constitution (1989) s. 173 a pardon is possible for someone "concerned with or convicted of" an offence; the Constitution implies guilt when it says "concerned with". Since it is the statement that is being construed and not the Constitution, and defamation is in the eyes of the ordinary person and not a lawyer one would expect the court to accept that guilt is implied.)

In *Nxumalo v Nxumalo* (Swaziland 1982-86) the statement was to the effect that a fraudulent faith healer was a "close associate" of the plaintiff, which it was held would suggest to the ordinary reader that he was a party to the other's conduct.

Activities Against the State

Many such activities would be criminal offences, for example collaborating with the rebels during the Nigerian civil war, of which a "natural ruler" was accused (*Uyo I v Nigerian National Press Ltd.* (1974); see also *Dafe v Tswinor* (1967)). The same was probably true when in Zambia a prominent politician was said to have sent people for guerrilla training to Angola (*Times Newspapers v Kapwepwe* (1973)), or when it was said that the police had invited the plaintiff to help in investigation of a document which the authorities claimed to be anti-government (*Odu v Daily Times of Nigeria* (1977)), and in *Odongkara v Astles* it was held that the allegation amounted to one of treason (Uganda 1970). An allegation that the plaintiff had been detained, at least under a regime which had the power to detain without the necessity to establish the commission of an offence, may convey suspicion of either an offence, or some anti-government activity; it was held to be defamatory in Nigeria (*Adewusi v Sketch* No. 2 (1978)). In *Ohanbamu v Midwest Newspaper Corpn.* (Nigeria 1974), it was defamatory to say of the plaintiff "his Biafra", suggesting sympathy with the secessionists.

In Kenya it was held that it was not defamatory for the defendant to complain to the police that the plaintiff (chair of the ruling party) had made a mistake in electing the President, and should step down from his party position; this did not allege sedition or any conduct which would lower the plaintiff in others' estimation (*Nzoma v Kasoa* (1989)).

Immorality

Allegations of immorality are defamatory - whether rather general such as "Judge tells teacher 'you are a bad woman'"(*Omo-Osagie v Okutubo* (Nigeria 1969)) or more specific, such as that the plaintiff has lied (*Magennis v Malawi Press Ltd.* (1961-3) - the plaintiff "would write any kind of lies"; *Awolowo v West African Pilot* (Nigeria 1962) - the plaintiff "lied" in autobiography) or has committed adultery or fornication. Such allegations may injure plaintiffs professionally as well as personally, as with a lecturer who was accused in the press of having an affair with a student (*Nthenda v Alade* (Nigeria 1974)), or a personnel manager accused of "rampant sex mania" (*Ezega v Embechem Ltd.* (Nigeria 1981))! The former of course was defamatory of the student as well; in *Bolokor v Alade* (1982) one of the students named was awarded ₦3000 damages.

In *Ijeh v Daily Times* (Nigeria 1977, p. 374) it was held, *obiter*, that it would not be defamatory to say of a polygamist that he had a girlfriend - though it would be different if one said he had a mistress. (*Ijeh v Sketch Publishing Co.* (1978) arose out of a similar report in another newspaper. Apparently three newspapers reported that the plaintiff had obtained money for his girlfriend although at the inquiry which was being reported the evidence was about his sister!) It is defamatory to say of someone monogamously married that he had a girlfriend (*Musonda v Zambia Publishing Co. Ltd.* (1976); it is to be assumed that the marriage was monogamous though this is not stated - the observations are *obiter*).

Private Parts

It seems that quarrelsome behaviour in many African societies may involve insulting remarks about the genitalia of the other party or even of his relatives, as in *Sakyiwaa v Amponsah* (Ghana 1974) - vagina like a monkey's and smelling (and was a prostitute). And "To refer to a person in a paternal position as a man born prematurely when such reference of his birth refers to his mother's sexual organs is a most serious abuse to such a person" - *Sello v Tihedi* (Lesotho 1953). In one Seychelles case it was held defamatory to describe a woman as incapable of having sexual intercourse (*Dookun v Ramtohul* (1971)). There was no discussion of why this was defamatory - and it is impossible to tell if there was any "customary" influence at work. Customary imports into received law have generally been rejected: for example, a Zambian judge said the suggestion that the plaintiff had a long penis, and a reference to the plaintiff's mother's clitoris, though insulting, were not defamatory (*Mdambo v Changu* (1979)).

Imputations as to Profession etc.

It is defamatory to say that a person is incompetent or inefficient - as with a doctor accused of being responsible for a smallpox outbreak (*Masson v Issaac* (Mauritius 1914)); a medical assistant described as a "quack", and among those "who get their medicine from doctors from Nairobi but forget to bring their brains with them" (*Kajima v East African Newspapers (Nation Series) Ltd.* (Kenya 1972)); a secondary school head accused of ruining the school (*Okon v The COR. Advocate* (Nigeria 1961)); the plaintiff alleged to have taken money to erect stand at trade fair but not done the work (*Okusanya v WAATECO* (Nigeria 1974)); in *Clarke v Nigerian Ports Authority* (1977), the defamatory statement included allegations that the plaintiff's ability to plan for and control subordinates was poor, as were his judgment, time-keeping and integrity, that he showed "signs of immaturity" and spent time "unnecessarily nosing around". It was actionable to say that the plaintiff was appointed only due to a bending of the rules and favouritism (*Jegede v Daily Times of Nigeria Ltd.* (1980) - appointment to chair of Law in University of Lagos) or that he claimed to have qualifications which he did not have (e.g. *David-West v Goodwill Press & Bookshop Ltd.* (Nigeria 1983), *Musajjalumbwa v Uganda Eyogera Ltd.* (1993)). Dereliction of professional duty is equally actionable, including that a doctor refused to attend a patient (*Charlesworth v Sleeman* (Zanzibar 1897), *Obu v Medical & Health Dept. Workers' Union* (Nigeria 1980)), or that the plaintiff has broken the terms of his employment (*Juma v Continental Office Products Ltd.* (Nigeria 1971)), given away his employer's trade secrets (*Aruna v George-Taylor* (Nigeria 1974)) or broken the ethical standards of his profession - as with the nurse who was alleged to have made sexual advances to patients (*Gyang v Ilyasu* (Nigeria 1977)).

Lawyers are not infrequent litigators about their professional honour. It was defamatory to suggest that a lawyer is incompetent (e.g. *Mkandawire v Zambia Publishing Co.* (1979)) one had shown a statement by his client to his opponent (*Aghahowa v Aguebor* (Nigeria 1957); see also *Lardner v Sketch Publishing Co. Ltd.* (Nigeria 1979) - where it was alleged the plaintiff "falsely" and "fraudulently" took over property entrusted to his care). A Mauritian court held it was actionable to say of a barrister that he was a "sophist". The court said that in "common parlance" sophism is "false reasoning" and might indicate lack of judgment. The court held the words were not defamatory or slanderous in the legal senses of the words, by which it meant under the Penal Code. It held that statement did not come within Art. 288 of the Penal Code because it was neither an allegation of fact nor an insult, but was actionable because it might have a prejudicial effect, as a "quasi-delict" under Art. 1382 of the Code Civil (*Galéa v Roussel* (1891)). It has been held not defamatory of a lawyer that he lost a case (*Akomolafe v African Newspapers of Nigeria Ltd.* (1990)).

In one Ugandan case a head teacher accused a colleague of having fomented a pupils' strike (*Busulwa v Kakongoro* (1976)), almost trivial in comparison with one in which a school teacher sued the parish priest who had accused him of being drunk in class, being constantly absent, having sexual intercourse in front of his pupils, being uncooperative and incompetent (*Ssejjobi v Rwabigonji* (Uganda 1977)). A permanent secretary was said to have subordinated his professional responsibilities to his personal convenience, and been guilty of economic crimes (*Asiodu v Abodunde* (Nigeria 1979)), and a Commissioner of Police was described as "debauched" (*Omolowo v Punch Ltd.* (Nigeria 1985)). All these were defamatory.

Corruption and Abuse of Office

A statement in general terms alleging corruption by public servants will be actionable (e.g. *African Newspapers of Nigeria Ltd. v Coker* (1973)) as would a statement that one had taken a bribe (e.g. *Dina v New Nigerian Newspapers* (1986)), or an oath to conceal corruption (*Dalumo v Sketch* (Nigeria 1972); also *Mutemba v Zambia Newspapers Ltd.* (1972) - held not to refer to the plaintiff). There are many cases, including *Tharia v Morrison* decided in Zanzibar in 1910. It is no less defamatory of politicians. One of the best known Nigerian examples was the accusation that a federal Commissioner (equivalent of Minister under the military government) had corruptly enriched himself (*Tarka v Daily Sketch* (1978)).

To say that one has abused or taken undue advantage of an office - even a past office - whether salaried, political or honorary, is defamatory "it is strongly believed that Alhaji Babalola is using his influence as a former police officer to sweep his case under the carpet" was held defamatory in *Babaḷola v African Newspapers of Nigeria Ltd.* (Nigeria 1980). An Attorney-General and DPP were accused of "unprecedented interference with the course of justice in a free country, deplorable and deliberate contempt of court by the DPP" (*Farmer v Uganda Argus* (1964); see also *Yanni v Sierra Leone Daily Mail* (1967-68)). In this group one might include a Minister who was said to have used his position to enrich himself (*Johnson v Daily Times* (Nigeria 1966)) and a Nigerian state governor defamed by a report which said "Governor Bisi Onabanjo arrived in England with a 14-man entourage in the style of an Arab Sheikh from an oil-rich kingdom. Those on junket with him are his wife, his ADC Police, his Protocol Staff, Ministry officials, his personal staff of cooks, stewards and his aunt" - all at public expense (*Onabanjo v Concord Press of Nigeria Ltd.* (1982) pp. 80-1). It was defamatory of an alderman to say that he had made a statement to the press giving incorrect information calculated to bring his colleagues into disrepute (*Palmer v Boston* (Sierra Leone 1960-1)). An army officer was defamed by the allegation that he personally brandished a gun at the defendant with whom he was having a land dispute, and also brought soldiers with him (*Ajala v Showunmi* (Nigeria 1977)).

A leading member of the management of a parastatal sued for an article which (as translated) was headed "Come and See Tribalism", which alleged that all the people employed came from only two ethnic groups, and that proper appointments processes were neglected - and also that another form of abuse was taking place in that "Many girls who know nothing about typing are being employed as clerks just because they happen to have beautiful faces" (*Maskini v Mbugus* (Tanzania 1975)).

Trade union officials also sue: it was defamatory to suggest that the plaintiff had been taking money from foreign trades unions, was building a personal empire and should be barred from trade union activities (*Eshiett v New Nigerian Newspapers Ltd.* (1978)). In *Ijeh v Daily Times of Nigeria Ltd.* (1977) it was held defamatory to say of a trade unionist that while on a delegation to a convention in the US he asked for a personal gift of $2000 for his girl friend (the real sting of the defamation being that he used his position to feather his own nest). Many of these allegations would also be defamatory of private individuals - for example it was defamatory to say of a trade unionist that he was associated with someone engaged in subversive activities, but it would hardly have enhanced the reputation of anyone (*Anunobi v Nigerian National Press Ltd.* (1964)).

Extravagance

Accusations of extravagance may imply misconduct too to some extent, but this need not be so. A natural ruler who was said to have encouraged by his example an extravagant life-style sued successfully (*Adetona v Drum* (Nigeria 1972)). In countries with officially socialist philosophies such an allegation would presumably be more serious. But many African governments call for restraint. A Nigerian couple whose wedding photograph was used to illustrate an article about extravagant wedding receptions sued for defamation; they failed, though the court did not clearly address the question of whether an allegation of extravagance is or can be defamatory (*Omotayo v African Newspapers Ltd.* (1986)).

Defaming Politicians

Many cases in most countries involve politicians; they, like others, are defamed if someone says that they have been guilty of a criminal offence - for example that although someone had been tried and acquitted of murder his innocence had not been fully established (*Awolowo v Kingsway* (Nigeria 1969)), or that a rival candidate has threatened one's life (*Amiekhai v Okwilage* (Nigeria 1962)). In *Williams v West African Pilot* allegations of the following were held defamatory: "bribery of the electorate, electoral fraud, the employment of thugs and ex-convicts for mass impersonation at an election and the buying of the conscience and allegiance of candidates who have won an election on different platforms" (Nigeria 1961), at p. 881). In a more marginal case from the same era Chief Okotie-Eboh had "intrigued to kick Dr Azikiwe upstairs" [presumably to the Governor-Generalship]; this was held to suggest trickery and deceitfulness (*Amalgamated Press of Nigeria Ltd. v Okotie-Eboh* (1963)). Chief Obafemi Awolowo in Nigeria succeeded in suing for the allegation that he had tried to stir up ethnic discord (*Awolowo v West African Pilot* (1962)); ten years later he successfully sued the *Economist* for a very oblique suggestion that he might have been involved in stirring up labour unrest to hasten the end of military rule (*Awolowo v The*

Economist Newspaper Ltd. (1972)). It was actionable to say that the Leader of the House used his position to suppress debate (*Enahoro v Associated Newspapers of Nigeria Ltd.* (1960)), or that a Minister referred to traders as "economic Shylocks", since it made the Minister appear irresponsible (*Okeke v Mkpanam* (Nigeria 1962)).

Rather imprecise pieces of invective have been held defamatory: "a wolf among men and lambs, a parasite who thrives at the expense of the people, a wicked and unsympathetic man who has broken the custom of the area and deprived the people of their rights thereunder, a cheater who posed as a saviour and a trouble-maker" (*Nwangwu v Nwankwo* (Nigeria 1962)) or "a rolling-stone-gather-no-moss politician, great failure and expert trouble-maker"(*Wallace-Johnson v Yanson* (Sierra Leone 1960-1)). Nigerian delegates to the constitutional conference preceding independence were defamed by allegations that they spent their time shopping or with girl-friends rather than attending the meetings, to the discussions at which they were incapable of contributing (*Edukugho v Proprietors of the "Sunday Times"* (1958)).

Chief Obafemi Awolowo was a most frequent politician plaintiff, but he was run a close second, though not over such an extended period of time, by Kapwepwe, whom we have seen accused of training guerillas. It was also defamatory to accuse him of receiving funds from the Government of South Africa; in the same case he complained (as did Awolowo in one case) that he had been accused of tribalism. The judge said,

> It is, of course, not libellous to say of a politician, who is in opposition to the Government, that he attacks the Government. At the time of the libel Zambia was not a one-party state and the plaintiff was the leader of an opposing party...Intrinsically there is nothing wrong in supporting one's own tribe or clan. Pride of tribe, pride of clan and pride of family are natural and everyday feelings. What is worthy of condemnation and is, quite apart from Government policy, condemned in Zambia, is the use of such feeling to introduce dissension and division in the nation. I am fully satisfied that an accusation of tribalism without qualification is not generally accepted in Zambia in this pejorative sense, and that such an accusation would tend to lower the person so accused in the public esteem...(*Zambia Publishing Co. Ltd. v Kapwepwe* (1974) p. 298 (Doyle CJ)).

This judicial tolerance of allegations of tribalism is somewhat surprising, and out of line with what courts, and, I am sure, people, in Africa generally think "tribalism" connotes. In Zimbabwe Eddison Zvogbo sued for being described as an "unashamed regionalist" (*Zvogbo v Kingston's Ltd.* (1986)). In another case arising out of the same publication the court observed (*Zvogbo v Mutjuwadi* (1985) pp. 337-8),

> It is common knowledge in this country and the court takes judicial notice that the Prime Minister and many other prominent politicians have spoken against racism, tribalism, nepotism and regionalism. Anyone displaying such tendencies might be despised in our society.

In *Peckover v Muyu* (Kenya 1970) the plaintiff succeeded, when the allegation was he had "the old colonial mentality", practised racial discrimination and had shown disrespect for thc President.

In other cases, and other countries, the courts have held it defamatory to accuse a public figure of departing from the national, or party, philosophy. In Tanzanian cases the courts have stressed the national commitment to Socialism and the demands this makes upon the leadership (see Mtengeti-Migiro, 1985; Goulbourne, 1976). For example, it was defamatory to say that a person was unfit to be a Leader because he owned many houses which he let out and was therefore exploiting the people (*Hassan v Manyori* (1979)).

In Zambia a plaintiff objected to: "A good number of leaders are hangers-on and lack depth and dedication to the humanist cause". The plaintiff seems to have extracted "hangers-on" as though it was particularly obnoxious, although it is not clear why (*Zulu v Times Newspapers (Zambia) Ltd.* (1985)). The Supreme Court itself said that the whole sentence seemed to mean some people have not made "any significant contribution to the appropriate national cause"; one might have expected that they would hold that alleging lack of commitment to the ruling party ideology was defamatory of a former Solicitor-General but they did not. Possibly the problem was the over-ambitious nature of the pleadings: the plaintiff alleged that this meant he was "Undesirable and a disgrace in the Zambian society"; the court felt that this was far-fetched.

Some courts have held that politicians must expect a degree of criticism, and this is not necessarily to be found defamatory. A Zimbabwean court said (*Zvogbo v Kingston's Ltd.* (1986) p. 323),

> ...no public figure can expect to escape criticism, disapproval, complaint and even hostility at times in respect of some of his decisions and actions. Provided that these protests are kept within the bounds of moderation, and do not impute improper, immoral or otherwise dishonourable conduct to the plaintiff, the author's constitutional rights of free expression will be protected. In fact many

> a public figure welcomes constructive criticism and debate, and would echo Oscar Wilde's remarks in *The Picture of Dorian Gray* "...there is only one thing in the world worse than being talked about, and that is not being talked about".

These are brave words, but do not really amount to a great deal in practical terms. As in some other cases in which similar sentiments were expressed, the outcome was to hold that the words in question were defamatory.

"Natural Rulers"

Many African societies were ruled in pre-colonial times by their own kings and many retain some prominent position, although not necessarily much political power, today. We have seen that the Kabaka of Buganda failed because his perception of his treatment by Obote would not have been shared by all Ugandans (*Kiwanuka v Obote* (1965)). Courts have held that it was defamatory to say that the plaintiff (in Nigeria) achieved the conferment of his title by duress (*Akpojaro v Bendel Newspapers Corporation* (1981)), or that a Chief in Uganda had disappeared from his post (*Ndawala v Uganda Printing and Publishing Co. Ltd.* (1966)).

In *Okafor v Ikeanyi* (1979) the Supreme Court of Nigeria reached a rather remarkable decision, holding that a statement to the effect that a vote of no confidence had been passed in the plaintiff in his capacity of natural ruler, and that he had been deposed, was not defamatory. The statement had been made that the plaintiff had "wantonly violated" the terms of the Chieftaincy Agreement, but the court held that the reasonable man would not jeer at a chief who had lost his title, but would sympathise with him (p. 114). Less surprisingly, it was held not to be defamatory to say that a ruler had abdicated (*Bulus v Suleiman* (Nigeria 1982)) (it might, the court said, be injurious falsehood, which would require proof of malice). Another Nigerian court held it was not defamatory to say that a natural ruler deprecated an amnesty given to former rebels at the end of the civil war (*Nigerian Chronicle v Peterside* (1978)); the trial judge (Inko Tariah J) had found the defendants liable. Another newspaper described one section of a town's community as "strangers" meaning that they had arrived more recently (and could not provide the local ruler); this was also held not to be defamatory (*Olukaiyeja v Kwara State Printing and Publishing Corporation* (Nigeria 1980)).

Religion

Some cases are the outcome of the explosive mixture of religion and politics. A Muslim Minister of Education in Uganda successfully sued for the allegation that he advocated the forceful conversion of Catholic girls to Islam (*Mayanja v White Fathers* (1960)) and a former Minister of Home Affairs in Tanzania for the allegation that he pressed for "too rapid Muslimisation of the police force" (*Maswanya v African Buyer and Trader (Publications) Ltd.* (1981)). In the latter it was observed that it was particularly offensive in Tanzanian society "which denounces all forms of discrimination and believes in equal opportunity for all regardless of such considerations as race, sex or religion" (p. 223). In Mauritius the plaintiff sued successfully for an allegation that he fomented discord between different branches of Hinduism (*Gujadhur v Moonasing* (1935)).

Among the "pure" religion cases, it has been held in Nigeria that an action could be brought for saying that a Christian preacher used "paganic practices" and "enchantments" that did not come from the Bible (*Bandele v Daily Times* (1974)), and for describing the teachings of a church as "pernicious" (*Oke v Gansallo* (1923)). A modern Nigerian equivalent is perhaps *Registered Trustees of the Rosicrucian Order v Awoniyi* (1994).

In *Sketch v Ajagbemokeferi* (1989), the Nigerian Supreme Court held *obiter* it was not defamatory to say that a chieftaincy title conferred on the plaintiff because of his preaching was worthless and un-Islamic, and that holders of such titles would go to hell. Oputa JSC observed (p. 706) "...is it not a dangerous departure from known legal procedure to make the civil Courts arbiters in matters of sin, heaven and hell?" The Court of Appeal had held that it was defamatory to say that one would go to hell. The Supreme Court on the other hand, as these remarks suggest, seems to have been keen to stay out of religious controversy, rather as the courts have out of ethnic issues.

Witchcraft

Witchcraft is often taken very seriously, even today, and allegations of witchcraft have been held defamatory; in a criminal case in Swaziland, brought by an inyanga, or "witch doctor" (*R v Mathebula* (1977-78)) the statement was "You must bring me a human head". He complained that it was suggested he killed people. In *Olowo v Attorney-General* (Uganda 1972) the phrase used was "unexplained powers". A Nigerian judge pointed out that a mere allegation of witchcraft has led to lynching (*Olapade v Sketch*

Publishing Co. Ltd. (1978)). A witchcraft allegation would be especially defamatory if the plaintiff were a ordained clergyman (as in *Nkalubo v Kibirige* (Uganda 1973)). But it could be argued that the *reasonable* person does not believe in witchcraft, a view apparently taken by the South African courts in the late nineteenth century *(Ex parte Du Plooy* (1893) quoted by Poulter (1970, p. 143)). There is a well-known Nigerian criminal case - *R v Gadam* (1953) - in which it was held that a belief in witchcraft offered no defence to a charge of murder. But this case surely reflects judicial judgment of what is acceptable in terms of public policy, rather than a serious estimate of what people actually believe. What do courts think they achieve by refusing to recognise that an allegation of witchcraft is defamatory? Maybe they are essentially saying "I don't believe in witchcraft so clearly no reasonable person will"? Or are they denying something which, in the case of indigenous judges, they find embarrassing to admit about their own society? Or are they using the law of defamation to express disapproval of such beliefs? (See Chapter 4.)

The situation would be perhaps even more difficult for those administering customary law. A Sudanese writer has suggested (Makec, 1988, p. 212),

> although I do not believe that there are people possessing such power, I would submit that imputation of *wuuth* or *peeth* (dangerous supernatural powers) to one of the families locally believed to possess such power would not amount to defamation.

If the family was not known to have such powers the statement would be defamatory.This view, albeit respectful of tradition, seems to hold its own problems: what relief is there for a family which wishes to dissociate itself from a past of attributed supernatural powers - and which may perhaps face criminal charges if it simply submits to such allegations?

Others

Among the other allegations in various cases we might mention, that a well-known businessman has used his party connections to obtain government loans (*Odutola v West African Pilot* (Nigeria 1960)), and that another prominent businessman exploited his workers and public funds, was funded by the CIA, and lived in wanton gluttony and self-indulgence indifferent to the plight of the majority of his fellow-countrymen (*Bakare v Oluwide* (Nigeria 1969)). It was defamatory to say that a person kept a slave

(*Ogundelu v Solarin* (Nigeria 1980)), or had brought a private prosecution from political motives(*Yanni v Sierra Leone Daily Mail* (1967-68)).

On the other hand, to take a couple of examples of *non*-defamatory statements: it was held not defamatory to describe someone as an "ingrate and an opportunist" (*Oshuntokun v Babalola* (Nigeria (1992)). Nor was it defamatory to say of a bank that it opened at 10 p.m. in order to pay ₦20,000 to the Chairman from his account, even if the mandate to pay was on the back of his business card. The payment, the Court said, "may be unorthodox, but that does not make it defamatory of the Bank" (*Union Bank Ltd. v Oredein* (Nigeria 1987)).

Disclaimer Notices

Notices in the press or in the form of circulars disclaiming responsibility for and warning the public against certain people have generated so much litigation that they merit separate consideration (for English authority see *Muligan v Cole* (1875); *Beswick v Smith* (1907)). A simple statement that a person is no longer employed and the defendants will no longer take responsibility for him is unlikely to be considered defamatory (*De Souza v George Bros. Ltd.* (Uganda 1956-7); see also *Caltex v Oddie* (Kenya 1955); *Banda v Zambia Publishing Company Ltd.* (1982)). A judge held that a statement to the effect that the plaintiff was no longer with the company, that "He therefore has no further authority whatsoever to transact any business on behalf of this company" and that anyone who dealt with him did so at his own risk, was not capable of a defamatory meaning; it would have been different, the judge suggested, had the notice been headed "Caution" or said the plaintiff had been dismissed; as it was the ordinary person would not believe that the plaintiff had been dismissed or been dishonest but had resigned and the defendants were just protecting their interests (*Inneh v Midwest Line* (Nigeria 1977) (Unurhobo J); Gatley p. 33 fn 80 also suggests that a notice headed "Caution" might be defamatory). A statement in the *Daily Times* in Nigeria to the effect that a person had been "presenting himself as the personal representative of the Cameroonian Ambassador" was held libellous (*Visas v Daily Times of Nigeria Ltd.* (1975)), as was a statement in an East African paper which added to the disclaimer "He escaped after he was found guilty of being untrustworthy with this Company's money" (*Daily Nation v Mukundi* (Kenya 1975)). Similarly a statement that the plaintiff had been dismissed for professional misconduct was defamatory (*Atoyebi v Odudu* (Nigeria 1990)), as was an even a more cautiously worded statement: that the plaintiff was not the Manager of the company and he had no authority to present himself as such or to transact any business on behalf of the company (*Obikoya v Ezenwa* (Nigeria 1973)).

Not all cases concern ex-employees; in *Bakare v Ibrahim* the warning was against a business associate of the defendant (Nigeria 1973). (For this point a fuller discussion is at first instance (1970).) And in *Onwuka v Utaegbulam* (1977) the Aba Zone of the Nigerian Medical Association published a notice referring to publicity about alleged cures for certain medical conditions; they said that they knew of no such cures, and that the plaintiff who had been interviewed in the previous publications had been suspended from the NMA, and dissociated themselves from "such false claims". The case is reported only on procedural issues; we do not therefore know whether the court would hold the statements to be defamatory.

It is difficult to convey a warning to members of the public without being defamatory, unless one uses language so bland that the warning may not get home. Someone who wishes to make such a warning to protect both himself and the public should take care to remain within the bounds of the defence of qualified privilege.

Financial Credit

The East African Court of Appeal said (without citing authority - it might have cited *Sim v Stretch* (England 1936)), "It is well settled that a mere statement that a man owes money is not *per se* defamatory" (*Singh v Notkin* (Kenya 1952) p.119). And in Nigeria it was held not defamatory to say that the plaintiff had not paid his rates - pointing out that failure to pay could well be due to some innocent reason such as inadvertence (*Osisanya v Lagos City Council* (1974)).

There is, of course, a difference between refusing to pay one's debts and being unable to do so. There has been some difference of view between authors as to whether, in the case of a non-trader, an allegation of insolvency (which of itself suggests inability not refusal to pay) is defamatory (in the case of a trader, an oral statement to this effect is actionable *per se* - see Chapter 4). There is authority in both directions, and it has been suggested that the best approach is for the court to take account of the circumstances of the plaintiff in deciding whether he has been defamed (Hudson, 1990, citing the U.K. cases *AB v CD* (1904), *Boaks v Associated Newspapers* (1967)).

There have been several African cases holding it defamatory to say that the plaintiff could or would not pay his debts, either expressly, or by implication - as by saying that his house is to be auctioned on the instructions of mortgagee (*Karunwi v Wema Bank* (Nigeria 1973); *Mutual Aids Society v Akerele* (Nigeria 1966)). Examples of express statements are trying to avoid paying business debts, such as *Hassan v Kassardjan Construction Ltd.* (Ghana 1964); being stranded, "destitute", in Germany having failed to pay hotel bills (*Zambia Publishing Co. v Kakungu* (1982); also *Duguid v Storey* (Malaŵi 1923)). A judge in Malaŵi held that it was not defamatory simply to say that the plaintiff had had a default judgment for debt entered against him, but where the statement was published in a bulletin for the information of bankers and commercial concerns the words could be taken as implying that he was insolvent (*Madumuse v Press Furniture and Joinery Ltd. (1984)*, quoting *Khembo v Blantyre Print & Packaging* (1980) (both Skinner CJ)). In *Kuye v Nigerian National Press* (1963) it was held defamatory to say that the plaintiff had been sued to recover an overdraft, because it suggested insolvency. (For English authority (relied on in *Kuye*) see *Stubbs v Russell* (1913) and *Stubbs v Mazure* (1920) and Gatley, para. 55.) Allegations of trying to avoid the payment of taxes may reflect as much on one's obedience to law as on one's financial credit - and is certainly defamatory. (In *Economides v S. Thomopoulos & Co. Ltd.* (Nigeria 1956), it was unsuccessfully pleaded as a popular innuendo.)

It is, of course, a breach of contract for a bank to fail to honour a cheque if there are funds in the account; in *Grindlays Bank (U) Ltd. v Kayondo* (Uganda 1976), the bank was sued in both contract and defamation (and see *Ashubiojo v African Continental Bank Ltd.* (Nigeria 1966)). However, it is not entirely clear in what circumstances words written on the cheque by the bank will be defamatory. The common expression is "refer to drawer" or the abbreviation "R/D". The English authorities are divided (*Flach v London & S.W.Bank Ltd.* (1915), *Sterling v Barclays Bank Ltd.*(1930), *Plunkett v Barclays* (1936), *Pyke v Hibernian Bank Ltd.* (Ireland 1950), cited in *Alabi v Standard Bank of Nigeria Ltd.* (1976)). Gatley suggests that the words are capable of a defamatory meaning and should be left to the jury (para. 56); he also observes *ibid.* n. 57),

> It is submitted that it would not be unreasonable for a jury to find, in the light of their knowledge of worldly affairs, that the usual reason for writing "R/D" was want of funds to meet it

(which is just what the court did in the *Grindlays* case in Uganda - above). In *Coker v Standard Bank of Nigeria Ltd.* (1976) the judge held that "referred to drawer" was libellous. Unfortunately, his reasoning is not entirely clear; indeed, at one point he says counsel for the defence had not sought to contend that the endorsement was not libellous (p. 177). There have been other cases in Nigeria going both ways: in *Adeleke v National Bank of Nigeria Ltd.* (1978) the cheque was "returned unpaid" which was held to be defamatory; in *Evuleocha v Barclays Bank of Nigeria Ltd* (1977), counsel for the plaintiff conceded that the expression could not be defamatory after counsel for the defendant had cited *Flach, Plunkett* and *Alabi* (above) - on the last he was clearly wrong to concede the point as the phrase used was quite different. In at least one East African case the court held it was not defamatory (*Dogra v Barclays Bank* (Kenya 1974)).

In *Alabi v Standard Bank of Nigeria Ltd.* (above) the bank had written "effects uncleared" on the cheque. The judge said (p. 414)

> It seems to me that the words "effects uncleared" in their ordinary connotation denote that at the time the cheque was presented there were not sufficient funds available for drawing against in the customer's account merely because a cheque or cheques credited to the account had not at that moment in time been cleared. My own view is that it is not reasonably possible to regard these words as reflecting upon the solvency or upon the integrity of the customer.

But two years later another Nigerian judge held that the same expression *was* defamatory (*Adamolekun v Akanbi* (1978) p. 78). He thought that in Nigeria,

> The average man in the street would have concluded that a payer whose cheque was returned was impecunious or bankrupt until he had proved the contrary...the reaction...would be one of contempt of the payer and consequent injury to his trade, profession or financial credit.

These are only findings of fact and not of law and in the ultimate analysis it must be left to the judge, though one does wonder how a judge can decide how a reasonable Nigerian businessman would make this evaluation (in this case the judge had heard evidence of the reaction of one person). Finally, in *Animashaun v Standard Bank of West Africa Ltd.* (Nigeria 1968) it was held not to be defamatory to say that the plaintiff's cheque had been "countermanded", "cancelled" or "revoked".

Very few of the cases have involved holdings that statements were *not* defamatory.This suggests that the question of what is "defamatory" gives rise to relatively few practical problems. Plaintiffs, and judges, recognise defamatory statements when they see them, and plaintiffs on the whole only sue for statements which are clearly defamatory.

8 Publication

"There must...be a recipient of the information not himself being the plaintiff" (*Jonathan v Athuman Khalfan* (Tanzania 1980) p. 178).

Another Person

If the plaintiff cannot prove that the offending matter was published to anyone other than the plaintiff himself, he will fail (as in *Moiro v Naileklet K.J. Zablon* (Tanzania 1980), *Asaolu v Olaiya Fagbemi Ltd.* (Nigeria 1982); *Nsirim v Nsirim* (Nigeria 1990). Publication is used in this context in the sense of "communicated" - the "making known of the defamatory matter" (Lord Esher in *Pullman v Hill* (England 1891)). It is not a tort to attack the plaintiff's character to his face with no third person present (see *Dickson v Enwere* (Nigeria 1967)). It has been said that in systems of customary law the rule is the same (McCullough, 1971). However, as mentioned before, abuse is often actionable under customary law, and it may be that publication to a third person is not then required. In some jurisdictions the criminal offence may be committed without publication to any person other than the one defamed; it will depend upon the wording of the legislation - see s. 374 Nigerian Criminal Code, s. 40 Newspapers Act of Tanzania.

Husband and wife were treated as one to the extent that communication by the defendant to his or her spouse is not publication - at least in older cases (e.g. *Wennhak v Morgan* (England 1880)), although some say the authority is weak ("slender judicial authority" said the Irish Law Reform Commission (1991, 4.18), coming out in favour of its abolition (*ibid.*, 4.23). In Africa there is the risk that, as with other questions like evidence of one spouse against another, communications between spouses of customary marriages would be treated differently from those between spouses of monogamous marriages. Communication to the spouse of the *plaintiff* is publication (e.g. *Theaker v Richardson* (England 1962)), a rule lacking logic perhaps, but reflecting reality since often it is precisely to one's spouse that one would not wish a statement to be communicated.

Any other person will be treated as a third person. The servant or agent of the plaintiff or of the defendant is a third party for this purpose.

> Even a confidential communication to one individual, if defamatory, is actionable in law. It does not matter how the individual stands in relation to the plaintiff...A plaintiff may rely on publication to his agent, even if the agent has invited and procured the publication, so long as it has not been instigated by the plaintiff (*Jonathan v Athuman Khalfan*, p. 175, citing *King v Waring* (England 1803)[1]).

A few cases have touched on the question of whether a company, which for most purposes has a separate personality from its members and officers, is "another person" for the purposes of publication of defamation. One plaintiff argued that, when he opened a letter defamatory of himself in his capacity as Chairman of a company, there was publication to the company through himself as its agent. The court gave short shrift to this argument, observing that "what actually occurred could only have resulted in a blow to Louw's own self-esteem but in no loss of reputation" (*Grindlays v Louw* (Rhodesia 1979) p. 194). They also rejected his argument that he was bound to disclose the communication to the company (since the statement alleged improper interest on the plaintiff's part in contracts of the company). In effect the court said this was not information, being untrue to his knowledge. Members of the East African Court of Appeal said, *obiter*, that they thought publication to a director of matter defamatory of the company was not publication, though they cited no authority (*Kenya Litho Ltd. v All Africa Trading Co.* (1973); the court below took a different view). With respect, the Court of Appeal view would seem questionable, although it might be appropriate where a "one-man" company is involved. A Nigerian judge held that publication to *servants* of the company was sufficient (Omusin J in *Osezuah & Co. (Nigeria) Ltd. v Guinness (Nigeria) Ltd* (1980)). He cited *Salvalene v Darby* (England, unrep., see Gatley, para. 222) on this point, to the effect that publication to an officer may be sufficient. Gatley contrasts *Insurance Research Services v Associates Finance* (USA 1955).

It may happen that a publication about more than one person is made only to those people. Is this publication to each of the statement about the other or others? *Obiter*, a Seychelles court agreed with Gatley that it was publication (*Sedgwick v Lepaire* (1967); for Gatley see now para. 222 n. 10, citing US authority).

There is no publication if the reader or hearer did not understand the statement, because he did not understand the language (*Price v Jenkins* (England 1601)), or because he was ignorant of some extrinsic fact that made the statement defamatory, or which connected it to the plaintiff (*Knuppfer v London Express* (England 1944)).

Proof of Publication

In many situations publication is presumed: for example that a postcard or a telegram is published to the employees of the post office, or post and telegraph department (*Huth v Huth* (England 1915) p. 39 (postcard); *Sim v Stretch* (England 1935); *Pfeiffer v Steffens* (Tanzania 1930: telegram - a criminal case)), or a conversation to the operator in an operator-connected call. Some African judges are less prepared to assume the communication was published to the intended recipient, in the case of a letter posted. Yinka Ayoola J said that he would not assume that the Nigerian post office had actually delivered a letter (despite English authority: *Warren v Warren* (1834), where the letter had been postmarked and its seal broken, and *Shipley v Todhunter* (1836)). However, his remarks were *obiter* as the case actually concerned a letter delivered by a messenger, which he, quite rightly, said he would not assume without proof had been delivered (*Okwuwe v Onifade* (1981)). A Malaŵian judge took a more positive view of postal services (*Malaŵi Railways v Bhadhurkan* (1986) p. 437, applying *Warren* and *Shipley*) while an East African court said that there was a reasonable presumption (presumably rebuttable) that if a carbon of a letter had reached its destination, the top copy and other carbons had done so too (*Davies v Mohanlal Karamshi Shah* (Kenya 1957)). However, in *Moiro v Zablon* above, it was held that, although the letter to the plaintiff was marked "cc" others, there was no evidence that the copies had even been posted. Spry (1976, p. 15) says that at first instance the court in *Kenya Litho Ltd. v All Africa Trading Co.* (1970) held that there was publication as soon as the letter was posted which "would seem clearly to have been made *per incuriam*".

Once copies of a book or newspaper have been sold it will be presumed it is read (e.g. *Awoniyi v Registered Trustees of the Rosicrucian Order (AMORC)* (Nigeria 1990) p. 64). Indeed, publication to the employees of the publisher and printer will be presumed. In the case of newspapers, Nigerian authority seems to be a little unusual. It is not uncommon for the plaintiff to call as a witness someone who actually bought the newspaper (e.g. *Asiodu v Abodunde* (1979)), or a library may produce a copy, as in the *Awoniyi* case. One would have thought that an admission by the defendant that he had published the paper would do as well. However, the Supreme Court said "The admission that the Daily Times was printed and published did not of itself establish publication" (*Ajakaiye v Okandeji* (1972)). If by this confusing use of "publication" the court meant there is no evidence that sales actually took place, it is probably unobjectionable: Gatley says there must be evidence showing a probability that sales took place (para. 1289n. - citing *Trimble v*

Central News (South Africa 1933)). But a later judge went too far when he said, "the rationale behind the authority would appear to be that in cases of libel, the mere fact that the document containing the words complained of is admitted to be published by the defendant, would not constitute 'publication' that would ground libel unless a third person testified that he had read the said words complained of" (*Thievent v Daily Times* (Nigeria 1979)), for, as we have seen, it is unnecessary to show that anyone actually read the material.

Who is Liable?

Dictating to a secretary (*Gidando v Chief Imam of Odo-Ado* (Nigeria 1962)) (or a public letter writer) is publication (although if the letter is otherwise privileged this publication will be covered - *Boxius v Goblet Frères* (England 1894)). However, in a Kenyan case Madan JA held in effect that publication to a secretary was not publication (*University of Nairobi v Mbuthia* (1980)):

> Personal assistants and secretaries have become an indispensable adjunct to the running of establishments both in the public and private sectors...As regards a stenographer who is also a private secretary...provided the occasion is one in which the communication is both delivered and received in the ordinary course of business and duty respectively the writer or publisher of the communication should be treated as one person with his stenographer or personal secretary as if he were performing the function himself in person instead of physically projecting the stenographer or private secretary to do it as another separate and independent individual.

This line of reasoning suggests no publication. However, Madan J seems actually to have been saying that there was a species of qualified privilege; the difference being that malice would defeat the latter. His observations were *obiter*, and not endorsed by Law JA (who relied upon *Bryanston Finance v de Vries* (England 1975)).

A person who signs a letter (*Gidando v Chief Imam*) or instructs his secretary to type and send one without signing publishes it. A legal practitioner who writes and sends a defamatory communication on behalf of a client is that client's agent and both will be liable (*Mutual Aids Society v Akerele* (Nigeria 1966) p. 261, *Odebunmi v Ademokun* (Nigeria 1976)). The situation would be different if the agent published unauthorised statements. So in a Malaŵian case the defendant, who had obtained a default judgment against the plaintiff, was held not liable for the act of his solicitor who sent a statement about the judgment for publication in a bulletin for the information of banks and credit granters. Skinner CJ said (*Madumase v Press Furniture and Joinery Ltd.* (1984)),

> The scope of the employment in a debt collection matter is to collect the money by way of demand, judgment and execution and I cannot see how the publication of the judgment is a matter incidental to any of those acts or in any way a mode of doing them.

In *Boagya v Boakye* (Ghana 1981) the plaintiff failed, *inter alia*, because he did not show that the defendant had authorised the gong-gong beater to say that the plaintiff had stolen his sheep. A person will, however, be liable on the usual principles if he ratifies an otherwise unauthorised statement by his agent (*Odebunmi v Ademokun* (Nigeria 1976)) or for defamatory statements by a servant in the course of his or her employment (see the discussion in *Eigbe v Capital Hotel Ltd. (Sheraton)* (Nigeria 1993) p. 97). (For other cases, from England and elsewhere, including *Citizen's Life Co. v Brown* (England 1904), see Gatley, para. 941.)

Everyone involved in the production of an item will be liable. As a Ugandan court (*Opoka v Munno* (1990-91) p.18) said,

> In the first place there is publication by the author of the defamation to the publisher for which the author is solely liable. Secondary [*sic*] there is the publication by the author and publisher jointly to the printer for which both of them are jointly liable. Then comes the publication of the printed matter to the public for which the author, publisher and printer are jointly liable.

(See also *Gyang v Ilyasu* (Nigeria 1977), Fiebai J quoting Gatley 6th. ed. para. 625; *Jakande v Concord Press* (Nigeria 1982).) There are many cases against newspaper proprietors (e.g. *Williams v West African Pilot* (Nigeria 1961)). In *Leal v Hitié* (Mauritius 1882) one defendant was held liable on the basis of being the owner, and licensee, of the printing press, although she was assumed to have known nothing of the matter printed, and in *Robertson v Michel* (Mauritius 1927, p. 83) the court observed that the 1837 statute requiring a declaration of the place of printing and name of the printer of a newspaper was "enacted precisely for the purpose of fixing responsibility for the contents of a newspaper and it would be defeated if one of the signatories could be allowed to disclaim responsibility". The distributor (e.g. *Awolowo v Kingsway* (Nigeria 1968) and the library which lends the item (e.g. *Vizetelly v Mudie's Select Library* (England 1900)) will also be liable.

Gatley now points out (para. 1289n.) that the assumption that someone other than the author has read the material is less easy to assume when journalists themselves directly input the materials onto the computer from which it is automatically typeset - though I have a feeling this is rare in African newspapers. The only people who have any defence at common law based on their ignorance of the defamatory content may be the distributors and libraries (see Chapter 17 which also discusses suggestions that printers should have a defence). Plaintiffs commonly sue newspapers and not the author of the article, or the originator of the remark, complained of. It has been proposed in Zambia that there should be a requirement for the originator also to be sued. The Attorney-General in rejecting this said,

> A newspaper...ought not to publish wildly irresponsible statements in the knowledge and expectation that after all someone else will be held responsible (Law Development Commission, 1984, p. 8).

If publication was not intended by the defendant, his liability will depend on whether he ought to have foreseen the possibility of publication. If the communication was sent to the plaintiff who chose to publish it the defendant will not be liable - as in the Nigerian case in which the police sent a statement to the plaintiff stating negligently that he had a conviction, which the plaintiff (rather remarkably) showed to a prospective scholarship sponsor (*Okotcha v Olumese* (1967); see also other Nigerian cases - *Emessiri v Sanomi* (1977) where Aluyi J held the plaintiff had himself shown the letter to others, *Isah v Ajaokuta Steel Co. Ltd.* (Nigeria 1985) and *Bia v Murray* (Sierra Leone 1954)). The Supreme Court of Sierra Leone held that it was not foreseeable that the plaintiff would repeat an allegation of her own unfaithfulness to her husband who then put her out of his house for three days (*Johnson v Smith* (1963), citing *Speight v Gosnay* (England 1891)).[2] There *may* be situations in which it is incumbent upon the plaintiff to show the communication to others, in which case its author might be liable for publication (if one was credibly told one was suffering from AIDS one would surely have a duty to tell one's sexual partner?). An argument that there was a duty to communicate failed in the *Louw* case (above). If the plaintiff authorised or requested the publication, as the plaintiff in *Jonathan v Athuman Khalfan* (above) had instigated one of the communications of which he complained, the defendant will not be liable.

In slander there will be publication if the defendant spoke within what he should have realised was the hearing of others, such as a railway compartment or public rooms in a hotel, to take two Mauritian examples

(*Bouffé v Lemaire* (1886) and *Wing Fo Chan Kun v Sam Zee Moi* (1955) (in the latter case the court said the defendant was not so drunk as not to know what he was saying!). In another Mauritian case it does not seem that the publication issue was properly addressed: the defendant had been "dressing down" the plaintiff in private but a third person came on the scene in time to hear part of the conversation. Whether this was foreseeable was not discussed (*Stockdale v Le Blanc* (1918)).

If the defendant knew that the plaintiff was illiterate or blind, and would have to ask someone else to read the letter to him he will be held to have published it (*Jackson v Staley* (Canada 1885), applied in *Na Kaura v Ikeawujo* (Nigeria 1976)). There is one West African Court of Appeal case of doubtful reasoning. The plaintiff was told by his superior "I am going to get you sacked". The superior then gave the plaintiff a letter to deliver to the company management; the letter was not in an envelope, and the plaintiff, who was illiterate, asked someone to read it for him and discovered that it was defamatory. The court reversed the trial judge and held that there was no publication to the third person. They said, "It is his misfortune to be illiterate, but that is no reason for holding the defendant responsible for this publication which was brought about by the plaintiff himself diverting the form out of its routine course" (*Bia v Murray* above, p. 372). Is this not rather hard on the plaintiff, when this could have been avoided by putting the form in an envelope, or sending it by some other messenger?

In an Indian case, the plaintiff could read Urdu (Persian) script (as opposed to the Devanagari (Hindi) script in which the letter was written. It was held that the defendant was not liable for the publication necessitated by the plaintiff's asking someone to read the letter to him if he did not know that the plaintiff did not read Urdu (*Mahendra Ram v Harnandan Prasad* (1958)). A similar situation might arise in, for example, Nigeria, if a person able to read Arabic script received a letter written in Hausa in Roman script.

There will be publication if the defendant sent a communication to the wrong person by mistake, as in a Ugandan case in which the letter was sent by error to the plaintiff's father instead of to the plaintiff (*Arvind Anand Kati v CL Elder* (1965), see also *Fox v Broderick* (Ireland 1864)). If father and son had the identical name, presumably it would be a question of fact whether the defendant ought to have known and realised the implication of this. Similarly, if in a particular family, to the knowledge of the defendant, parents opened letters for their children (or husbands their wives' letters) the defendant ought to foresee publication. Suppose such behaviour was likely in a particular community to the knowledge of the defendant, but he knew nothing of the domestic arrangements of the particular family? This can be looked at by analogy with cases on secretaries opening letters to their bosses, (see e.g. *Delacroix v Thevenot* (England 1817), where the defendant knew of the practice in the plaintiff's firm; and Gatley, para. 231, n. 45). In *Emessiri v Sanomi* (above) Aluyi J suggested *obiter* that if the letter had been sent to the plaintiff's office and opened by his clerk there would have been publication to the clerk. In one English case the defendant delivered a letter by hand, in the sort of (brown) envelope which in England was used for business rather than personal communications, addressed to the plaintiff of whom it was defamatory. It was opened by her husband who thought it was just a circular. It was held there was publication (*Theaker v Richardson* - above). There is no reason to suppose that a similar finding of fact would be appropriate where such envelopes are used for all types of letters.

Repetition

A person who repeats a defamatory statement is liable - it will be no defence to say he was simply repeating what someone else began, and it is no help to say "it is rumoured that" (*Watkin v Hall* (England 1868)).

But is the originator liable for other people spreading his statement further? As we have seen, he will be liable if he ought to have foreseen this, because, for example, the recipient needed a person to read the letter for him. He will be liable in other situations for foreseeable repetitions (*Weld-Blundell v Stevens* (England 1920); for a recent English example see *Slipper v British Broadcasting Corporation* (1991)). The Supreme Court of New South Wales discussed the repetition on the radio of a restaurant review; the purpose of the repetition was to comment on the style of the review; even so the court held it was open to a jury to decide that a repetition was foreseeable. They observed that the very purpose of such a review was repetition, though the object of the repetition in this case was rather different (*Williams v John Fairfax Group Pty. Ltd.* (1991)).

Some cases have involved newspaper reports of the defendant's words. Akpata JSC (*Ejabulor v Osha* (Nigeria 1990) p.195) said,

> It would amount to turning a blind eye to an obvious fact to hold that a slanderous speech held at a press centre was not authorised to be published.

On the other hand, he said (p. 192)

> It seems to me plain and reasonable that where by chance reporters were present when the slanderous speech was made but not at a press conference

> and the author knew of their presence and was conscious of the likelihood of the speech appearing in a newspaper he will not for that reason alone be rendered liable for the publication of the speech without some sort of request by him, expressly or implicitly, that the speech be published. In such a situation there would be the presumption that the reporters exercised their own discretion in publishing the offending speech. Only the reporters and the newspapers that publish the slanderous speech will be liable for the publication.
> It is however a different consideration in respect of a defamatory speech made at a press conference.

Karibi-Whyte JSC added (p. 220) "It is accepted law that liability for publication of a libel may arise either from publication or authorisation". The East African Court of Appeal said "authorisation should very readily be implied when a person has agreed to give an interview to a press reporter" (*Lalobo v Lakidi* (Uganda 1971)). In *Kiwanuka v Obote* (Uganda 1965) Sheridan J said, "I would have thought that although the first defendant did not expressly authorise, the reporting of his speech might be inferred from his knowledge that a reporter was present getting information for his paper". (See Gatley, para. 237 citing *Wills v Hardcastle* (USA 1902), *Parkes v Prescott* (England 1869) p.179, *Lyons v Prescott-Decie* (England 1925), *Hay v Smither* (England 1911) *inter alia*.)

The emphasis on "authorisation" in these cases is perhaps misguided, at least to the extent that they suggest that authorisation is a pre-requisite to liability. Ultimately it is a question of fact - ought the defendant reasonably to have foreseen that his statement would be published? The English Court of Appeal has emphasised that these cases fall within the usual principles of remoteness of damage in tort *(Slipper v BBC,* above, esp. Stocker LJ, p. 175)

A Zimbabwean judge said (*Maketo v Medical Investments (Pvt) Ltd.* (1988) p. 13),

> [S]uch consequential liability is usually limited to those circumstances which were identified by LOPES L.J. in *Speight v Gosnay* as follows:
> (1) where the defendant authorized or intended the repetition
> (2) where there was a moral duty, to the defendant's knowledge, on the other person or person to repeat the matter, or
> (3) where the repetition flows in the ordinary and normal course of events fron the original publication.

He then went on to say, somewhat surprisingly in part (p. 14),

> It is my view that if a person makes a defamatory statement against another in the course of an interview with a newspaper reporter, all three of these circumstances apply.

Surely a reporter is not under a *duty* to report everything which is said to him in interviews?

If the original statement was oral but the foreseeable repetition was in writing, the defendant will be liable for slander for the original statement and liable for the repetition - relevant in *Kiwanuka* and *Lalobo* (though no such issue would arise in Zimbabwe where the libel/slander distinction is not recognised).

There would not, of course, be liability for a libel which was the result of misreporting what the defendant said. In *Lalobo v Lakidi* the plaintiff failed because he had not shown that what was in the newspaper was what the defendant actually said, and the court said that accuracy of reporting could not be assumed. In *Fletcher v Bardoh* (Gold Coast 1882), the plaintiff was non-suited when he sued on the basis of a letter which had been written at the defendant's dictation; the defendant said that he had actually dictated something different.[3]

A Seychelles case went rather far in holding a defendant liable; he composed a defamatory song, and had a recording made of himself singing it with his band. He gave the recording to someone who was preparing a programme for the French broadcasting service, ORTF. Apparently without the defendant's authorisation another employee of the local radio station made a copy and it was broadcast over Radio Seychelles. The said the defendant ought to have anticipated that such a broadcast would be made, he had not prohibited it, it was the natural and probable consequence of his act and he was as much liable as if he had authorised the publication (*Kim Koon v Wirtz* (1976)).

A broadcasting organisation will be liable at common law for any defamatory content, even though they did not know that any defamatory observations were going to be made - as might well occur with a live broadcast. As Gatley says, there is no reason to give such organisations protection which is not given to other sorts of media which are liable regardless of knowledge (para. 245n). In a Mauritian case, however, it was held that no liability under the Civil Code attached when during a live broadcast of popular, topical songs (*segas*) one of the singers insisted he wanted to sing about the plaintiff in defamatory terms, and the altercation this caused was heard over the radio until the announcer switched off the microphone. It was held there was an absence of *faute* (fault) as required by the code, and that liability would only attach if the defendants were in a position to control what was happening. Having administered rum to the parties was not sufficient! (*Curé v Universal Sound Equipment Co.* (1941)).

But if the defamatory matter is published on premises - posted on a notice board or scrawled on a wall - the common law is closer to Mauritian law: there will not be liability unless the occupier of the libel-bearing premises fails to take advantage of a reasonable opportunity to remove it (*Byrne v Deane* (England 1937) p. 837; *Hellar v Bianco* (USA 1952), see Gatley, para. 225 n. 29). There might even then be a statutory defence if the defamatory nature of the words is not apparent. Under the equivalent of s. 4 of the English 1952 Act, the defendant would have to show that the author of the words was not malicious, which might be difficult - indeed impossible if the statement was anonymous! (s. 4(6)) (see Chapter14).

Multiple Publications

Every publication gives rise to a separate cause of action - and every copy of a book or newspaper is a separate publication (*Duke of Brunswick v Harmer* (England 1849)), and every reception of a broadcast, too.

> A slander spoken to an audience is one publication to all the members of the audience who heard and understood the words. But a libel in the form of a letter delivered to several individuals is a separate publication to each addressee

(*Oforka v Anisiuba* (Nigeria 1979) p. 136 (Obi-Okoye J)); the publication of the letter will only take place to those who read it, of course - though this may be presumed, as we have seen. The Faulks Committee in England recommended that if proceedings have been concluded by judgment, settlement or discontinuance the plaintiff should not be allowed to bring a further action on the same defamation without the leave of the court (Cmnd 5909, p. 80), which is in fact the law in some Australian states, such as the New South Wales Defamation Act 1974.

Notes

1. In fact this case, taken from Clerk & Lindsell on *Torts* (now para. 21-61n), did not discuss the agency issue, but is solely concerned with the possibility of the plaintiff instigating the communication.

2. For a rather similar English case to *Johnson* see *Parkins v Scott* (1862). Some cases have treated publication by the plaintiff as a variety of consent, e.g. *Phakisi v Phakisi* (Lesotho 1954). As Poulter (1970) 144 observes, when mentioning this case, absence of publication seems the more appropriate analysis.
3. This would be a constant hazard in societies in which illiteracy - and public letter writers - were common. The Illiterates Protection Acts in some jurisdictions at least provide that someone who writes at another's dictation should give his name and address.

9 Who Can Sue?

Introduction

The first section of this chapter emphasises that A cannot sue for defamation of B, and it then goes on to discuss what happens where the defamation refers to the dead, or where the plaintiff is a non-human person.[1]

No Vicarious Defamation

One cannot sue for defamation of another person, even a very close relative.[2] We can infer from the observations of a Nigerian court, to the effect that a statement is not actionable just because it causes damage to the plaintiff if it is not defamatory of him, that it thought that a statement that a young man had been charged with a criminal offence was not defamatory of his father (*Omo Bare v Odukomaiya* (1973) p. 59).

There may be situations in which a statement referring to A defames B by implication (for example, to say that someone is a bastard defames his parents). But in *Sketch v Ajagbemokeferi* (Nigeria 1989, p. 697) Wali JSC suggested that where the words complained of were to the effect that the plaintiff had been given a worthless chieftaincy title, an innovation unacceptable to Islam, they defamed those who had awarded the title, rather than its recipient. Is this right? The aspersions would seem to be as much upon the person who accepted the title as upon those who granted it.

In another intriguing Nigerian case the Court of Appeal held that a religious organisation, the Rosicrucian Order, could not sue for remarks which were defamatory of its founder, "Harve Spencer Lewis is not a party. Neither the plaintiff nor those who believe in him [i.e. Lewis] or his teachings can sue for any alleged libel of and concerning him". (*Awoniyi v Registered Trustees of the Rosicrucian Order (AMORC)* (1990) p. 64. The issue did not arise in the Supreme Court.) The trial judge (Edem Koofreh J) had said "If the so-called Christians decided to join AMORC, was it right for the defendants to publish invectives against the plaintiffs and immoral and debasing things against its leader Mr H. Spencer Lewis?"[3] The line seems very fine; if the whole object of the sect, as here, is to propagate the beliefs of the founder, is it really possible to take the view that the remarks do not attack the organisation and its members (though individuals who wanted to sue would have to confront the "class libel" issue discussed in Chap. 5)?

Defamation of the Dead

Under the common law, an action for defamation, like other "personal actions", would die when either party died. Most African jurisdictions have, like England, abrogated this rule by statute (the English Act is the Law Reform (Miscellaneous Provisions) Act of 1934). However, defamation was one of a small number of actions which were excluded from the effects of this legislation.

A Zambian writer suggested that defamation actions, like others, ought to survive the death of either party. He said,

> This is particularly desirable in Zambia where the dead are revered. It is believed by some that our destiny is decided by our ancestors. While this traditional belief, like others, has no scientific basis and may be dismissed as mere superstition, its advantage as a bond in the family, and therefore in society as a whole, must be recognised (Molotsi, 1984, p. 77).

He went on to suggest that it was unfair that a plaintiff should be deprived of the opportunity to vindicate his reputation because the defendant has died, or a defendant deprived of costs if an unmeritorious plaintiff should die after losing the suit but before paying the costs.

"[I]f the dead are defamed, neither their personal representatives nor their family can sue to protect their reputation, unless the allegation reflects on the living" (*In re Aluko* (Nigeria 1992) p. 347). In a Ghanaian case the plaintiffs complained that a history of certain Ga customs had defamed their grandmother/great grandmother; this, they said was defamatory of them because they "will be considered the descendants of a thief or burglar" (*Oppon v Advance Press* (1980)). The judge dealt with this as a question of "class libel", that is, could the plaintiffs claim that they, out of all the descendants of the maligned lady, had been especially defamed. It seems unlikely that an English court would have held any living person to have been defamed, and it is a pity that the judge does not make a specific finding whether in Ghana it is in fact defamatory of a person to say that his grandmother was dishonest. So to hold might well accord with traditional views as reflected in customary law. As Francis Deng (1965, pp. 560-1) put it in the Sudanese context,

> In as much as solidarities in Africa centre in the family...it is clear that defamation is necessarily contrary to family interests...and anything which spoils a man's name threatens to reflect on his family. Protection of the family is therefore an important factor in the law of defamation.
> ...The person defamed need not be a living member of the family. The logic of maintaining the name of a dead man means that he can be defamed in his death.

The English Committee on Defamation recommended that the cause of action should survive the death of either party, but if the plaintiff died before the action was commenced, remedies should be limited to an injunction and any actual or likely pecuniary damage. In the case of defamation of the already dead, the Committee recommended a new cause of action: specified relatives should be able to sue for a declaration that the statement was untrue, for an injunction, and for costs. The period for which the reputation of deceased individuals was to be protected was to be limited to 5 years after death (Cmnd 5909, para. 423). Molotsi, above, did not recommend a change of the law in this respect, because this would inhibit historians and biographers too much, and Robertson and Nicol (1992, p. 55) criticised the notion on the basis that the plaintiff, being dead, could not be cross-examined.[4]

The Corporate Plaintiff

In principle a corporation may bring an action in defamation as may any other person. The statement in Halsbury's *Laws of England* is to the effect that a corporation may sue "unless the imputation is solely against its individual officers or members" (Vol. 28 para. 25). If the latter is the case the corporation cannot sue even if the statement led to perfectly foreseeable damaging consequences to the corporation. In a Hong Kong case a mission sued, but the court held that the statements were defamatory only of a doctor and a missionary employed by the organisation. Although the mission had suffered a serious decline in donations it could not sue (*The President in Hong Kong of the Basel Evangelical Missionary Society v The Hong Kong Sheung Po Co. Ltd.* (1912)).

A company can sue for damage to its trading reputation; the leading English case is *South Hetton Coal Co. v North Eastern News Association* (1894). A Nigerian company was tried and acquitted of hoarding beer contrary to price control legislation. A newspaper item referring to beer hoarded by the company was held to be defamatory. Belgore JSC said,

> a corporate body suing for defamation...can sue for loss of profit, shortfall in turnover or anticipatory loss but not for natural grief and distress, and not for social disadvantage...A company is a legal person but it is inanimate. It has got no personal feelings of grief or distress...It is because of these special attributes of a company that in an action in defamation, a company does not need to prove special damage or even financial loss to recover damages for the injury to its reputation in the way of its trade or business (*Duyile v Kelly Ogunbayo & Sons Ltd.* (1988) p. 611, citing *Lewis v Daily Telegraph* (England 1964)).

It seems that the trial judge had fallen into error by applying to the defamation context concepts developed by the courts to pin criminal liability on companies. He referred to the notion that the state of mind of a company's managers can be treated as the state of mind of the company (citing Denning LJ in *Bolton Engineering Co. Ltd.* (England 1957) pp. 172-3, as quoted in *Trenco (Nigeria) Ltd. v African Real Estate and Investment Co. Ltd.* (1978) p. 24). The judge had awarded damages to the company because of the grief and distress felt by the managing director, saying this could be treated as the state of mind of the company.[5] However, a " company which has ceased to carry on business cannot be injured by words which reflect on the method by which it conducted its affairs"- *ACB Ltd v Sodeinde Bros. (Nigeria) Ltd* (1980), citing *Dupont Co. v Nashville Banner Co* (USA 1925) p. 189, Gatley [now para. 954n]).

There are a few other African cases involving artificial persons: a company could sue for the allegation that it had not paid its workers for months and was far behind in completing a contract (*A.W. Ibe & Co. Ltd. v The Reveille Printing and Publishing Co. Ltd.* (Nigeria 1975)). The point does not seem to have been raised in the case of *Ebuwa v United Africa Company* (Nigeria 1955), where UAC was the successful plaintiff; the allegation was of racial bias. It was held that it was defamatory for a newspaper to publish a statement that the Government was considering cancelling the certificate of the plaintiff insurance company because it had not measured up to expectations (*Nigerian Amicable Assurance Co. v Mercantile Press* (1977); for English examples see Gatley, para. 954). A doubtful decision was reached in Malaŵi where it was held that a corporation could not sue for an allegation of corruption (*Malaŵi Railways v Bhardukhan* (1986)).[6] A Ugandan court had no problem in holding that such an action could succeed (*Construction Engineers & Builders Ltd. v The New Vision* (1994)). A court in Mauritius declined to follow the English courts in their caution about permitting companies to sue. An association, which both counsel treated as a corporation, succeeded in claiming damages for an allegation that it organised a farce and theatrical performance for political purposes under the guise of rewarding acts of bravery. The judge said,

> Of course a libel may be of a nature to cause moral prejudice if applied to an individual, and yet not similarly affect a Society, but there is no principle of the law itself which excludes a Society or *personnalité morale* from the benefits of moral damages merely because it is a Society (*Hospitaliers Sauveteurs v Newton* (1909) p. 146, Brown J).[7]

The Nigerian Court of Appeal declined, by a majority, to allow an incorporated religious organisation to sue. The Court of Appeal said that so far as the defendant's statements suggested the plaintiff was satanic, evil or sinister it could not sue since "it has no mind of its own to do any of these" (*Awoniyi v Registered Trustees of AMORC* (1990) - in the Supreme Court the decision hinged on a different issue). As a non-trading organisation it could not complain of injury to its trading reputation. Uwaifo J cited the Supreme Court in *Duyile* to the effect that "loss of earnings, loss of profits, and loss of goodwill" could be sued for, but held that the plaintiff had none of these to lose. Kutigi JCA dissented and held that the reputation of the plaintiffs had been affected, and that since they had lost huge numbers of members leading to financial loss they could sue (quoting Gatley 7th. ed. para. 888).

Elsewhere, authorities are to the effect that non-trading corporations may sue for statements affecting their property, financial position or calling, and this has been applied to religious or quasi-religious bodies; in *Church of Scientology v Globe and Mail* (Canada 1978, p. 241) it was observed *obiter* that a non-profit company may sue without the necessity to prove special damage provided that the allegation touched its property or financial position or its trade or calling, and if that trade or calling were religion that could be very wide. Provided AMORC was indeed a body corporate it would seem that the majority of the Court of Appeal was in error in depriving it of a remedy on the grounds stated. While it is true that an artificial body has no mind, it can surely be accused of association with evil.

In a recent case in which the English Court of Appeal held that there was no necessity - indeed it was positively undesirable - to allow a local authority to sue for defamation, relying to some extent upon the European Convention on Human Rights; the criminal law is the appropriate means for protecting government (*Derbyshire County Council v Times* (1992)). The House of Lords (1993) reached the same conclusion by a rather different route, namely that it represented the common law, and it was unnecessary to invoke the Convention (applied in *Ballina Shire Council v Ringland* (Australia 1994)).[8] In *Societé Hospitaliers Sauveteurs v Newton* (above, p. 147) it was stated, *obiter*, that a municipal corporation, even in Mauritius, could not be awarded moral damages: "It has an object and duties defined by law, its resources are provided by the collection of revenue by means quite independent of voluntary public support. Any attack on its reputation cannot prejudicially affect its work or its existence."

It has been suggested that even private corporations - at least large ones - ought to be unable to use the law of defamation.[9] Such corporations have a public character in terms of the economic, and often political, power which they wield, and are given special status by virtue of incorporation and limited liability; a corollary ought to be exposure to public scrutiny; the same treatment is proposed for non-profit companies, and possibly even for small companies (Patfield, 1993). The traditional approach of the common law has been to view the affairs of companies as appropriate topics for "fair comment", but this still requires a sub-stratum of fact (see Chapter 15). The Hong Kong Court of Appeal has refused to extend the *Derbyshire* principle to a University, even on the basis of a Bill of Rights (*Hong Kong Polytechnic University v Next Magazine Publishing Ltd.* (1997)).

Other Bodies

The English law has recognised the right of trades unions to sue for defamation, being placed in a rather different position from that of other unincorporated associations by statute.[10] Other unincorporated associations cannot sue, since they have no personality (e.g. *Ezekwe v God's Kingdom Society* (Nigeria 1957), *Oke v Gansallo* (Nigeria 1923)). Individual members could only sue if the statement affected them as individuals, and even then cannot bring a representative action on behalf of all the members (*Jenkins v John Bull* (England 1910); see Gatley, para. 971 esp. fn. 90).

Partnerships, like trades unions, may bring actions for defamation in the name of the partnership, for allegations which affect the reputation of the partnership (*Le Fanu v Malcomson* (England 1848)).

Roman-Dutch Jurisdictions

In pre-independence Zimbabwe two associations of traders sued for allegations that they corruptly made allocations of foreign exchange on behalf of the government (*Association of Rhodesian Industries v Brook* (1972)), as did a newspaper publishing company accused of irresponsible and slanted reporting (*Rhodesian Printing and Publishing Co. Ltd. v Howman N.O.* (1976)). However, more recently it was argued that an artificial person cannot sue for defamation, on the basis that in Roman-Dutch law defamation provides a remedy for outraged feelings, not for economic loss, and a corporation has no feelings to be outraged. The judge pointed out that in South Africa this issue was whether an artificial entity could sue in defamation (the *actio iniuriarum* - see Chapter 2) when damages would be presumed, or could only sue under the *lex Aquilia* which would require proof of special damage (see Burchell, 1985, Chapter 6). He took the view that in modern circumstances there was no justification for a distinction between natural and artificial persons, nor for one between trading and non-trading corporations. He suggested that the issue could be viewed as one of evidence rather than of substantive law, and that therefore English rather than Roman-Dutch law should apply (by virtue of the Civil Evidence Act). The judge held that the plaintiff had standing to sue for the allegation that the plaintiff had attempted to bribe customs officers (*Boka Enterprises (Pvt) Ltd. v Manatse* (1989)). With respect, surely what must be proved in order to establish a cause of action is not properly to be described as a matter of the law of evidence. The South African courts have had no difficulty in holding that corporations can sue in defamation. In 1989 the Appellate Division held that both a trading and a non-trading corporation can sue, - the latter only "if a defamatory statement concerning the way it conducts its affairs is calculated to cause it financial prejudice" (*Dhlomo v Natal Newspapers (Pty) Ltd.* (1989) p. 945, Rabie ACJ). This case is actually cited by the judge in *Boka* but in such a way as to suggest it came to his attention too late to be a factor in his own judgment.

The court in *Dhlomo* reserved the question of whether there might be public or legal policy reasons for not permitting certain types of body to sue. This was returned to in a subsequent case (*Argus Printing & Publishing Co. Ltd. v Inkatha Freedom Party* (1992) - it seems to be essentially the *same* case). The Appellate Division said there was no policy reason for depriving a political party of the right to sue. The law was already sufficiently flexible (through the question of whether the statement was defamatory, and the defences of fair comment and qualified privilege) to make allowance for political debate. Practical problems might arise in defining "political parties" for this purpose. Freedom of speech must be balanced with protection of reputation. And US (see Chapter 22) and English authority were essentially dismissed as arising from different political, social and legal contexts (including the *Derbyshire* case - before the House of Lords decision).

Notes

1. There may be other legal obstacles to suit not specific to defamation, as with a Kenyan civil servant who instituted an action for slander; the Attorney-General obtained a court order restraining him from proceeding until he had obtained the consent of the Attorney-General to bring an action arising out of his employment, as required by the Civil Service Code of Regulations - *Ogola v Wasike* (1978). In Nigeria, however, it was held that similar civil service rules could not be used to take away a citizen's rights to go to court - *Obu v Medical and Health Dept. Workers Union* (1980) pp. 361-2. The latter approach is preferable.
2. Contrast customary law where it may be actionable to cast aspersions upon someone's parent - or even just to name him or her. E.g. in Hausa it is an insult to say "*Ubanka*"- "your father". And see Deng (1965, p. 560) "Anything which spoils a man's name threatens to reflect on his family" - see below.
3. This is taken from a pamphlet written by the defendant (Anon, 1988). No doubt it is possible for defamation of one person to be defamatory of another, but it is not really possible to decide from this short pamphlet (containing extracts from a 106 page judgment) whether the judge even addressed his mind to the issues.
4. It is usually assumed that defamation of the dead can be the subject of a criminal prosecution - but only there was an intention to injure the living. The law in the Republic of Ireland is similar and recently a judge held that libel of the dead was not included within the criminal offence - *Hilliard v Penfield Enterprises Ltd.* (1990), relying upon Stephen J in *R v Ensor* (England 1887) (see McGonagle (1990)). Gatley, para. 1594, says in the text that the law is as in the first sentence in this note, but comes down in a footnote in favour of the requirement that the living also should be defamed.

   In African countries criminal law is statutory; the Tanzanian Newspapers Act No. 3 of 1976 s. 39: it is immaterial whether the person defamed is living or dead, but in the latter event the consent of the DPP is required for prosecution. In Mauritius, the material must be "calculated to throw discredit on or be hurtful to the feelings of the family or relatives of the deceased" - art. 288 (2) PC. A surviving distinction between the tort and the crime is that truth alone is not a defence for the latter: the publication must have been in the public interest also, e.g. Tanzanian Newspapers Act s. 41 (a).
5. However, there may be circumstances when the criminal cases are relevant for deciding who is the directing mind of the company - see Gatley para. 954 fn. 23; one of the leading English cases is *Tesco Supermarkets v Natrass* (1972).
6. The judge relied upon *Mayor of Manchester v Williams* (England 1891), but this was a case about a *municipal* corporation; Gatley pointed out it had been criticised (para. 958); in any event, recent English authority suggests local

government bodies should not be able to sue - see below. In fact there is authority, not mentioned in the Malaŵi case, e.g. *Metropolitan Saloon v Hawkins* (England 1859) p. 90 (Pollock CB), itself criticised by Gatley, para. 956.

7. *Societé* is used of company as well as association in French. In French law *personnalité morale* means having separate legal personality - e.g. Weill & Terré (1983, p. 155).
8. There had been earlier authority limiting the right of local authorities to sue for defamation, see *Mayor of Manchester v Williams* above (though see also *Bognor Regis UDC v Campion* (England 1972)).
9. An argument rejected by Bell J in England, in a case in which McDonald's sued Greenpeace members. He said, "There may be an argument...that very large corporations should not have the right to sue for defamation under English law...If ever there was a matter for Parliament to decide as elected representatives of the people, rather than an individual judge, it would have to be something like that" (Vidal, 1997, p. 173).
10. Gatley, para. 970, maintains that this remains the case, by virtue of the Trade Union and Labour Relations Act 1974 despite *EEPTU v The Times* (1980). Trade Union legislation in common law African jurisdictions tends to be based on, older, English legislation.

10 The Defendant's Fault

This is a topic on which the common law, Roman-Dutch law and French law are somewhat alike in that each at first glance requires some moral fault, but in most circumstances this turns out to be unnecessary.

The Common Law

The traditional form of pleading - that the defendant was "malicious" - is just a piece of pleader's embroidery, and is quite unnecessary to a *prima facie* case. In the Nigerian case of *Akintola v Anyiam* (1961) the judge rejected the defendant's argument that he had had no defamatory intention, quoting Lord Loreburn in *Hulton v Jones* (England 1910) p. 28: "A person charged with libel cannot defend himself by showing that he intended in his own breast not to defame or that he intended not to defame the plaintiff, if in fact he did both." Another example is *Balfour Beatty Ltd. v S.A.T Wadda* in which the defendants had by mistake indicated in their tax return that they paid rent to the plaintiff (Gambia 1983).

Hulton's case is one of a famous trio of English cases (all cited in *Akintola*), the others being *Cassidy v Daily Mirror* (1929), where the defendants could not really have known that the plaintiff existed at all, *Hough v London Express* (1940), and *Newstead v London Express Newspapers* Ltd. (1940) (for the facts see Chapter 6). Eventually legislation provided a defence to newspapers which committed innocent defamation (see Chapter 14). The Kenyan Court of Appeal felt unable to depart from those English precedents, because they had been followed by the East African Court of Appeal, and because Kenyan legislation (based on the English) assumes the correctness of those English decisions (*The Nation Newspapers Ltd. v Chesire* (1984), citing *East African Standard v Gitau* (Kenya 1970); see Chapter 5).

In India a statement that a person carrying on a certain business had been arrested for smuggling opium which was true of one person was held to be defamatory of the plaintiff, of whose existence the defendants were unaware but who carried on business in the same place. However, the Madras High Court held that the English rule, as exemplified in *Hulton v Jones*, was contrary to natural justice, equity and good conscience and refused to apply it (*T.V. Ramasubba Iyer v A.M. Ahmed Mohideen* (1971)).

Fleming (1992, p. 540) observes that by this rule "creative literature is unnecessarily victimised". The various committees in different parts of the common law world which have considered the law have generally not recommended any change in this respect. Some have suggested that a right of reply would be a better approach (e.g. Robertson & Nicol, 1992, p. 60; see also Chapter 20). In Zambia, however, it was suggested that the rule in *Hulton* should be reversed and the defendant should not be liable unless he intended the words to refer to the plaintiff (Zambian Law Development Commission, 1984, pp. 12-13). This was a proposal of the Acting Chief Justice, endorsing the suggestion of Hodgin (1973) that the dissenting view of Fletcher Moulton LJ in *Hulton* should be accepted. Although the existing strict liability rule may cause grave injustice, is it right to change it with respect to the reference to the plaintiff issue and not with respect to the issues of the meaning and defamatory nature of the words?

Other Systems

In the Roman-Dutch jurisdictions, and in Mauritius, on close analysis the law is similar to the common law, though not identical.

> In defamation, as in all *injuriae*, the intention of the perpetrator is vital. But the court cannot dive into the mind of a defendant, it can only interpret his language as it would be understood by reasonable men; he is assumed to have meant what his language thus interpreted would convey.

These words of Innes CJ (*Sutter v Brown* (South Africa 1926) p. 163) were quoted by a Zimbabwean judge in 1988 (*Velempini v Engineering Services Workers' Committee for City of Bulawayo* (Muchechetere J)). The latter held that there was no intention to defame the plaintiff; but he reached that decision upon a reading of the words - and indeed, on the basis of how he believed the ordinary reader of the article would interpret it, a process very similar to that adopted by the common law, except that the latter system would not even purport to draw any conclusion about the intention of the defendant.

A court in South West Africa (now Namibia) said in 1937,

> I think it is now established that, notwithstanding the theory that *animus injuriandi* is the basis of an action for defamation, the presumption of the existence of *animus injuriandi* that flows from the publication of defamatory

> words is rebutted if the defendant proves "that his case falls within certain definite and recognised categories of privilege, exemption or excuse, and if he does not prove that, it will not avail him to show that in fact he had no intention to injure the plaintiff" (*Barry v Bayer* (1937) p. 97, citing *Mankowitz v Geyser* (South Africa 1928), *Tothill v Foster* (South Africa 1925)).

Modern South African cases, however, have held that intention to defame is an essential requirement of the tort, though such intention is inferred from the existence of the defamation (*Suid-Afrikaanse Uitsaaikorporasie v O'Malley* (1977)). In *Nxumalo v Nxumalo* (Swaziland 1982-86, p. 225) it was observed that it would be a defence under Roman-Dutch law to show that one had no intention to injure the plaintiff but had some other lawful purpose in mind. However, in the case of the press there is strict liability, putting it in the same position as under the common law (*Pakendorf v De Flamingh* (1982)).

The conceptual structure of Mauritian law is also at first sight different from that of English law, although in the end the result, and even the reasoning, is often very similar. The basic provision of law is the omnibus art. 1382 of the *Code Napoléon*, which requires "*faute*" (literally fault) on the part of the defendant. One of the classic French commentaries (Savatier, Vol. I, Nos. 4 and 35) is quoted in *Forget v Presse Mauricienne* (1958, p. 251) (my translation),

> The principle which directs a civilised society is that no-one has the right to harm another. In such a society, all damage caused by one person to another in a manner which the first could have foreseen and avoided, generates a presumption of fault and responsibility.

Thus a defamatory statement will be presumed to have been made with malice (*Lesage v Mason* (1976) p.178; *Forget v La Presse Mauricienne* (1958) p. 252, citing the French case D. (1877)). In French law the defendant may in some circumstances rely upon his good faith as a defence. In *Lesage v Mason* the court, (p. 179), mentions the French position, but also makes the point that no Mauritian court has decided precisely how far French law is relevant. It also observes (p. 180) that in France good faith may mean a number of things: it may refer to absence of criminal intention, or to good motive, which does not excuse a crime. A few recent Mauritius cases, relying on French authority, have held plaintiff must establish "*faute*", but the defendant must, in order to escape liability, show good faith arising from "*faits justificatifs*" ("justificatory facts") (*Boodhoo v Sun* (1992)). (On French law see Carter-Ruck (1992, p. 328) setting out the elements of the defence of publication in good faith: valid objective, absence of animosity, restrained language and having checked on the reliability of the statement.) In *Curé v Universal Sound Equipment Co. Ltd.* (1941) inability to stop the broadcast was held to negative *faute*.

Insanity and Inebriation

The basic approach of the common law would suggest that neither inebriation nor insanity should excuse - though they might negative actual malice. If the hearers or readers of the statement knew of the condition of the defendant, it would surely be appropriate for the court to hold that the words would not have been taken seriously - by analogy with "mere abuse".

Gatley suggests that drunkenness is irrelevant to liability for defamation (para. 937, citing *Kendrick v Hopkins* (England 1580) "*qui peccat ebrius, luat sobrius*" (who sins drunk pays sober)), although it might be a ground for mitigation of damages - for which he says there is no English authority. There is a Mauritian case in which the defendant claimed he was drunk, but the court held he had known what he was saying, nor is it clear what the consequences might have been (whether absence of liability or reduced damages) had they found otherwise (*Wing Fo Chan Kun v Sam Zee Moi* (1955)).

The situation so far as insanity is concerned seems obscure (no doubt because most people have better sense than to sue the insane). Lord Esher seems to have suggested that an inability to understand the nature and quality of his act would generally exempt from civil liability - at least he said that if a person did understand this he would be liable (*Hanbury v Hanbury* (a divorce case, England 1892) p. 560, quoted by Gatley, para. 934). There is a Southern Rhodesian case in which the defendant suffered from a nervous disorder and had the emotional reactions of a child of eight. However the court held that he knew that what he was doing was wrong. The court said it was surprised that the plaintiff took the statements, some of which were "clearly wild and exaggerated" so seriously, and took these facts into account in awarding damages (*Vaughan v Ford* (1953)).

11 Truth and Public Benefit

Some systems of law require not only that the statement be true but that the defendant also show some public benefit served by his statement. This is true of "civil law systems" including that of Mauritius and Roman-Dutch law, and the requirement has been introduced into Australia, too. The common law, however, in civil though not in criminal matters, is satisfied with proof of the veracity of the allegation.

Truth

The traditional term of art for this defence in the common law is "justification" but it is known in some parts of the world, perhaps with slightly more accuracy, as "truth". The English Committee on Defamation, (Cmnd 5909, para. 129) recommended that the defence be renamed, and in New Zealand this change actually occurred in the Defamation Act of 1992. Perhaps if the defence were named "truth" it would prevent error such as seems to have happened in *Osho v Cooperative Bank Ltd.* (Nigeria 1985): the plaintiff's complaint was that the bank failed to record that he had paid a cheque into the account of the college of which he was bursar, with the result that he was queried by the auditors. The judge held that the bank had failed to record the payment-in due to the plaintiff's own failure to complete the paying-in slip properly. The judge said, "To my mind, the reason thus given amounts to justification which constitutes a valid defence to a tort of defamation" (p. 81).

The underlying idea is that the law will protect a reputation only against unmerited attack. "The truth of the imputation is a complete defence to an action of defamation because the plaintiff has no right to a character free from that imputation and if he has no right to it, he cannot in justice recover damages for the loss of it" (Odunlami J in *Ogundelu v Solarin* (Nigeria 1980) p. 170 - this is essentially a quotation from Gatley, now para. 351). As Belgore JSC put it in another Nigerian case (*Din v African Newspapers of Nigeria* Ltd. (1990) p. 222),

> A man is entitled to his good name and to be called what he is. But if in a man's life he happens to have a blur [sc. blot?] and that blur is with the

sanction of the law recognised as such, it is no libel to point it out, even if it is done for mischief.

Instances of reliance upon this defence are relatively rare, especially in African cases. A wise defendant only pleads justification when he is fairly confident of his ability to satisfy the court that what he said was indeed true. If he persists in stating that his original remarks were true but fails to establish this by evidence, the court is likely to take the view that he has been obstinately compounding his original act and may even increase any damages it awards against him (see *Ezekwe v Otomewo* (Nigeria 1957 upheld 1958); more recently *Tutumor v Igbindolor* (Nigeria 1981)). Thus the Supreme Court of Nigeria said, "In our view, the unsuccessful attempt to justify the charge of corruption...gravely aggravated the case against the defendants. We entertain no doubt that the defence was a mere repetition of the libel" (*African Newspapers of Nigeria Ltd. v Coker* (1973) p. 396; see also *Adewunmi v Oshinowo* (Nigeria 1977) p. 197). For other unsuccessful pleas of justification see *Akurefe v Sketch Publishing Co. Ltd.* (Nigeria 1971); *Pedro v Orafidiya* (Nigeria 1974); *Gidando v Chief Imam of Odo-Ado* (Nigeria 1962); *Mumba v Singoyi* (Zambia 1975); *Mwanza v Zambia Publishing Co.* (1981).

The New Zealand Committee on Defamation (1977, para. 135) rejected a suggestion that statute should state that a plea of truth should not of itself be a ground for increasing damages, taking the view that the law was already adequate, being that additional damages should not be awarded unless the defendant had caused additional damage to the plaintiff's feelings and reputation.

There have been a few African cases in which the defence has been successfully raised. The well-known Nigerian journalist and educationist Tai Solarin, wrote in the press accusing the plaintiff of treating his house-girl like a slave. Evidence was produced to show that the girl had to work very hard, was under-nourished and ill-treated, even chained to a bucket. The judge held that the allegation had been justified, taking into account the dictionary definition of a slave as "Person compelled to work very hard for someone else" *Ogundelu v Solarin* (above). In *Saraki v Soleye* (Nigeria 1972) the defendant had failed to plead justification, but the judge indicated that he would have found the statement justified. Justification succeeded in the unreported case of *Fajebe v Uphaday* (Nigeria 1967) (Adefarasin J), in *Din v African Newspapers* (above) and *Odukoya v Sketch Publishing Co.* (Nigeria 1979), in which the allegation of rigging a beauty contest was held justified (see also *Adekoya v Ogunnaiya* (Nigeria 1980)). In *Adapoe v Pospisil* (Ghana

1974) both justification and qualified privilege succeeded. In *Registered Trustees of the Rosicrucian Order AMORC (Nigeria) v Awoniyi* (1994) the Supreme Court of Nigeria upheld the Court of Appeal in deciding that the plaintiff organisation was secret and satanic society - "It is satanic to say that Jesus Christ was a member of secret societies and an advocate of occult teachings" (Wali JSC at p. 419). Fair comment, which would have been the more obvious defence, was not properly pleaded. In *Banda v Zambia Publishing Co. Ltd.* (1982) the judge found that the statement was not defamatory, but he also held it to have been justified. In *Naphazi v Protea Assurance Co. Ltd.* (Malawi 1980) the judge held that the words were not actionable as slander, but also held they were justified. (Other Nigerian examples are *Visas v Daily Times of Nigeria Ltd.* (1975), *Onwuchekwa v Onovo* (1974); *Ogbuatu v Daily Times of Nigeria Ltd.*)

What Must Be Shown

It is not enough that the defendant *believed* what he said to be true.

> A man in good faith may publish libel believing it to be true and it may be found by the jury that he acted in good faith, believing it to be true, but in fact the statement was false. Under those circumstances he has no defence however excellent his intention.

(Lord Loreburn in *Hulton v Jones* (England 1910) p. 23/24 quoted by Olatawura JSC in *Atoyebi v Odudu* (Nigeria 1990) p. 401, see also Nnaemeka-Agu JSC at p. 403, citing *Peters v Bradlaugh* (England 1884) and *Truth (NZ) Ltd. v Holloway* (New Zealand 1960); also *Tutumor v Igbindolor*, above p. 222).) In *Nthenda v Alade* (Nigeria 1974) the judge said "A Bona Fide belief in the truth of the story will not exonerate the editor...from liability". One of the leading English cases is *Sutherland v Stopes* (1925), where Lord Shaw said (p. 75), "In a plea of justification the defence that a matter of opinion or inference is true is not that the defendant truly made that inference or truly held that opinion, but that the opinion and the inference are both of them true", quoted, for example, in *Mwanza v Zambia Publishing Co. Ltd.* (1981) p. 237.

A Ghanaian husband reported that his wife had had an affair with the plaintiff. Part of his defence was that he genuinely believed this to be the case because his wife had told him so. This belief, however honest, was not sufficient justification (in fact qualified privilege succeeded) (*Buachie v Samman* (1980)). In a Tanzanian case the defendants had complained to the authorities that the plaintiff was holding someone prisoner by witchcraft. The High Court on appeal rejected the defence that the defendants had been told this was true by a local witchdoctor - *Romani s/o Modesti v Amiri s/o Kitego* (1969).

If the defendant has passed on a rumour, even if the original statement was phrased as "I am told" or "it is rumoured that", or even if the original source was identified; it will not be sufficient justification for the defendant to show that he *was* told, or that there were indeed such rumours, or that the sources were usually reliable. The defendant must prove the substance of what was rumoured or that what he was told and repeated was true (*Hassan v Kassardjian Construction Ltd.* (Ghana 1964), *Shah v Uganda Argus* (1972), *Truth (NZ) Ltd. v Holloway* (New Zealand 1960); see also *Nekyon v Tanganyika Standard Ltd.* (Uganda 1964) quoting (*obiter*) Lush J in *Watkin v Hall* (England 1868) p. 403)). Lord Denning said,

> If the report or rumour was true, let him justify it. If it was not true, he ought not to have repeated it or aided in its circulation. He must answer for it just as if he had started it himself (Lord Denning in *Associated Newspapers v Dingle* (England 1964) quoted in *Zvogbo v Kingston's* Ltd. (Zimbabwe 1986) p. 320).

And a court in Mauritius observed,

> We cannot hold that the repetition of that which is libellous or slanderous is no evil, merely because it has been invented by another. As great an injury may result from the repetition as from the first invention and the person who repeats it, by the publication of it, gives greater weight to the libel (*Leal v Hitié* (1882) p. 54).

Secondly, the defendant is not permitted to prove *something else*, however discreditable to the plaintiff. When the allegation was one of fraud it was not enough to show that the conduct of the plaintiff had been "irregular and therefore reprehensible"; the allegation was that money intended for a conference was fraudulently paid into the plaintiff professor's personal bank account; in fact the money was so paid, in breach of usual procedures, but not for the personal use of the plaintiff (*Adamolekun v African Newspapers* (Nigeria 1982)). In another Nigerian case the allegation was that the tarmac laid by the plaintiff company at the airport sank; this was not justified by proof that the wheels of a high-loader sank into the tarmac (*Akin Taylor & Co. Ltd. v Daily Times of Nigeria Ltd.* (1976)). Even more closely related allegations may not be proved; a Nigerian judge said (Uche

Omo JCA in *Lana v University of Ibadan* (1987) p. 265, citing *Sun Printing Assurance v Schenck* (UK 1900)),

> Normally, a defence of justification simpliciter, involves a defendant in proving the precise imputation complained of. "If the words impute a specific offence e.g. stealing a watch, it is not enough to prove that the plaintiff was guilty of another offence though of the same character e.g. stealing a clock."

If the defamatory statement alleged a course of conduct, the defendant will be permitted to prove this by proving individual acts (indeed he could do little else). But if he can prove only one or two isolated occurrences he is likely to fail. Describing the plaintiff as a "libellous journalist"was held not to have justified by proof that the plaintiff had libelled on one occasion (*Wakely v Cooke* (England 1849)). This was applied in a Malaŵian case in which it was held that an allegation that someone writes all sorts of lies was not justified by proving that he once published a statement with reckless indifference to truth (*Magennis v Malawi Press Ltd.* (1961-3)). And in *Chong Leung v Selvon* (Seychelles 1978) the defendant failed to justify statements such as the plaintiff "*se ridiculise comme toujours*" (makes a fool of himself as always), and "*pondit des niaiseries dignes de lui*" (delivered himself of inane remarks worthy of him). In Tanzania, where the defendant had alleged, *inter alia*, that the plaintiff never allowed subordinate staff to sit examinations related to their jobs, the judge said that could not be justified by evidence that on one isolated occasion he refused to do so *(Eyakuze v Editor of Sunday News* (1974)).

It is sometimes said that what must be established as true is the "substance or sting" of the libel (e.g. Cmnd 5909, para. 128). The "justification must be as broad as the charge" (*Ogundelu v Solarin* (above) p. 170). The same approach is adopted in Roman-Dutch law (see, for example, *Jensen v Acavalos* (Zimbabwe 1993) p. 227). Public interest in the publication must also be shown (see below).

> A plea of justification means that all the words were true and covers not only the bare statements of facts in the alleged libel but also any imputation which the words in their context may be taken to convey

said Collins MR in words quoted approvingly by Karibi-Whyte JSC in Nigeria (*Digby v Financial News Ltd.* (1907) p. 509, quoted in *Din v African Newspapers of Nigeria Ltd.* (1990) p. 221). And if the defendant had made comments as well as statements of fact he must justify these too (*ibid.* citing

Sutherland v Stopes (England 1925); see also *Mwanza v Zambia Publishing Co. Ltd.* (1981) p. 237, also citing *Sutherland*). A judge in Zambia observed, "In a plea of justification I consider it is irrelevant to plead that expression of opinion was 'fair' or 'impartial'...the test which I intend to apply is whether or not the expressions of opinion were correct" (*Mumba v Singoyi* (1975)). If the comments are fair, based on fact and on a matter of public interest the defendant may be able to raise the defence of fair comment, but that is a different defence (Chapter 15). And that defence is only available if the defendant was not malicious, whereas if he can prove the *truth* of the comments his malice, if any, is irrelevant. Thus the judge in *Palmer v Boston* (Sierra Leone 1961) was wrong when he said, *obiter* (p. 106), that malice would have destroyed the defence of justification.

If some trivial discrepancy remains between what was said and what the defendant is able to prove he will not fail in his plea. In *Alexander v Railway Executive* (England 1865) the libel was to the effect that the plaintiff was fined £1 with three weeks' imprisonment in default of payment; the defendant proved that he had been fined £1 with the alternative of two weeks, and justification succeeded (cited in *Onwuchekwa v Onowo* above; see also *Visas v Daily Times* (Nigeria 1975)). Annan J said in Ghana (*Boohene v Abeyie & Abura Printing Works Ltd.* (1969, quoted in Date-Bah, 1973b, p. 40)),

> ...if there is no real difference between the allegation charged and the evidence adduced in proof of it such as would have any effect on the judgment of a reasonable man then the defence...succeeds.

In *Lana v University of Ibadan* the plaintiff complained of a statement in the University's *Bulletin* stating that he had wrongly claimed that two articles of his had been published in a learned journal. In the event the defendant proved that the plaintiff had, inaccurately, claimed that the articles had been *accepted* for publication. The Court of Appeal held the defence established; as Uche Omo J said, "the *sting* of the libel in my view would appear to be in *the false listing*. That has been proved" (Nigeria 1987) p. 265 (emphasis in original). But in *Nyam v Rwang* (Nigeria 1978) the allegation was that the plaintiff held an illegal meeting. The defendant showed that there had been a meeting to discuss the alleged misconduct, or removal of a chief, but this did not make the meeting illegal.

In *Dumbo v Idugboe* (1983) the allegation, in a newspaper announcement, was that the plaintiff had been "removed from office" as a director "with immediate effect". The Nigerian Court of Appeal and Supreme Court held that the words were, by virtue of their publication in the press, and by the resonance of the words quoted, defamatory, as they suggested removal for incompetence. They also held that proof that the defendant was indeed removed was not sufficient to justify these defamatory implications. This case may seem to be very close to the borderline, and can only be understood, perhaps, in the light of current circumstances, when removal "with immediate effect" had become a catch phrase for the removal by the government of all sorts of public servants for corruption and other deficiencies.

If there is more than one separate allegation in the defamatory statement, there is a difference between the position at common law and under statute - where such exists. At common law a defence of justification will fail if any charge remains unproved, although the plaintiff will get damages only for the statements which have not been shown to be true (*Helsham v Blackwood* (England 1851)).

Under the legislation, however, where there are distinct charges "a defence of justification shall not fail by reason only that the truth of every charge is not proved if the words not proved to be true do not materially injure the plaintiff's reputation having regard to the truth of the remaining charges" (Lagos Law s. 7, Abia etc Law, s. 8, Delta, Ogun and etc., s. 11, s. 8 of the legislation in Kenya and Sierra Leone, s. 6 in Zambia). This was paraphrased by Uche Omo JCA in *Lana v University of Ibadan* (p. 265):

> Its effect is to broaden the defence of justification by allowing a defendant to succeed in that defence where he can prove the truth of only parts of several charges (Parts) of a libel and show that the plaintiff's reputation has not been materially injured by the truth of the part(s) of the libel not proved.

Another Nigerian judge suggested that one object of the provision was to eliminate cases in which plaintiffs succeeded on very technical grounds, leading to awards of contemptuous damages (*Obu v Medical & Health Dept. Workers Union* (1980) p. 367).

There have been very few cases on this provision in any jurisdiction (see *Truth (NZ) Ltd. v Avery* (New Zealand 1959), *Anders v Gas* (England 1960)). While it would not be difficult to see that, for example, a person who is proved to have stolen 100,000 naira, kwacha or whatever, will be precluded by this section from claiming damages for an unproved accompanying allegation that he stole 50 kobo or ngwee from someone else, it is not always going to be clear whether what has been proved is so serious that what has not been proved can be ignored (see the interesting observations of Gatley, para. 367, fn. 51, on the question of establishing the relative severity of allegations). In one Nigerian case it was held that the allegation that the plaintiff had refused to treat a co-worker "on the point of death" had been proved; his reputation would not be materially injured by further allegations, not proved, that he had refused to treat the patient the previous day (not on the point of death, presumably), and that he had said that he would not treat a laundry man (*Obu v Medical & General* above). And in another it had been shown that the plaintiff had used a knife to damage a drum, and threatened people with it, and the failure to prove that he had "bought" the knife did not further damage him (*Oforka v Anisiuba* (1979) p. 142). In *Nzenwa v Kwara State Printing & Publishing Corpn* (Nigeria 1980) Araka CJ held that once it was shown that there was truth in the allegation that donations were used to pay for the transportation of girl friends and "club comforters" for the football team, it did not matter that the further allegation of money going into private pockets was proved. With respect this seems to be carrying the section too far.

At common law, as Savage J in Nigeria put it, "There is a string of authorities to the effect that a defendant cannot justify part of a libel unless he can show clearly that the statements are severable" (*Awolowo v Concord Press of Nigeria Ltd.* (1982)); according to Gatley, (para. 368) the string of authorities include *Clarkson v Lawson* (England 1829) (the allegation was that the plaintiff was suspended 3 times; the defendant could only prove one; held that they could be severed and so the damages were reduced) and *Davis v Billing* (1891). This remains the case under the legislation - indeed the English Court of Appeal has held that the benefit of this section will only apply where the allegations are contained in separate words, and that the justification must be of words of which the plaintiff complains (*Polly Peck (Holdings) plc v Trelford* (1986) p. 103).

Even if the defendant had alleged in his publication that the plaintiff was both a thief and a murderer, the plaintiff might choose to sue only for the former, and the defendant could not plead or prove the truth of the latter (see *Plato Films v Spiedel* (England 1961)). As the Press Council in the UK said to the Faulks Committee:

> Under the law as it stands at present, a plaintiff can bring an action in respect of one untrue defamatory statement which he has selected from a number of others which were true. Plaintiffs do do this. Where this is done, section 5 of the Defamation Act 1952 does not entitle the defendant to plead as a defence that the plaintiff's reputation was not materially injured having regard to the truth of the other defamatory statements on which the plaintiff has not relied.

The Committee recommended that the section be amended in order to make it possible for the defendant to rely on the truth of the whole publication (paras. 133-6).[1] A similar proposal was also made in Zambia.[2]

There is a New Zealand case which seems to exemplify the problem: the plaintiff was accused of despising "bureaucrats, civil servants, politicians, women, Jews and professionals"; he chose to sue on the allegation about despising Jews and it was held that evidence as to the truth of the other allegations could not be led (*Templeton v Jones* (1984)). However, this has been doubted by the Court of Appeal in England which held that the plaintiff can only ignore part of the statement, making it impossible for the defendant to justify other parts, if the statement consists of separate and distinct allegations. If the allegations have "a common sting" they cannot be so separated. The court said that it seemed to them that the words in *Templeton* were capable of meaning "that the plaintiff was an intolerant bigot, preaching the politics of hatred in the hope of political advantage" and that the "Jews" allegation could not be separated out. The Court went on to hold that in the case in front of it the allegations were not distinct and separate (*Polly Peck (Holdings) plc v Trelford* (1986); the passage quoted is at p. 102).

Public Benefit

Under the *criminal* law, the defence of truth only avails if it was in the public interest that the statement be made (Northern Nigeria Penal Code s. 391(2), Criminal Code (southern states of Nigeria) s. 377, Tanzania Newspapers Act s. 41). The defence was introduced into English law by s. 6 Libel Act 1843 (Lord Campbell's Act), held in *R v Coker* (1928) to be applicable in Nigeria as a statute of general application.

But what about civil, as opposed to criminal, law? In some of the states of Australia, e.g. Queensland, which have codified versions of the law of defamation, and where the provisions of the Criminal Code, in this instance s. 376, are applied in civil suits, truth is only a defence if publication was also in the public interest. This is not on the whole the case in Africa, even in those countries which apply versions of the Queensland Criminal Code, such as the 'Southern states' of Nigeria. The New Zealand Committee (1977), however, took the view that

> the law of defamation is not the appropriate means for the prevention of "muck-raking". A public benefit requirement would go beyond publications which are malicious and would affect all defamatory publications. The criterion of "public benefit" is a vague concept and would cause difficulties for

> publishers and legal advisers where the words are true. As result public discussion might be unnecessarily inhibited to the detriment of the public (para. 118).

Recent English committees have taken rather the same view (e.g. Cmnd 5909, para. 138). Although it may be true that public benefit is a vague concept, the courts have had precisely that sort of responsibility thrust upon them when they apply bills of rights; and there is a public interest requirement in some statutory defences (Chapter 14).

Interestingly, a customary court in Nigeria held that an allegation of thieving was actionable even if it was true that the plaintiff had stolen many years ago; it was wrong to take up the matter now (*Ocheikwu v Ode* (1963)).

Roman-Dutch Law

Public benefit is a well established feature of Roman-Dutch law. The *locus classicus* is a case of 1892,

> As a general principle, I take it to be for the public benefit that the truth as to the character or conduct of individuals should be known. But the worst characters sometimes reform, and some of the inducements to reformation would be removed if stories as to past transgressions could with impunity be raked up after a long lapse of time. Public interest, as I conceive it, would suffer rather than benefit from any unnecessary reviving of forgotten scandals. But the commission of recent offences against the law or against society stands on a different footing. It is generally for the public interest that others who might have any dealings with the guilty individual should be informed of his true character, and it is a sufficient protection to the innocent that the burthen of proving the truth of the defamatory words lies upon him who uttered them

(*Graham v Ker* (South Africa 1892), quoted by Beadle CJ in *Mahomed v Kassim* (Rhodesia 1973) p. 9, whence the "*locus classicus*" description also derives. The same passage was quoted in the South West African case of *Barry v Bayer* (1937)).

In a Rhodesian case it was held that where the audience already knew the truth the public benefit requirement could not be satisfied, since no question of informing them arose. On the other hand, the plaintiff received only nominal damages (*Mohammed v Kassim* (1972)). Other instances of public benefit have included information about government, and public officials (e.g. *Jensen v Acavalos* (Zimbabwe 1993), where the statement was conveyed to the plaintiff's superiors in the City Council, and the conduct alleged would reflect on the Council (pp. 230-1)), the apprehension of criminals, and fraudulent conduct. However, it seems that the making of statements about sexual misbehaviour does not fall in the same category; Poulter (1970, p. 134) gives South African authorities, and mentions that in *Graham v Ker* above, it was held that an imputation of miscegenation was held to be in the public interest, but observes "The latter case is not good law in Lesotho" (fn. 73) - nor would it now be so in South Africa. Where a magistrate, after rising from a sitting as a licensing court, had said to the plaintiff's lawyer that he did not like the plaintiff because he had made a false application before him six years previously, it was held that the public benefit requirement was not satisfied (*Barry v Bayer* above).

Mauritius

In Mauritius, the interaction of the Civil and Penal Codes, and of French and English law, introduces a "public interest" requirement. Section 6 of the English 1843 Libel Act, which introduced the public interest element in criminal cases was effectively reproduced as art. 79 of the Criminal Procedure Code in 1852, replacing an earlier provision to the effect that truth was a defence only when the allegation was in support of a denunciation to the Ministère Public (*Cordouan v Jardin* (1883)). If a statement is civilly actionable by virtue of constituting an offence under the Penal Code, it remains illicit unless a defence to a criminal charge is available. "The defence founded upon Art. 79...is as competent a defence in a civil action for personal libel as it is in a criminal prosecution for the same cause" (*Le Cernéen v Laurent* (1901) p. 56). The court does suggest that possibly the same argument does not apply if the defamation if not of a "person" since art. 79 referred to "personal libel", unlike the English Act. This would only have validity if a statement about a body was not a crime under the Penal Code. However, the Mauritian courts have no difficulty in holding statements about corporations actionable, and the Indian Penal Code specifically states that defamation may cover a body. The law is now to be found in art. 288 proviso (i) of the Penal Code: in the case of "truth", the public interest requirement must also be satisfied. But suppose that the statement is actionable *not* because it is a criminal offence, but as a *delit civil*? (see Chapter 3). In *Le Cernéen v Laurent* the court held that the defence would be applicable here, too, and required as well as truth "some reasonable and legitimate motive" (p. 56). In a later case the court held that when the Penal Code was not in issue, the "public interest" requirement did not apply, and truth alone would be a defence (*Oliver v Rochecouste* (1940) p. 62). They also held that the public interest requirement was satisfied, however, since it was transgression of the Pharmacy Ordinance that was in issue. In French law, under art. 35 of the law of the press of 1881, truth is a defence (though since 1944 references to events more than 10 years old have been excluded - see Carter-Ruck, 1992, p. 329).

If the statement is *untrue* (or cannot be proved to be true) the defendant will fail unless he can show an occasion of privilege, in all systems (Chapters 13 and 14). A South African court of first instance held that the public right to know about serious allegations of misconduct by a public official outweighed the fact that they were shown to be untrue (*Neethling v du Preez* briefly summarised by Feltoe, 1993, p. 50). However, this was reversed on appeal in 1994.

Pleading and Proof

The defendant must be able to *prove* it is true, and must, therefore, plead the defence (*Bardi v Maurice* (Gold Coast 1954)). The defence must be pleaded specifically; it is not enough simply to traverse the words "falsely and maliciously" which are ritually included in the statement of claim (e.g. *Obikoya v Nigerian National Press* (1971); see also Gatley, para. 1106). In England it has been held that the defendant must plead specifically which meanings he intends to justify: *Lucas-Box v News Group Newspapers Ltd.* (1986).

More recently, however, the Irish Law Reform Commission has recommended a definition of defamation which includes the fact that the statement is "untrue", saying,

> It is in principle unsatisfactory that the plaintiff should be relieved of the burden of proving all essential ingredients of the wrong which he has alleged (Ireland, 1991, para. 7.21).

The dissenting minority, however, asked,

> Do we wish to live in a society in which one person may with impunity publish a hurtful and damaging statement about another as long as it remains impossible or difficult for that other to prove that the statement was untrue? (para. 7.25)

The recommendation of the majority cannot be viewed in isolation from their recommendation for the creation of a defence (to a claim for *general damages*) that the defendant exercised reasonable care in attempting to ascertain the truth of the allegation (para. 14.26(1)).

What is the standard of proof? A case in Seychelles held that proof beyond reasonable doubt was not required, relying upon English authority, and Gatley. Proof on a high degree of probability was required (*Moulinié v De Comarmond* (1972), citing *Hornel v Neuberger* (England 1957), *Blyth v Blyth* (England 1966), and Gatley (now para. 1395)). Many years ago a court in Southern Rhodesia held that proof must be beyond reasonable doubt (*Thurtell v Ford* (1939)). The court relied upon an English decision of 1839 (*Willmett v Harmer* (1839)), as well as on South African decisions. In Malaŵi the courts have reached contradictory decisions, the more recent favouring the stricter, beyond reasonable doubt, requirement (*Naphazi v Protea Assurance Co. Ltd.* (1980) p. 465) - *obiter)*. The more recent case is *Malaŵian Rlys. v Bhadurkhan* (1986) p. 443 (not mentioning *Naphazi*, but relying on English cases).

The modern approach of the English courts is rather different; one of the leading authorities is *Bater v Bater* (1950, p. 459) where Lord Denning said that the degree of proof required in a civil court depends upon the subject matter, and that specifically it requires a higher degree of probability where fraud is alleged, but not so high as a criminal court, and *Hornal v Neuberger* where he said, "The more serious the allegation the higher the degree of probability that is required; but it need not, in a civil case, reach the very high standard required by the criminal law". Of the last observations, Gould V-P said,

> I think what is implicit in that passage represents the trend of modern authority but I would not construe it as indicating that there may never be an overlapping of civil and criminal standards. In my opinion there might well be circumstances in civil action and there might be a charge of a crime so heinous that a judge would be amply justified in demanding its proof by such a preponderance of probability as would suffice to discharge the onus in at least some type of criminal prosecutions. In the instant case I agree that a higher standard of care was required than a bare preponderance of probability and generally that nothing less than clear evidence should suffice to establish an allegation of crime in justification of a libel (*United African Press v Shah* (Kenya 1964) p. 340).

Crawshaw and Newbold JJA were in agreement, citing *Ilanga v Manyoka* (Tanzania 1961), a trespass case, which itself relies upon both *Bater* and *Hornal*. The *Shah* case was applied (without discussion) in *Kateera v Kayondo* (Uganda 1976).

Of Gould V-P's words the judge in a later Tanzanian case (*Eyakuze v Editor of Sunday News* (1974) pp. 201-2, upheld by the EACA, 1975) said,

> ...these observations...are so appropriate to the circumstances of East Africa...that they were, I think, unnecessarily guarded to make it appear that he was not differing with that great English judge Lord Denning. But the fact is that he did differ[3] and certainly the views of Denning that there can be no overlapping of civil and criminal standards, while they may be appropriate for the English Society, cannot be appropriate for Tanzania, where within the Socialist context, antisocial crimes or even misconduct of the kind alleged against the plaintiff attract greater attention. Therefore although the observations of Gould quoted above were obiter, I would respectfully adopt them and say that in Tanzania the standard of preponderance of probability should not be adopted in civil cases involving allegation of crimes and that nothing less than clear evidence should suffice to establish an allegation of a crime in justification of a libel

while in yet another Tanzanian case the judge said,

> I can think of no rationale for the law to look with favour at a person charged with, say, corruption in a criminal court and to abandon a plaintiff in a civil court who is imputed with the same offence (*Jonathan v Athuman Khalfan* (1980) p. 184).

He consequently required proof beyond reasonable doubt. With respect, the consequences of conviction in a criminal court are more serious than the successful raising of a plea of justification in a defamation suit. And should a prosecution be brought later it would be necessary to prove the allegation beyond reasonable doubt. These decisions make it potentially more difficult for the press, for example, making allegations of corruption, to rely on the defence of justification.

Under the Nigerian Evidence Act, however, allegations of criminal offences must be proved beyond reasonable doubt (s. 137(1)). And it has been said "the subsection would apply where a defendant in an action for libel pleaded justification of an allegation that the plaintiff had committed a criminal offence" (*Ikoku v Oli* (1962) p. 199, also *Pedro v Orafidiya* (1975), *Sobayo v Daily Times of Nigeria Ltd.* (1977), *Abe v Odo* (1983) - allegation that plaintiff stole gravel from parties' common employer (it is not clear to me why qualified privilege was not relied upon since the allegation was made to the police; maybe there was malice); *Adeyinka v Balogun* (1980); see also Aguda, 1980b, 255).

At common law the fact of conviction cannot be used to prove in a civil case the commission of the offence (*Hinds v Sparks* (England 1964); *Hollington v Hewthorn* (England 1943) - "still part of our law notwithstanding general agreement that it is bad law" (Umezinwa J in *Aneke v Star* (Nigeria 1979)). Some African countries at least have followed this approach (see *Figueredo v Editor Sunday Nation* (Uganda 1968) a defamation case, citing *Hinds v Sparks*; *Cosmas v Faustini* (Tanzania 1971) - quoting the AIR *Commentaries on the Criminal Procedure Code* which was the same as that applied in Tanzania: "The finding of a criminal court is not conclusive in a civil court and the latter is bound to decide the question for itself" (6th. ed. Vol. 1)). On this basis a Nigerian court erred when it held allegations justified on the production of a report of a government inquiry (*Bello-Osagie v Concord Press Nig. Ltd.* (1983)). The normal defence in such a case would be one of privilege. However, the newspaper had jumped the gun and published a report which accurately reflected the report but before the report had even been submitted to the government. Some common law jurisdictions have declined to apply this rule (e.g. *Jorgenson v News Media (Auckland) Ltd.* (New Zealand 1969)), and it has now been reversed by statute in England (Civil Evidence Act 1968 s. 13).[4] Hodgin (1972, p. 79) recommended that the English rule be adopted in East Africa, as did Osei in Ghana (1970, p. 94). (It is raised for consideration in Zambia in the Working Paper on Defamation (Zambian Law Development Commission, 1984, p. 26.)

If the plaintiff has been *acquitted* of an offence which the defendant alleges he committed, this does not preclude the defendant, if he is sufficiently audacious, pleading justification and proving it if he can. In at least one Nigerian case such an attempt failed (*Akurefe v Sketch* (1971), while in one English case, where the charge was of murder, it succeeded (*Loughans v Odhams Press Ltd.* (1963))!

Notes

1. They also proposed that the law should make it clear that proof of "substance or sting" is enough; the latter point was in response to the suggestion that some older cases required proof of the literal meaning of the words.
   The New Zealand Committee took the view that even the Faulks recommendation did not cover the latter point adequately, and proposed an additional provision spelling out that it is enough if what is proved does not differ materially from the charge in the publication - New Zealand, 1977, paras. 112-5. This proposal was included in the 1988/1990 Bill (see Todd, *et*

al., (1991) para. 17.9.2. The Irish Commission made a recommendation to similar effect: para. 7.4.

2. The Attorney-General's comment that this adds nothing to the existing law fails to grasp the point.
3. With respect it is not clear to me that this is really so, the more so since *Ilanga* was based on the two Denning decisions.
4. Under the English 1996 Act s. 12 the conviction is only to be *conclusive* proof of the commission of the offence in the case of the *plaintiff* to the defamation action.

12 Absolute Privilege

The defence applies in certain situations, and protects whatever the motive for making the remarks of which the plaintiff complains, and an action brought against someone who acted in a clearly privileged situation can be struck out *in limine*, as was done in *Foley v Asfour* (Nigeria 1970) (for an English example see *Law v Llewellyn* (1906)). The privilege attaches to court proceedings, legislative houses, and communications between officers of state; there is also the more doubtful case of communications between solicitor and client. Courts would probably be reluctant these days to extend the privilege.[1] Whether communications between spouses are privileged is dealt with in Chapter 8 as a matter of publication.

Statements in, or Related to, Judicial Proceedings

At common law, judges cannot be sued for anything which they say or do in court (see *Fray v Blackburn* (England 1863), *Anderson v Gorrie* (England 1895). In *Boyo v Atake* (Nigeria 1970) a member of the Bar unsuccessfully sued a judge for having him incarcerated for contempt). Modern English authority (*Sirros v Moore* (1975)) suggests that all judges are protected even if acting without jurisdiction - formerly it used to be thought that the judges of inferior courts were not protected if they were acting without jurisdiction, and ought to have realised they had no jurisdiction (*Calder v Halkett* (1839)).[2] In African jurisdictions the protection may be statutory. Some of the statutes refer to protection from liability for *acts* done, while others refer to acts done and things said; Olowofoyeku (1992, pp. 116) points out that in Nigeria only the legislation of Abia etc., refers to words spoken: High Courts Law s. 55 and Magistrates Courts Law s. 76. That legislation may provide protection only to judges acting within their jurisdiction (for example, in the Kenyan Judicature Act, s. 6), or to those who believed in good faith they were acting within their jurisdiction. The Gambian District Tribunal Ordinance, Cap. 49 s. 26 had such a provision, applied in *Njundu Touray v Jerreh Jabang* (1963) a false imprisonment and malicous prosecution case. One might assume that words are a sort of act. However, there is authority for the view that common law immunity for acts was not as wide as that for words (Olowofoyeku, *op. cit.* and 1993, p. 126-8, citing Brazier, 1976, p. 398,

Schwartz v Smith (Canada 1964)). If so, could the common law still be looked to for the immunity for words? Although there is some authority for this (*Schwartz v Smith* above), and there are good reasons for a wider immunity for words (Olowofoyeku, 1993, pp.127-8), the argument seems to have one general drawback, namely that those who drafted the legislation surely intended it to contain the whole of the law on judicial immunity, including for words. There is another problem specific to Nigeria: that the law would be different in some states of the federation from others. Finally, it should be observed, there has not been total agreement that judges ought to have such sweeping immunity for their words (see Coleridge CJ (diss.) in *Dawkins v Paulet* (England 1869) p. 11). However, there may be something to be said for full judicial protection in countries where governments (and others) are not fully convinced of the virtues of judicial independence.

For behaviour outside court the judges can be sued like any other person (*Barry v Bayer* (South West Africa 1937) p. 77, citing Gatley, 2nd. ed., p.190; the *Barry* case involved a licensing magistrate; the case does not discuss whether he would have had absolute or qualified privilege). Their immunity does not extend to the administrative functions which many of them will also have. So when the Chief Justice of Botswana was sued by a court clerk for remarks he had made in discussing her employment with the Acting Chief Magistrate, the defendant's judicial status offered no protection (*Ngope v Quinn* (1987)), although, like others performing similar functions, he could rely on qualified privilege (see High Court (1987) - qualified privilege applied on the facts). A commentator has written (Othlogile, 1991, p. 133), "In future judges will find it difficult to be zealous in investigating any act in the discharge of their administrative function", and seems to suggest that such administrative functions be taken away from the judiciary. There seems no good case for treating the judiciary so very differently from others who have to bear the responsibility for their professional actions, although it is true that the situation of the judiciary made this case especially difficult, especially the small size of the judiciary, which meant that *ad hoc* judges had to be appointed from South Africa to hear the case at first instance (*ibid*. p. 111). It is also the case that in any country a litigant in dispute with a judge particularly where there is an issue of credibility of the judge's evidence, faces a difficult situation, as pointed out by Amissah J in the Court of Appeal (*ibid*. p. 125).

Protection at common law would no doubt apply to assessors, who sit in some courts to advise on customary law by analogy with the assumption, made in England, that jurors have the privilege (Gatley, para. 392).

Counsel also enjoy a similar privilege (*Munster v Lamb* (England 1883)), and under English law this privilege extends to everything said in court. In South Africa, and, therefore, one would assume, in other Roman-Dutch jurisdictions, advocates have only qualified privilege (see *Pogrund v Yutar* (1967) and Gatley, para. 383 n. 20).

Other participants in the trial have privilege, including prosecutors - like the Malaŵian tax clerk presenting the case in court for failure to pay income tax, *Mkumba v Attorney-General* (1988) p. 150. Witnesses are privileged for what they say or write in their capacity as witnesses (*Dawkins v Lord Rokeby* (England 1875) quoted in *Mandavia v Mangat* (Kenya 1954), a case on a disciplinary tribunal under the Kenyan Advocates' Ordinance, *Seaman v Netherclift* (England 1876)). The privilege attaches also to documents submitted as evidence by a witness (*Dawkins v Lord Rokeby*). Suppose a witness, while giving evidence, makes some remark which is utterly unrelated to the case or the questions he has been asked as well as being defamatory? There is Indian authority, and English judicial *dicta*, to the effect that such a witness may be liable (*Jiwan Mal v Lachhman Dass* (India 1929), *Seaman v Netherclift* (above).

The Mauritian Criminal Code (s. 290 in the Code as amended in 1909) specifically provides a defence in civil and criminal defamation cases for words spoken or documents produced in court. This extends to judges, magistrates, parties, witnesses, advocates, attorneys or agents. The section previously contained no reference to civil cases, but after it was amended the courts held that it did provide a defence to civil action, despite appearing in the Penal Code,[3] and in 1936 it was held that it was intended to introduce the English defence of absolute privilege (*Decotter v Winson*; more recently *Ructoo v Nohur* (1969)). However, the restriction to words and documents actually *in court* means that the defence remains narrower than the common law one (see below); *Rault v Bacorisen* (1983) could not therefore involve *absolute* privilege: the statement complained of was made by a solicitor trying to arrange a settlement of this case; the court said, *obiter*, that it was privileged, but did not specify why. However, if the words were foreign to the cause in issue, a right of action exists for third parties, and even for the parties to the original litigation (provided, in the latter case, the court reserves the right to sue to the parties).[4]

In common law systems, for how far before the actual hearing does this privilege extend? There is a relationship between this immunity and that given to counsel from action for negligence (*Saif Ali v Sydney Mitchell & Co.* (England 1980) pp. 215, 220), which in English law covers only matters closely connected with the litigation (*ibid.*). However, in Nigeria the negligence immunity is more limited: the Legal Practitioners Act 1964 preserves the common law rule giving immunity to legal practitioners, *in front of the court*. One would expect the courts to extend absolute privilege at least to pleadings used for their proper purpose (see the Scottish case of *Rome v Watson* (1898)). Pleadings not being public documents, but prepared for communication to the other side in litigation, absolute privilege does not extend to making them public (see Chapter 14).

Witnesses' privilege clearly attaches to affidavits produced in connection with litigation (e.g. *Foley v Asfour* (Nigeria 1970) relying on *Munster v Lamb* and *Seaman v Netherclift*, *inter alia*), and to statements made by a person who is being interviewed by a lawyer with a view to possibly being called as a witness (*Beresford v White* (England 1914) also *Sanjeev Reddi* v *Koneri Reddi* (India 1926)), or giving a proof of evidence to a lawyer (*Watson v McEwan* (England 1905); this case was distinguished by the appeal court, sitting in Bombay, in *Tharia v Morrison* (Zanzibar 1910) because the collection of statements by the Director of Public Works was at too early a stage to be in contemplation of litigation). An English court held that the investigations done by a hospital in a post mortem which they reported to the police and led to the plaintiff being charged with murder were covered by absolute privilege (*Evans v London Hospital Medical College* (1981)); otherwise the accepted privilege for what was done after proceedings were started could in many cases be nullified by the disgruntled litigant saying they were suing for the investigations, not for the evidence later given on the basis of the investigations. (The court also said that it was unlikely that *counsel* would have privilege at so early a stage - p. 191.)

In the 1970s there was a brief vogue in Nigeria for making allegations against prominent figures by means of affidavits. The Advisory Judicial Committee pointed out that no special privilege attached to a statement simply by virtue of its being in the form of an affidavit (*Daily Times*, Sept. 11 and 18, 1974, and Ewelukwa, 1977, p. 47). (An English case is *Maloney v Bartley* (1812).) Privilege only applies to affidavits prepared for litigation.

There is Indian authority to the effect that a petition to a magistrate to begin criminal proceedings (under the equivalent of s. 88 of the Nigerian CPC - person likely to cause breach of the peace) has absolute privilege (*T.G. Nair v Melepurath Sankunni* (1971)), and the same would be true of any other step initiating legal process (e.g. *Hodson v Pare* (England 1899)).[5] In Tanzania it was held that a magistrate could not sue a party who complained in a petition of appeal that he had lost because the magistrate had an "amorous relationship" with the defendant's wife. Kwikima J said,

> ...justice would be in jeopardy if litigants were scared to allege misconduct on the part of magistrates just because they were not in a position to prove them should they be called upon to do so. I suppose a magistrate has to accept as a fact of life the prospect of being vilified without being able to do anything about it (*Nkulu v Mkungile* (1972) p. 70).

(The learned judge does not specify whether the privilege is absolute but this is to be assumed, especially since "nothing can be done about it"!)

In *Aghahowa v Aguebor* the plaintiff had been engaged by the defendant as his lawyer but then dropped out and appeared for the other side ((Nigeria 1957); see the Australian case *Troughton v McIntosh* (1896)). The defendant wrote a defamatory letter of complaint about the plaintiff's conduct to the Judge of the High Court, the Chief Magistrate, the Magistrate and the Superintendent of Police. Since the suit in question was already pending, the communications were held to be absolutely privileged (other than that to the Superintendent of Police who could do nothing).

A Tanzanian court took a view which seems somewhat different from that of the Nigerian court: the defendant wrote to the Chief Justice after the hearing of a civil case, but while judgment was reserved, complaining that the judge was not impartial. To quote the judge in the defamation litigation:

> [T]the defendant suggested that he was protected by absolute privilege. He said: "since I took this affair to the Chief Justice, I was in a court of law, even if it be under a mango tree". Unfortunately, he was wrong in his understanding. Going to the Chief Justice, wherever he happens to be, does not constitute judicial proceedings. ....in writing to the Chief, the defendant did not do so in the course of a judicial proceeding. He only communicated to him in his capacity as an administrator. (*Jonathan v Athuman Khalfan* (1980) p. 183.[6])

Qualified privilege did apply.

In *Payne v Cole* (Nigeria 1899) a party to litigation wrote to the judge alleging that the Registrar had taken a bribe. The Full Court held that the letter was not part of the proceedings before the court, since it could not influence any matter connected with those proceedings, nor was it a stage in proceedings against the Registrar. It was not therefore absolutely privileged - although qualified privilege applied. (Edlin Ag. CJ dissented; he held that since the Chief Justice, to whom the complaint was made, could have dealt with it in a summary way under s. 70 Supreme Court Ordinance, it could be considered as "preferring a complaint" to which absolute privilege would apply. He said *Johnson v Evans* (England 1799) - holding that there is no action for words preferring a complaint - applied; this was distinguished by the majority.)

A party to litigation will have the privilege of counsel if he conducts his own case, and the privilege of a witness when he gives evidence. Privilege would also attach to other statements - for example an unsworn statement from the dock in a criminal case, or for an affidavit (e.g. *Foley v Asfour*, above, *Adene v Oyeyemi* (Nigeria 1969) or for the instructions to his lawyer for the preparation of pleading and so on (*Lincoln v Daniels* (England 1962)). A Sudanese court held that the privilege applied to a party who initiated protest proceedings on a promissory note. It declined to distinguish these from other types of proceedings, and held that "The privilege...covers everything done by the ordinary courts of law in the course of their normal duties whether involving adjudication on a contested cause or otherwise"(*Ali Mahmoud Obeid v Barclays Bank (DCO) Shendi* (1959)).

Quasi-judicial Proceedings

Absolute privilege would not - naturally enough - apply to an *illegal* court, as in the case of a body purporting to exercise criminal jurisdiction as a customary court in Nigeria when these had been abolished (*Agoaka v Ejiofor* (1972)). In *Trapp v Mackie* (England 1979, p. 384), Lord Diplock described recognition of the tribunal by law to be a *sine qua non* for the application of absolute privilege; *a fortiori* it would not apply to an illegal body. Whether a body attracts privilege depends on how closely it approximates to a court; the line is not easy to draw (see Gatley, para. 401 ff). On appeal from Tanzania, the East African Court of Appeal said that it was taking into account the procedure of the body in question (a transport licensing authority) and the nature of the decision it was to take (*H. Suleman* Ltd. *v Sayani* (1963)). (Among the major English cases cited are *Royal Aquarium v Parkinson* (1892) and *Copartnership Farms v Harvey-Smith* (1918).) The House of Lords suggested as relevant the authority under which the body acts, the type of question into which it has to inquire, its procedure and the consequences of its decision (*Trapp v Mackie*, above). The court will take account of whether the body can compel the attendance of witnesses (see *Dawkins v Lord Rokeby* (England 1873)), whether it sits in public (*Addis v Crocker* (England 1961), whether it takes evidence on oath (in *Suleman v Sayani* above, the court quoted from the English Report of the *Committee on Administrative Tribunals and Inquiries* (Cmnd 218 (1957) para. 82) to the effect that absolute privilege ought to be available at least to tribunals which take evidence on oath, and observed that this means that at present such privilege was not available to tribunals) and so on; but there is no check-list of criteria which must be satisfied before absolute privilege applies (Gatley, paras. 403 and 405). If its decision is not final, in the sense that it merely makes recommendations, absolute privilege may not apply, but it may do so if the body's decision is a "step leading directly to the determination of an issue by the body who appointed it" to quote Lord Fraser in *Trapp v Mackie*. Privilege will not apply if the body's functions are really more administrative than judicial (*Suleman v Sayani, Royal Aquarium* case above).

Absolute privilege has been held to attach to a military court of inquiry (e.g. *Dawkins v Rokeby*),[7] and various sorts of professional disciplinary bodies (*Mandavia v Mangat* (Kenya 1954); *Marrinan v Vibart* (England 1963) and the letter written to the Attorney-General in *Aghahowa v Aguebor* (above) - that case cites *Lilley v Roney* (England 1892)). All these involved lawyers - contrast *Saraki v Soleye* (1972) pp. 280-1: the Nigerian Medical Council does not have judicial function with respect to complaints against doctors. Tribunals with procedures very close to courts - such as rent tribunals - will obviously be covered. A writer in Nigeria suggested that bodies set up under the Tribunals of Inquiry Act ought to attract absolute privilege. They hear evidence and counsel may appear before them, and their recommendations, although not binding, may have far reaching consequences for individuals (Sogbesan,1971). This reasoning, however, would apply to many bodies which have been held not to attract absolute privilege, like the Bar Council (*Lincoln v Daniels* (England 1962) - privilege does not apply to Bar Council though it does to the Benchers of an Inn).

What about arbitration? In theory this is based on the agreement of the parties. In reality one party very often has no choice. And the modern trend is towards making arbitration increasingly final. A leading book on arbitration suggests that whether there is absolute privilege will depend on the type of arbitration: how close it comes to a court, as we have seen is relevant for other bodies. They suggest, however, that this is illogical, since if the point is that "those who take part in the administration of justice by a means recognised and sanctioned by law should be entirely uninfluenced by the possibility of proceedings for defamation" it should apply to any type of arbitration (Mustill & Boyd, 1981, p. 357).

Bodies *not* attracting absolute privilege include merely domestic tribunals which derive their authority from the consent of the parties (*Hope v J'Anson* (England 1901), *Omenwa v Okonkwo* (Nigeria 1963)), and this covers conciliation bodies (see *Tadd v Eastwood* (England 1985) cited by Mustill & Boyd)). This would embrace customary arbitration: in *Osumanu v Taribabu* (Ghana 1977) such arbitration was held to attract *qualified* privilege. A transport licensing authority was held in East Africa to be exercising administrative rather than judicial functions, although its procedure was formal and quite like that of a court (*Suleman v Sayani* above); (see also *Attwood v Chapman* (England 1914) (liquor licensing) - but see the views of Gatley, para. 408 fn. 23). In the former Western Region of Nigeria the non-statutory anti-corruption officer inquired into and reported upon allegations of corruption; he was held not to be "quasi-judicial" in his function (*Majekodunmi v Olopade* (1963)). In Mauritius a committee of inquiry conducted by the General Manager of Railways was also held to be insufficiently like a court to attract absolute privilege (*Drieu v Amode* (1881); and another court held, applying what it considered would be the approach of the English courts, that the proceedings of an inspector under the Companies Ordinance would not be absolutely privileged (*Decotter v Winson*; this case contains a lengthy review of the English authority at the time, including *Re Grosvenor and West End Terminus Hotel Co. Ltd.* (1897), and *Royal Aquarium*). Specific legislation may also confer complete immunity upon officials or bodies who would not meet the common law criteria (see *Drieu v Amode*, p. 110, referring to Ordinances 17 and 18 of 1934 which conferred immunity upon witnesses before Commissions of Enquiry set up by the Governor or the Council of Government).

Legislative Bodies

The basic rule providing for absolute privilege for proceedings of legislatures is laid down in legislation.[8] The English legislation is the Bill of Rights 1688 Article 9 "That the freedom of speech, and debates on proceedings in Parliament ought not to be impeached or questioned in any court, or place out of parliament". (See Gatley, para. 422n. for the wider implications of this including that the validity of a report of a legislative committee cannot be questioned - *Dingle v Associated Newspapers* (England 1960).) The bar has been held to be effective to prevent a defendant as well as a plaintiff from relying on what was said in Parliament (*Prebble v Television New Zealand Ltd.* (NZ 1994)).[9] Very similar words appear in at least some African statutes (e.g. Legislative Houses (Powers and Privileges) Law, Cap. 59 Ondo State of Nigeria s. 3; Basutoland [now Lesotho] National Council (Powers and Privileges) Proclamation No. 16 of 1960, s. 3 (see Poulter (1970), p. 136) (no doubt replaced by more recent legislation). But additional provision may also be made:

> No member shall be liable to any civil or criminal proceedings, arrest, imprisonment or damages by reason of anything which he may have said in the House or by reason of any matter or thing which he may have brought before the House by petition, bill, resolution, motion or otherwise.

(Lesotho, s. 4; there is a variety of wording (see, for example, the Ugandan National Assembly (Powers and Privileges) Act Cap. 249 quoted in Veitch (1973) p. 81). The Ondo statute also goes on to confer all privileges enjoyed by members of the UK House of Commons: s. 8.) Privilege may also be given to those who give evidence before legislative committees (e.g. Uganda Act s. 14). In situations not covered by the words of the legislation - for example a letter written by a legislator to some government body or functionary - the courts would have to fall back on the common law, under which such a letter is probably not absolutely privileged (see Gatley, para. 424, suggesting that a letter by an MP to a Minister criticising a statutory board is "probably not" a "proceeding in Parliament" in England). The phraseology of the Nigerian legislation is different, and the fact that, under the two most recent, US-type Constitutions of that country, Ministers are not members of the legislature would make it less likely that privilege would be held to apply. The common law privilege extends to proceedings of committees of any legislative house (see *Gaffin v Donelly* (England 1881)). (This is sometimes provided by statute expressly and would cover the evidence of witnesses to such committees as well as their members.) Absolute privilege would also attach to a petition to a House (*Lake v King* (England 1680)).

A member will not be protected if he chooses to repeat (orally or by publishing his speech) outside the legislature the words he spoke within. Then his only hope of protection would be *qualified* privilege if he published it only to those with an interest in the subject matter (*Wason v Walter* (England 1868)). A Ugandan MP held a press conference which he said was to respond to a challenge to repeat his words outside Parliament. However, the court held that in fact he could not be said to have "impliedly repeated, adopted or approved" his own words in Parliament (*Onama v Uganda Argus* (1968) p. 516). He did make some fresh allegation which was defamatory, however. The case of *Prebble v Television New Zealand* (above) may cast some doubt upon whether such a person would be liable if he "adopted" rather than repeated his words in Parliament, for this would involve calling into question something said there.

Statutory provision is made for reports, papers and proceedings published by or under the authority of a legislative house - taken from the

English Parliamentary Papers Act of 1840 s. 1. A defendant who wishes to rely upon this privilege must give 24 hours' notice to the plaintiff and bring a certificate of a specified officer stating that the report or other document was published by or under the authority of the House in question (in Ondo legislation (above) the Speaker or Clerk of the House, in Malaŵi the Speaker - National Assembly (Powers and Privileges) Act Cap. 2:04, s. 24). The court will then stay the proceedings. *Extracts* from such reports attract only qualified privilege - see next chapter. This provision is usually restricted to legislatures: it would not cover reports published by a Minister or any part of the executive (see English Committee on Defamation (Cmnd 5909) para. 223). In Zambia, however, it extends to reports published by order or under the authority of the Cabinet (Defamation Act s. 16).

It was held in Ghana that a pronouncement of the supreme legislative body - military and unelected - had absolute privilege at common law (*Attisogbe v Harlley* (1972)).

It has been suggested that,

> ...the fact that the defence of absolute privilege protects statements made in Parliament means in practice that the politicians themselves operate as a two-way conduit of public scrutiny. It is common in the context of the Westminster system of government that allegations of corruption, malfeasance and impropriety are first voiced on the floor of Parliament by opposition and independent politicians freed from the threat of defamation litigation (Edgeworth & Newcity, 1992, p. 59).

This reasoning has often been inapplicable to African legislatures. Where there is a one-party state there are no opposition or independent MPs; legislatures have tended to rubber-stamp government policy, and the sort of committee system which can encourage less partisan examination of the executive has been a rarity. All this may be changing (see Chapter 1).

Statements between Officers of State

There is an established but unclear category of absolute privilege attaching to communications between high officers of state in the course of their duty. It has been held to cover a Cabinet Minister and his immediate junior minister (*Chatterton v Secretary of State for India* (England 1985)), and an ambassador reporting to the head of his government (*M. Isaacs Ltd. v Cook* (England 1925)), and communications between embassy officials within the embassy of a friendly foreign state: (*Fayed v Al-Tajir* (England 1987)). It may not go below the level of minister (suggested *obiter* in *Szalatney-Stacho v Fink* (England 1946)).

There have been few African instances. In Zambia it was held not to apply to a letter from a Provincial Commissioner to a Paramount Chief, conveying a message from the colonial Governor (*Ngandu v Price* (1960) - a very brief report). The plaintiff was a member of the Legislative Council, and advisor to the Chief; on the facts there was held to be qualified privilege. In Uganda this privilege was held not to arise in the case of letters written by a County chief to the Administrative Secretary with copies to Security Officers (*Gunigina v Wakabala* (1975) citing the *Royal Aquarium* case). In Gold Coast in 1915 it was held that a report from a District Commissioner on an election to a stool did not fall within the *Chatterton* class of absolutely privileged communications though there is no discussion of reasoning (the case was actually brought in slander of title) (*Aluwah v Bartlett*).

Outside the governmental sphere it has been held to cover a communication between a major-general and the adjutant-general of the British army (*Dawkins v Lord Paulet* (1869)). It has been suggested that it does not cover a Commissioner of Police and his Deputy (*Merricks v Nott-Bower* (England 1965)).

Solicitor and Client

There is some English authority to the effect that communications between solicitor and client are absolutely privileged (*More v Weaver* (1928)). However, there are powerful House of Lords *dicta* (*Minter v Priest* (1930)) and a strong current of non-judicial opinion (for example the Irish Law Reform Commission Report (Ireland 1991, p. 20) against. There seem to be no African cases.

Notes

1. In 1992 a court in England said it should not be extended to statements provided by an ex-employee to the social security authorities when applying for benefit, this not being a judicial or semi-judicial situation - *Purdew v Seress-Smith*.
2. Apparently New Zealand draws no such distinction: superior and inferior courts judges both lose the protection if acting beyond their jurisdiction: *Nakhla v McCarthy* (1978).
3. "That an article which deals with civil as well as criminal immunity should appear in the Penal Code is merely an example of those mental aberrations

which, from time to time, attack the draftsman" - Tracey Watts J *Decotter v Winson* (1936) p. 77. This "aberration", of course, only continues that which allows primary liability to depend on the Criminal as well as the Civil Code. The history is actually extremely complex: In the nineteenth century art. 299 of the Penal Code of 1838 (based on art. 23 of the French Law of 17 May 1819) provided a defence for criminal and civil actions, as explained by LeConte J in (1936) p. 91, where he reproduces the newer Fench version - art. 41 of the Law of 29 July 1881, and the Mauritian art. 299. In 1875 it was said,

> Where the wrong for which damages are claimed is caused by an action having been raised or by injurious statements having been employed by a suitor in connection with judicial proceedings, proof of good faith will exclude "faute" and constitute a valid defence if it be not made merely with the view of causing useless annoyance to the opponent, that is if the allegation be really pertinent to the issue involved

- *Malot v Constantin* (1875) p. 93, citing *Dalloz Périodique* 52-1240 and authorities cited in Dalloz, *voce* "Responsabilité" No. 112. And earlier the court said "the jurisprudence of French Courts proceeding on principles equally applicable here has recognised a certain privilege as attaching to acts and words even if injury result therefrom if they are done or employed in connection with a suit".

In 1901 (Ord. 23 of 1901) art. 290 was substituted, with a defence for criminal cases only, by a draftsman intent on separating civil and criminal liability. The draftsman was Pigott, who as judge in cases like *Legrand v Thatcher* (1896) insisted that the two were separate (see Brown J in *Loumeau v d'Unienville* (1909) p. 164). However, the court in *Loumeau* felt it had to interpret the words as they stood, and that the defence to civil actions had disappeared. That same year the article was amended to its present state.

4. This proviso "For no very apparent reason...[was] reintroduced and tacked on to the provisions of the new article" - Tracey Watts J in *Decotter v Winson* (1936) p. 77, while Nairac CJ said (p. 110) that the proviso "Unfortunately...cut down the privilege".

Originally the judge could decide that even words not foreign to the case should be suppressed, and order their originator to pay damages. In *Malot v Constantin* (pp. 89-90) the court suggested that this introduced into Mauritian law a provision similar to that in English law under which an immaterial statement could be ordered expunged and "satisfaction" ordered - quoting Lord Mansfield in *Astley v Younger* (1759).

Another issue in this case concerned the original drafting of the proviso to the effect that a court could suppress the words or award damages *when deciding upon the merits of the case*. But in this instance the merits of the earlier case were never decided because it transpired that the case was brought in an incompetent court: the court held that this did not prevent the plaintiff relying upon the proviso to section 299 - otherwise a person could deliberately bring an action in an incompetent court and obtain the protection of the Article. The original provision even allowed the judge to suspend the responsible advocate or "ministerial officer" - see pp. 90-91 where the history of Art. 290 is set out.

5. If this is done maliciously there may be liability for the separate tort of malicious institution of proceedings, a point made in the Ghanaian case of *Panagiotopoulos v Plastico Ltd.* (1965). The position would be somewhat similar under Mauritian law, though it would not be conceived of as a separate tort (see Chapter 3). Legal proceedings started with malice or bad faith can be actionable - see *Migale v Punchoo* (1943) p. 57 quoting Dalloz,1939 No. 16 p. 242, and No. 25 p. 285. In *Migale* permission was given to proceed with an action for maliciously applying for a new trial.
6. The printing of the report is very confused, and this quotation goes from page 183 to 185.
7. For a more recent example from Sri Lanka (which applies Roman-Dutch law) see *Balthazar v Hulangamuwa* (1987).
8. In Seychelles the argument was made that a member of a colonial legislature could not enjoy such a privilege. However, it was held that the protection (contained in the Seychelles Penal Code s. 192(1)(a)) was not repugnant to s. 5 of the Colonial Laws Validity Act, and that anyway the establishment of the legislature created absolute privilege by implication: *Chenard & Co. v Arissol* (1947) upheld by the Privy Council (1949).
9. The case has been controversial, see e.g. Sharland & Loveland (1997), and s. 13 of the English Defamation Act 1996 makes it possible for a Member of Parliament to waive the privilege.

13 Qualified Privilege Generally

Introduction

The notion underlying this, the most frequently invoked defence, is that there are certain situations in which the freedom to speak honestly outweighs the need to protect reputations. This means the statement is protected even if it turns out to be untrue (courts have sometimes shown some confusion over this and held privilege not to apply because the statements were untrue). Blackburn J (*Danes v Snead* (England 1870) p. 611 quoted in *Abasi v Williams* (Nigeria 1942)) said:

> The result of decided cases is that where a person is so situated that it becomes right in the interests of society that he should tell to a third person certain facts, then if he, bona fide and without malice, does tell him it is a privileged communication, i.e. a communication protected by the occasion.

Rather more informative as to when the interests of society do give rise to the privilege is a dictum of Lord Atkinson:

...an occasion where the person who makes the communication has an interest or a duty, legal, social or moral, to make it to the person to whom it is made, and the person to whom it is so made has a corresponding interest or duty to receive it (*Adam v Ward* (England 1917) p. 334).

While an occasion of *absolute* privilege protects all communications (with a few possible exceptions), an occasion of *qualified* privilege protects only communications to which the requisite duties and/or interests attach. In *Monyamane v Anderson* (Botswana 1987) the court held there was no occasion of privilege: the matter which concerned the plaintiff was outside the agenda of the meeting convened by the defendant.

The Duty to Communicate

Courts are in their element in deciding whether a person has a *legal* duty to communicate (any sort of legal duty would be covered, for example contractual or under statute (see *Mihaka v Wellington Publishing* (New

Zealand 1975)). A moral or social duty is a more difficult concept. Jibowu FJ quoted Lindley LJ (*Stuart v Bell* (England 1891) p. 350) in *Economides v S. Thomopoulos & Co. Ltd.* (Nigeria 1956):

> I take moral or social duty to mean a duty recognised by English people of ordinary intelligence and moral principle, but at the same time not a duty enforceable by legal proceedings, whether civil or criminal.

A Ghanaian was told by his wife that she had had an affair with the plaintiff. After the end of the marriage the husband told this to the Director of Education for whom both the allegedly adulterous pair worked, and to her parents (and to the head of the women's section of a secret society to which all three belonged, but no decision about privilege of this communication seems to have been made). It was held that the first communication was privileged because everyone had a duty to bring dereliction of duty by a public officer to the attention of the authorities (the dereliction was on the part of the plaintiff who was alleged to have made use of his position). The second communication was also privileged because "Under customary law there existed a moral as well as a legal duty to report the conduct of one of the spouses to their respective parents for investigation and settlement" (the latter rationale was undermined somewhat by the defendant's refusal to accept family mediation - although the court itself did not draw this conclusion) (*Buachie v Samman* 1982). A Rhodesian judge said "a member of the public has a right - it might almost be said a duty - to call the attention of a head of department to actions of a public servant which are detrimental to the public interest" (*Ling v Palfrey* 1943 p. 169 (quoted in *Parsons v Cooney* (1970) p. 81)).

Many of the cases concern reports to authorities. In the Gambian case of *Balfour Beatty Ltd. v Wadda* (1983) the defendants erroneously told the Commissioner of Income Tax that the plaintiff was their landlord. They were held protected by qualified privilege as they had a legal duty to file their tax return including expenditure. In *Economides* the report had been made by the defendant about the plaintiff, whom he had just dismissed, to the tax authorities suggesting that the plaintiff might be trying to evade taxes. Jibowu FJ said:

> ...it is considered a moral or social wrong for a citizen to refrain from giving information at his disposal which might help the police to bring a criminal to book...(p. 12)

and by analogy decided that the defendant did act in pursuit of a duty. He did not make it entirely clear how much significance was to be attached to the fact that the defendant reasonably expected to be asked by the tax authorities about the plaintiff's emoluments. However, he had previously quoted Hamilton LJ in *Greenlands Ltd. v Wilmhurst* (England 1913) p. 535:

> privilege must depend on the relations of the parties, on the duty thereout arising, and on the occasion which is used or abused, not on the mere accident who spoke first. When this is critical it is on account of the nature of the duty, the discharge of which may or may not be consistent with volunteering the statement. There is no general rule that statements which would be privileged if made in answer to an inquiry cease to be so when the informant has not waited to be asked.

Hamilton LJ also observed that volunteering information, acting as a "busybody", might be evidence of malice (*ibid.* quoted in *Isibor v Bendel Transport Services Ltd.* (Nigeria 1980), Akhigbe J).

Reports to the police to the effect that the plaintiff is suspected of an offence will attract qualified privilege, even if there is no explicit legal duty to report. For examples see *Rwekanika v Binamungu* (Tanzania 1974) (quoting at length what is now Gatley, para. 484); *Johnson v Evans* (England 1800); *Yohana Mujuni v Isaya s/o Bakobi* (Tanzania 1969); *Manneh v Sanang* (Gambia 1967); *Umeh v Okoye* (Nigeria 1985) also referring to *Balogun v Adeyanju* (Nigeria 1985). In Tanzania the principle has been introduced into cases brought under customary law (e.g. *Tumanieli v Aisa d/o Issai* 1969).

In *N'Jie v Edmondson* (Gambia 1957) it was held that a lawyer was justified in reporting to the acting DPP, when he was instructed to sue another lawyer for something which was also a criminal offence; this was because the rule in *Smith v Selwyn* (England 1914) would apply, namely that the action in tort could not be brought until the defendant had been prosecuted for the criminal offence, which was a matter for the DPP.

In these cases not only is the defendant acting as a responsible citizen in making the report, but the recipients have an interest (indeed a duty) to receive complaints of this nature. Into the same category one might place other cases about reports to government functionaries, beginning with colonial period cases of reports to the administration. Members of an Oman in Gold Coast were held to have had a duty to write to the District Commissioner complaining about the stool clerk (*Yankum v Abaka* (1926-9)). The court said, "The District Commissioner admits the right of the Oman to make complaints to him, and it would render the administration of this country extremely difficult, if this right were to be hampered by the fear of proceedings for defamation..."(p. 115). They went on to say that the defendants were fulfilling a public *duty*. (See also *Doryume v Awah II* (Gold Coast 1913)). In Northern Rhodesia it was held that a communication from the Provincial Commissioner to a Paramount Chief had qualified privilege (*Ngandu v Price* (1960)). The Commissioner was the channel of communication between Government and the Chief and he had a duty to advise the Chief on all matters connected with the administration of the Chiefdom. The suggestion that the privilege was *absolute* was rejected (see also *Aluwah v Bartlett* (Gold Coast 1915)). In *Dikey v Odeniyi* (Nigeria 1960) the defendant, a member of the public, wrote a letter to the chairman of the appropriate education committee accusing the plaintiff, a headmaster, of immoral behaviour with pupils. This was held to be privileged. Again it is not clear how much relevance was attached to the fact that the letter was written at the request of the committee chairman. After independence government informants have the same sort of protection: *Nkalubo v Kibirige* (Uganda 1973) involved a report by the lay leader of a church to the District Commissioner about a dispute in church; it was held that the DC had an interest in knowing of situations that might lead to breach of the peace. Similarly in Tanzania, letters complaining of the plaintiff's mismanagement of the affairs of a mosque were sent to the local sheikh, the local branch of the ruling party, the Muslim Welfare Society and the Village Development Comittee, all of whom were held to have an interest either in the affairs of the mosque or in the preservation of peace (*Athman Lusahu v Sadiki Athumani* (1966)).

A communication from an inspector for Lusaka City Council reporting his suspicions of the sales manager in the Council's Liquor Undertaking Section to the Mayor, Council officers and Councillors was held to be privileged: the defendant had a duty and the recipients had at least an interest (the Councillors) and some a duty (Mayor and officers) (*Mumba v Singoyi* (Zambia 1975). And in *Jensen v Acavalos* (Zimbabwe 1993) the defendant had an interest in writing to council officials to complain about the plaintiff, who was employed by the Harare City Council and they had an interest in receiving the complaint. In Nigeria a motor company which had employed a contractor to erect a stand at a trade fair was held to have a moral duty to write to the Permanent Secretary, who was in charge of the fair and who had proposed the contractor, when they wished to complain about the contractor's incompetence (*Okusanya v WAATECO* (1974)).

Privilege will also attach to statements made to bodies and officers whose responsibility it is to uphold professional standards. In *Saraki v Soleye* (Nigeria 1972) the defendant, Permanent Secretary in a State Ministry of Health, made a report to the Nigerian Medical Council on the plaintiff's clinic. The defendant was held to have a duty to make and the Council to receive the report, and it was held to have qualified privilege. As we have seen, a report about a lawyer or a court official which can be viewed as part of court proceedings (Chapter 12), or as a formal step towards instituting disciplinary proceedings (as was the case with the letter to the Attorney-General in *Aghahowa v Aguebor* (Nigeria 1957)) will have *absolute* privilege. Other complaints about such people will attract qualified privilege, provided they go to the right quarters (see below).

Others held to be under duties include employees informing their employers of what they believe to be dereliction of duty by fellow-employees (e.g. *Adapoe v Pospisil* (Ghana 1974), *Ngbemaneh v Rothstein* (Nigeria 1976)), an employer who is requested to give a reference for a former employee (e.g. *Ayoola v Olajure* (Nigeria 1977)). It seems the former employer need not wait for an inquiry (*Pattison v Jones* (England 1828)), though the court pointed out that the fact that he volunteered is relevant in deciding on malice. In *Parsons v Cooney* the court said it doubted whether the privilege would apply where the servant had already been working for the new employer for some time and giving satisfactory service ((Rhodesia 1970) p. 79). Other examples are a bank asked about the credit worthiness of a customer (though this will only apply when the customer has agreed to the reference being sought, for otherwise the bank must treat the customer's financial affairs as confidential: *Tournier v National Provincial Bank* (England 1924)), and the police if they are asked whether a prospective scholarship holder has a criminal record (*Okotcha v Olumese* (Nigeria 1967)) - here the plaintiff asked for the report, but no doubt the result would be the same if the prospective scholarship grantor had done so. And family relationships too may give rise to a moral duty - for example a person might tell a close relative if he has reason to suspect the other's intended spouse of being unsuitable (e.g. *Todd v Hawkins* (England 1837) *Fairman v Ives* (England 1822)).

The importance of the duty requirement was emphasised in the English Court of Appeal in 1915 (*Adam v Ward*), when it cast doubt upon an earlier statement (in *Mangena v Wright* (England 1909)) namely:

> A communication by a public servant of a matter within his own province concerning the conduct of a person who is for the time being taking a public

> part, the matter being one of public interest as to which the public are entitled to information, may be a privileged occasion on the part of that public servant.

The Court doubted this, unless there was a duty on the civil servant to publish (p. 304). However, this same statement was quoted with approval many years later in East Africa (*Shah v Uganda Argus* 1972). A statement so broad was unnecessary either in *Mangena* or in *Shah*; the English court seems to have been determined to defeat the plaintiff from every available angle, since he was obviously considered to be a disloyal citizen of the Empire, in fact a black South African.

The difficulty comes in anticipating when the courts will hold that a person is being a mere busybody who has no duty of any sort to report what he believes to be true but unsavoury facts about the plaintiff to someone who has an interest, or even duty to receive them. One may expect the courts to give protection to people whose statements are intended to lead to the enforcement of the criminal law. At the other end of the scale is a case like *Watt v Longsdon* (England 1930): though an employee who suspected a fellow employee to be engaging in immoral sexual behaviour while on company business had a duty to tell their employer, he had none to tell the man's wife. The wife presumably had an interest, and had the communicator been a member of the family a duty would probably have been held to exist. There may be a right-minded view in Uganda or Nigeria, say, about reporting suspects to the police; is there necessarily one about telling people about their spouse's misdemeanours? Behaviour that might be thought of by European societies as being a "busybody" might not be so characterised in African societies which tolerate or even encourage far more involvement of extended families in the affairs of nuclear families. In *Dewhirst v Larkins* (Uganda 1911) it seems that the ultimate recipient had an interest - in knowing that the General Manager of the Uganda Company had been warned not to use him for auditing as he was friendly with a known fraudster. The case does not explore what duty the defendant had in making the statement, and must be regarded as doubtful. In this I would respectfully disagree with Spry who says "There is also a qualified privilege attaching to friendly acts" (1976, p. 33). At least this does not entirely square with cases like *Watt*.

An Interest in Communicating

Very often it is not easy to draw a line between duty and interest: a person who reports what he believes is an imminent crime could be said to be acting in pursuit of a duty or (if he would be affected by the crime) in his own interests. A parent who reports a teacher for immoral relations with pupils will be carrying out a duty and perhaps protecting the interests of his own children; no doubt the defendant in the Ugandan case of *Ssejjobi v Rwabigonji* (1977) would have succeeded had he not been malicious. He reported the plaintiff school teacher to the District Education Officer, and claimed he did so in pursuit of his moral and legal duty as parent of a pupil and also as pastor.

A person who had a dispute with his neighbour, an army officer, wrote complaining that the officer had come with armed soldiers and demolished his property and had himself "stood around brandishing a revolver". The letter to the Chief of Army Staff who had power to punish the officer and the Director of Army Public Relations who had a duty to inquire into the complaint were held to be privileged. (*Ajala v Showunmi* (Nigeria 1977), citing *Fairmain v Ives* (England 1882)). A letter from an election candidate to the police asking for protection against a rival who, he said, had threatened to kill him, was privileged (*Amiekhai v Okilage* (Nigeria 1962)), as was a letter from a man who believed his two young sisters had been sexually interfered with by the plaintiff, written to the housing authorities asking to be allocated a new flat on these grounds (*Obasuyi v Ezeighu* (Nigeria 1991)). Privilege covered a letter by a creditor to the police trying to stop a debtor running away (*Hassan v Kassardjian Construction Ltd.* (Ghana 1964)), and a letter to the Chief Justice alleging that the Chief Registrar had solicited a bribe (*Payne v Cole* (Nigeria 1899)). In *Jonathan v Athuman Khalfan* (Tanzania 1980) it was treated as obvious that such a letter would have qualified privilege; the judge said that the fact that the Chief Justice advised the defendant to put his complaint in writing shows the reciprocity between complainant and Chief Justice (p. 185). The privilege was also held to apply when a government contractor told the Director of Public Works that the Superintendent of the PWO took bribes (*Tharia v Morrison* (Zanzibar 1910)), and when the local administration wrote to the manager of the only petrol station in town complaining about the constant breakdown in supplies, and copied the letter to the company for which the manager was agent (*Kapondeni v Mapulanga* (Zambia 1984)). Other examples are *Mwange v Kayiwe* (Uganda 1970) - a District Council complained to the relevant government Minister that the Secretary-General of the District Administration failed to carry out his duties, was negligent, a drunkard, a thief and a smuggler - and *Mosi v Mobil Oil Ghana Ltd. Kumasi* (Ghana 1964) - involving a letter to the employer of a tanker driver suggesting that he had tampered with the petrol loaded by the defendants.

Privilege will also apply if the defendant is asking questions with a view to verifying some information that affects his interest. One defendant had been told that the plaintiff (with whom he was already involved in litigation) planned to enlist the help of X to purloin some documents from the defendant's lawyer's office. When the defendant made inquiries of X to try to verify this story, he was held to have qualified privilege (*Abasi v Williams* (Nigeria 1942)).

Common Interest

People in some common enterprise have a common interest in the success of the enterprise. An employer has qualified privilege in telling employees why one of their number has been dismissed (*Hunt v Great Northern Railway* (England 1891), cited in many African cases). However, one Nigerian judge said,

> The malpractice was such that would naturally involve the company in financial losses. That, in my view, is indicative of sufficient interest to justify the company in publishing the circular informing the rest of the employees of the findings of the Panel of Inquiry and the aftermath of the inquiry. I am also of the view that correspondingly the outcome of the inquiry must be of curiosity and interest to the generality of the employees, especially the honest and dedicated ones who have interest in the progress of the company (*Isah v Ajaokuta Steel Co. Ltd.* (1985) p. 1173).

This comes perilously close to identifying interest with curiosity. One might say that it is the less honest employees who have the interest in knowing the consequences if they are tempted to offend! But employees involved in a particular aspect of the company's business have an interest in knowing about possible irregularities in that aspect, as when employees of two companies were present at a meeting where it was alleged that one of the companies was receiving payment from the other for work which had not actually been done (*Osezuah & Co. (Nigeria) Ltd. v Guinness (Nigeria) Ltd.* (Nigeria 1980)).

The court in a Zambian case (*Nyirenda v Kapiri Glass Products Ltd.* (1985)) had an interesting approach:

> ...in view of the indication of the legislature that there should be effective participation of workers in the affairs of the undertaking, matters of competence or otherwise of managers are of common interest to all members of the undertaking, that is both management and workers.

There was thus privilege for publication of the dismissal of the plaintiff (formerly Purchasing Manager) to some of the workforce. Several cases have involved communications to or from trade union representatives, as where union representatives alleged at a joint meeting with management that the plaintiff used corporation labour to erect his own house - it was held that union and management had a common interest (*Giwa v Ajayi* (Nigeria 1992)). In *Namugera v Uganda Bookshop Press* (Uganda 1974) the court said the defendants were "under an obligation" to send a copy of a letter of dismissal to the Union secretary (though it does not spell out the source of the duty), and that the Shop Stewards were interested parties. In *Kilonzo v Tam* privilege covered a meeting at which the plaintiff was accused by his employer in the presence of two shop stewards (Kenya 1970). In *Ezaga v Embechem Ltd.* (Nigeria 1981) it was held that management and union had a common interest in resolving disputes.

Many cases have involved relationships of a business nature such as a company and its shareholders (e.g. *Lawless v Anglo-Egyptian Co.* (England 1869)), or a business and its customers. So a notification that a salesman was no longer working for a company would be privileged on the interest basis if sent only to customers (*Daily Nation v Mukundi* (Kenya 1975)). One plaintiff was a member of an Association of sub-contractors employed by the Zambia-Tanzania Road Service Ltd. At the request of the latter a letter was posted on the Association's notice-board stating that the plaintiff's lorry had been involved in stealing from the defendants. Georges CJ said,

> If, in fact, the plaintiff was a party to the theft of copper by his servants from the defendant company's lorries, every member of the Association would have an interest in knowing this - not only from the point of view of the action which the defendant company was likely to take against them as sub-contractors, but also in their own interests to protect their freight from possible theft (*Chimala Stores v Zambia-Tanzania Road Services Ltd.* (Tanzania 1970)).

A letter from a farming co-operative to the District Commissioner complained of record keeping by the plaintiff millers, which if inaccurate would affect payment to defendants by the DC; it was held there was a common interest (*Das Puri v The Kenya Farmer's Association (Co-operative) Ltd.* (Kenya 1946-7)). And in a Tanzanian case the defendant wrote to the Commissioner for Lands saying that he did not wish to go on with a land transaction in which the plaintiff lawyer was acting because of the lawyer's dereliction of duty. He also wrote to the bank with which the deeds of the property in question were deposited; it was held he had qualified privilege for these communications (*Mangat v Sharma* (1968)).

The dissemination of information among members of business communities about alleged bad credit risks may be privileged, as of interest to both disseminator and recipient. Lord Dundas drew a distinction in words quoted by a Malaŵian court:

> The information complained of was circulated by the defenders among their own members in legitimate self-defence; they are not persons who trade for profit in the characters of other people (*Barr v Musselburgh* (Scotland 1912) p. 180, quoted by Skinner JC in *Madumuse v Press Furniture and Joinery Ltd.* (1984)).

Skinner CJ went on to hold that since the bulletin in question was sold for profit, privilege did not protect either the publishers or their contributors; the situation would have been different if the privilege had been based on the publication's reproducing a court register (see next Chapter).

An announcement made to a student body about disciplinary action would attract qualified privilege, whether it involved examiners, invigilators, examinees (*Bridgeman v Stockdale* (England 1953)), parents or school authorities (*Dikey v Odeniyi* (Nigeria 1960)). Other examples are members, and governing body, of a religious organisation or sect (*Laughton v Bishop of Sodor and Man* (England 1872)), as in an old Zanzibar case in which a communication to all members of an Indian caste was held to be privileged because the purpose was to inform them that the plaintiff had been excommunicated from the caste (*Velji v Hirachand* (1910)).

Response to Attack

A particular type of 'interest in communicating' privilege arises where the defendant is protecting himself against attack, usually where he is refuting allegations made against him by the plaintiff (see *Adam v Ward* (England 1917) cited in very many African cases e.g. *Majekodunmi v Olapade* (Nigeria 1963), *Moiro v Zablon* (Tanzania 1980)). This may extend to rebutting an attack on one's property (*Norton v Hoare (No. 1)* (Australia 1913) or on the reputation of a close relative (*Bowen-Rowlands v Argus Press Ltd.* (England 1926 (see Gatley, para. 517) - a daughter defending her recently deceased father); also *Israel v Portland News Pub. Co.* (USA 1936) - widow and sister of deceased; and see the critical note by T.H.B. (1936)).

A letter to the shareholders of a company accusing a former manager of stealing the company's business was held privileged because the plaintiff had attacked the defendant before the same audience (*Hoare v Jessop* (Kenya 1965)). A letter in a newspaper from a Town Clerk replying to a statement made by an alderman calculated to bring his colleagues into disrepute was held privileged (*Palmer v Boston* (Sierra Leone 1960-1)).

The defendant should restrict his comments to matters reasonably germane to the attack, and he is entitled to defend himself only to the same audience before which he has been attacked. However, the court will take account of the circumstances: a little latitude may be permitted in terms of the content of what the defendant says (for example *Kateera v Kayondo* (Uganda 1976) in which the defendant, exasperated with letters received from lawyers of a Building Society and his inability to convince them that he was not a defaulter, wrote to the Building Society describing the lawyers as mad men!) Similarly in terms of the audience, at least if the only way the defendant can reach those before whom he has been attacked is to address a rather wider group.

Duffus J (*Majekodunmi v Olapade* (Nigeria 1963) p. 17 (see also *Kitto v Chadwick* (Uganda 1975)) quoted Lord Oaksey in *Turner v M-G-M Pictures Ltd.* (England 1950, p. 470):

> There is, it seems to me, an analogy between the criminal law of self-defence and a man's right to defend himself against written or verbal attacks. In both cases he is entitled, if he can, to defend himself effectively, and he only loses the protection of the law if he goes beyond defence and proceeds to offence. That is to say, the circumstances in which he defends himself, either by acts or by words, negative the malice which the law draws from violent acts or defamatory words. If you are attacked with a deadly weapon you can defend yourself with a deadly weapon or with any other weapon which may protect your life. The law does not concern itself with niceties in such matters ... They had, therefore to adopt other means of defence, but provided that they were means of defence and not of offence or attack, they are not evidence of malice, but merely the adoption of the most effective method of defence available

And a Cameroon court said (*Wilson v Ntoko* (1972), O'Brien Quinn J),

> Taking all the correspondence into account, and the insults, taunts and provocation given by each side, I consider that both sides left themselves, to use a pugilistic expression, "wide open" and, to continue in the same vein, were "swinging wildly" at each other. In these circumstances while the reply may have been very insulting, it itself was provoked by language equally

insulting, and I would hold that the reply was fairly relevant to the attack and did not go beyond it in extent and character of publication.

In most of these cases the defamation relates to the "attacker", as it were, but this is not necessarily so. In one East African case the defendant company replied to the Inspector of Mines about safety precautions, in terms which one of their employees took exception to. He said that his employers' letter suggested that he had lied to an inquiry, and misled the inspector. This occasion was held to be privileged (*Williamson Diamonds Ltd. v Brown* (Tanzania 1970) cited in *Moiro v Zablon* (Tanzania 1980); see also *Banda v Pitman* (Malaŵi 1990)). *The West African Pilot* tried unsuccessfully to argue that it had a duty to leap to the defence of Dr Azikiwe (at the time Governor-General of Nigeria - but, more important, no doubt, were political links, Azikiwe being the founder of the paper) (*Awolowo v West African Pilot* (1962)).

In an unreported case the plaintiff lawyer had written an offensive letter to the defendant (a Divisional Police Officer) on behalf of his client in which he had said among other things that behaviour like that of the defendant had "compounded the ills of the last Republic". The defendant replied rather tartly, describing the plaintiff as a "village petitioner". *Obiter* (since it was held there was no publication) the court suggested qualified privilege applied - though this would have applied only to a publication to someone who had seen the plaintiff's letter (*Emessiri v Sanomi* (Nigeria 1977)).

In *Majekodunmi v Olapade* (Nigeria 1963) the defendant had been reported to the Anti-Corruption Officer by the plaintiff and had defended himself largely by attacking the plaintiff. The court held that he had gone beyond defence to attack and did not have the defence of qualified privilege: "A person cannot, however, in his defence, charge his accuser with offences unconnected with and not relevant to his defence of the charge against himself, only for the purpose of discrediting the statement or testimony of his accuser" (p. 167). It does not seem to have been argued that there was qualified privilege by virtue of the nature of the recipient of the complaint, rather than by virtue of self-defence (absolute privilege was rejected). However, malice was found.

Elections

An elector may warn fellow electors, in the same constituency, of what he believes to be information which would make a candidate unsuitable for office (*Wisdom v Brown* (England 1885)). At common law a candidate has the same privilege as any other citizen, and is protected by privilege if he communicated what he believed to be true about a rival candidate to the electors (*Braddock v Bevins* (England 1948); communication to the general public is a different matter however - *Templeman v Jones* (New Zealand 1984)). However, "the prevailing opinion in England was that Lord Greene had gone too far in *Braddock v Bevins*" (*ibid*. p. 457), and in that country, and in most jurisdictions where legislation modelled on the English 1952 Act applies, a candidate is deprived of qualified privilege for statements made by or on his behalf even if it is made to electors and even if made by an elector (see Appendix). In Lagos State in Nigeria (Defamation Law s. 12) the law covers local government and Parliamentary elections leaving State Assembly elections to be governed by the common law, a curious consequence of the legislation having been passed before Lagos State existed. The common law also still exists in jurisdictions which have no legislation based on the English 1952 Act, and in Kenya, where Members of the National Assembly resisted the change, one of them saying,

> I think this clause must go, this must go completely, and forever because we as politicians must have - we want to have - a larger latitude in expressing ourselves (quoted by Hodgin, 1973, p. 83).

Adjudicatory and Arbitral Bodies

Bodies which do not approximate sufficiently closely to courts, or to those which operate by virtue of contractual agreement rather than by law, such as arbitration, have qualified rather than absolute privilege (on which see Chapter 12).

Village Meetings and Associations

It is perhaps a little surprising that there are not more attempts to argue that some sort of privilege attaches to community meetings. In one Nigerian case the defendants had been told by a third party that the plaintiff had paid a native doctor to kill them. This they reported to a clan organisation in the town where they lived. The trial judge had held that this organisation was in a position to investigate and settle the matter, but the Court of Appeal said,

> If the respondents had reported the matter to the police, they would have been protected under the defence of qualified privilege because the latter has interest and or duty to investigate crime. It is my view that the respondents have no

> social or moral duty to communicate the slanderous words to members of the Nise Youth Organisation whose powers of sanction if any is not disclosed (*Amata v Enekwachi* (1986)).

This was perhaps a case which ought never to have got into the "English" court system at all, although its doing so may be attributable to the fact that the parties who were all Igbos were in Makurdi (not in Igboland).The trial judge was perhaps closer to realities than the members of the Court of Appeal. The police would probably have told the parties not to bother them with such matters, whereas there is some reason to believe that the meeting reached a more helpful outcome when the chairman suggested that the defendants had been duped by their informant. The ultimate reason the matter got to court was the refusal of the warring relatives to settle the matter peacefully.

On the other hand, in another "Igbo" case, the judge took a more "community-oriented" approach. He said that,

> all the age-grade societies[[1]] and youth leagues in the village have a common interest in the affairs of the village and of each other and usually attempt to settle any dispute in a society

and held that the communication to the societies was privileged (*Oforka v Anisiuba* (1979)). In yet another Nigerian case the judge held that a village meeting was privileged (it seems he was talking about qualified privilege), even if it could be said that the meeting constituted an illegal court (see *Agoaka v Ejiofor* (1971), and *Omenwa v Okonkwo* (1963)), having no power to try criminal cases. He insisted,

> [F)or in a native village society, it is traditional for the public at large to lay all social and moral questions, as a matter of duty, before the elders. This duty goes at times as high as allegations of theft, bribery and poisoning and practice of witchcraft. The elders hear all these questions and regard it as their social, moral and sacred duty to question into them for the health of the society and safety and freedom of the citizens (*Akubuike v Nwokoro* (1979) p. 569).

And in Tanzania a meeting called by the party leaders in a village to discuss issues of law and order was held to be the occasion of qualified privilege. The presence of non-party members did not destroy that privilege since the topic of the meeting was of concern to all villagers (*Novati Joseph v Sebastian Muzo* (1978). A more traditional Tanzanian village meeting has also been held to be the occasion of privilege: the headman called a meeting and asked the defendants whose cattle had been stolen whom they suspected and they named the plaintiffs. The court said that it was common practice for the government to ask the public for the name of suspected cattle thieves and the plaintiffs were lucky that the headman examined and exonerated them (*Yamo v Achieng* (1970)).

Excess of Privilege

"This reciprocity is essential," Lord Atkinson said (*Adam v Ward* (England 1917) p. 334). Thus in the earlier discussion it has almost always been necessary to say *to* whom the communication was made *and* by whom. Defences of qualified privilege have sometimes failed because statements were made to the wrong people. If only some recipients had no interest, it will be only for publication to them that the defendant will be liable, and the defendant is said to have "exceeded the privilege". In *Nyirenda v Kapiri* (Zambia 1985) publication to the Senior Labour Officer was excessive: because the requirement to inform the Officer of dismissal of employees had been removed (Employment (Special Provisions) Regulations SI 135 of 1975). There is an old Ugandan case in which the defendant had made his defamatory remark at dinner apparently in the hope that one of his guests would pass on the information to the affected plaintiff. The court, holding privilege applied, quite failed to discuss whether this roundabout way of communicating was necessary (*Dewhirst v Larkins* (1911)).

A complaint against a member of the House of Assembly, to the local authority, was not privileged because the authority had no interest or duty to deal with the matter (*Nwangwu v Nwankwo* (Nigeria 1962)). A litigant was held entitled to complain about a lawyer to the judiciary (see also the Mauritian case *Esnouf v Chauvot* (1962)) but not to the Inspector-General of Police (there being no allegation of a criminal offence) (*Aghahowa v Aguebor* above). And it was held that an allegation that the plaintiff intended to kill the defendant would have privilege if made to the Commissioner of Police, the Inspector-General of Police, the Attorney-General of the Federation, but not to the General Officer Commanding the 3rd. Infantry Division who could do nothing to remedy the complaint (*Eke v Oriji* (Nigeria 1976)). In *Tackyie v Kabbah* (Ghana 1956) a letter sent to three others than the addressee was excess of privilege. (See also *Malaŵi Railways Ltd. v Bhadurkhan* (1986)).

These cases seem to require a remarkable degree of sophistication on the part of members of the public about who has the power to inquire into or to discipline whom. As Mbanefo CJ said in *Nwangwo v Nwankwo* (above p. 98):

> The appellants are illiterates and unsophisticated people and can hardly be expected to appreciate the difference between what are and what are not part of the duty and function of the Council. And they probably do not appreciate they could take any complaint to anybody but to the Council. Unfortunately, a bona fide belief that the Council has the duty and interest to hear the complaint when in fact they have none does not make the occasion privileged.

A majority of the Irish Supreme Court recently held that there was authority to the effect that even an honest and reasonable belief that one was making a complaint to the right quarters did not give rise to privilege if objectively the quarters were the wrong ones (*Hynes-O'Sullivan v O'Driscoll* (1988) citing other Irish cases: *Reilly v Gill* (1951) and *Kirkwood Hackett v Tierney* (1952)). Interestingly, the court quoted Macnaghten LJ in the Privy Council approving a judge's direction to the jury to the effect that an honest but mistaken belief as to the proper authority would not deprive the defendant of privilege (*Jenoure v Delmège* (1891 from Jamaica)) "Perhaps it is to be explained as being as favourable as possible to the defendant in a defendant's appeal" (Gatley, para. 534n). But English authority seems to be to the contrary effect (*Hebditch v MacIlwaine* (1894) - though see *London Association for the Protection of Trade v Greenlands Ltd.* (1916) where it was held that a *bona fide* belief that a person making an inquiry about the plaintiff's credit had a legitimate interest was enough to give rise to privilege. Both were cited in *Hynes-O'Sullivan* at p. 355). And in a 1916 Ugandan case the judge said,

> The fact that a person making a complaint believes that the person to whom he addresses the complaint is the proper person to receive it, is, as a general rule, immaterial if, in fact, he was not so (*Bulchand Thadani v Wahid Ali Khan* p. 229 (Walker AJ);

There is no indication of what the significance of "as a general rule" might be. (Other African examples are *Farmer v Uganda Argus* (Uganda 1964) p. 578, *Atoyebi v Odudu* (Nigeria 1990) p. 399, *Amata v Enekwachi* (Nigeria 1984) p. 421 all citing *Hebditch v McIlwaine.*) The Ghanaian court in *Hassan v Kassardjan Construction Ltd.* (1964 above p. 174) seems to have been more generous.

A mistake of a different kind occurred in a Kenyan case in 1944: the defendants believed that the plaintiffs had kept incorrect records, and made a complaint to the District Commissioner. The court held that the occasion and the relationship which gave rise to the privilege was already in existence, and the privilege was not destroyed by the mistake (*Das Puri v Kenya Farmers' Association (Cooperative) Ltd.* citing *Davidson v Barclays Bank Ltd.* (England 1940)). It could hardly be otherwise, since mistakes of fact must give rise to many communications for which qualified privilege is then claimed.

It was excessive in a different sense to write to the Sikh community throughout Kenya, concerning a school in one town (*Singh v Singh* (1967)). A similar problem faces those who seek qualified privilege for publications in the press (see next chapter). Normally even a disclaimer notice published in a newspaper will not have privilege (see *Daily Nation v Mukundi* (Kenya 1975)); Nnaemeka-Agu said in a Nigerian case, "..he did not confine the publication of the defamatory matter to the professional colleagues of the appellant and the respondent and, perhaps, his client. He went ahead to publish to the whole world" (*Atoyebi v Odudu* (1990) p. 406). By way of contrast, in *Chimala Stores* (Tanzania 1970) Georges CJ pointed out that there was no evidence that anyone other than members of the Association and their agents visited the office where the offending letter was displayed.

Privilege may be exceeded by telling the recipient more than he has any interest in knowing. The Finance Officer, the Housing Officer and the Recruitment Officer of the University of Nairobi needed to know that the plaintiff's services with the University were being terminated; they did not need to know that it was because he was suspected of theft (*University of Nairobi v Mbuthia* (Kenya 1980)). A more flexible (maybe too flexible) approach was taken in an old Ugandan case: the angry defendant had complained that the plaintiff had been negligent when his true complaint was that his family had been wrongly charged for medical treatment; he was held to have privilege (*Bulchand Thadani v Wahid Ali Khan* above).

Is publication to a secretary or public letter writer in excess of privilege? If the communication to the ultimate recipient was privileged the communication to the defendant's secretary would have the same privilege (*Clarke v Nigerian Ports Authority* (Nigeria 1977); *Edmondson v Birch & Co.* (England 1907) (cited in *Saraki v Soleye* (Nigeria 1972)); *Osborn v Boulter* (England 1930); *Bryanston Finance v De Vries* (England 1975); *Boxius v Goblet Frères* (England 1894); *Aruna v George-Taylor* (Nigeria 1977).[2] The same would apply if the defendant could only write, or the plaintiff could only read, by using the services of a public letter writer; in *Aghahowa v Aguebor* (Nigeria 1957) the privilege attaching to the communication to the public letter writer was absolute; in *Na Kaura v*

Ikeawujo (Nigeria 1976) where the plaintiff could not read English, the inevitable publication to the letter writer had qualified privilege. (In this case the *only* publication to a third party was to the letter writer.) Otherwise a letter dictated to or written for a typist can be used as the basis for an action for defamation (*Bryanston Finance v De Vries*, Lord Denning MR dissenting). It was held, *obiter*, by a court in Kenya, that publication to the defendant's own secretary would, in effect, be privileged even if other publication of the letter was not, but this was an unusual, even unique, approach (*University of Nairobi v Mbuthia* (1979)).

Whether publication to the *recipient's* secretary or other people is privileged may depend on circumstances. In a Ugandan case when a copy of a defamatory but privileged letter was handed to the plaintiff's secretary without an envelope, it was held that this publication was not privileged (*Mwange v Kayiwe* (Uganda 1971)); the defendant should have taken reasonable steps to avoid the publication to the secretary. In *Saraki v Soleye* (above), privilege was not destroyed by the communication being read by people in the Nigerian Medical Council's office, for this was "in accordance with the reasonable and usual course of business". In an East African appeal it was held (*obiter* since it was also held the words were not defamatory) that sending a statement by telegram and not in code (although it would have been possible to use code) did not take the communication out of the protection of privilege if the use of the telegram was reasonable (*Heebels v Westerdijk* (Kenya 1950) citing *Williamson v Freer* (England 1874) and *Robinson v Jones* (Ireland 1879)). One would imagine that the gravity of the statement, the urgency of the situation and the extent to which the telegraph clerks would be able to understand it would be factors in deciding the reasonableness of the method of communication.

Oral statements may raise their own problems. A Nigerian court held that the fact that a third party was accidentally present when the defendant made a complaint against the plaintiff to the police did not necessarily take away the privilege. It observed, *obiter*, that if the accuser raised his voice or knowingly made his allegations in the presence of a third party the judge could leave it to the jury (!) to decide whether this indicated malice (*Anyamele v Ihenacho* (1979); see also, e.g. *Toogood v Spyring* (England 1834)).

The court in an old Gold Coast case seems to have confused excess of privilege and malice, and said that making a communication to those without the requisite interest or duty shows malice. The result is no different, although there might be differences in terms of burden of proof. The court went on to make some interesting remarks about the meeting at which the words were said:

> In this colony it is the custom for a chief never to speak or allow himself to be spoken to on topics affecting him and his people except in the presence of his elders and councillors. And I understand that very often a considerable body of his less important subjects attend all public meetings in the result of which he is interested whether as accuser or accused. This being the custom, I am unable to hold that the presence of the followers ...is evidence of any ill-will on the part of the defendant (*Doryume v Awah II* (1913) p. 791).

It would have been preferable in analytical terms to rest the decision on the interest of the community, which the judge also thought existed, rather than on the malice approach, but the result certainly seems satisfactory, and in effect extends to traditional forms of government some degree of the protection enjoyed by the imported organs of legislation and adjudication.

Other Systems

There are relatively few "qualified privilege" cases in Mauritius. There are a few older cases in which the courts behaved as though English law were applicable (e.g. *Drieu v Amode* (1881) where the plaintiff was a railway clerk, accused by the defendant trader, when asked by an audit clerk of the railways why he ceased to use the railway, of taking bribes; and *Cordouan v Jardin* (1884) p. 43 - response to attack). However, it is now clear that one route to deciding whether a statement is made with fault is by inquiring whether it constitutes an offence (see Chapter 4). Under the Penal Code there are certain defences, coming immediately from the Indian Penal Code, but ultimately derived from English law, which resemble certain types of qualified privilege. These include the good faith censure of one person by another who is in authority over him; or in good faith to prefer an accusation to those in authority; or an imputation in good faith for the protection of the person making the imputation, or the public good; or to "convey a caution" for the good of the recipient of the caution, or of some person in whom the latter "is interested", or of the public (art. 288 exceptions h-j).

Are these provisos effective to remove civil liability, as they are to remove criminal? It has been held in a number of cases that where defamation takes a form "contemplated by the Penal Code the defences open to a party by virtue of the provisos to the section are competent defences to a civil action in damages" (*Roy v Bhookun* (1956) p. 121, citing *Cordouan v Jardin* (1883), *Le Cernéen v Laurent* (1901), *Laurent v Brebner* (1907)). In one case it was held that the art. 288 provisos do apply to civil cases, but that proviso (i) - imputation as to *character* made in self defence - cannot cover allegations of negligence, carelessness or ignorance in a doctor, for these went much further than an attack on character (*Laurent v Brebner*). But there is also a line of authority to the effect that the art. 288 provisos have no impact on civil liability, which derives some of its force from the fact that art. 290 (the "absolute privilege" provision) explicitly mentions both civil and criminal liability (*Forget v La Presse Mauricienne* (1958) p. 250). However, this is not quite the view taken in the case of *Lesage v Mason* where the court held the defences could be relied upon in a civil case if the plaintiff himself relied upon the Criminal Code to establish *prima facie* liability (p. 172).

It is clear that the art. 288 provisos were never intended as a statement of defences in civil cases, and to the extent that they do not one must look at French law. It has been said that there is no general principle analogous to that underlying qualified privilege in French law (*Forget v Presse Mauricienne,* p. 252). There is, however, the defence of "good faith" (see p. 137 above). And:

> ...an action for damages may lie under the provisions of Article 1382 *et seq.* of the Code Napoléon in respect of a defamatory statement, notwithstanding that the communication was made *bona fide* if, in fact its contents were untrue and made recklessly, negligently or imprudently (*Hanning v Curé,* p.7).

(Tracey Watts J seemed to think this state of affairs required legislative attention.) "Recklessness, negligence and imprudence" here refer to art. 1383. So, if a statement is defamatory any defence (whether it be an art. 288 proviso, assuming such is effective as a defence, or good faith) will itself be defeated if recklesness, negligence or imprudence is shown (e.g. *Mancini v Desvaux* (1908); the case also seems to suggest that if art. 1383 of the Civil Code is relied upon *ab initio*, no question of the Penal Code defences can arise). In *D'Avoine v Ozoux* (1897) there was held to be no liability since the defendant had acted upon reasonable evidence when he passed on a statement to the owner of the sugar estate at which the plaintiff was an overseer (and the defendant the manager), which led to the plaintiff's dismissal. The defendant had shown "proper discretion" in passing it on and there was no *faute* or imprudence. This would seem to suggest no breach of art. 1383 (the summary is very brief). Proof of actual malice is, of course, destructive of any claim of good faith.

Few cases have referred to French law in this context, however. One is *Rault v Cownie* (1958) which referred to the defence to an action of "slander" "to express one's thought in a certain circle according to the circumstances of time and place",[3] and more particularly in this case to the right to give information on another. In the latter case, however, it was clear that liability might attach if care was not taken in giving the information, and the greater the prejudice that might be caused, the greater the care that should be taken in verifying the facts (p. 307), a view which corresponds to the impression of Tracey Watts J quoted above.

There have also been Mauritian cases which appear to rely on French law, and involve defence to attack as a form of privilege (e.g. *Laurent v Issac* (1915)) In *Morel v Rivet* (1931) this was rejected, on the basis that the plaintiff's own words had criticised the defendant's political party, but could not be considered an attack on the defendant, and also that the defendant's response was irrelevant to the criticisms. Provocation is more likely to reduce damages than eliminate liability (see Chapter 19).

Roman-Dutch law seems fundamentally similar in effect to the common law (e.g. *Vincent v Long* (South Africa 1988, p. 47), quoted by Boberg (1989, p. 61)), although the precise implications of the requirement of *animus injuriandi* - the intention to injure - have occasioned a good deal of controversy (*ibid.*).

Side-stepping the Defence

The House of Lords held that a person writing a reference can be liable in negligence (*Spring v Guardian Assurance plc* (1993) reversing the Court of Appeal which had agreed with *Bell-Booth Group Ltd. v AG* (New Zealand 1989)). One effect of this is to avoid the effect of qualified privilege.

Notes

1. For an account of an age-set system see Nsugbe (1974) Chap. IV p. 58ff.
2. This case has a curious history: it originally reached trial in 1974 when there was no defence argued since the defendant's lawyer had withdrawn from the case because he "could not find his client".
3. "*d'exprimer sa pensée dans un certain cercle selon les circonstances de temps et de lieu*" from Savatier Vol. 1. The case quotes Savatier notes 86 and 88.

14 Defences for the Press I: Statutes and Privilege

African judges seem to have little enthusiasm for the press, and have frequently emphasised that the press has no special rights (e.g. *Shamuyarira v Zimbabwe Newspapers (1980) Ltd.* (1994)); in this they are very much in the English tradition (e.g. *Blackshaw v Lord* (1980)). There are a few situations in which the press has some special protection, even at common law, and there are some defences under statute which are applicable only to the press (and other forms of news media). Before discussing these, however, there are two statutory, limited exemptions given by statute to the press from the usual rules to the effect that absence of knowledge that one was defaming the plaintiff is no defence.

Lord Campbell's Act

The Libel Act 1843 is a statute of general application in force in jurisdictions which have received English statutory law at that date, and not abrogated it (it is assumed to be applicable in Nigeria: *Edukugho v Sunday Times* (1958)). It provides in section 2 (see Appendix) a defence for newspapers and periodicals (which are not defined) that can establish that they were innocent and non-negligent.

The defendant must, when he files a statement of defence which incorporates this plea, pay a sum of money into court by way of amends (a requirement, as opposed to an option to pay into court, was added by the Libel Act 1845 s. 2). If the plaintiff wishes he may take this money out in full satisfaction of his claim (*Bell v Northern Constitution Ltd.* (Northern Ireland 1943)). (Rules of court will deal with taking out money paid into court. In Nigeria see, for example, Order 18 r. 2 (Bendel, Ondo etc.); (Aguda 1980a paras. 27.14, 27.15, 27.41)). If he chooses not to do so and the matter comes to trial, the defendant must prove (i) that the libel was inserted without (a) actual malice or (b) gross negligence (for a non-African example, see *Bell v Northern Constitution Ltd.* (above)) and (ii) that either before the action or at the earliest opportunity after the action was started he inserted a "full apology" (on which see *Lafone v Smith* (England 1858); if the newspaper appears less frequently than once a week the plaintiff may choose in which publication the apology is to appear); and he must plead the payment in, which will therefore be known to the court.[1]

The English statutory provisions have been copied in most of the African legislation,[2] although it also provides a new defence (next discussed) which is less demanding. If the defendant fails in his defence under s. 2 (or equivalent), but the amount awarded to the plaintiff is no more than the sum the defendant paid into court, the defendant may have to pay *all* the costs of the action (*Oxley v Wilkes* (England 1898)), contrary to the usual rule on payment into court: if the plaintiff is awarded no more than the amount paid in the plaintiff must pay the defendant's costs *from the date of the payment in*. If the defendant wins on the s. 2 issue he gets judgment and his costs but the plaintiff still gets something - either the whole sum paid into court (*Dunn v Devon (No. 2)* (England 1895)), or only the amount awarded as damages (up to a maximum of the sum paid into court) (*Gray v Bartholomew* (England 1895) (*obiter*), *Veale v Reid* (England 1904)); Gatley seems to prefer the former (paras. 837-5). It may be wiser for a defendant whose only defence is absence of malice and negligence, to pay a sum into court under the usual rules. Certainly, for these various reasons, the Lord Campbell's Act defence is extinct in England (Gatley, para. 876).

In fact it does not seem to be relied on in Africa either. A defence based on s. 2 was struck out because the defence had not pleaded the payment into court in one case; however, the judge said he would have found the defendants liable anyway, because they were negligent - the statement was clearly libellous and the defendants should have taken steps to find out if it was based on facts (*Edukugho* above).

Under s. 1 of the same Act an apology may be used in mitigation of damages (see, for example, *Edukugho* but the apology there had lost a lot of its value through delay).

"Unintentional Defamation" Under the Modern Legislation

The English 1952 Act s. 4 (see Appendix) provided a defence which has been copied in the legislation of those African jurisdictions which have "1952 model" legislation. In *The Nation Newspapers v Chesire* (1984) the court observed that the defendant had not made use of the defence under the Kenyan legislation (either section 12 - the Lord Campbell's Act defence - or s. 13 - unintentional defamation). The defence is not restricted in its terms to the press, but has its main potential use in that context.

A person who wishes to make use of this defence must first make an offer of "amends" - an offer to publish a "suitable correction" and a "sufficient apology," taking reasonable steps to bring this to the attention of those who would have read or heard the original statement. This offer must be made as soon as practicable after the defendant realises the words may be defamatory, the defendant must make it clear that this is indeed an offer under this legislation and the offer must be accompanied with an affidavit showing all the facts on which the defendant is relying as establishing that his publication was innocent (s. 6 English Act).

The "person aggrieved" (plaintiff if the action has started) may at this point accept this offer and the parties will try to agree on the correction, apology and how it is to be publicised. If they cannot agree the matter will be referred to the court whose decision will be final. The court can then order the defendant to pay costs to the plaintiff, and also to pay any expenses arising from the publication (s. 6(4)).

But the plaintiff may choose not to accept the offer, and sue. The defendant will have a defence if he can establish that he made the offer of amends as prescribed by the statute, and secondly that he published the original statement "innocently" (s. 6(1) (b). In establishing this innocence the defendant may not go beyond the facts he stated in the affidavit accompanying his offer of amends (s. 6(2)). "Innocently" means (s. 6(5)):

> *either* the publisher did not intend the words to refer to the plaintiff and did not know of any circumstances (i.e. true innuendo) by virtue of which the words might be considered to apply to the plaintiff
> *or* the words were not defamatory on their face and the defendant did not know of any circumstances (again a true innuendo) which might make them defamatory.

Finally the defendant must show he was not negligent (if the defendant is not the author he must show that the original author was without malice - s. 6 (6). Gatley (para. 838n.) suggests that "malice" here cannot have the usual meaning of misuse of the occasion and must have the more "popular" meaning of intention to injure the plaintiff). If the defendant fails to establish any one of these elements (see *Ross v Hopkinson* (England 1956)) he loses his case and damages will be awarded in the usual way (his apology if any will become relevant to damages). If the defendant proves all the elements, he is entitled to judgment.

Kneller JA (*The Nation Newspapers v Chesire*, p. 21) commented that the burden on the defendant under these sections was a heavy one, while the Faulks Committee in England said (para. 281):

(a) The procedure required involves too much expensive rigmarole, in particular the need to collect the evidence and incorporate it in an affidavit which must be served with the offer of amends. This process has numerous grave disadvantages:-
   (i) it is laborious, time-consuming and expensive;
   (ii) the publisher is in a grave dilemma; if he omits to collect all available evidence, he cannot use any evidence subsequently obtained; if he leaves no stone unturned, he may be held not to have made the offer as soon as practicable.

(b) The burden placed on the publisher, if he is not the author, to establish positively that the author wrote the words without malice is exceedingly onerous, and might be quite impossible (e.g. in the case of an anonymous letter).

The Press and Privilege

Resort to the press is a temptation into which many aggrieved people have fallen, and often leads to the court holding that privilege has been exceeded, as a Mauritian club which had excluded the plaintiff found - press publication was held to be "*publicité excessive*" (*Bouvet v Mauritius Turf Club* (1963)).

Newspapers which have argued for some general privilege arising from a duty to inform the public have usually received short shrift from the courts. Lord Shaw's observation: "The freedom of the journalist is an ordinary part of the freedom of the subject, and to whatever lengths the subject in general may go, so also may the journalist (*Arnold v King Emperor* (India PC 1914)) was quoted in a 1933 Mauritian case (*Daurat v Le Cerneen* (1933) p. 17; see also another Mauritian case, *Wright v L'Homme* (1868)). The 1933 court observed that French law is to similar effect (p. 18, quoting Fabreguettes, *Traité des délits politiques and des infractions par les parole, l'écriture et la presse*, (Treatise on political delicts and infractions of the law by speech, writing and the press) "*Le journaliste est responsable de ses paroles et actes aux mêmes titre et degré que toute autre personne, ni plus ni moins*" (the journalist is responsible for his words and deeds in the same way and to the same degree as everyone else, no more no less).)

A Nigerian judge dismissed the argument that the newspapers have a moral and social duty to publish items about events such as the turbanning of a chief and should be protected in the absence of malice as "balderdash"

(*Bulus v Suleiman* (1982)). Nor could a Zambian newspaper claim privilege for reports of alleged corruption (*Eastern Province Co-operative Marketing Association Ltd. v Zambia Publishing Co. Ltd.* (1970)). A Nigerian judge rejected an argument to the effect that public figures should have thick skins (*Enahoro v Association Newspapers* (1960)); and a Tanzanian defendant who said "I...thought it advisable to write this story regarding the threatened strike with the hope that if the story is read by higher authority, they could take some action to avert the strike" received an ironic response from the judge at first instance: "..they cannot say that they addressed this article to those authorities alone when their paper is read by all and sundry all over East Africa and the world. What was the public supposed to do after reading the story, march in a procession to prevent the strike?" (*Eyakuze v Editor of Sunday News* (1974) p. 200)). Far from supporting a special privilege, one Nigerian judge suggested restricting the protection of the press:

> I must suggest that the defence of qualified privilege is due for review. It is high time the law treated every defamatory publication in a newspaper, magazine, radio and television in this country as carrying with it a presumption of express malice: it will no longer be for the plaintiff to plead and prove malice in fact; instead the defence of qualified privilege must carry with it the burden to satisfy the court that the publication was not actuated by express malice, which of course includes improper motive or partisan fanaticism (Obi-Okoye CJ in *Bulus v Suleiman* above).

Rare examples of judges sympathetic to newspapers' claims of qualified privilege, are in Zambia, where the plaintiff was the manager of a state-owned bus company, and the judge observed,

> The management of UBZ affected no doubt the vast majority of the population in their daily lives, indeed in the conduct of their business. As I see it, not alone were the public interested in the contents of the article but it was in their interests that they be apprised of the widespread complaints of others and of the arrogance and indifference of the principal officer of the company (*Mwanza v Zambia Publishing Co. Ltd.* (1981))

and Nigeria:

> The defendants making the publication here are media organisation(s), the publisher and printer of the weekly newspaper the "Sunday Sketch". They have a duty and interest to inform the general public and the people receiving are the general public....The whole publication shows that the content is of

> public interest against the background of cultural or Economic Revolution that responded to the present economic recession or crunch. A traditional ceremony causing 27,49 [*sic*] Jets to land in a town in 2 successive days, and where cows, horses, expensive cars and large amounts of money were freely given away should interest the general public about the "Rich and their Pleasures during these Austere Times" (*Union Bank Ltd. v Oredein* (1987) (*obiter*)).

And the Court of Appeal, over Ayoola JCA's energetic dissent, held in *Nigerian Television Authority v Babatope* (1996) that there was qualified privilege for a television broadcast about alleged corruption in a political party. These cases are unusual, to say the least.

But it has been in Tanzania that the courts have recognised the widest qualified privilege for the press: privilege was held to attach to a newspaper report alleging tribalism and corruption in the publicly owned Tanzania Zambia Road Services (*Maskini v Mbugus* (1975)); Law JA, dissenting, said that there was no privilege, partly because the defendant knew that the labour troubles which were highlighted in the article had been settled. Privilege was held to attach to articles in Party newspapers about the removal of the plaintiff from a Party position. The judge said, "Obviously other Party members had an interest in receiving the communication and the paper had a like interest and duty in fact of making the communication" (*Heri Idd Ngungu v Editor of Uhuru/Mzalendo* (1979)); however, non-Party people apparently read these papers. There seems some risk of giving Party newspapers a privileged position denied to other papers; a particularly questionable approach to take where the party is the ruling party, and even more so in a one party state as Tanzania was at the time. But in *Saba v Tanganyika Standard* (1979) about an article accusing the Personnel Manager of a Public Corporation of irresponsibility and sexual harassment, the defence failed.

Sometimes accurate reports of government statement have been held to attract privilege; it was said of a Government release in Uganda,

> It was an important public announcement and although the respondent newspaper was under no physical obligation to print any Government or Ministry announcement, it was under a strong moral obligation to do so as the newspaper was a medium of mass information for the public of Uganda and the Government of Uganda relied on this newspaper for the propagation of its policies and public announcements (*Shah v Uganda Argus* (1972)).

It has been emphasised that this only applies where the public interest requires the publication to be made (Gatley, para. 562 quoting *London Artists v Littler* (England 1968) p. 619)). This presumably requires the court to do more than simply accept that the government thinks it is important, but it still gives to the media which are controlled by government and which are happy to report little else than government news a privilege not enjoyed by those media trying to place before the public an alternative view. However, it should also be pointed out that in many jurisdictions, of which Uganda is not one, there is statutory protection for accurate reports of government statements (see below).

Much more usually the press has been denied reliance on qualified privilege, even if statutory, as the Nigerian Broadcasting Corporation was unsuccessful in arguing that being established by statute to broadcast gave it a special privilege (*Mukete v NBC* (1961)). The same *Uganda Argus* that was protected when it published a government statement had no such benefit when it published a report alleging that the Attorney General had instructed the constitutionally independent DPP to stop a prosecution (*Farmer v Uganda Argus* (1964)). The Chief Justice held that this matter was of interest to only a small section of Baganda society - a remarkable conclusion based on the evidence of the reporter himself.

The press will be protected by the privilege of the author of an item who is, for example, defending himself legitimately before the public at large (see *Adam v Ward* (England 1917); *Shah v Uganda Argus* (1972)), but a newspaper might lose that privilege by its own malice even if the author had none (which follows from *Egger v Chelmsford* (England 1965)). With respect the East African Court of Appeal was wrong in *Daily Nation v Mukundi* (Kenya 1975) p. 316 to suggest that a newspaper could not have derivative privilege.

However, there are certain situations in which the press has a degree of protection which is specifically granted to it, or which, in the nature of things, can only be taken advantage of by the press, which are now discussed.

Privilege of Reports at Common Law

At common law there is a qualified privilege which applies to reports of proceedings in legislative houses (and their committees) (*Wason v Walter* (England 1868)) and proceedings in court (*Kimber v Press Association* (England 1893) cited in, e.g. *Lardner v Sketch* (Nigeria 1979), and *Khembo v Blantyre Print & Packaging Co. Ltd.* (Malaŵi 1980), though this case does not make it clear whether the basis of the privilege was common law or statute). (In *Kayondo v New Vision Printing and Pub. Corpn.* (Uganda 1990-91), the judge talks in terms appropriate to qualified privilege (p. 98) and of absolute privilege (p. 99); the latter is clearly wrong.) The public are permitted to attend court proceedings; newspaper reports simply provide information to those who are unable to attend. So if the proceedings were held *in camera* no privilege attaches to the report (*Kimber* above, see also *Furniss v Cambridge News Ltd.* (England 1907) (Barnes P) "The privilege given to reports of proceedings in court is based upon this, that as everyone cannot be in court, it is for the public benefit that they should be informed of what takes place substantially as if they were present" (quoted in *Lardner v Sketch*, above, p. 281)). The privilege is not restricted to the press.

The report need not be contemporaneous (*Wason v Walter*, above, p. 95; the judge in *Kayondo v New Visions*, above, was wrong on this point), but it must be accurate. A report will not be fair if one or two passages are picked out rather than a picture of the whole proceedings being given (see the summary of the law by Abott J in *Oweh v Amalgamated Press of Nigeria Ltd.* (1957)). Reports of court proceedings, too, may be abridged but must not give an inaccurate impression of what occurred (*Omo-Osagie v Okutubo* (Nigeria 1969); *Ajao v Sketch Publishing Co. Ltd.* (Nigeria 1978) citing *Hope v Leng Ltd.* (England 1907)). A Ugandan court was prepared to overlook some inaccuracies which it attributed to the carelessness and poor English of the reporter and the paper's somewhat sensational style, but added nothing to what was actually said; an example was "fictitious" instead of "vexatious" (*Kayondo v New Vision*).

A report of foreign legal proceedings will also have qualified privilege, but only if local readers would have a legitimate interest, as concerning a citizen of the country in which the publication is made perhaps, or throwing light on the administration of justice in that country (e.g. *Webb v Times Publishing Co. Ltd.* (England 1960)). It is assumed that a similar principle would apply to reports of debates in a foreign legislature. Poulter (1970, p. 137n) points out that in South Africa the reports of foreign legislatures did not have privilege (*Benson v Robinson & Co. (Pty) Ltd.* (1967)). However, there was no special South African interest in this case. Poulter suggests that "it is more in accord with Lesotho's constitutional guarantee of free speech that such reports should be protected". The Zambian Law Development Commission (1984, p. 7) proposed that reports of proceedings in foreign courts and legislatures should have a blanket statutory qualified privilege. The English 1996 Act s. 15 and Schedule 1 grants the same privilege to reports of legislative proceedings as to those of foreign courts.

How much further the protection extends is unclear. The bodies must be such that it is in the public interest that there be publicity for the proceedings (*Perera v Peiris* (Privy Council 1949)) and must be open to the public (*Wason v Walter* above, cited in, e.g. *Ajao v Sketch* (Nigeria 1978)). It has been extended in the Nigerian context to tribunals of inquiry (e.g. *Ijeh v Daily Times of Nigeria* (1972) - newspaper report of evidence to Tribunal of Inquiry into Activities of Trades Unions (under the Tribunals of Inquiry Decree); also *Ajao v Sketch* above). The privilege has been applied to reports of coroners' courts and the UK General Medical Council (*Lynam v Gowing* (Ireland 1860), *Allbut v General Council of Medical Education and Registration* (England 1889)).

This common law privilege has been relied upon in a number of African cases - more often than not without success, usually because of inaccurate or incomplete reporting. In *Oweh v Amalgamated Press of Nigeria Ltd* (above) the judge said:

> Nowhere in his speech did Mr. Otobo say, as alleged in the opening sentence of the words complained of, that the plaintiff "is one of the N.C.N.C. crooks referred to by Dr. Azikiwe". Finally, on this point, the publication was not even "of a single speech" - but only a garbled version of that part of a single speech which impugned the plaintiff's character.

In *Eyo v Eastern Nigeria Information Service* (1963) the report accurately summarised evidence on a point but went on to say that the judge had said he believed it. This was not true, and though "Not every inaccuracy destroys the privilege; if the report is on the whole fair and accurate, a small error on a point that is not very material would not affect it"(p. 145), this error went beyond that. Inaccurate reporting defeated the privilege for a newspaper even though its report of a trial had been based on a Bulletin put out for the press by the Police Public Relations Department (*Igbongidi v Midwest Mass Communication Corporation* (Nigeria 1976)),[3] and where the report had said the plaintiff was to be "detained for questioning", while the Chief Magistrate had actually said he and others would be "handed over" to the police *Bello (Haroun) v Oyebola* (Nigeria 1977). Since the ordinary person might well think "handing over" involved some deprivation of liberty, this shows that the press are unwise to use their own words in reporting court cases.

On the other hand, in *Ijeh v Daily Times* (above) the gist of the original statement, in evidence to a Tribunal of Inquiry, was that the plaintiff had used his position as a member of a United Labour Congress delegation to the United States to obtain a personal gift. The purpose of the gift as alleged by the witness had been for the plaintiff's "sister", but the newspaper said for his "girlfriend". Ayoola J (citing *Hope v Leng*, above) said

> The test in my view, is whether the discrepancy gives a substantially different impression of what transpired at the proceedings to the detriment of the plaintiff. In short, the discrepancy must be such that its existence gives the report a defamatory imputation; that if it had not been made, its absence would have made an appreciable difference to the position of the plaintiff.

Privilege extends to extracts of registers which legislation requires to be kept, such as registers of court judgments or of bills of sale; publication of copies or extracts, provided they are fair and accurate, assist in the objective of informing the public. The privilege is not lost by virtue of the fact that publication is for profit; leading cases are *Fleming v Newton* (England 1848), and *Searles v Scarlett* (England 1892). In the Malaŵian case of *Madumuse v Press Furniture and Joinery Co.* (1984) Skinner CJ said that the facts before him were not covered by these cases (the information was not a copy of a register).

Privilege has been denied to reports of documents initiating legal proceedings which are not public documents, such as the statement of claim (*Lardner v Sketch Publishing Co.* (Nigeria 1979)), the First Information Report beginning a prosecution under the Nigerian Criminal Procedure Code, (*Bello (Mustapha) v Oyebola* (1974)) or the writ (*Daily Times of Nigeria Ltd. v Williams* (1986)). The Court of Appeal in Nigeria in the last named case regretted that it was bound by the reception legislation to apply the common law *of England* as it preferred that of the United States in which reports of the pleadings are privileged - namely *Campbell v New York Post* (1925).

Absolute Privilege for Reports of Proceedings

"A fair and accurate report in any newspaper of proceedings publicly heard before any court exercising judicial authority shall, if published contemporaneously with such proceedings, be privileged" (English Law of Libel (Amendment) Act of 1888, s. 3); a newspaper is printed at intervals of not less than 26 days (see Newspaper Libel and Registration Act 1881 s. 1 referred to in s. 1 Law of Libel Amendment Act 1888). Presumably this applies as a statute of general application in African jurisdictions which have not copied the English legislation; in *Ogbuatu v Daily Times of Nigeria Ltd.* (1976) the judge said the pleadings raised section 3 of this Act, though he went on to hold that the report was not accurate; this case was from Kano which does not have the 1952 English model legislation. In *Ikoku v Zik's Press* (Nigeria 1950) s. 4 of the same Act was referred to. Although the section does not specify, it has been taken in England to confer *absolute* rather than merely qualified privilege (*Farmer v Hyde* (1937), *McCarey v Associated Newspapers* (1964)).

The Zambian Act (relied on in *Mumba v Zambia Publishing Co.* (1982) and *Hodges v Times Newspapers Zambia Ltd.* (1979)), the Sierra Leone and Kenyan Acts and the Laws of Eda, Delta, Ogun, Oshun, Ondo and Oyo States in Nigeria, picking up the English decisions, say that *absolute* privilege is to apply. The rest of the Laws in Nigeria simply, like the English Act, say "privileged"; one would imagine courts would follow the English authorities and hold the reports to have absolute privilege. However, in one Nigerian case the Court of Appeal seems to have thought that it conferred qualified privilege only, and was effectively the same as the common law (*Daily Times Nigeria Ltd. v Williams* (1986)); Ademola and Kolawole JJCA decided on the basis of the common law while Nnaemeka-Agu JCA relied upon the statute and held that it coincided with, and therefore excluded, the common law rule (p. 544); Ademola JCA also referred to "qualified privilege" in the same breath as s. 10 of the Lagos statute (p. 538). The African legislation follows the English lead and restricts the privilege to reports of courts within the country, except for that of Lagos which rather remarkably refers to proceedings in Lagos. Thus in Lagos there is statutory (probably absolute) privilege for reports of proceedings in Lagos, statutory qualified privilege for reports of proceedings elsewhere in the Commonwealth (see below), and only common law (qualified) privilege for those of proceedings in Nigeria outside Lagos! Hodgin (1973, p. 79) says that arguments in Kenya to the effect that courts in East Africa ought to be covered in view of the existence (at the time) of the East African Community and of the East African Court of Appeal were not accepted.

Most of the pieces of legislation require the publication to be "contemporaneous", though the Kenyan Act omits this word. According to Gatley (para. 633) there is no English decision on the meaning of "contemporaneous". He suggests it should be taken to mean "as nearly at the same time as the proceedings as is reasonably possible, having regard to the opportunities for preparation of the report and the time of going to press or making the broadcast".

The 1888 English Act applies only to newspapers, as do the Zambian and Kenyan Acts, but the Nigerian and Sierra Leone legislation, like the English 1952 Act s. 9, extends this statutory privilege to broadcasting. The definition of "newspaper" has also been changed. In Kenya, Zambia and Lagos it is a news (or advertisement) publication, published at intervals of not more than 36 days. In Sierra Leone, and the Delta/Ogun model legislation in Nigeria no time limit at all is prescribed. In Abia model statutes the interval is three months. In each of these countries - Kenya, Nigeria, Sierra Leone and Zambia - the protection is given to newspapers published within the country only, so a foreign newspaper report, even of a local case, would not be absolutely privileged.

There are only a few cases clearly relying on any of these provisions. In *Omo-Bare v Odukomaiye* (Nigeria 1973) the judge mentioned the Act, but seems to have held that it applied to a report of proceedings in Ibadan which, as this was a Lagos case, would clearly be wrong. On the other hand he also mentioned *Kimber v Press Association* (above) on common law privilege, and held the report to have *qualified* privilege (see also *Omo-Osagie v Okutubo* (Nigeria 1969)). A Ugandan court also held privilege to apply without, apparently, making it clear whether it was absolute or qualified, and what the basis for the privilege was *(Kalungi v Munno Publications* (1971)). Only the English 1888 Act could have provided a statutory basis. In Zambia it was unsuccessfully argued that a court attempting reconciliation between the parties was not a "court" for the purposes of this legislation (*Hodges v Times* (1979), citing *Kimber v Press Association*). In Nigeria a court held the protection unavailable because the paper had coloured the account of what was said in court, stating that the plaintiff had been detained, whereas in court it was said that a subpoena had been served on him and he was *rumoured* to have been detained (*Adewusi v Sketch Publications* (1978) [No. 2]; the case being reported was itself a defamation case: *Tarka v Sketch Publishing Co. Ltd* (1978)). The Kenyan provision was applied in *Gautama v East African Newspapers (Nation Series)* (1971). The court said that in judging the fairness and accuracy of the report the court should look at the whole ruling and the background (see Spry, 1976, pp. 32-3).

Statutory Protection for Reports of Proceedings of Legislatures

Section 3 of the English Parliamentary Papers Act of 1840 provides a qualified privilege for any publication of an extract from or abstract of any proceedings of a legislature or any parliamentary report or paper or note provided it is extracted or abstracted from a publication by or under the authority of the legislative house (for absolute privilege for official reports of proceedings see Chapter 12). This provision appears in the various pieces of legislation in Africa, which may also cover broadcasting (Legislative

House Act (Federal and Lagos) s. 27, Anambra, Imo, Cross River and Rivers Laws s. 47, Bendel, Ogun, Oyo and Ondo Laws s. 21 and remaining States s. 18 Defamation Act of Zambia s. 16, Kenyan Act s. 11). The protection only applies if the publication was in good faith and without malice (*Mangena v Wright* (England 1909)). This defence was rejected in *Enahoro v Associated Newspapers* (Nigeria 1960) because the report was grossly inaccurate, indeed reckless, and could not therefore be *bona fide*.

Other Reports Privileged Under Statute

The English Law of Libel Amendment Act 1888 s.4, which would apply, where appropriate as a "statute of general application" (it was presumed to be applicable in Nigeria in *Ikoku v Zik's Press* (1950)), gives protection to certain reports, a privilege which is lost if the plaintiff can show that the defendant was asked to insert in the newspaper "a reasonable letter or statement by way of contradiction or explanation of such report or other publication, and has refused or neglected to insert the same" (this proviso was not satisfied in *Ikoku*). The reports covered are those of public meetings and of various local government bodies, school boards, select committees of the legislature; the section also covers the publication of notices or reports issued by government departments and the police, at the request of the body issuing the statement (see Appendix). Only fair and accurate reports are privileged, and the privilege will be lost if malice exists.

In the jurisdictions with "modern" Defamation Acts or Laws a fundamentally similar provision applies (based on ss. 7 and 16 and the Schedule of the 1952 English Act). It differs in some major respects: there are now two distinct lists of bodies; one is of bodies the reports of which are privileged without any provision about requests for explanation or contradiction. The other is of bodies the reports of which lose privilege if the plaintiff requested the defendant to publish a statement by way of explanation or contradiction and he refused to do so (that is similar to the 1888 provision). In England under the 1952 Act the first list contains reports of courts, legislatures, public inquiries and courts-martial in the Commonwealth,[4] of international bodies and conferences, with the addition of registers required to be open to the public in the UK, and notices published on the authority of UK courts; and the second list corresponds to the 1888 list with the addition of various bodies for the advancement of religion or learning, trade, sport and so on, and of the general meeting of a public company. (In fact, although not specifically mentioned in the 1888 Act, companies are covered - see *Ponsford v Financial Times Ltd*. (England

1900)). However, to take one example, the Sierra Leone statute rather surprisingly includes in the first list the legislature of Sierra Leone - but not of other legislatures, public inquiries within Sierra Leone but not elsewhere, as well as registers required to be open to the public. Each individual statute must be perused to see what bodies are covered.[5]

A further difference is that protection under the modern legislation extends to broadcasts. And a requirement in the 1888 Statute that notices from government departments, the police etc. should be published *at their request* has disappeared. The privilege is in addition to, and not in derogation from, any common law privilege.

There have been several Nigerian cases: a summary of a news bulletin issued by a Ministry of Information was protected (*Akurefe v Sketch* (1971)). The judge explained (p. 17) that "the report may be condensed but not coloured or unfair as a result of its omissions or abridgement. It need not be a complete report, provided it presents to the reader an accurate picture" (see also *Kimber v Press Association* (above), *Cook v Alexander* (England 1974)). The defence applied to material derived from an Army Public Relations Directorate statement; the Supreme Court rejected the argument that the army was not a department of government (*Din v African Newspapers of Nigeria Ltd.* (1990)). The section (9 of the Lagos Law) was applied in *Guobadia v Bendel Newspapers Corp.* (1980), and in *Eda v Bendel Newspaper Corporation* (1982) (s. 12 Bendel State Defamation Law), for a Police public relations handout. The defence was rejected in *Anunobi v Nigerian National Press* (1964) because the "report" was just a news item, and in *NTA v Babatope* (1996) on the ground that "public meeting" does not include a press conference. A claim for statutory privilege for a notice (the Police Crime Diary) issued by the police failed because there was no evidence that it was issued for public information (*Oloyede v Sketch Publishing Co. Ltd.* (Nigeria 1977)), and also because the summary was not fair and accurate: the paper said the plaintiff had been invited for questioning whereas the original document said the police had received a petition making allegations. Another claim failed because, although the information had emanated from the police, publication was not made on the authority of a *superior* police officer, as required by s. 10 and the schedule to the Defamation Law of Anambra State (*Ilonuba v Star Printing & Publishing Co. Ltd.* (1979)).

An Australian court has indicated that a similar privilege covers only formal statements and not titbits of gossip from official sources (*Forster v Watson* (1944)). In England the privilege applied to a television programme to enlist the help of the public in apprehending a suspected offender (*Boston v Bagshaw* (1966)), and the English Court of Appeal refused to apply the provision to the report of information extracted "like teeth" from a public servant - this was not "issued" (*Blackshaw v Lord* (1984)).

A Nigerian court decided that a summary of a Government White Paper was not privileged under the 1961 Act because the document did not *say* it was issued on behalf of a Government department or officer of State (*Coker v Daily Times* (1969)). This has been strongly criticised as being illogical (Sogbesan, 1971, p. 48 citing *Boston v Bagshaw* above in which Denning MR inferred from the evidence that the statement in question was issued by the police). The Nigerian court also held that the protection of the proceedings of a commission of inquiry did not cover its conclusions; Sogbesan (*ibid.*) suggested that these ought to have privilege at common law, a possibility not considered by the court. No such argument was addressed to the High Court in England in *Tsikata v Newspaper Publishing plc* (upheld by the Court of Appeal 1997)[6], concerning an article in the *Independent* which included the conclusions of the Azu-Crabbe Special Investigation Board into the murder of three Ghanaian High Court Judges in 1982 but the judge did hold that the findings and recommendations of a fact-finding body were, "as a matter of ordinary English" part of the proceedings, and "In the case of a body appointed to hold a public inquiry, the report of its conclusions must I think have been pre-eminently the part of its 'proceedings' which Parliament had in mind".

Inaccurate summaries will not be protected (e.g. *Duyile v Sketch Publishing Co.* (Nigeria 1988), in which it seems the newspaper had not even seen the Price Control Board public announcement when they published the news item), but here is no requirement that summaries of proceedings be contemporaneous (*Tsikata v Newspaper Publishing*).

The main issue in the *Tsikata* case centred round the requirement (sub.-s. (3) of the various statutes) that the publication be for the public interest and be of matter of public concern. Captain Tsikata argued that there was no public benefit served by a British newspaper publishing an item on the Investigation Board ten years after its original publication. However, the courts held that there was legitimate interest in the United Kingdom in the affairs of a Commonwealth country, and that this remained true especially since Captain Tsikata was still a member of the government of President Rawlings, and that the latter was a candidate for imminent election. Nor was this diminished by failure to include subsequent developments including the decision of the Attorney-General not to prosecute Captain Tsikata, observations by a Special Tribunal on the failure of the main witness to cross-examine Tsikata (and the pre-execution retraction by that witness of his allegations). It was held that it did not; the Court of Appeal observed that it was difficult for newspapers to assess the weight of subsequent developments, and they might even be unaware of them. Ultimately the application of the provision must depend on the circumstances of each case.

The defence failed when a newspaper had printed a notice issued by the local authority about difficulties in collecting the rates, naming the plaintiff as one of the defaulters. The judge held that the defendants had pleaded public benefit, but had failed to plead and prove public concern (*Esiso v Ethiope Local Government* (Nigeria 1980)). (For English authority holding that both must be satisfied, see *Kelly v O'Malley* (1889) p. 64; *Boston v Bagshaw* (above).

Where a request for explanation or contradiction is made it must state specifically what is to be published; a general request is not sufficient (*Khan v Ahmed* (England 1957), approved in *Akurefe v Sketch* (Nigeria 1971)). Whether the defendant's response was adequate is a question of fact. It must be published in the same newspaper as the original publication and should not be hidden away or printed in small print (Gatley, para. 677). In the case of a broadcast correction the aim should be to reach the same audience as heard the original broadcast.

Mauritius

Among the defences set out in the Mauritian Penal Code art. 288 is:

> publish an impartial and accurate report of the proceedings of any public meeting, or (except when neither the public nor any newspaper reporter is admitted) of any meeting of the Council of Government, of the Municipal Council or of any Board created by law.

A New Defence for the Media?

Under the Codes applicable in Queensland and Tasmania there is a qualified privilege defence for the media. It seems to apply where the purpose of the publication was to give information to the readers as members of the public (*Caldwell v Ipec Australia Ltd.* (1975)). It has been argued that such a defence should be more widely available and that the present state of the law, affording the press little more protection than anyone else, is a hindrance to investigative journalism (e.g. Robertson & Nicol, 1992, p. 87ff). The Australian Law Reform Commission, however, took the view that it was not the law which inhibited investigative journalism in Australia but factors like expense; they were prepared to go only as far as proposing an expansion of the "reporting" privilege, notably to include all accurate reports of material from identified sources, provided dissemination was in the public interest (Australia, 1979, paras. 166-181).

A Working Paper in Zambia proposed

> a statutory defence of qualified privilege for newspapers and other news media in respect of publication of matters of public interest where the publication is made in good faith without malice and is based upon evidence which might reasonably be true

provided there was a statement by way of explanation or correction and appropriate apology. It also proposed a defence of good faith criticism of persons or institutions (Zambian Law Development Commission, 1984, pp. 5-6);[7] these proposals have not become law.

In one Nigerian case the defendant newspaper had published a statement to the effect that an insurance company had not measured up to standard; this was based upon a statement in the Government *Gazette* which had subsequently been withdrawn but not publicly. Possibly the defendant could have succeeded under the existing fair report provisions, as an accurate report of a statement put out by a department of government. Oddly enough it was not argued on this basis, but was treated by the judge as fair comment - but comment it certainly was not (*Nigerian Amicable Assurance Co. Ltd. v Mercantile Press Ltd.* (1977)). A general defence of fair report would meet a case like this - provided the defendant had identified their source. Such defences would not avail newspapers which are simply careless in checking their sources - as in the case in which a newspaper editor admitted in evidence that "We just published what we heard. We did not check to find out whether the story was false or true" characterised by the judge as "recklessness in excelsis" (*Obayiuwuana v Muhammed* (Nigeria 1986)).

It has sometimes been suggested that constitutional protections for free speech, which sometimes specifically mention the press, could also be used as the basis for extended qualified privilege; the Editor of the *Bulletin of Zimbabwean Law* says after the summary of *Shamuyarira* (above) "Should the starting point for our law still be the common law, or ss. 11 and 20 of our Constitution?". However, this has, as we shall see in the last chapter, received little support in the African courts.

Notes

1. In other contexts, payment in should not be pleaded or made known to the court lest it influence the Judge's mind; see, for example, Order 19 r. 6 (Lagos) (Aguda 1980a, paras. 27.29-30).
2. The Lagos Act does not reproduce this provision. In the unlikely event of a defendant relying on s. 2 of Lord Campbell's Act, it could perhaps be argued that its omission from the Lagos Act was deliberate.
3. It does not appear that the defendants tried to rely on the statutory protection given in some circumstances to statements accurately based on material issued for the information of the public by a superior officer of police see below.
4. The legislation actually said Her Majesty's dominions outside Great Britain. However, this now means, by virtue of the British Nationality Act 1981, Sch. 3, the Commonwealth. The 1996 Act replaces the schedule.
5. See Appendix I. Some countries adopted the English interpretation provision in Part II of the Schedule of the 1952 Act. This referred to India (which was the only Republic within the Commonwealth at the time), Sudan and New Hebrides (which were respectively Anglo-Egyptian and Anglo-French condominiums at the time). It would be necessary to cross-check with, for example, Interpretation Acts, or Acts passed at the time of independence or achievement of republican status of other countries, to see whether they spell out some expanded meaning of "Her Majesty's Dominions".
6. In August 1997 the plaintiff was refused leave to appeal to the House of Lords, although it was reported that he still intended to proceed with the case on the basis of malice (*Independent* 25.8.97).
7. The Attorney-General saw no objection to these proposals.

15 Defences for the Press II: Fair Comment

Introduction

"Fair comment on a matter of public interest" represents the right which every citizen has to express his views upon matters of public concern, provided they are indeed *views* and presented as such. "..[I]t is in the public interest to have free discussion of matters of public interest" (Scott LJ in *Lyon v Daily Telegraph* (England 1943)). The defence is in fact most often resorted to by newspapers - with a notable lack of success on the whole in Africa - but is available to any citizen. "The right to comment on a matter of public interest is not the peculiar privilege of the press" (*Currimjee Jeewonjee & Co. v Millien* (Mauritius 1948, p. 56) citing *Campbell v Spottiswoode* (England 1863)). For examples of pleas of fair comment raised by defendants other than newspapers, see *Adedipe v Falaiye* (Nigeria 1955-56) where the defendant was a Member of a regional legislature, *Ibrahim v Bakare* (Nigeria 1973), (first defendant/appellant a businessman); *Saraki v Soleye* (Nigeria 1971) (defendant was Permanent Secretary in the Ministry of Health and Social Welfare).

Roman-Dutch law and common law would seem to be the same; Zimbabwean cases judges have set out the following requirements,

(i) the allegation in question must amount to comment;
(ii) it must be fair;
(iii) the facts upon which the comment is made must be true;
(iv) the comment must relate to a matter of public interest

(*Zvogbo v Kingston's Ltd.* (1986), quoting from the headnote in *Marais v Richard* (South Africa 1981); the judge referred to *Crawford v Albu* (South Africa 1917), as the *locus classicus* on fair comment; see also *Tekere v Zimbabwe Newspapers(1980) Ltd.* (1986) p. 286). A common lawyer would have put it precisely the same way.

Courts, and lawyers, have often found difficulty with the distinction between this defence and that of qualified privilege; *Hoare v Jessop* (Kenya

1965) is an example (see below). One Nigerian court quoted Gatley (para. 703, 7th. ed., quoted in *Concordia Press of Nigeria Ltd. v Obijo* (1990) p. 314):

> In the defence of fair comment the right exercised by the defendant is shared by every member of the public....In that of qualified privilege the right is not shared by every member of the public, but is limited to an individual who stands in such relation to the circumstances that he is entitled to say or write what would be libellous or slanderous on the part of anyone else.

While another Nigerian judge (Obi-Okoye CJ in *Oforka v Anisiuba* (1979) p. 139) said, neatly:

> The defence of justification means that what the defendants wrote is true. Fair comment must be based on true statements of fact. But qualified privilege is in spite of the falsity of the statements.

Matters of Public Interest

A person's private life is not a matter for comment, unless it impinges upon his performance of a public duty (see *David-West v Goodwill Press & Bookshop Ltd.* (Nigeria 1983) p. 377 - Fakayode CJ quoting himself in *Rotimi v African Newspapers of Nigeria Ltd.* (1979) quoting Gatley (now para. 732)). "It cannot be reasonably argued that the private life of a subject is a matter of public interest" said d'Unienville J in *Daurat v Le Cernéen* (Mauritius 1933) p. 21; see also English cases: *Wilson v Reed* (1860); *Seymour v Butterworth* (1862); *Silkin v Beaverbrook Newspapers Ltd.* (1969); *London Artists Ltd. v Littler* (1969); *Merrivale v Carson* (1887). In one Nigerian case the judge held that the plaintiff's political views could not be viewed as part of his conduct as a public servant (*Okon v COR Advocate* (1961)). The conduct of government and politics, both at national and more local levels are matters of public interest: examples include *Adedipe v Falaiye* above (a Member of House of Assembly could comment on the behaviour of the plaintiff in his capacity as a member of the Native Authority), *Enahoro v Associated Newspapers of Nigeria Ltd.* (Nigeria 1960) (conduct of Minister), *Williams v West African Pilot* (Nigeria 1961) (conduct of party leaders in election), *David-West v Goodwill Press & Bookshop Ltd.* (above) (conduct of former Commissioner for Education in State government). So is the administration of justice (e.g. *Woodgate v Ridout* (England 1865), *Bweupe v Attorney-General* (Zambia 1964) quoting Lord Atkin in *Ambard v*

A-G of Trinidad and Tobago (Privy Council 1936) p. 709 (the "justice is not a cloistered virtue" speech)). More specifically, efforts (or lack of effort) to eliminate corruption would be an appropriate subject of comment.

> Corruption is commonly known in this country as one of the evils which the Government of this country has set out to eradicate. It is within living memory that a lot of actions had been taken by the Government in pursuance of this crusade. The issue of corruption therefore can rightly be said to be a matter of wide public interest in this country (*Tarka v Sketch Publishing Co. Ltd.* (Nigeria 1978) p. 274).

Anything that involves the use of public money is a suitable topic for comment whether it is in services for the public, or the allocation of government loans (*Odutola v West African Pilot Ltd.* (Nigeria 1960)), or indeed any other use of the "taxpayers' money". Similarly in the case of health care: at least where there is public supervision. As one judge said

> In my opinion the conduct of a private venture of such a kind that it affects and relates to a whole community and its interests and affects public health generally is a matter of public interest. It certainly is in the interest of the public that when its members go into a private hospital or clinic their lives should not be exposed to any danger (*Saraki v Soleye* (Nigeria 1971) p. 282).

The forms of worship (*Kelly v Tinling* England (1865)), and the doctrines of a religious group of any sort may be commented upon, at least if it opens its doors to the public - or if its activities affect the public (see *Prisloo v Levy* (South Africa1936)). Nigerian cases involving religion include *Sketch v Ajagbemokeferi* (1989) and *Awoniyi v AMORC* (1990); in neither case was there any extended discussion of the defence, since the Court in each case achieved the result it clearly wished to achieve (namely absence of liability) by another route. In *Gathercole v Miall* (England 1846) the administration of a charity set up by a clergyman was held not to be a suitable subject of comment. However, if it receives tax concessions as a charity, or and if it receives donations from the public, it would seem there ought to be the possibility of public comment.

The public interest extends to all public institutions, such as schools (e.g. *Okon v COR Advocate* (Nigeria 1961)) and universities: "Ahmadu Bello University is a public institution and its affairs including those of its lecturers are matters of public interest and are subject to fair comment by members of the public including the defendants" (*Nthenda v Alade* (Nigeria 1974) pp.

478-9)). Bello SPJ presumably meant the affairs of the lecturers so far as they related to their duties as such.

The conduct of a private business will in many circumstances not be a matter of public interest. But the situation would be different if the business was carrying out government contracts (as in *A.W. Ibe & Co. Ltd. v The Reveille Printing and Publishing Co. Ltd.* (Nigeria 1975)), or if the business is so large that it affects a substantial section of the public (*South Hetton Coal Co. v N.E. News Association* (England 1894)). Mysterious fires in textile factories were held *obiter* to be a matter of public interest (*Nigerian Textile Mills v Punch Nigeria Ltd.* (1986)), as was the use of flour at a time when it was rationed in Mauritius (*Merven v Millien* (1945)).

A company which invites the public to subscribe for shares invites public comment as well (e.g. *Ibrahim v Bakare* (Nigeria 1973)), as does someone who asks the public to offer financial or other support to a project (e.g. *Campbell v Spottiswoode* (England 1863), *Jenner v À Beckett* (England 1871), *Dakhyl v Labouchere* (England 1908)), including a Nigerian football club which raised donations from the public (*Nzenwa v Kwara State Printing & Publishing Corpn* (1980)). "Appeals of every kind through the Press and platform are daily being made to the public intelligence, the public conscience and the public pocket. Whatever the nature of these appeals, or the position of those who make them, discussion is clearly invited and that discussion is free" (Clerk and Lindsell, 1995, paras. 21-162).

The arts which are offered to the public become a matter for comment, by professional critics and the public generally (see *Turner v M-G-M Pictures* (England 1950), *Thomas v Bradbury, Agnew* (England 1906)). "Every kind of literary production placed before the public is the subject of fair comment" *(Awoniyi v AMORC*, above: Uwaifo JCA (*obiter*)); the same is true of less artistic productions, including a beauty contest to choose "Miss Nigeria" (*Odukoya v Sketch* (1979)) though it is hard to see what room was left for fair comment when the judge had found every aspect of the allegation true. A rare African case on artistic endeavours came from Nairobi, although the facts originated in Uganda, where the plaintiff had been commissioned to paint an official portrait of Idi Amin, then Head of State. A sergeant in the army was reported as saying he "thought the artist must have painted the wrong man by mistake"! The defence of fair comment succeeded (*Dawson v East African Newspapers (Nation Series) Ltd.* (1975)). Mauritian cases include one where a newspaper review of a play had referred to one of the actors as a "clown". The court held that this was not actionable if it was not in bad faith, an approach in effect similar to the common law, although the latter would say there is protection unless there is malice (*Forget v Maurice*

Press Ltd. (1964), citing Savatier, *Traité de la Responsabilité Civil Tome I* para. 89(b)). The court took account of the fact that the performance was clearly controversial, in deciding whether the defendant was in good faith. In another case it was held there was no basis of fact for the comment; the court seems to have approached the question as though the common law applied. The supposed basis of fact was that the plaintiff's writings had to be reshaped by someone else before they could be published (*Millien v Giraud* (1938)). And in *Roy v Bhookun* (Mauritius 1956) the plaintiff complained that after he wrote two articles in the press the defendant sent out a circular letter inviting others to participate in a competition to find the grammatical and other errors in those articles.

What is an appropriate object of public interest and comment must be judged in the context of time and place: "The courts now treat many more matters as being of legitimate public concern or interest than would have been the case in the nineteenth century" (Gatley, para. 731). And the interest must be legitimate; Fakayode CJ quoted Lord Denning:

> Whenever a matter is such as to affect people at large, so that they may be legitimately interested in, or concerned at what is going on; then it is a matter of public interest on which everyone is entitled to make fair comment (*David-West v Goodwill* above, p. 378, quoting Denning in *London Artists Ltd. v Littler* (England 1969) p. 391).

With respect, the learned judge was wrong to go on to summarise this by saying that a matter is a matter of public interest if it affects, concerns or interests the public; Lord Denning was saying that the interest must stem from the affecting. Curiosity is not enough.

Comment not Fact

Many of the African defendants have been simply unable to show that what they said or wrote was an expression of opinion and not a statement of purported fact. In *Dawson v East African Newspapers* above, Spry Ag. P took the view that the statement of the sergeant was of fact not comment - a slightly surprising view, I suggest. The test is whether the reasonable member of the public, reading or hearing the words in their context, would have taken them as comment (*Grech v Odhams Press* (England 1958)). A good example is the imputation of motive; this may well be a matter of opinion, but can be stated in such a way that it is a statement of fact (e.g. *Bardi v Maurice* (Gold Coast 1954)). It has been held not to be comment to say someone is suffering from heart disease (*"Munyonyozi" (Publishers) v The Lukkiko of Buganda* (Uganda 1923)). But even such a statement might be couched in a way which was opinion rather than fact. Gatley (para. 699n) suggests that newspaper headlines will usually be taken as statements of fact, but editorials will more readily be construed as comment. A headline "Alleged Love Advances. Nursing Officer Sacked" was held to be a statement of fact (*Gyang v Iliyasu* (Nigeria 1977)).

In *Nthenda v Alade* (above) Bello SPJ, holding no comment, quoted from Gatley (now para. 697):

> A comment is a statement of opinion on facts. A libellous statement of fact is not a comment or a criticism on anything. It is comment to say that a certain act which a man has done is disgraceful or dishonourable; it is an allegation of fact that he did the act so criticized.

In *Ohanbamu v Midwest Newspaper Corporation* (Nigeria 1974) the remarks made in the article in the defendant's newspaper went far beyond comment - the defendant's article said the plaintiff disseminated falsehood, and referred to his "shallowness and immorality" (though even these words might be comment if based on facts?). And in *Ebuwa v UCA Ltd.* the West African Court of Appeal reached the same conclusion on the statement that (*inter alia*) the UAC discriminated against African licensed buying agents of palm oil in its management of bulk oil plants (Nigeria 1955). In *Nekyon v Tanganyika Standard Ltd.* (Uganda 1964) Udoma CJ doubted whether the offending article, apart from its headline "Curbs on Ministers, Rumours" could be comment - and, with respect, it is hard to see quite how even these words could be construed as comment. In Zimbabwe, a judge said that the statements: "his behaviour is not always, perhaps, what Mugabe expects of leaders" and "Zvogbo, sources within Zanu say, is an 'unashamed regionalist'"...would be taken by the reasonable reader to be statements of fact: the reader would regard the first as being "founded upon unrevealed information in the possession of the publisher", and would read the second as indicating that the plaintiff had declared himself as a regionalist (*Zvogbo v Kingston's Ltd.* (1986) p. 322 - the judge took the last quotation from *Waring v Mervis* (South Africa 1969) p. 545; see also *Tekere v Zimbabwe Newspapers* (1986)). Another Zimbabwean court held that "Zimbabwe's export reputation has been harmed in that Arab state" by the conduct of the plaintiff was comment though framed as fact (*Prakash v Wilson* (1992) p. 301)). This would seem to be a borderline case: the Supreme Court seems to have read the statement as though it really said, "This sort of behaviour will damage our reputation".

The decision of the House of Lords in *Telnikoff v Matusevitch* (1992) has been strongly criticised for somewhat restricting the material which may be used in deciding whether a statement is comment (Robertson & Nicol, 1992, p. 81). The statement complained of was in a letter to a newspaper, commenting on an earlier article in the same paper. The majority of the House held that in deciding whether the letter contained comment as opposed to statements of fact the earlier article could not be considered. Only if the statements were comments could the earlier item be looked at to decide whether those comments were fair.

The Comment Must Be on Facts

This is really a further aspect of the same question: the statement will only be a comment if it is based upon facts, and those facts are true - unless privilege applies.

> Fair comment is, as I understand it, a judgement on or a criticism of qualities, merits or demerits, founded on true facts. It is not, and never has been a baseless and malicious attack on the character of another grounded on statements of fact wholly imaginary and damaging. (*Ezekwe v Otomewo,* Onyeama J (Nigeria 1957)).

In *A.W. Ibe & Co. v Reveille* (Nigeria 1975) the defendants had given sufficient factual information to ground the observation that the plaintiffs were "inefficient". In *Oke v Gansallo* it was held that the doctrines of the United Native African Church were "demonstrably false and untrue" when considered in the light of orthodox Christian doctrine, and there were therefore facts which could ground a charge that they were "pernicious" (Nigeria 1923, p. 117 - see below). A modern view would be that religious doctrine is not susceptible of being held "true or false" by a court - but this was the 1920s and the judge seemed to welcome the opportunity to denounce churches of which he disapproved.

The case of *African Newspapers v Coker* (Nigeria 1973) involved an interesting variant of the problem. The newspaper (*The Tribune*) maintained that it had commented on the report of a Tribunal of Inquiry, but had omitted all mention of the Government White Paper which itself commented on the Report. The Supreme Court said of this (pp. 395-6),

> ...it is the crux of the case against the defendants in this appeal as indicating a deliberate act of "*suppressio veri, suggestio falsi*" and therefore must have some effect on any defence of fair comment. It is trite law that to sustain the defence of fair comment the whole of the facts must be correctly and fairly stated, or the premise upon which the comment is based must be the whole truth. Anything short of these would destroy the defence of fair comment.

In fact the court went on to agree with the trial judge that the articles in question were not really even comments on the report.

The burden of proving the truth of the facts rests upon the defendant. In the jurisdictions with English pre-1952 common law rules failure to prove the truth of every statement of fact upon which the comment was based will be fatal to a defence of fair comment. A judge quoted Lord Porter: "In a case where the facts are fully set out in the alleged libel each fact must be justified and if the defendant fails to justify one, even if it be comparatively unimportant, he fails" (*Kemsley v Foot* (England 1952) quoted by Dickson J in *Odutola v West African Pilot* (Nigeria 1960)). Under the legislation:

> In an action for libel or slander in respect of words consisting partly of allegations of fact and partly of expressions of opinion, a defence of fair comment shall not fail by reason only that the truth of every allegation of fact is not proved if the expression of opinion is fair comment having regard to such of the facts alleged or referred to in the words complained of as are proved (based on s. 6 of the English Act).

This has hardly figured in any African case; it was mentioned in *Africa Newspapers v Coker* (above, p. 396). Onalaja J said that he was applying it in *Ajala v Are* (Nigeria 1985) p. 518 but it is not clear how or why. In most cases in which this defence has failed either the statement complained of was one of fact rather than comment, or the supposed facts relied on fell far short of the truth. (The fullest discussion is in *Truth (N.Z.) Ltd. v Avery* (New Zealand 1959), see *Broadway Approvals v Odhams Press* (England 1964), *London Artists v Littler* (England 1969).)

The one circumstance in which a comment may be held to be fair even though the "facts" in question may be untrue is if the facts are themselves contained in a privileged statement (*Mangena v Wright* (England 1909)). Thus a newspaper could comment in an editorial upon statements made by a legislator, or the findings of a committee of inquiry. The defendant must show, however, that he has given a fair and accurate report of the privileged occasion (*Brent Walker Group plc v Time Out* (England 1991)).

Facts Must Be Referred To or Identified

The reader must be able to tell what is fact and what comment (*Nekyon v Tanganyika Standard* (Uganda 1964), citing *Andrews v Chapman* (England 1853)). The facts may actually be stated in the same place as the comment, but a newspaper will often comment in its leader column on factual material reported elsewhere in the same day's or a recent issue. A review of a book or film obviously cannot reprint every aspect on which it might comment; it is enough that the film or book are in the public domain (see *Kemsley v Foot* (England 1952)). But if the review misdescribed the object of the review and then commented on the erroneous "fact", it would be no defence to say "but the public can go and check the facts for themselves" (e.g. *Merrivale v Carson* (above)). There should be some specificity about the facts: one assumes it would not be enough for a reviewer to say "This was an appalling performance" without indicating in what way it was appalling. The readers will be expected to know notorious facts; in *Kemsley* v *Foot* (above) a headline said "Lower than Kemsley" above an attack on a newspaper. To attribute any meaning to this one needed to know that Kemsley was the proprietor of another newspaper. The same facts made it clear that the statement was a comment.

In *Oke v Gansallo* (above) the judge examined at some length the teachings of the church as set out in its Constitution, as they related to polygamy - which it did not encourage but tolerated. The judge does not appear to have addressed his mind to the question of whether this teaching was adequately referred to in the report in question (issued by the Diocesan Synod of the Anglican Church). The passage from the report quoted by the judge (p. 110) gives no indication of the nature of the "pernicious" teachings. It would have been possible for the plaintiff to make a *Kemsley v Foot* argument: that the facts - or here the doctrine - was so well known that it would have been known to the readers. There is no indication that this was so, and anyway this was years before *Kemsley* - and the original report treated the Roman Catholic church to the same invective, which church would have shared little with the African Communion, certainly not the acceptance of polygamy which so upset the judge. Also in the *David-West* case (Nigeria 1983) the judge (*obiter*) seems to have said that comment on a Commission of Inquiry would have been protected; but it does not seem that the statements in question had appeared in the article complained of - and the report of the Inquiry seems to have been unpublished so members of the public would not have had access to it when reading the article.

Fairness

The comment should be fair; it seems to be on this basis that the defence failed for two of the three defendants in the odd case of *Bweupe v Attorney-General* (Zambia 1964). The plaintiff (a High Court judge) had made the, rather foolish, statement, that special constables did not exist, when he meant they had exceeded their powers. The Minister responsible for special constables made a speech saying that the plaintiff was wrong, that he was shocked, and demanded an apology. The judge held that fair comment protected the defendants from liability for the implication that the judge was ignorant, but that the demand for an apology went too far. But it hard to see how the demand for an apology was actually defamatory. It is not necessary that the court should agree with the comment before it can be held to be fair. The judge in *Oke v Gansallo*, above, in holding that the United Native African Church was "clearly wrong and...teaching what is false and untrue" (p. 117), and the judge in *Mullery v Stevenson-Delhomme* (Seychelles 1955), when he held that the plaintiff *was* "undesirable", when all he needed to hold was that the statement to that effect was comment, seem to have gone further than they need.

Does the defence require that the defendant was honest, or that a fair person *could* have held that opinion? Or that an *honest* person *could* have held the view? Or must the defendant show both elements - the subjective and the objective? Some African cases tend to suggest the last. In *Cobbett-Tribe v Zambian Publishing Co. Ltd.* (1977), the court held both that no reasonable person could infer corrupt motives in the Law Society (which was opposing detention without trial), and that anyway the defendants did not honestly believe it. The High Court in Malaŵi said fair comment must be the honest opinion of the defendant and "warranted by (the) facts in the sense that a fair-minded man might reasonably draw from them that inference" (*Malaŵi Railways v Bhadurkhan* (1986) p. 433 (Makuta CJ)). Ayoola J suggested, in *Adetona v Drum* that honest comment is not necessarily fair (Nigeria 1972, citing Lord Alverston LJ in *Bell v Bashford* (England 1912)).

In fact the question is rarely directly addressed. Many of the cases, on close inspection, turn out to be less than helpful. Sheridan CJ in *Kihika v Buringuriza* (Uganda 1962) quoted an English case (*Hedley v Barlow* (1865) p. 230)):

> ...comments must be fair, that is, conceived in a fair spirit - in the spirit of fair discussion - and not in a spirit of reckless or inconsiderable [sc.

> unconsidering?] imputation. That which is recklessly defamatory can hardly be deemed fair.

This seems to place the emphasis upon the attitude of the defendant, perhaps suggesting that honesty is the key issue. The emphasis is somewhat different from that of Lord Esher in *Merivale v Carson*: "Would any fair man, however prejudiced he may be, however exaggerated or obstinate his views, have said that which this criticism has said?" ((England 1887) p. 280, quoted in *Yanni v Sierra Leone Daily Mail* (1967-8), p. 106). Strongly held and expressed, even prejudiced, views, are not necessarily beyond the scope of this defence (*Turner v M-G-M*; *David-West v Goodwill*, above).

Until recently it was indeed very difficult to see from the English judicial pronouncements and from the books what "fair" should really mean (see Sutherland,1992, p. 281). Recently the House of Lords has stated that the defendant does not have to show that the views were honest; the test is "whether any (fair-minded) man, however prejudiced and obstinate, could honestly hold the view expressed" (*Telnikoff v Matusevitch* (1992, p. 354)). Actual honesty would go to questions of malice. There is still room for different perceptions of what the House decided. The word "fair-minded" does not actually appear in the speech of Lord Keith, but it does in the judgment of Lloyd LJ which he was approving. Without that word the text seems almost devoid of content, with it one is left wondering whether being fair-minded is compatible with being prejudiced! Either way, there is validity in the view of the Faulks Committee (Cmnd 5909 para. 251) that the defence should be named simply "comment" (see Sutherland, above, p. 281). New Zealand, through statute, has gone the other way and renamed the defence "honest opinion" and made honesty the key element - Defamation Act 1992 s. 9.

It is possible, however, that a slightly different, and anomalous, rule applies where the comment goes so far as to impute dishonourable motives to the plaintiff, and that such a comment is only protected when it is the *correct* inference to draw from the facts. Cockburn CJ in *Campbell v Spottiswoode* (England 1863, p. 776) said,

> I think the fair position in which the law may be settled is this: that where the public conduct of a public man is open to animadversion, and the writer who is commenting upon it makes imputations on his motives which arise fairly and legitimately out of his conduct so that a jury shall say that the criticism was not only honest but well-founded, an action is not maintainable

(see also *Dakhyl v Laboucherie* (England 1908), *Hunt v Star* (England 1908)). Lloyd LJ mentioned this in *Telnikoff* and said that the case before him did not fall into the class. Gatley (para. 724), who plumped for "honesty" as the general test, seemed to favour the "fair-minded person" test in this context - citing *Peter Walker Ltd. v Hodgson* (England 1909).[1] Fleming observed "It is open to serious doubt whether this Victorian period piece should survive into the more robust atmosphere of our present public life. Nothing has been heard of it for a long time ..." (1992, pp. 590-1). Actually, something has been heard of it in Mauritius. However, although the court in *Lesage v Mason* ((1976) pp. 186-7) quoted *Campbell v Spottiswoode* including the reference to the statement being "well-founded", it satisfied itself with holding that the defendant was not honest, and that the inference was not one which a "fair-minded man" might reasonably have made; the court seemed unaware that it was not fully applying *Campbell*. The court mentioned three earlier cases: *Celestin v Sandapa* (1917), *Tranquille v Le Mauricien* (1929), *Deane v Le Mauricien* (1932). In *Hoare v Jessop* (Kenya 1965, p. 229) Crabbe JA said (emphasis supplied),

> If the facts are true and the comments thereon, which are honestly believed to be true, impute corrupt or dishonest motives, the defendant must succeed *if the imputation is warranted by the facts*.

In some cases the court will hold that to impute an improper motive in not so much a comment as a statement of fact, in which case this issue will not arise (as in *Bardi v Maurice* (Ghana 1954)).

Whose Honesty?

This defence is used mainly by news media - which constantly give publicity to materials of which they are not the originators. If the test of "fairness" was honesty and this were to be required of the medium as well as the author then the press could not publish views with which it disagreed, which would preclude controversy in letters columns, for example. (Not to mention the problem of deciding who is to hold the view of the news medium: the owner, editor or who? - see Rogers, 1981, p. 227.) The Supreme Court of Canada seems[2] to have held that each publisher who claims fair comment should hold the opinion honestly (*Chernesky v Armadale Publishers Ltd.* (1978)).[3] However, the House of Lords decision in *Telnikoff* is in this respect more favourable to press freedom, since the test of "an honest person *could* hold this view" does not require the defendant to show that anyone *did* hold it.

Pleading Fair Comment

One way to plead the defence is: "The said words are fair and bona fide comment on a matter of public interest" (Gatley, para. 1130). The defendant must then give particulars of the facts on which he is relying and also of the matter of public interest on which he says he is commenting (*Kemsley v Foot* (England 1952)).

The other plea is the "rolled-up plea": "Insofar as the words complained of consist of statements of fact, they are true in substance and in fact; and insofar as they consist of expressions of opinion they are fair comment made in good faith and without malice on the said facts which are matters of public interest" (Gatley, para. 1131 n. 4). The plea was approved in *Penrhyn v Licensed Victualler's Mirror* (England 1890). This plea is virtually extinct in England (*Control Risks Ltd v New English Library Ltd.* (1990)) having lost its advantages because the Rules of the Supreme Court (Order 82 4 r. 3) provide that the defendant must give particulars stating which he alleges are statements of fact and of what facts and matters he relies on in support of the allegation that the words are true. The same rule applies in at least some African jurisdictions (e.g. Lagos (Order 16 r. 19); Ghana High Court (Civil Procedure) Rules O. 19 r. 23A applied in *Standard Engineering Co. Ltd. v New Times Corporation* (1976)). It has been suggested that this English rule should apply elsewhere in Nigeria (other than Lagos which has it explicitly), by virtue of the provisions applying English rules of court where there is "no provision" in Nigeria (*Odutola v West African Pilot* (Nigeria 1960) p. 32 - see High Court of Lagos Act s. 12, Order 35 r. 10 High Court Rules, Bendel etc. s. 35 High Court Laws (Northern States), s.16 High Court Laws, (Eastern States). See Aguda 1980a paras. 52. 39-40. Actually, in *ibid.* para. 18.25, Aguda says these particulars must *already* be given, citing *Simonds v Dunne* (Ireland 1891)).

It has been held in most modern cases that the rolled-up plea is a plea of fair comment and not of justification: *Sutherland v Stopes* (England 1925) cited in *Odutola*, above where Dickson J went on to describe the difference between the two defences:

> It is quite true that although, as we have seen, a plea of fair comment is different from a plea of justification, the defendant is entitled to prove, and indeed must prove, that the facts on which his comments are based are true, notwithstanding such facts are defamatory of the plaintiff and there is no plea of justification. The two defences are similar, to this extent, that in the plea of fair comment the defendant must show that there is a foundation of fact well

> and truly laid on which the comment is based; but conclusions inferred as matters of opinion have not to be proved as facts. On the other hand, the mental attitude of the commentator is material to the issue of fair comment, but immaterial to the issue of justification.

Dickson J (presumably the same judge) used similar language in *Figueredo v Editor, Sunday Nation* (Uganda 1968)). The defendant should therefore not be permitted to argue, in the defence of fair comment, that statements of fact are true except insofar as these facts support his comment (see *Saraki v Soleye*, above, where the defendant could not argue justification because it had not been pleaded). And if the underlying statements of fact are themselves defamatory, he should plead justification (or privilege) with respect to them (*Broadway Approvals v Odhams Press* (England 1965)). If the plaintiff complains only of something which the defendant maintains was a comment, he should plead justification in the alternative (as is possible - e.g. *Broadway Approvals*, *Tarka v Sketch* (Nigeria 1978)) if there is any possibility that the court will decide it is *not* a comment, or that the subject matter was not one of public interest.

A Note on Mauritius

In *Lesage v Mason* (p. 184) the court said,

> A defendant must first show that all the allegations of fact in the words complained of are true and, secondly, that the comment upon those facts was a *bona fide* and fair comment on a matter of public interest.

In the case of criminal defamation the Penal Code art. 288 provides:

> Provided that no offence shall be held to have been committed under this section when the writing or words -
> (iii) are a fair and *bona fide* comment or criticism of the conduct of any person touching any public question, and respecting his character so far as his character appear in that conduct, and no further.

However, according to this very case (p. 179), Penal Code defences only apply to a civil case which would not be actionable but for the Penal Code, and where the plaintiff relies upon the Penal Code. Examples of the defence in reliance on the Penal Code are *Ducray v Rohan* (1906) and *Roy v Bhookun* (1956). It has been held that English law can be relied on because French and English law are the same (*Forget v La Presse Mauricienne Ltée* (1958)).

However, the overriding requirement of good faith in Mauritius would suggest that the House of Lords approach in *Telnikoff* could not be applied in that country.

Notes

1. See also Cmnd. 5909 paras. 161-9, which recommends the abolition of this special rule for imputations of dishonourable motives, a step taken in the New Zealand Defamation Act 1992 s. 12.
2. Rogers (1981, p. 227) suggests that the majority view is not quite as clear as this, but that the minority in the Court thought that was what the majority thought!
3. The Libel and Slander (Amendment) Act 1980 of Ontario reverses this decision by providing that the defence is not lost if a person "could hold that opinion" - new s. 25 to cap. 243 Revised Statutes of Ontario (see Gatley, para. 730 n. 51).
   The New Zealand Defamation Act 1992 s. 9 provides: if the author is the defendant he or she must show that the statement was his or her honest opinion. If the author was someone else, but was the employee or agent of the defendant it must be shown that the opinion did not purport to be that of the defendant and that the latter believed it was the genuine opinion of the author. If the author was not the employee or agent the requirement of not purporting to be his/her opinion still holds, but the defendant must also show that he/she had no reasonable cause to believe it was not the opinion of the author.

16 Malice

Malice operates to defeat a defence of qualified privilege or fair comment (for an example of the former see *African Press v Ikejiani* (Nigeria 1953)). If the defendant pleads one of these defences, the plaintiff is not *obliged* to plead malice: he may try to convince the court that the occasion was not privileged, or the comment not fair (see Nnaemeka-Agu JSC in *Atoyebi v Odudu* (Nigeria 1990)). We are concerned here with "express malice", not the "malice" which the law presumes to exist in any defamatory statement, and which need not be proved (or pleaded: *Clarke v Molyneux* (England 1877) p. 247). The Supreme Court of Nigeria observed:

> We think it is necessary to stress here that the word "maliciously", as usually pleaded, has a technical meaning. We think that in the pleadings, sufficient care should be taken to draw a clear distinction between this "technical malice", if we may say so, and actual malice. In our view, each has a definite role to play at the trial. It should always be borne in mind that, once the plea of fair comment or qualified privilege is made out...the inference of malice is rebutted, and the burden is thrown upon the plaintiff of showing "express malice" against the defendants (*Bakare v Ibrahim* (1973) Ibekwe Ag. JSC).

(The old rules, which may still apply in some parts of Africa did not require the additional pleading of express malice, see below.) In the context of qualified privilege, the situation was well put by a Zambian judge:

> When it is the duty of a person to make a given communication, "good faith" is inferred automatically on his part because the "duty" or "interest" is presumed to be his only motive for doing so. The presence of "duty" or "interest" rebuts the presumption of legal malice...It is here where a party is required to show that motives other than duty or interest alone caused the making of the slanderous communication (*Musiwa v Chanda* (1985) p. 246, Mr. Commissioner Kabamba).

The plaintiff failed on appeal because he had not pleaded express malice; the plea "falsely and maliciously" in the statement of claim was not enough.

The Meaning of Malice

Malice means an improper motive - that in a case of qualified privilege the defendant was not genuinely acting to perform a duty or protect a legitimate interest, and in the case of fair comment was not exercising the right to make an honest observation on a matter of public concern.

> Actual malice does not mean personal spite or ill-will and it may exist even though there is no spite or desire for vengeance in the ordinary sense. Any indirect motive other than a sense of duty is what the law calls malice. Malice means making use of the occasion for some indirect purpose. (*Oweh v Amalgamated Press of Nigeria Ltd.* (1957) (Abbott J)).

(See also *Bakare v Ibrahim* (Nigeria 1973), where a large number of English cases defining malice are referred to: *Dickson v Earl of Wilton* (1859) p. 793, *Stuart v Bell* (1891), *Turnbull v Bird* (1861) 175 ER at 1171, and *Browne v Dunn* (Scotland 1893).) As one Ghanaian judge said, "Annoyance and malice are two different things" (*Yankum v Abaka* (1926-9)). Nor are stupidity or obstinacy the same as malice (*Bank of West Africa Ltd. v Appenteng* (Ghana 1972) p. 169, quoting Lord Porter in *Turner v M-G-M* (England 1950) p. 463, where he points out that they may in extreme cases be evidence of malice). A court in East Africa said (*Bulchand Thadani v Wahid Alikhan* (Uganda 1916)),

> It is no evidence of malice in the defendant to show that his informants were malicious [citing *Hennessy v Wright* (England 1888) p. 445[1]]. nor that he failed to exercise a sound discrimination [citing *Pater v Baker* (England 1847)], nor that the words were exaggerated, for "a man may use excessive language and yet have not malice in his mind" [quoting *Neville v Fine Arts etc.* (1895) p. 170], nor that his statements are now admitted or proved to be untrue [citing *Caulfield v Whitworth* (England 1868)].

With respect, though none of these in itself amounts to malice, the third, and possibly the second, would seem to be some evidence of it (see below).

Spite

In many cases, however, the defendant has lost because his motive has precisely been to injure the plaintiff, or what one might call "spite"; as Lord Diplock says in *Horrocks v Lowe* (England 1975), this is the most common improper motive pleaded. In *African Newspapers v Coker* (1973), the

Nigerian Supreme Court quoted *Selman v Isaac* (England 1869, p. 886), "But if you can infer from the circumstances attending the publication that it was really made not with a view to the information of the public but for the purpose of injuring some individual, the publisher will be liable...", apparently holding that some such motive existed in the case before them.

It was malice to accuse others of misappropriating money for a local project not out of a genuine desire to see justice done but because the accusers themselves had been excluded, properly, from the benefits of the project (*Adoki v Adoki* (Nigeria 1977)), and for a contractor to report the PWD Superintendent for taking bribes in order to get him removed because he was holding down the rates paid (*Tharia v Morrison* (Zanzibar 1910)). In *Okon v COR Advocate* (Nigeria 1961) the defendants had attacked the competence of the plaintiff in running a school. Their motives were held to be improper: "I am of the opinion that the third defendant intended by this article, in referring to the office of the plaintiff to punish him for his effrontery in writing something in his private capacity against the C.O.R. State Movement" (p. 25), and "the third defendant was trying...to catch votes for leaders of his party for election into the Calabar Urban County Council" (p. 26). Similarly, it was malicious to try to damage the reputation of the plaintiff to harm him politically and enhance the prospects of the defendant's own party (*Oweh v Amalgamated Press*, above).

No Belief in Truth

Where qualified privilege is involved, the objective truth of the statements is not in issue; Nyalali CJ was quite right to criticise the lower court judge for this confusion: "I am of the view that the learned trial judge misdirected himself in law in finding malice on the basis of the falsehood of the allegation" in *Moiro v Zablon* (Tanzania 1980, p. 277).

The absence of an honest *belief* in the truth of what he says on the part of the defendant, however, is strong evidence of malice, so a defendant was malicious when he persisted in making allegations although he had been told after several police investigations that they were false (*Tackyie v Kabbah* (Ghana 1956); see also *Bulchand Thadani v Wahid Ali Khan* (above, p. 232), and *Kitto v Chadwick* (Uganda 1975)). In *Chimala Stores v Zambia-Tanzania Road Services Ltd.* (Tanzania 1970) Georges CJ said, "If they did not believe their allegation to be true, then clearly there would be malice" (p. 220).

In fair comment, where the dishonest defendant is the author, courts have sometimes held the comment was not fair (e.g. *Adetona v Drum* (Nigeria 1972)) and sometimes that the defendant was malicious (e.g.

Obaseki v Omo-Osagie (Nigeria 1953)). However, the House of Lords recently emphasised that the defendant is not obliged to show that the comment is the expression of his own views (*Telnikoff v Matusevitch* (1992)). If the plaintiff shows that the defendant did not actually believe the statement it is more logical to treat this as evidence of malice. Sutherland (1992, p. 282) suggests absence of belief is not enough *per se* to establish malice, though the English authorities are unclear (comparing (at 285) *Thomas v Bradbury* (1906) p. 641 with *Merrivale v Carson* (1887)).

Reckless indifference as to whether a statement is true or, in the case of a comment, fair will also normally defeat a defence: a person who does not care about the truth or fairness can hardly have had a proper motive (*Enahoro v Associated Newspapers* (Nigeria 1960) quoting, at p. 227, *Royal Aquarium and Summer and Winter Garden Society v Parkinson* (England 1892) p. 454; and *Mangat v Sharma* (Tanzania 1968) where anger led to recklessness). As Brett MR said (in *Clarke v Molyneux* (England 1877) p. 248, quoted in *Thadani* (above) p. 233, *Rwekanika v Binamungu* (Tanzania 1974) p. 390, and *Chimala Stores v Zambia-Tanzania Road Services* above),

> If it be proved that out of anger, or for some other wrong motive, the defendant has stated as true which he does not know to be true and he has stated it, whether it is true or not, recklessly, by reason of his anger or other motive, the jury may infer that he used the occasion, not for the reason which justifies it, but for the gratification of his anger or some other indirect motive.

(See also *Royal Aquarium and Summer and Winter Garden Society v Parkinson* (1892) p. 444, quoted in *Thadani* at p. 235.) Carelessness is a different matter; that the defendant did not take care to check the truth of what he said is not itself malice; it might possibly be evidence of it: "The defendant's carelessness in not investigating the truth of the story did not, in my view, negative the absence of recklessness or malice" (*Zambia Publishing Co. v Kakungu* (1982) p. 171, Ngulube DCJ; see also *Balfour Beatty Ltd. v Wadda* (Sierra Leone 1983)).

Belief that the facts were true does not preclude malice:

> He may be moved by hatred or dislike, or a desire to injure the subject of the libel, and may be using the occasion for that purpose, and if he is doing so the publication will be maliciously made, even though he may believe the defamatory statements to be true (*Watt v Longsdon* (England 1930) at 154-5 (Greer LJ) quoted in *Hoare v Jessop* (Kenya 1965) p. 223).

(See also *Ssejjobi v Rwabigonji* (Uganda 1977).) On the other hand, Lord Diplock said in *Horrocks v Lowe* (1975) p. 147 (now the leading English authority),

> Judges and juries should, however, be very slow to draw the inference that a defendant was so far actuated by improper motives as to deprive him of the protection of the privilege unless they are satisfied that he did not believe that what he said or wrote was true or that he was indifferent to its truth or falsity.

The trial judge had held that while honest the plaintiff was suffering "gross and unreasoning prejudice". However, both the Court of Appeal and the House of Lords declined to hold that this amounted to malice.

However, there may be circumstances in which a defendant is under a duty to report something, even if he does not believe it to be true. In *N'Jie v Edmondson* (Gambia 1957) the defendant lawyer wrote to the Attorney-General passing on a complaint from his client about another lawyer, expressing no personal opinion. Taking into account all the circumstances, including that it would take time to contact the client who was far away for more information, the Privy Council held there was no evidence of malice. The defendant had been instructed to take proceedings against the plaintiff. Under the rule in *Smith v Selwyn (*England 1914*)*, since the allegations against the plaintiff imputed a felony, criminal proceedings ought to be taken first and the defendant really had no option but to report the matter to the Attorney-General.

Proof of Malice

Inference of malice may be from the language used (e.g. *Obaseki v Omo-Osagie* (Nigeria 1953); *Musiwa v Chanda* (Zambia 1985)) from the behaviour of the defendant in court (*Turner v M-G-M* (England 1950) - for an example, see *Tanganyika Transport v Nooray* (1961)). Other indicators may be the defendant's behaviour elsewhere, as in *Banda v Pitman* (Malaŵi 1991), where the defendant had told the plaintiff that the consequences which the latter anticipated would flow from the defamatory letter would serve him right), or the existence of a long-standing bad relationship with the plaintiff (e.g. *Ajala v Showunmi* (Nigeria 1977)).

The language used in the original statement - "intrinsic evidence" - may be evidence of malice because of its excessive violence or other quality. In *Obaseki v Omo-Osagie* (above) malice was inferred from the words: "iniquitous, woeful exploitation and Hitlerite oppression" and "a man of low mentality". In *Ezekwe v Otomewo* (Nigeria 1957) the defendants had mentioned the "arrogance, ignorance and the spiritual wickedness" of the plaintiff. However, pungency of language, even exaggeration, are not necessarily evidence of malice (see *Adam v Ward* (England 1917) p. 339, *Laughton v Bishop of Sodor & Man* (England 1972) p. 508, and *Turner v M-G-M* (England 1950), p. 470-1, all quoted in *Hoare v Jessop* (above) p. 225). "A man may use excessive language and yet have no malice in his mind" said Lord Esher in *Nevill v Fine Arts Co.* (England 1895) p. 170, quoted in *Thadani* (above at p. 233). "While the language in the newspaper article in this case may suffer from slight exaggeration, nonetheless I see no evidence of malice therein" said the judge in *Mwanza v Zambia Publishing Co. Ltd.* (1981, p. 243). In *Kitto v Chadwick* (Uganda 1975, p. 144), it was said that a letter was "undoubtedly couched in peremptory and threatening language, but in view of the appellant's apparent reluctance to supply the information, I do not consider the language to have been oppressive in the circumstances". This is particularly so where the defendant is responding to an attack (*Adam v Ward*; *Kitto v Chadwick*; *Akin-Olugbade v Iro* (Nigeria 1980, p. 290) (Bada J quoting Gatley)). Passion and hurt pride is not the same thing as showing malice (*Hassan v Harding* (Sierra Leone 1967-8)). And a certain astringency of language is by no means uncommon in literary and other artistic criticism; a rare African example is *Forget v Maurice Press Ltd.* (Mauritius 1964) where a newspaper criticism of a play referred to an actor as a "clown", but this was held not actionable (under essentially French law). And the Vice-Chancellor of the University of Ibadan said in evidence in *Ekanem-Ita v Fetuga* (Nigeria 1991) that "Exhibit P. 18 was written in a harsh language which is characteristic of letters in the University of Ibadan. He further stated that Exhibit P. 15 was equally harsh", and the court held there was no malice!

A mere failure or refusal to apologise is not itself to be taken as evidence of malice (*Ayoola v Alajure* (Nigeria 1977); *Mumba v Singoyi* (Zambia 1975) (quoting Lord Denning in *Horrocks v Lowe*)) although repeating the defamation might well be (Gatley (para. 1355) cites *Neill v Henderson* (Scotland 1901, p. 390)); *Tackyie v Kabbah* above was a strong case since police investigation had shown the allegation to be unfounded. It seems that in *African Newspapers v Coker* (Nigeria 1973, p. 396) the Supreme Court of Nigeria took the plea of justification as evidence of malice. Gatley (para. 1354) says "It may be that in some cases an unsuccessful plea of justification may be evidence of malice" (quoting *Broadway Approvals v Odhams Press* (England 1965, p. 825) citing *Simpson v Robinson* (England 1848)). However, this will not always be an appropriate inference (for example *Buachie v Samman* (Ghana 1982) citing *Pape v O'Driscoll* (England 1909)). In *Coker* the Court also said that the defendant newspaper was essentially repeating the original allegations, drawn from the Saville Tribunal report and ignoring the Government's subsequent White Paper (p. 396, see Chapter 14).

If the defendant believed that what he says was true, his failure to check it will not defeat the defence (e.g. *Suleman Ltd. v Sayani* (Tanzania 1963)). In *Mumba v Singoyi* above, the defendant may have been hasty and even irrational in making his judgments, but not malicious. However, in *Ukpoma v Bademosi* (Nigeria 1979) the court concluded that there was evidence of malice in the number of discrepancies between the letter circulated by the defendant to civil service departments and the statement from the Public Complaints Commission on which it purported to be based. Overall, malice was perhaps found too readily. In a Rhodesian case in 1970 the court held that the inference of malice was "irresistible" from the defendant's refusal to give evidence, and to attempt to explain his "patently false" statement (*Parsons v Cooney* (1970)). Such inferences should be made with care, for the issue is the state of mind of the defendant at the time of the publication (see below; however, see also *Broadway Approvals v Odhams Press* (England 1965)). The *obiter dictum* of a judge in Uganda to the effect that "it is not necessary for the plaintiff to prove affirmatively what the defendant's improper motive was, all that he needs to do is to disprove the existence of a proper motive" is perhaps doubtful (*Ssejjobi v Rwabigonji* (1977)). Courts should not be too ready to draw inferences of malice (*Horrocks v Lowe* (England 1975)).

Evidence of malice has included attacking the plaintiffs on the basis of 8-year old events *(Williams v West African Pilot* (Nigeria 1961)), and the defendant's writing his letter about the plaintiff anonymously (*Mumba v Singoyi,* above). Publication of the statement to an unnecessarily wide audience *may* be evidence of malice. As was said in *Toogood v Spyring* (England 1834) quoted in *Abasi v Williams* (Nigeria 1942),

> I am not aware that it was ever deemed essential to the protection of such a communication that it should be made to someone interested in the inquiry, alone, and not in the presence of a third party. If made with honesty of purpose to a party who has any interest in the inquiry (and that has been very liberally construed) the simple fact that there has been some casual bystander cannot alter the nature of the transaction. The business of life could not well be carried on if such restraints were imposed on this and similar

> communications and if, on every occasion on which they were made, they were not protected unless strictly private.

But if the defendant deliberately involved someone else, or could easily have avoided being overheard, the situation may be different (*Toogood v Spyring*). In *Doryume v Awah II* (Gold Coast 1913) the court indicated that if the defendant had engineered the presence of extra people at the meeting that might have indicated malice. In the case of written communications excess of privilege may mean that some communications are not privileged (Chapter 13), but it does not necessarily mean that there was malice in the privileged communication (though it might be some evidence of malice).

Malice Must Be the Motivating Factor

The malice must have been the *dominant* factor (*Horrocks v Lowe* above). The court in *Hoare v Jessop* (Kenya 1965) was prepared to recognise that there was some evidence of malice, but held that the circulation of the statement complained of was motivated by the desire to put the defendants' own side of the story. Crabbe JA said (p. 222) of the trial judge:

> If, however, he meant that at the time of the publication the defendants bore ill-will for the plaintiff, that would not be sufficient to enable the plaintiff to succeed though the existence of such ill-will would be a material factor to consider in determining whether the publication of the words was activated by malice.

Pleading

English Rules of Court now (Order 82, r. 3 (3)) make specific provision in connection with qualified privilege and fair comment, and this has been copied in some African jurisdictions (e.g. Order 16 r. 18 of the 1973 Lagos High Court Rules): malice must be pleaded (*Bakare v Ibrahim* (Nigeria 1973) applied in *Ajala v Are* (Nigeria 1985)) - as must particulars of the facts and matters from which that malice is to be inferred. In Tanganyika in 1963 (*Suleman v Sayani*) the old provision (Order 6 r.10 of the Indian Code of Civil Procedure) remained - that it was enough to allege malice "as a fact without setting out the circumstances from which the same is to be inferred" (p. 608). There was English authority to the effect that if malice was alleged in the statement of claim it did not require to be pleaded again in the reply (*Smith v Lewis* (1917)); therefore the plaintiff, having pleaded the usual ritual words about falsely and maliciously, could argue express malice - which he did unsuccessfully. Similarly in Kenya, the High Court observed that there had been several amendments to the Rules but not to this rule (*Saifudin Taherali Patwa v Mustafa Mulla Heptulla* (1975)).

Malice Where There are Joint Tortfeasors

Where the defence of qualified privilege is in issue the malice of one person does not infect his fellow defendants. In the leading English case (*Egger v Chelmsford* (1965)) out of a committee of ten who instructed that a libellous letter be written on a privileged occasion, seven were malicious. It was held that the rest were still entitled to the defence, as was the assistant secretary who actually wrote the letter. The court thought the secretary would not lose his privilege even if all the committee were malicious, provided the secretary himself had no malice (Gatley has doubts - para. 788 fn. 50).

If one joint tort-feasor is vicariously liable for another who is malicious the former also loses his privilege (*Egger v Chelmsford*; for example, see *Tanganyika Transport v Nooray* (Tanzania 1965)).

In the case of fair comment, if the person who made the comment is malicious, some would take the view that the comment cannot be described as fair, and no-one can claim the protection of the defence (Gatley, para. 789). In *Thomas v Bradbury, Agnew & Co.* (England 1906) the publishers did not argue that they were not infected by the malice of the contributor, although it is not clear he was a servant (see Rogers, 1981, p. 233). The House of Lords has emphasised that the fairness of comment is to be judged on the basis of the comment itself, and not of the belief of the defendant (*Telnikoff v Matusevich* (1991)). The potential of this approach for protecting freedom of comment by the press would be substantially undermined if the plaintiff could vitiate the defence by showing that someone else was malicious. The logic of the Lords' position is that the fairness of the comment depends upon the comment alone, and the position of any individual defendant upon his behaviour alone. If the plaintiff could show not only that the author was malicious but that the publisher was aware of that malice, this would be substantial evidence of the publisher's own malice.

Notes

1. A case brought by the Governor of Mauritius against *The Times*!

17 Innocent Dissemination

This is the only defence recognised by the common law which amounts to saying "I did not know that the publication was defamatory".[1] Certain people who have played a part in the dissemination of a libel, but no part in its production, can plead that they did not know that the publication contained anything defamatory, that it was not of a character likely to contain a libel, and were not negligent in not knowing (derived from the findings of the jury in *Emmens v Pottle* (England 1885)). The defence amounts to a denial of publication; the plea in *Emmens* was "never published". However, since the onus is upon the defendant (*Vizetelly v Mudie's Select Library* (England 1900)) it seems most appropriate to discuss it as a defence. It may be available to a wholesaler or retailer or a library (see *Vizetelly v Mudie's Select Library Ltd.* - with *Emmens v Pottle* one of the principal English cases; both these were relied on in the *Awolowo* case, below). Other cases are *Sun Life Assurance v WH Smith* (England 1934) and *Goldsmith v Sperrings* (England 1977). Observations in the latter case were *obiter*, since the point in issue was whether the plaintiff was abusing the process of the court by suing the distributors in order to deny an outlet to the satirical journal *Private Eye*, rather than seeking to vindicate his reputation.

The principles are admirably illustrated by the Nigerian case of *Awolowo v Kingsway Ltd.* (1968): the defendants sold *The One Eyed Man is King* in which Chief Awolowo was libelled. They were held liable; the very reason the booksellers had stocked the book was that it concerned Nigerian politics. The judge said,

> I...think that a book seller who undertakes the sale of a book which known to him is written about a particular locality or geographical area and contains the names of the people of that place and their activities ought to read through such book to satisfy himself that it does not contain a libel on the people of whom it is written.

A similar approach obtains under Roman-Dutch law; in a Zimbabwe case (*Zvogbo v Kingston's Ltd.* (1986) citing *Trimble v Central News Agency Ltd.* (South Africa 1934)) the judge observed (p. 325),

> The magazine Drum appears to consist, at least in part, of political news and comment, and it is printed and published in South Africa, a country which is politically hostile to Zimbabwe. In these circumstances, it is my view that the defendant distributes this magazine, and any other of a similar type, without first checking their contents, at its peril.

It would be perfectly possible for a distributor to read an item and be unaware of its libellous content in, for example a case like *Cassidy v Daily Mirror* (England 1929). Gatley (para. 241n.) says it is not clear what the position is - whether the fault lies in not having realised that the publication might contain any libel, or in not realising that it contained the particular libel which is complained of. Any newspaper *may* contain a libel, but it probably impossible for the distributor to read every issue, to see if it is libellous, and Gatley mentions the recommendation of the UK Royal Commission on the Press (Cmnd 6810, paras. 19.39-19.46) that the defence should be available unless the defendant ought to have known that the publication contained the specific libel. (He refers to *Sun Life Assurance v WH Smith* and *Goldsmith v Sperrings* above.) The test should perhaps be whether there is anything about the particular issue which should have alerted him - and should be viewed in the context of the realities of the business (see the remarks in *Trimble v Central News* quoted by Gatley, para. 242n). On the other hand, it might be argued that some newspapers are so scurrilous, and sell by virtue of this, that the distributor ought to to assume that they contain something defamatory rather than the contrary! These considerations would presumably go to the question of negligence which should, as usual, be assessed in the circumstances. There is not the same urgency to get books onto the shelves.

This defence is not available to the author, editor, publisher or even the printer (see *Newton v City of Vancouver* (Canada 1932)). The English Committee on Defamation said (Cmnd 5909, para. 304),

> The management of a printing company or firm cannot possibly read all the material submitted for printing. Those directly concerned with the actual printing (compositors, proof-readers, etc.) know what words and sentences are in fact printed, but are not equipped to and cannot be expected to evaluate them from the defamation angle.

Changed technology has been a factor in changed attitudes: now that much printing is done from camera-ready copy or computer disks, very often no-one in the printing concern actually reads the material. The English 1996 Defamation Act s. 1 creates a new defence for printers, producers and distributors of books and those who process and distribute other forms of medium, provided that they took reasonable care and did not know and had no reasonable grounds to believe that they were contributing to the publication of a defamatory statement.

The defence was unsuccessfully raised by an Australian television company in whose live broadcast defamatory remarks were made. It was held that the company was not a subordinate distributor but an originator of the statement. There were policy reasons against extension of the defence; the possibility of the author of the defamation being overseas was mentioned as one possible complication (*Thompson v Australian Capital TV Pty. Ltd.* (1995)). The English 1996 Act s. 1 gives a defence to broadcasters of live programmes who have "no effective control" over the maker of a statement, and indeed to operators of other communications systems.

Under Mauritian law the innocent dissemination argument would come under the broad defence of absence of fault. Indeed, as we have seen, a radio company was held not liable for a live broadcast (*Curé v Universal Sound Equipment Co. Ltd.* (1941)). In France the defence of good faith requires proof of the valid objective in publishing, the absence of any personal spite, restraint of expression and that necessary precautions were taken to check on the veracity of the statement (*Carter-Ruck on Libel and Slander* (1992), pp. 328-329), it is not clear that all these requirements were satisfied in the *Curé* case.

Note

1. It has been suggested that this defence does not survive a correct construction of the Defamation Act provision (s. 4 of the English Act) (Crystal-Kirk, 1988). The various writers, and law reform commissions, seem to presume otherwise, and in *Awolowo v Kingsway Ltd.* (Nigeria 1968) the judge held the defences were distinct, and the abandonment by the defendants of the statutory defence did not preclude their relying on the common law one.

18 Other Defences

Consent

If the plaintiff has consented to the publication of particular words (*Moore v News of the World* (England 1972)) to a particular audience (*Chapman v Ellesmere* (England 1932)) he cannot then complain of the publication (*Monson v Tussaud's* (England 1894) cited in *Saraki v Soleye* (Nigeria 1971)). Examples are, not unnaturally, rare, but *Saraki v Soleye* is one; the background was that there had been a report on an inspection of the plaintiff's clinic, then the plaintiff's letter of protest in which he said he was taking the matter to the Nigerian Medical Council. Finally the defendant (Permanent Secretary in the Ministry of Health) wrote to the plaintiff, copy to the Council. The judge held that the plaintiff had consented to the defendant's letter "to the extent to which [it] relates to the subject-matter of the plaintiff's letter...i.e. the report of Dr. Shona" (p. 278). In essence the plaintiff had agreed to the Council's being informed of what the plaintiff himself had already been told. The judge described the defence (pp. 277-8):

> The requirement of the law...is that if it can be proved that the plaintiff expressly or impliedly assented to, or acquiesced in, the publication of the defamatory matter, no action will lie...Where the defence relies on the assent of the plaintiff the evidence of assent must be clear and unequivocal.

Another plaintiff invited a potential witness to hear what was being said by the defendant - who obligingly repeated his statement - but this was held not to amount to consent (*Okoro v Adogwu* (Nigeria 1982) citing Gatley, paras. 246-7). A less convincing case comes from Rhodesia. A magazine published a letter from the plaintiff challenging the magazine's correspondent to say where and when the plaintiff had made a particular remark. Below the letter the magazine purported to do just that. The plaintiff said this implied that he was a liar. The court held that he had assumed the risk of this occurring (*Fortune v African International Publishing Co (Pty) Ltd.* (1976)). It said that in many cases a challenge amounted to saying "I dare you to say xxx and if you do I'll sue", but this was not so here. I should have thought it was a more likely interpretation of the plaintiff's challenge than that he was saying, "I deny that I said that, but if you insist I am not telling the truth I shall meekly accept it".

In Mauritius a court found that the plaintiff had provided information about himself, knowing that it would be published, in a journal called *Appel pour nos Missions* [Appeal for our Missions] - in an article portraying him as a chicken thief reformed by the discovery of religion (*Ardor v Girou* (1935) citing Dalloz, *Code Annoté*).

Accord and Satisfaction

The plaintiff cannot sue if, contractually or under seal, he has agreed not to do so. The most likely situation is that the plaintiff has agreed not to bring an action if the defendant will publish an apology, and possibly make some payment. The plea was raised in *Akintola v Anyiam* (Nigeria 1961) but failed because the defendant had not done what the plaintiff had asked: he had not paid the sum of £1,000, and although he had published an apology (headed "Correction") this had not been in the terms requested by the plaintiff.

In *Ibe & Co. v Reveille* (Nigeria 1975) the plaintiff's lawyer had demanded publication of a rejoinder. The letter ended "if you fail to publish the rejoinder it will be clear that your company is greatly actuated by malice against our clients. In that event legal action will be taken to vindicate our clients' good name and dispel the wanton charge of inefficiency". The judge interpreted the letter not as promising not to sue if the rejoinder was published but as amounting to an acceptance that malice was not involved if the rejoinder was published. With respect I would read the original offer as saying that if you do not publish the rejoinder we shall sue - with the implication that if they did publish, the plaintiffs would not sue. The publisher should be careful to clarify what is being agreed; where the plaintiff's lawyer had said "Our client would be *willing to consider* withholding this action providing you publish a retraction", the court held this did not amount to an undertaking to withdraw (*Prakash v Wilson* (Zimbabwe 1992)).

A release to, or satisfaction reached with, one person responsible for a defamatory statement operates a bar against suing the other joint tortfeasors (*Howe v Oliver* (England 1908)); Spry (1976, p. 49) says this seems to have been overlooked in the case of *Lalobo v Lakidi* (Uganda 1969). However, the courts will readily infer that the agreement is a covenant not to sue the individual, and that the plaintiff has reserved his right to take action against the others (*Bryanston Finance v De Vries* (England 1975)). Where the agreement was a settlement with one tortfeasor *after* judgment a court said it would offend common sense if it was construed to release the other (*Watts v Aldington* (England 1993)).

Statutory Limitations and Protection

As with torts generally, once a certain period of time has elapsed, no action can be brought. Two questions arise: how long is the period, and when does it start to run? The answer to the first is surprisingly complex, for historical reasons. Under the Statute of Limitations of 1623, in force in some African jurisdictions which do not have locally enacted legislation, an action for slander must be brought within two years (s. 2). This provision has been reproduced in post-independence Ghanaian legislation, but the period for libel is six years (Limitation Decree NRC Decree No. 54 1972, s. 2(9) for slander and s. 4(1)(a) for general tort actions). In Lagos, under the Limitation Act s. 10 the period for slander is three years (*Egbe v Adefarasin* (Nigeria 1987) turned on this); in Delta, Ogun and similar legislation in Nigeria the period for slander is six years (Limitation Law s. 4(a)). For libel, however, the period in *all* the Nigerian jurisdictions is six years. In Kenya, somewhat unusually, the limitation period is one year only for both types of action (Limitation of Actions Act s. 4(2) as amended by the Defamation Act s. 20 - held to affect existing causes of action in *Amrit Pal Aggarwal v Hamilton, Harris & Mathers* (1972)). In *Okoth v Wachira* (Kenya 1978) when a magazine was dated "May 1975", there was publication for the whole of that month, unless it was proved otherwise). In Tanzania the period for all types of tort actions is three years (Law of Limitation Act No. 10 of 1971, s. 3(1) and Sch. 1). In the Roman-Dutch jurisdictions, there is also a three-year limitation period (e.g. Prescription Act 1975 of Zimbabwe, applied in *Maketo v Medical Investments (Pvt) Ltd.* (1988)). Press representatives argued for a one-year period to the Zambian Law Development Commission (1984, p. 11).

A further complication is that there is a difference as to when the limitation period begins to run between, on the one hand, libel, and slander *per se*, and, on the other, slander actionable only on proof of special damage: "in the case of a suit for compensation for a wrong which does not give rise to a cause of action unless some specific injury actually results therefrom, the right of action shall accrue on the date when an injury results" (s. 6(e) of the Tanzanian legislation, for example). Even at common law, where a tort is not actionable unless damage occurs, there is no tort committed (Gatley cites *Saunders v Edwards* (England 1663), *Darley Main v Mitchell* (England 1885), *inter alia*). In *Egbe v Adefarasin* above the court observed *obiter* that the period would not run until damage occurred if the slander were not actionable *per se*, but in the event it was actionable *per se*. However, under the Statute of Limitations this normal expectation is displaced, and the time runs from when the words are spoken (Gatley, para. 854n), so in jurisdictions which apply this statute there is no difference between the causes of action on this point.

I would not claim that this information is either up-to-date or complete, and evidently care should be taken in referring to sources from England - where there is now a one year period, with a possible discretionary extension for both torts (1996 Act s. 5). This will apply to Seychelles (see Chapter 3).

Many jurisdictions retain colonial legislation providing a special short limitation period for actions against public servants, usually termed "Public Officers Protection Acts" or Laws, some giving periods as short as three months. In *Attisogbe v Harlley* (Ghana 1972) it was held that the same period applied under the Public Officers Act 1962 to the defendant who was Inspector-General of Police and Vice-Chairman of the National Liberation Council. It did not cease to apply if there was express malice. In Mauritius doubts have been expressed about the constitutionality about such special protection (*Beau Plan SE v Government of Mauritius and Sunnassee* (1993)).

There may be other limitations, such as that applying to the Nigerian Broadcasting Corporation, under which no writ could be issued until at least one month from the service of a written notice of intention to sue (e.g. Nigerian Broadcasting Act s. 61(2), applied in *Edibiri v NBC* (1978)).

Other examples of special protection exist such as that in the Kenyan Post and Telegraph Corporation Act (Cap. 411 s. 74) which states that the corporation and its employees are not liable for transmission in the ordinary course of the telegraph service of any defamatory telegram. Similar legislation is found elsewhere.

Provocation

This is not formally treated as a defence at common law, though words spoken in a quarrel may be treated as "mere abuse" (Chapter 5), words spoken in self-defence may be privileged (Chapter 13), and provocation may also be relevant to the assessment of damages (Chapter 19, and also the discussion in the Malaŵian case of *Hampton v Herkes* (1961-63)).

But Roman-Dutch law has a concept of *rixa*, or provocation. Some authorities do not treat this as separate from abuse or self-defence (Burchell,1985, p. 267, and Chapter 20 generally); and some consider that *rixa* is best translated as "anger" and is different from provocation (see

Boberg, 1989, p. 59). In a Botswana case it was said that the response in the case of *rixa* must be proportionate to the provocation offered (*Mosieman v Maswabi* (1977) p. 93 (the defence was not applied)).

"Lying"

Under Shona and Ndebele customary law in Zimbabwe there is a defence translated as "lying" (*kunyepa*) which amounts to saying that the defendant was talking nonsense and is the sort of person the community would not take seriously, indeed was a "lunatic". (This sentence is taken essentially from *Zijena v Maphosa* (1992) p. 429, where it was held that the defence did not apply because the defendant had not claimed to be insane. The court was relying on Goldin & Gelfand (1975).)

19 Damages

Introduction

Certain consequences measurable in financial terms may flow from a defamatory statement, but most of the loss is much less tangible, and such loss is normally compensatable - indeed is often compensated at a much higher level than the measurable losses.

Special Damage in Slander

Subject to certain exceptions, no action can be brought for slander unless special damage is proved (Chapter 4). Some authorities say special damage must be "capable of being estimated in money" (*Roberts v Roberts* (England 1864)). This expression adequately covers loss such as that of employment actual or prospective (*Longdon-Griffiths v Smith* (England 1950), *Ecklin v Little* (England 1890)), or loss of custom (*Bluck v Lowering* (England 1885), *Worsley v Cooper* (England 1939), *Sobayo v Daily Times* (Nigeria 1977)) but special damage embraces other things which really cannot be measured in pecuniary terms, such as loss of the hospitality of friends (*Davies v Solomon* (England 1871)) or loss of a spouse, actual or prospective. English examples of the last involving women plaintiffs are *Lynch v Knight* (1861) and *Speight v Gosnay* (1891); McGregor (1988) suggests that now a man might also be able to claim such damages. In *Johnson v Smith* (Sierra Leone 1963) the plaintiff complained that her husband had thrown her out of the house for three days. She failed because she had herself passed the defamatory statement on to her husband, but otherwise the court would have been prepared to award damages - citing *Ward v Weeks* (England 1830) and *Parkins v Scott* (England 1862). But the courts will not go so far as to include loss of friendship as such *(Argent v Donigan* (England 1892)), exclusion from a religious sect (*Roberts v Roberts* above) or illness caused by distress at the slander (*Allsop v Allsop* (England 1860)). A Nigerian court did accept social ostracism and the fact that community meetings of which the plaintiff was leader were moved to someone else's house, but it is not clear that this would satisfy the English criteria, which were not discussed (*Nweze v Ugwu* (1976)). But exclusion from buying and selling in the local market, and being denied payment made at the time of marriage of one's daughter would seem clearly to be special damage (*Nwankwo v Okeke* (1980)); the payment seems to have been made to members of a society (a sort of save and loan function?). The same case also involved suspension from membership of societies; the judge, who did cite Gatley, did not spell out the pecuniary aspect of this.

Having been prosecuted is not special damage for which damages will be given in this tort. This, a South West African Court said, would amount to giving damages for malicious prosecution in defamation (*Doll v Kaiser* (1939)). In Tanzania, (*Hamiei v Akilimali* (1971)) such damages were, erroneously, given.

Special Damage Generally

Apart from the special damage which is required to make most slander actionable, plaintiffs may also claim special damages in slander actionable *per se* and in libel, which is always actionable *per se*. A Mauritius example is *Pierre v Issac* (1914): the plaintiff lost his job as a shorthand writer because the defendant accused him of having falsified a record.

Causation and Remoteness

If the misfortune would have happened anyway, the plaintiff cannot hold the defendant liable. In *Okotcha v Olumese* (Nigeria 1974), the plaintiff claimed the defamation had cost him a scholarship: the judge held that the plaintiff would not have got a scholarship anyway (there was no evidence that he had admission to a university, or that the "sponsor" could pay). In an old Gold Coast case the plaintiff complained that the libel had led to his being expelled from Porto Novo by the King, and he lost house and stock worth £2500. He was awarded £150 on the basis that he admitted he had already been on bad terms with the King (*Macaulay v Taiwo* 1884). But if this loss would not have occurred but for the libel should he not have obtained full compensation?

The East African Court of Appeal declined to award special damages because the evidence suggested that the plaintiff's associates withdrew companionship and credit not because they thought less of him, but because they feared the displeasure of other members of the community (*Patel v Dhanji* (Kenya 1977)).The court had held that a statement to the effect that the plaintiff ought to be ostracised could be defamatory; does it make sense to hold that he could not sue when he *was* ostracised? Is the classic excuse: "It's what other people might think..." to deprive plaintiffs of damages?

The damage must be "the natural and probable result" of the words spoken - which seems to mean the foreseeable result (*Lynch v Knight* above). In a Malaŵian case damage was held too remote: the plaintiff was prevailed upon by a sugar company which employed him to sell an estate which was his personal property following a libellous statement by the defendant that suggested the plaintiff was trying to avoid paying his debts (*Duguid v Storey* (1923), relying on *Speake v Hughes* (England 1904)). An element of policy no doubt creeps in: the ostensible reason for excluding illness caused by distress is usually that it is too remote (*Allsop v Allsop* above), but it is clear that fear of encouraging groundless actions is also an important factor (see *Wilkinson v Downton* (England 1897) p. 60). Suppose the reaction which led to the damage was foreseeable but unreasonable? A Nigerian judge said, "It is an unreasonable man that lynches a suspect" (*Ilonuba v Star Printing & Publishing Co.* (1979) p. 167). But in some communities such behaviour must be considered foreseeable. On the other hand, courts might be reluctant to hold a defendant liable for such consequences and might well escape from the dilemma by holding that any attempted lynching of an alleged thief was unforeseeable.

A specific "remoteness" issue arises where the original statement of the defendant has been repeated by someone else; the implications of this issue have been discussed in Chapters 4 and 8.

Assessing General Damages

A Sudanese judge observed,

> General damages are given in defamation cases really for the purpose of vindicating the plaintiff's character and to show the world that the defendant acted wrongfully in publishing the libel or slander. (*Awwad el Kadi v Mohammed Hussein Badran* (1900-1931))

And in Nigeria, "compensation by damages operates in two ways - as a vindication of the plaintiff to the public, and as a consolation to him for a wrong done" (*Onabanjo v Concord Press* (1982) p. 94, quoting Windeyer J in *Uren v Fairfax* (Australia 1967) p. 150, as quoted in *Broome v Cassell* (England 1972)). In *Rook v Fairrie* (England 1941), the judge suggested that when sitting without a jury the judge's comments might serve a vindicatory function to the extent that the damages awarded might be less than those awarded by a jury. Later cases have rejected this approach (e.g. *Associated Newspapers* v *Dingle* (England 1964)).

> It is to be remembered that in a libel action the damages awarded are, *for the most part*, entirely without any real connection with any pecuniary loss at all. One is endeavouring to express in terms of money several different things which are not really susceptible of a money valuation in any true sense.

said Lambo J in *Akintola v Ayiam* (Nigeria 1961); the emphasised words accommodate the rare case in which the plaintiff in a defamation action can prove special damages in the narrow sense of specific items of pecuniary loss strictly proved, and the fact that loss of business and similar injuries having a clear relationship to money are taken into account in assessing general damages (e.g. loss of custom - *Ratcliffe v Evans* (England 1892)). The Nigerian courts took account of the fact that the plaintiff in *Anunobi v Nigerian National Press Ltd.* (1964) lost financially because he had to resign his trade union positions, and in *Odutola v West African Pilot* (1960) had not been renominated as chairman of the local authority because of the libel.

The same sorts of items which are accepted as actual (or special) damages for the purposes of slander not actionable *per se* can be proved as relevant to general damages for libel or slander actionable *per se*. So can the sorts of consequences which are not acceptable for slander not actionable *per se* such as loss of friendship (*Garbett v Hazell Watson* (England 1943)) or illness. According to Gatley no English court has ever awarded damages for illness, but there are cases elsewhere including Australia (*Rigby v Mirror Newspapers* (1963)); in Malaŵi (*Hampton v Herkes* (1961-63)) the court said that though the plaintiff claimed she had suffered in health this could equally be due to the strain of her divorce case and living openly with a man to whom she was not married.

The sorts of matters referred to in the previous paragraph are guides to the appropriate level of general damages (Gatley, para. 1321n), but are not required for success; other than in slander not actionable *per se* damage is presumed. Indeed, the words are still actionable even if they were not believed, as we saw earlier (except perhaps in Mauritius - see *Mahraz v Jenkins* (1899)). A judge in Zimbabwe said, "the fact that the words complained of did not achieve their objective does not make them less defamatory" (*Tekere v Zimbabwe Newspapers (1880) Ltd.* (1986) p. 290, citing *Buthelezi v Poorter* (South Africa 1975)). In *Lardner v Sketch* (Nigeria 1979) the court refused to take account of the fact that the plaintiff had been made Senior Advocate less than two years after the libel and reduce the damages. The English Supreme Court Procedure Committee (1991, para. X.4), however, thought that whether anyone believed the statement was very relevant to general damages.[1]

Non-pecuniary loss is recognised by the law of Mauritius, where it is known as "moral damage". A French writer observed that such damages are for things which cannot be evaluated in pecuniary terms, but afford the victim a sort of substitute satisfaction, and ultimately are fixed by the judges in an independent way (Planiol, quoted in *Tranquille v Rivet* (1930) p. 343, my rough translation).[2]

There are many occasions on which courts have indicated in broad terms the sorts of factors they will take into account.

> I am entitled to take into consideration the conduct of the plaintiff, his position and standing, the nature of the libel, the mode and extent of publication, the absence or refusal of any retraction or apology, and the whole conduct of the defendant from the time when the libel was published down to the very moment of the verdict (*Onabanjo v Concord Press* (Nigeria 1982) pp. 94-5 (Kolawole J); see also *Adewusi v Sketch Publications* [No. 2] (Nigeria 1978)).

Coker JSC in Nigeria said,

> Such an award must be adequate to repair the injury to the plaintiff's reputation which was damaged; the award must be such as would atone for the assault on the plaintiff's character and pride which were unjustifiably invaded (*Uyo I v Nigerian National Press Ltd.* (1974)).

These various factors will determine whether the damages should be "aggravated" to reflect their seriousness. Aggravated damages are compensatory, towards the top end of the range of such damages. They are to reflect the extent of the injury to the plaintiff, not the degree of wickedness of the defendant, except so far as this enhances the injury (see *Williams v Daily Times* (Nigeria 1990) for some discussion, and Gatley, para. 1452).

The Defamation Itself

Factors include the very nature of the defamation itself (*Pedro v Orafidiya* (Nigeria 1974)). Any statement "justified" or shown to be privileged must first be, as it were, subtracted (*Associated Newspapers v Dingle* (above)). In *Pierce v Channel* ((Mauritius 1973) p. 12) the court observed that the fact that the defendants had been able to show a number of instances of violence on the part of the plaintiff towards sailors, while not enough fully to justify an allegation of general brutal treatment, would have reduced the damages considerably, and in *Prakash v Wilson* (Zimbabwe 1992) the court held that most of the allegations had been shown to be true.

In *Ukpoma v Daily Times* ((Nigeria 1979) p. 361) the court referred to "serious and wild allegations", and in *Tranquille v Rivet* ((Mauritius 1930) p. 343) to a "violent and vituperative" attack. On the other hand in *Nwangwu v Nwankwo* (Nigeria 1962) Mbanefo CJ said "The petition of the appellants was couched in such general terms and in such English that one wonders how much effect the libel had on those who heard it", and reduced the damages from £500 to £100. The offending words were "a wolf among men and lambs, a parasite who thrives at the expense of the people, a wicked and unsympathetic man who has broken the custom of the area and deprived the people of their rights thereunder, a cheater who posed as a saviour and a trouble-maker". Similarly, in Mauritius the court awarded a small sum because of "the unlikelihood of serious damage to the Plaintiff's reputation from (the) ranting phrases" (*Robertson v Michel* (1927) p. 84), while in *Leclézio v Roussel* (1896) damages took account of the fact the "article belonged to the class of political criticisms, in which more or less violent language is customary".

The severity of the imputation must be judged in the context of the national society. As the judge put it in a Swazi case (*Kunene v Shabangu* (1979-81) p. 187):

> Although in many Western countries there has during recent decades been a general decline in the standard of morals and some acceptance of the so-called permissive society, unfounded imputations of immorality and adultery have always been regarded as serious defamation and in Swaziland adultery is still an offence for which by Swazi law and custom heavy penalties may be inflicted.

And in Nigeria (*Okoro v Adogwu* (1981) p. 16):

> In an African setting...to call someone a witch can result in shunning the person said to be a witch thereby leading to such a person losing the society of his friends, people and even children.

The context of current events may also be relevant. A Nigerian court seemed to take into account the fact that the allegation - to the effect that the plaintiff Director of a parastatal had been arrested in connection with a large fraud - coincided with a period when a large number of public officers were being dismissed. The implication seemed to be that the coincidence would asssociate the plaintiff in the public mind with these disgraced public servants (*Obayiuwuana v Muhammed* (1986)). And in Namibia the court pointed out that the plaintiff had been employed by the South African and South West African police forces, thus opposing Namibian liberation, and an attack on his loyalty to the new Government was particularly serious for him (*Smit v Windhoek Observer* (1991)).

Extent of Dissemination

Dissemination through the press, broadcasting (e.g. *Attorney-General v Kapwepwe* (Zambia 1974)), enhances damages (in *Rindos v Hardwick* (1994) the Western Australia Supreme Court based damages on the potential dissemination - 23,000 personal computers with access to a computer bulletin board).

> It is difficult to estimate the consequences of libel in a newspaper. As Best CJ said in *De Crespigny v Wellesley* [England 1829], it may circulate the calumny through every region of the globe. Those who read it may never read the subsequent explanation or the report of the trial; and some of them who read both may forget the result and be left with the general recollection that the plaintiff was a man of whom a discreditable story was reported in the paper. Libellous statements are printed by newspapers because they find that it pays; many of their readers prefer to read and believe the worst of everybody, and the newspaper proprietors cannot complain if juries remember this in assessing damages

said Farwell LJ (*Hulton v Jones* (England 1909) p. 183, quoted in *Lardner v Sketch Publishing Co.* (Nigeria 1979) p. 284). But a Nigerian judge set rapid correction against the large circulation of the defendant newspaper (*Adewusi v Sketch* (1978) [No. 2] p. 306). It is also rational to distinguish between the ephemeral publication and the longer lasting. An English court said,

> A newspaper, on the day after publication, is fit for nothing except lighting a fire or wrapping up fish and chips; the *Tatler* lives on in doctors' waiting rooms and may be read months or even years afterwards (*Winyard v Tatler Publishing Co. Ltd* (1991)).

Conversely limited circulation restricts damages (e.g. *Enahoro v Associated Newspapers of Nigeria Ltd.* (1960) p. 227; *Asiodu v Abodunde*

(Nigeria 1979)). In *Lawson v Mahor* (Nigeria 1975) publication was to one person only; in *Bouchereau v Guichard* (Seychelles 1970) to the plaintiff and one or two others. Courts may take into account the fact that several people may read one copy of a newspaper (*Enahoro*, above). In *Okon v COR Advocate* (Nigeria 1961) the judge pointed out that though the circulation was not large, the article was repeated in Efik to make sure everyone in the area could read it. A slander heard by a large group of people would call for heavier damages than one heard by few. (But it by no means follows that damages for statements heard or read by very few people are trivial (in *Odongkara v Astles* (Uganda 1970) only one person heard the statement, but sh/5000 were awarded and in *Aruna v George-Taylor* (Nigeria 1977) ₦4000 were awarded for a libel published to two people (one a stenographer).) Where liability depends on an innuendo, the court will bear in mind that the number of people who understood the statement in that sense may be limited (e.g. *Maskini v Mbugus* (Tanzania 1975)).

Status and Position

Traditionally in African societies the *relative* status of the parties would have been significant: penalties would have been higher for defaming someone of higher status than oneself. In a case applying Chagga customary law the court said that since the status of chief had "long become an anachronism" in Tanzania, the plaintiff could get only an ordinary goat and not a fattened one as compensation (*Herman v Ndava* (1971)). Judges in other countries have not always taken a similar view though the emphasis on relative status is no longer seen. In Ghana, for example, it was relevant to damages that the plaintiff "had greatly suffered because he was a royal" (*Benneh v New Times Corporation* (1981)) and . "...to defame a chief or *ohene* as the defendant did of the plaintiff is a serious matter and the assumption of European way of life has not, in my view, had much impact on our rich culture" (Edusei J in *Kofi v Nana Essia Eiku* (Ghana 1970) quoted by Date-Bah (1973a, p. 136)).

Attitudes to politicians tend to be ambivalent. While conceding that defamation of a Minister which casts a doubt on his capacities for that position, is grave, a Zimbabwean judge said (*Zvogbo v Kingston's Ltd.* (1986)), "...no public figure can expect to escape criticism, disapproval, complaint and even hostility at times in respect of some of his decisions and actions". In fact the general tendency is to award substantial damages to prominent politicians and holders of public office, referring to "exalted position" (e.g. *Jakande v Concord Press* (Nigeria 1982) (Governor of Lagos State)) and so on, or, in one case to the fact that the plaintiff held a national honour (*Omolowo v Punch* (Nigeria 1985) - Order of the Federal Republic - as well as career in public service); see also *Mayanja v Editor of Mulengera Newspapers* (Uganda 1992 - former Minister); *Asare v Gomade* (Ghana 1961); *Maswanya v African Buyer and Trader (Publications) Ltd.* (Tanzania 1981), p. 223: award of damages should be "commensurate with such high office"). But status can be a matter of opinion. Although one judge in awarding Simon Kapwepwe damages referred to his prominence and the fact he had been Vice-President (*Kapwepwe v Zambia Publishing Co.* (Zambia 1978)), a judge in a later case suggested that he was "of high repute only to a limited number of the community" (*Zambia Publishing Co. v Mwanza* (1979) p. 82).

The professional status of the plaintiff may be relevant. In *Nthenda v Alade* (Nigeria 1974) the judge said "I have also taken into account the mental suffering of the plaintiff for the pain of false accusation and the embarrassment it caused him in his profession as a teacher both in relation to his students and fellow lecturers". There have been many cases in which the profession of the plaintiff, as a lawyer (e.g. *Lardner v Sketch* (Nigeria 1979), *Daily Times v Williams* (above), *Mayanja v Editor of Mulengera Newspaper* (Uganda 1992)), or senior police officer (*Adewusi v Sketch* (above), *Odongkara v Astles* (above)) to take two examples, has been emphasised.

The social standing of the plaintiff is also considered (e.g. *Oredein v Laseinde* (Nigeria 1975) p. 146). One judge, in holding that the plaintiffs should have brought separate actions, said that since they had different statuses, some being educated, some illiterate, for example, different amounts of damages would be appropriate (*Ojo v Eguassen* (Nigeria 1977)). A Ugandan court emphasised that standing should be judged at the time of the defamation, and that "humble beginnings" left behind should not restrict damages (*Oboth v New Vision* (1993)). It has been suggested that an allegation of theft against a child would be taken less seriously than against an adult (*Janbaccus v Hosseny* (Mauritius 1957) p. 121).

How about economic status? A Nigerian judge observed that a Nursing Supervisor like the plaintiff earned ₦3,500 a year, and awarded ₦600 for the allegation that he had been sacked for making advances to patients (*Gyang v Iliyasu* (1977)). In a Sudanese case (*Saadani v Sassoun*, 1917) the Chief Justice said,

> ...the court is entitled to take into account among other things the financial position of the defendant. The (defendant) receives a salary of £E[Egyptian]11 a month and the damages awarded by the court amounted to nine months pay;

> that seems to me a great deal too much. I think the sum of £E15 is a fair sum to award as damages; it is not a great sum, but it is substantial and it shows that the court thought the plaintiff was justified in bringing the action and that he has vindicated his character successfully; in a small community like that of the Sudan that is really all that is necessary for the plaintiff's protection.

It is not at all clear on what authority this approach was used. The judge may have been influenced by some doubt about the mental balance of the defendant (Gatley mentions insanity as a possibly mitigating factor (para. 1431, citing *Yeates v Read* (USA 1838); in *Saadani* counsel for the defendant argued absence of malice as affecting liability not in mitigation). A more common judicial reaction is that there is no basis for mitigating the damages because of the limited means of the defendant. In *Doll v Kaiser* ((Namibia 1939) p. 6) the judge said "counsel for the plaintiff, without adducing any authority, advanced the remarkable proposition that the defendant's ability to pay is an element to be considered in assessing the damages" (though in a recent Namibian case the judge said "I will assume in favour of the defendant that his financial means are not comparable to that of a flourishing newspaper" (*Marais v Haulyondjaba* (1993) p. 176). Such factors may creep back in if the court considers the *relative* position of the parties in society, as the judge said he would in *Biryabema v Kakwere* (Uganda) having also said he was "not entitled to diminish the damages by reference to the limited resources of the defendant" (see also *Sentengo v Sempa* (Uganda 1967)).

Otherwise the economic position of the parties is taken account of only when exemplary damages are under consideration (see below).

Existing Reputation

If a person has no reputation to protect he should not be able to claim compensation for statements that would injure someone with a reputation to lose. The defendant is permitted to show that the plaintiff had "a general bad reputation" (*Scott v Sampson* (England 1882), *Associated Newspapers v Dingle* (England 1964)) - proof of which "is notoriously difficult to achieve, and it is therefore a weapon which is hardly ever used" (Supreme Court Procedure Committee (1991, para. 1.19)). This reputation must be in the area of life in which the defamation had attacked the plaintiff's reputation (*Plato Films v Spiedel* (England 1961)). It must relate to the time of publication of the defamation, not subsequently (*Associated Newspapers v Dingle; Thompson v Nye* (England 1850) cited in *Elechi v Daily Times of Nigeria Ltd.* (1980)). It is not virtue or vice that is in issue - but reputation; thus the defendant may not prove specific instances of bad behaviour (*Scott v Sampson*; *Hobbs v Tinling* (England 1929), distinguished in *Thakers v Chipunguhelo* (Tanzania 1965), applied in *Currimjee Jeewonjee v Millien* (Mauritius 1948)). (See, however, *Juma v Continental Office Products Ltd.* (Nigeria 1971).) In Malaŵi where the accusation was of being a "jumper" or one who goes from one man to another, the court said (*Hampton v Herkes* (1961-63) p. 381),

> these specific admissions of misconduct with one man, although prolonged, are inadmissible to prove general bad character. The two broken marriages, while they may indicate absence of judgment or even defects in the temperament of the plaintiff or possibly mere incompatibility, do not of themselves prove bad character. The plaintiff might have figured in a divorce case without having acquired a general reputation for unchastity.

In Zambia the suggestion has been made that "evidence of specific known past conduct of the plaintiff which is connected in time and substance to the statement of which the plaintiff complains should be admissible in evidence in mitigation" - essentially to reverse the rule in *Scott v Sampson* (Zambian Law Development Commission, p. 6). In England the Supreme Court Procedure Committee which recommended this change[3] observing (1991, para. III 7):

> (T)he plaintiff would have the right to challenge the factual basis of the allegations as well as their relevance to the quantification of damage. Moreover, if the defendant's version of events turned out to be wrong, the fact that he had chosen to raise them would be an aggravating factor just as is the case with a failed plea of justification.

It is also not permissible to adduce evidence of rumours to the same effect as the defamation (*Scott v Sampson*), or of other newspaper reports of the same statement (*Dingle v Associated Newspapers* above).

When the plaintiff was already serving a sentence of imprisonment for theft, the judge held that he could take this into account in assessing the damages since, "he must be presumed to have less reputation to lose than if his record had been blameless". But this did not impinge on his "(presumed) reputation for sobriety" (*Thakers v Chipunguhelo* (above) p. 86, citing *Hawkins v Express Dairy Co. Ltd.* (England 1940), for the proposition that such admitted dishonesty could be relied upon when it was part of the plaintiff's own case). In one case the plaintiff had the misfortune to have one of his own witnesses reduce his damages by saying that he had believed the defamatory statement as the plaintiff was "the sort of person who might do such a thing" (*Adedoyin v Nigerian National Press* (1964)). On the other hand the court may take into account the good reputation (deserved or not) of the plaintiff: in *Ukpoma v Daily Times* (Nigeria 1979, p. 361) the court stressed that the plaintiff had worked "without any blemish on his character, reputation and profession, until his voluntary retirement".

Conduct of Defendant

The attitude of the defendant, particularly whether there was evidence of malice or deliberate falsification, will be relevant to damages. Examples include *Lardner v Sketch* (Nigeria 1979), where the defence failed to check its allegations. The defendant may aggravate damages by showing signs of malice (see *Akintola v Anyiam* (Nigeria 1961)): by his behaviour at the time of the defamation (in *Williams v West African Pilot* (Nigeria 1961) the judge decided there was malice partly because the defendants had based their statements on 8-year old events); by the strength of the language used (e.g. *Obasekei v Omo-Osagie* (Nigeria 1956) - "iniquities, woeful exploitation and Hitlerite oppression", also *East African Newspapers (Nation Series) Ltd v Opondo* (Kenya 1974) or subsequently). Malice may be shown even at the trial itself: an attempt to discredit plaintiff at trial "portrays the publication as one based on prejudice and malice. It is a calculated attempt to disparage the plaintiff in his profession and thus injure his dignity and pride" (*Lardner v Sketch* above p. 284). *In Banda v Pitman* ((Malaŵi 1990) p. 197) - "the attitude of the defendant in court was...full of ill-will". A Mauritian court took into account the fact that this was the third time the plaintiff had succeeded against the same defendant for defamatory attacks (*Morel v Rivet* (1931)).

Evidence of lack of malice may go to mitigate the damages. In *Mutual Aid Society Ltd. v Akerele* (Nigeria 1965) the defendant was negligent (which is not evidence of malice), and also the plaintiff's wife could have sorted out the mistake sooner. In *Rasmussen v MacPherson Train & Co. (EA) Ltd.* (Kenya 1959) the fact that the statement was foolish not malicious was taken into account, as was the reckless rather than malicious nature of that in *Kihika v Buringuriza* (Uganda 1962); (Spry (1976, p. 46) also mentions *Chandry v Uganda Printing & Publishing Co. Ltd.* (Uganda 1966) and *Peckover v Muyu* (Kenya 1970) as examples of behaviour indicating lack of malice.)

Lord Esher observed (*Draed v Graham* (England 1890) p. 55) that the court may look at the conduct of the defendant before the action complained of, after it or at the trial - quoted in *Akin Taylor & Co. Ltd. v Daily Times of Nigeria Ltd.* (Nigeria 1976). However, the West African Court of Appeal observed that conduct of the defendant, whether in aggravation or mitigation of the damages, should bear some relation to the defamation, and not be some unrelated event (*Obasekei v Omo-Osagie*, above, interpreting *Pearson v Lemaitre* (England 1843)).

Although there is no actual defence for the press based on the fact that the report was from identified sources (see Chapter 14) in *Saunders v Mills* (England 1829) evidence of source (another newspaper) was admitted; in *Associated Newspapers v Dingle* it was observed that this goes to show lack of malice and "comparative innocence of conduct" (Lord Radcliffe). An African example is *Dina v New Nigerian Newspapers* (1986, p. 366). In *Times of Zambia v Wonani* (1983) it is not clear whether the paper identified the source in its pages, but they were held to have acted reasonably even though they did not verify the information, since it came from a usually reliable source. The general trend of the authorities given by Gatley is somewhat to the effect that the source must be indicated in the original publication (paras. 1434-6; e.g. *Mullett v Hulton* (England 1803)). In *Zambia Publishing Co. Ltd. v Kakungu* (1982), the source was identified, (as a Minister "of whom it is reasonable to assume an absence of irresponsibility and deliberate falsehood" as the court observed, p. 171), as it was also in *Times Newspapers Zambia Ltd v Kashita* (1982) (see also *Times of Zambia v Kapwepwe* (1973) - the fact that the news item came from an agency was a mitigating factor). In a Mauritius case the court accepted that the defendant had borne no ill-will to the plaintiff, and that what he wrote had been based on information supplied to him by Municipal Councillors, and that he considered that he was acting in the public interest (*Menty v Pierre* (1938)); it does not appear from the report that the original publication stated the source of the supposed information. To the extent that the idea is that it is less malicious to spread a story than to make up one's own, it would seem that evidence of source ought to be admitted, whether or not it was mentioned in the original publication.

An unsuccessful defence of justification is likely to increase the damages (e.g. *African Newspapers v Coker* (Nigeria 1973), *Kihika v Buringuriza* (Uganda 1962)). The manner of the defence has been held relevant also; in *Nthenda v Alade* (Nigeria 1974) the judge said:

> The cross-examination of the plaintiff by the defendant's counsel goes beyond an attempt to establish the truth of the publication but transcends the limit of that area into the life history of the plaintiff's female relations from his

> secondary school days to the present day of examination not only a repetition of the libel but an amplification. His cross-examination of these former girl friends served no other purpose than to embarrass the plaintiff.

In the Mauritius case of *Lacaze v Henry* (1909), where the defamatory meaning of one statement only became clear at trial as a result of the conduct of the defence, especially the cross-examination of the plaintiff, the judge quoted Odgers: "The defendant must be careful not to increase by such cross-examination the amount of damages that was to be given against him".

Apology

The defendant may mitigate the damages by offering an apology, at common law (*Smith v Harrison* (England 1856)) or under statute (s. 1 of the 1843 Act - see Appendix). Under the latter the apology must made before the action or as soon as possible after it is begun, and notice in writing of intention to rely on the section is required. A Nigerian judge said, "To merely publish an apology probably in an obscure portion of the offending newspaper or worse still in another newspaper does not satisfy this section. The plaintiff should be directly informed of the apology before it can be accepted in mititgation of damage" (*Nasamu v Herwa Press Ltd.* 1981). The section itself does not require that the publication be in the same newspaper. In *Edukugho v Sunday Times* (Nigeria 1958) the section was relied upon but the plea failed because of delay in publishing the apology. However, the judge took it into account at common law. An apology must be adequate: covering the sting of the defamation as observed in *Akpojaro v Bendel Newspapers Corporation* (Nigeria 1981) and not apparently reluctant (*Risk Allah v Johnstone* (England 1868)). In *Mayanja v The White Fathers* (Uganda) the judge referred to the "rather half-hearted apology" by the defendants. In *Amalgamated Press v Allen* (Nigeria 1961) the apology was headed "rejoinder" which detracted partially from its value. In *Wing Fo Chan Kun v Sam Zee Moi* ((Mauritius 1955) p. 65) the court said the defendant's apology was made "rather with a view to extricating himself from his own embarassments, than with the object of assuaging the plaintiff's wounded feelings", applying the words of the court in *Millien v Giraud* ((Mauritius 1938) p. 92). And it must be prompt - which factor significantly reduced any value of the apologies in *Edukugho* (above) and *Mayanja v White Fathers* (above). On the other hand, the plaintiffs can expect too much: in *Edukugho v Sunday Times* (above), the judge said it was unreasonable to ask for apologies to be inserted in seven consecutive issues of the *Daily Times* and three consecutive issues of the *Sunday Times*.

A Zambian judge attached considerable importance to apology (*Times (Z) Ltd.* v *Wonani* (1983) p.134):

> We agree with the submission that, an adequate apology does repair, to a considerable extent, the damage done to a plaintiff's reputation. We agree also that the news media, and indeed, any other defendant, should be given every incentive to apologise when they have made a mistake.

And the Zambian Supreme Court held that an apology will usually "virtually expunge" damages (*Times Newspapers Zambia Ltd.* v *Chisulo* (1984)). However, in *Smit* v *Windhoek Observer* (Namibia 1991) the court was unimpressed by the defendant's "half-hearted apology" which regretted not having adorned the original statement with quotation marks or a question mark.

Gatley (para. 1327) doubts whether mere *absence* of an apology should be taken into account, to increase the damages, citing *Morgan* v *Odhams Press* (England 1971). And in Rhodesia (*Haas* v *Greatermans Stores Ltd.* (1966)) it was said that absence of apology cannot aggravate damages, citing *Lynch* v *Agnew* (South Africa 1929). However, judges often speak as though this was a factor, including in Lesotho (which also applies Roman-Dutch law) - where a court said the defendant "made his allegations without any apparent reason and even after these allegations had been proved to be untrue...at no stage did he ever tender an apology to the plaintiff" referring to this as an aggravating feature (*Tale* v *Beale* (1974-5)). In *Oredein* v *Laseinde* ((Nigeria 1975) p. 7) the court said "The attitude of the defendant throughout is not one of remorse for tarnishing the reputation of this gentleman". In *Lardner* v *Sketch* above "the ugly and damaging impression created in this publication remained uncorrected until now", and in *Eshiett* v *New Nigerian Newspapers* ((1978) p. 289) the court mentioned "the stubborn refusal of the defendants to tender an apology" (see also *Malaŵi Railways* v *Bhadurkhan* (1986) p. 443). Some of these situations may have gone beyond the mere absence of an apology, as in Sierra Leone (*Yanni* v *Sierra Leone Daily Mail* (1967-68) p. 108) where the judge thought that a defendant (a Queen's Counsel) had exacerbated the absence of apology:

> The plaintiff on the other hand is a motor engineer, and a small man in the social scale when compared with the third defendant, and from the conduct of the case by the third defendant one could not help feeling that it was expected

> that the small man must remain quiet and not seek the protection of the courts even though he may have been libelled by someone higher up the social scale.

Failure to apologise may be excused if a response to the plaintiff's own attitude - *Gautama v East African Newspapers* (Kenya 1970).

Conduct of Plaintiff

The fault of the plaintiff, too, may affect the damages. If he has attacked the defendant so as to provoke him into the defamatory statement, this may, even though not enough in the circumstances to provide a defence of qualified privilege on the "self-defence" basis, operate as some mitigation of the damages (e.g. *Hampton v Herkes* (Malaŵi 1961-3) p. 382, *Affull v Yambah* (Gold Coast 1855) where damages were reduced because the defendant was provoked by slander). There are several Mauritian cases, e.g. *Gaudet v Ah-Kong* (1914), *Gujadhur v Moonasing* (1935). *May v Brown* (England 1824) shows that the defendant must have been aware of the plaintiff's defamation of him (otherwise he could not claim to have been provoked by it) and that they must concern the same subject-matter. It was suggested in a Zambian case that this line of argument will not succeed if the attack was on someone else (*Times Publishing Co. v Kashita* (1982) p. 166) but surely if the defendant were responding to an attack on someone close to the defendant this ought to be taken into account in mitigation; it would be a factor indicating an absence of malice. In *Ohanbamu v Midwest Newspapers Corporation* (Nigeria 1974) the judge took account of the plaintiff's own conduct in publishing an article critical of the Federal Government which provoked an "understandable outburst". A Mauritius court took account of the fact that the plaintff had attacked the defendant's close friend, and the defendant had "felt it his duty to retaliate" (*Gallet v Hay* (1934) p. 50), while in Seychelles it was held to be relevant that the libel was prompted by a studied insult in the press, by the plaintiff, to Seychellois generally (*Mullery v Stevenson-Delhomme* (1955)).

A Rhodesian court (*Rhodesian Printing and Publishing Co. Ltd. v Howman* (1967) p. 340) when not awarding "punitive" damages said,

> Where newspapers - and here they are the only newspapers - openly set themselves against the policy of the Government of the day on a very important national issue they must expect, so to speak, "to get as good as they give". This does not mean that the Government is entitled to defame the

papers, but it does lessen its moral blameworthiness if, in attacking them it oversteps the lawful limits into the realm of defamation.

Evidence of Plaintiff

It has been observed that "Libel plaintiffs are virtually obliged to go into the witness box" (Robertson and Nicol, 1992, 76). This is raised in the context of justification. However, there are two Nigerian cases in which the plaintiffs failed to appear, having left the country. The judges observed that their absence made it very difficult to assess the damages (*Constantini v Daily Times* (1983) and *Thievent v Daily Times* (1984)). These seem to have arisen out of the same publication. The judge in the first case awarded ₦2000 and the latter would have awarded ₦5000 (but he held the newspaper had not been published!)

Other Damages

At common law the defendant could not plead in mitigation of damages the fact that the plaintiff had received damages for the same libel published by another defendant (*Creewy v Carr* (England 1835), *Singh v Singh* (Kenya 1967)). However, under section 6 of the Law of Libel Amendment Act 1888 - still in force in some African jurisdictions - such evidence may be given where the defendant is being sued for a libel contained in a *newspaper* (e.g. *Oweh v The African Press Ltd.* (Nigeria 1959) before the new legislation was in force; the 1888 Act was referred to though not by name; the other case was *Amalgamated Press of Nigeria Ltd. v Oweh* (1958)). The 1888 provision would seem to apply in Tanzania and Uganda. And where legislation modelled on the English 1952 Act is in force that possibility of mitigation has been extended to *all* actions for libel or slander (see Appendix). There is no similar section in the Lagos Law so there the English 1888 Act will still apply.

In a Sudanese case the court refused to award damages because criminal proceedings had already been brought against the defendant; thus the plaintiff's reputation had already been vindicated, and no further sum should be awarded - the more so as the plaintiff could have sought compensation in the criminal proceedings (*Awwad el Kadi v Mohammed Hussein Badran*). This is somewhat remarkable; not the least because the judge seemed to think, without citing authority, that no English court would award damages in such a situation; he erred: only in assault was the complainant in English law required to chose between criminal and civil proceedings. Gatley quotes

Lush J: "(T)he person libelled...may both sue for damages and indict" in *R v Holbrook* ((England 1878) p. 46 - Gatley, para. 1595, n. 28). (For a Tanzanian case making the same point see *Cosmas v Faustini* (1971).)

Account will only be taken of the previous damages when they are indeed for the same defamation - on which point a defendant failed in one of the Kapwepwe libel actions (*Kapwepwe v Zambia Publishing Co.* (1978)). In another of those cases the court held that exemplary damages awarded in one case could not be deducted from compensatory damages in a later case: "Exemplary damages are not given as compensation but are punitive, and the result is a gratuitous grant to the plaintiff outside his proper compensation. To offset such sums against compensatory damages would in my opinion lead to anomalies" (*AG v Kapwepwe* (1974)). Nor indeed can they be offset against exemplary damages to be awarded against someone else.

The fact that the plaintiff chooses to sue only one or some of the potential defendants is no ground for the reduction of his damages, however (*ibid.*).

Other Factors

A Nigerian case held that the fact that the parties were related was no ground for reducing the damages (*Okoroji v Ezumah* (1961)). However, another Nigerian court held that the damages would not be put very high because the parties might be related and the court should try to avoid exacerbating already poor relationships (*Iwowo v Emelize* (1977)). In *Hamiei v Akilimali* (Tanzania 1971) the judge declined to award costs, because, *inter alia*, it might prejudice attempts at reconciliation, and strain even more the relationship between the parties, who were kin.

In *Awolowo v West African Pilot* (Nigeria 1962) the judge seems to have introduced an element of "national interest". He said:

> In my view, these types of libels are very pernicious in their effect, because they are capable of doing incalculable evil in our body politic. Tribes are people who are expected to work together will fall apart, because of the seed of suspicion and hatred sown among them by the writings of people who *erroneously* believe that they can constitute themselves into local versions of Sir Galahad - defenders of the weak and the helpless and to right the supposed wrongs they think are done to their pet idols.... In my own view, the libel in Suit No. 1/207/604 is very serious indeed because of its effect on the peace and tranquillity of this country. No one has the right to toy with the destiny of millions of people in the manner attempted in the offending passages.

Somolu J does not seem to have awarded punitive damages. The approach is not in accordance with authority and can be criticised as tending to enforce the criminal law (of seditious libel) through the civil courts. And yet one has sympathy for this in the context of an area of the law which seems to have so much more to do with compensating the elite for injuries which do not seem to have seriously affected them, than with the national interest.

Nominal Damages

Since libel, and sometimes slander, is actionable *per se*, once the ingredients of the tort are proved the plaintiff must win, but if the damage to the plaintiff's reputation is slight nominal damages may be appropriate. In jurisdictions without 1952 English-model statutes this might happen if the defendant has pleaded and proved justification so far as most of the allegations are concerned (see Chapter 11).

There are a few African examples of very small damages being awarded. In *Bradley v Delorie* (Seychelles 1937) Tracey Watts J said that the plaintiff's claim while giving evidence that he was only really concerned to vindicate his reputation amounted to a claim for nominal damages only; it seems that his brethren on the Court of Appeal did not take the same view. In Uganda 5shs. only were awarded to a plaintiff who was accused, in a letter published only to his father and that by mistake, of having stolen an ashtray (*Kati v Elder* (1964)). In *Aghahowa v Aguebor* (Nigeria 1957) defences of privilege had succeeded with respect to all except one recipient of the defamatory communication; in addition the judge said "I am satisfied that the plaintiff should not have acted and appeared for the defendant's opponent and that the defendant had a just grievance in the matter. Further the plaintiff has not refunded defendant's fees or any portion thereof", and he awarded £5 (₦10). In *Benson v West African Pilot* (Nigeria 1965) the judge said there was no loss to the plaintiff's reputation, but he awarded rather more than is customary for nominal damages, namely £100 (₦200). And in *Nation Newspapers v Chesire* (1984) the Kenyan Court of Appeal reduced the damages from 15/000shs. to 1000/-, clearly considering that the plaintiff had suffered no real damage to her reputation. If the court wishes to signal that the action should not have been brought at all, it can award contemptuous damages of the smallest coin (in *Obu v Medical & Health Dept. Workers Union* (Nigeria 1980) p. 371-2) the judge said he would have awarded 1k contemptuous damages if he had found the defendant liable at all).

Sometimes where nominal damages are awarded each party is left to bear its own costs (as in the Nigerian cases *Aghahowa v Aguebor* (1957) and *Oruware v David-West* (1965)). In England the plaintiff may in "exceptional cases" have to bear the defendant's costs (see *Red Man's Syndicate v Associated Newspapers* (1910) p. 395 (*obiter*)), but this would seem not to be possible in Nigeria at least, where the various rules of court provide that a successful party cannot be ordered to bear the full costs of the suit (Aguda, 1980a, para. 47.03). In Zimbabwe costs can be awarded on a more modest scale in cases of nominal damages (*Prakash v Wilson* (1992) - costs awarded on magistrates court scale).

Exemplary Damages

The words "exemplary" or "punitive" tend to be used indiscriminately to describe damages which are greater than required to compensate the plaintiff, but are in recognition of the particularly reprehensible conduct of the defendant. The House of Lords in *Rookes v Barnard* (1964) held that exemplary or punitive damages should not usually be awarded - unless the defendant has abused an official position ("Oppressive, arbitrary or unconstitutional conduct": Tobi JCA in *Onagoruwa v Inspector General of Police* ((Nigeria 1991) p. 648)), deliberately made a greater profit from his tort than he would have to pay by way of compensatory damages (an example is *Broome v Cassell & Co. Ltd.* (England 1972)), or statute specifically provides. Some Commonwealth jurisdictions dissented from this restriction; see *Australian Consolidated Press v Uren* (1969); however, the New Zealand 1992 Defamation Act s. 28 provides that punitive damages should be awardable only in the case of flagrant disregard of the plaintiff's rights. There is no consistent pattern in African jurisdictions. Nigeria and Zambia have the largest number of cases, and represent opposing approaches.

Nigerian cases appear to have accepted *Rookes* (*Adetona v Drum.* (1972), *Asiodu v Abodunde* (1979); in *Onagoruwa v IGP* (above) p. 647 Tobi JCA cited *Ezeani v Ejidike* (1964), *AREC Ltd. v Amaye* (1986), *Eliochin v Mbadiwe* (1986), *Williams v Daily Times* (1990) and *Ilouno v Chiekwe* (1991) as cases relying on *Rookes*; not all are defamation cases). Hakeem Ogunniran (1992) argues that *Rookes v Barnard* is not binding in Nigeria.The problem is the Supreme Court does seem to have endorsed it, especially in *Williams v Daily Times*. There are a few cases in which the size of damages seems hard to explain on any other basis, however. One judge spoke of "Punishment for defamation", awarding ₦8,000,000 (*Olatunbosun v Madaki* 1989, Ogunniran, *op. cit.* pp. 121-2). The other case discussed by

Ogunniran, also unreported, is *Akilu v Fawehinmi* (1989): ₦5,000,000 was awarded, notionally as "aggravated damages" (for some background to this suit see Chapter 1).

The courts in Zambia, on the other hand, have rejected *Rookes v Barnard*:

> Zambian society is in a state of development, of much less sophistication than that of England. Its two daily newspapers are in a very powerful position by reason of the fact that many persons are ignorant of their rights and many others are afraid to assert them. Daily newspapers, and no doubt many other organisations and persons, are in a position to do great good and great harm. I see powerful reasons why the court, in awarding damages, should have the power, where a person wantonly, maliciously or contumeliously does great harm, to give such damages as will bring home to him that tort does not pay and will restrain him in the future from indulging in similar conduct (*Cobbett-Tribe v Zambian Publishing Co.* (1973) p. 21, approved by Supreme Court in *Times Newspapers v Kapwepwe* (1973) p. 301).

And exemplary damages have also been awarded against the state in connection with radio and television broadcasts (*Attorney-General v Kapwepwe* (1974)).[4]

In the last *Kapwepwe* case mentioned, the trial judge had considered the behaviour of the defendant the more reprehensible because it was the state with a monopoly of broadcasting. But at least one judge in the Supreme Court took the view that possibly less in the way of exemplary damages was necessary against the state.

> Exemplary damages are given for the purpose of bringing home to a defendant the error of his ways. In the case of Government it is impossible reasonably to award a sum that would hurt the Government pocket. The use of the award of exemplary damages is to induce Government to discipline its servants whose action has resulted in loss to Government, and so as to serve as a deterrent for future cases. In my opinion it is not necessary to give extravagant sums for this purpose (Doyle CJ, p. 215).

One Tanzanian judge thought that exemplary damages ought not to be awarded against a government newspaper and said he was assuming that the motives of such defendants were not "a selfish desire for 'hot news' to enable them to sell more copies for profit" (*Eyakuze v Editor of Sunday News* (1974) p. 219).

The whole Kapwepwe saga, incidentally, shows very clearly the potential for over-compensation of plaintiffs by the award of exemplary damages. Simon Kapwepwe was defamed in a statement originating with an ex-member of his political party. The statement was embraced with enthusiasm by the government whose news agency issued a press release which was taken up by the two newspapers (both Government owned) and the broadcasting media. In 1972 Kapwepwe got judgment by default against all three news media. Against the *Times of Zambia* he obtained K10,000 compensatory damages and K10,000 exemplary damages (1973). The publishers of the *Daily Mail* settled for K10,000. Finally the Government was ordered to pay K10,000 compensatory and K10,000 exemplary damages for the broadcast defamation. The plaintiff received therefore K50,000 for defamation for which the appropriate compensatory damages, the courts seemed to agree, was 30,000.

The Government and its media were not finished with Mr Kapwepwe, nor he with them. He was seriously libelled by the *Daily Mail* and brought two more actions (*Zambia Publishing Co. v Kapwepwe* (1974), *Kapwepwe v Zambia Publishing Co.* (1978)). In the second the court declined to award separate exemplary damages. The amount awarded as compensatory damages was sufficient to punish as well (see *Rookes v Barnard* (above) p. 1228, *Broome v Cassell* (above) pp. 1059-60). Baron DCJ went on to say, in effect, that since aggravating conduct by the defendant will be reflected in "compensatory" damages - as we have seen above - the only factor left to consider will be whether the resultant amount is enough to punish the particular defendant in the light of his means: a very rich defendant can only be punished or deterred by higher damages (p. 20).

Proposals in Zambia to accept the *Rookes* approach were endorsed by the Attorney-General. He also said,

> damages should never be awarded to "fatten" anybody and I would venture to suggest that so long as we recognise the principle of exemplary damages it is important that the quantum should be kept within reasonable limits and should not be excessive (see Zambian Law Development Commission 1984) .

Although the East African Court of Appeal embraced *Rookes* on appeal from Uganda and Kenya (*Kiwanuka v AG of Uganda*, *Obongo v Municipal Council of Kisumu* (Kenya 1971)), a judge in Tanzania rejected it as inappropriate for that country. He said firstly that the government or public servant category was too uncertain: "In our socialist oriented one party state almost every instrument in society is geared at development and a matter of interest to the public at large." Party functionaries, and those of party affiliated organisations, of trade unions, parastatals and even of private enterprise since this was monitored in the public interest would have to be included (*Jonathan v Athuman Khalfan* (1980) p. 189; Wambali (1989) regrets that the Court did not take up the challenge to discuss this aspect of the case). (Will judges in Tanzania take a different view as the country moves away from socialism and the one-party state, one wonders!) And so far as the "profit" category was concerned, the judge was impressed by the reasoning in *Uren v John Fairfax* (Australia 1967):

> I wonder...why the law should look with less favour on wrongs committed with a profit making motive than upon wrongs committed with the utmost degree of malice or vindictiveness, arrogantly or high-handedly with a contumelious disregard for the plaintiff's rights.

Rather than concluding that there should be no exemplary damages at all, he preferred a broader application of such damages, and imposed them in this case: "For his cruelty of mind, his persistence in the libel and his contumelious disregard for the plaintiff's rights, and in the hope that he may recall this occasion with advantage, I am satisfied that the defendant merits punishment" (p. 191). He went on to reject suggestions that there should be a relationship between exemplary damages and what might be imposed upon criminal conviction;[5] because the damages would go to the plaintiff and not the state, and because criminal penalties were not always adequate, he actually awarded twice the statutory maximum for the offence, saying "I cannot...espouse the subordination of a civil court's discretion to the edicts of a criminal code".

Recent Ugandan cases have been a little confusing. In 1992 a judge referred to the requirement of being "oppressive, arbitrary or unconstitutional" - the words of *Rookes v Barnard*, but without any reference to that case (*Acire v Engola* (1992)). But in 1993 (*Oboth v New Visions Newspaper*) the Supreme Court seems to have assumed that the "old" law still applied, citing *Davies v Shah* (Kenya 1957[6]) as though it was still good law - though they did not actually award punitive damages. Presumably the court was not referred to *Rookes* or *Kiwanuka*.

Courts in Zimbabwe, too, speak of exemplary damages. It is possible, however, that the practical effect of this is to award what some countries, including the UK, would describe as "aggravated damages" (although in *Rhodesian Printing and Publishing Co. Ltd. v Howman* the judge did refer to things which "may call for aggravation of damages to reflect an element of penalty" (1967) p. 340). In *Khan v Khan* (1971) the Appellate Division in Salisbury (Harare) said that exemplary damages are well recognised in English and South African law - at a time when this was no longer really true of the former. They quoted Lord Atkin on the subject of punitive damages, in a case (*Ley v Hamilton* (1935) described in *Rookes* (pp. 1230-1) as "strong authority for the view that insult offered and pain given are matters for compensation and not for punishment"). The factors mentioned in *Khan* - severity of the libel, failure to apologise, and suggestion in cross-examination that the plaintiff was "a woman of low repute" - were the sorts of factors usually used to affect the size of compensatory damages, and, indeed, the amount was not large.

A South-West African court (*Doll v Kaiser* (1939) pp. 6-7) said,

> [A] civil court never awards damages for the purpose of preventing people from committing delicts; punitive damages in that sense do not come within the purview of a civil court [citing *Wilson v Halle* (South Africa 1903)]. It is true that the cases sometimes speak of vindictive or exemplary damages, but the sense in which these terms are used is explained in the judgment of MASON, J., in the case of *Gray v Poutsma* [1914 p. 211], ...
> "there is sufficient authority for declaring that exemplary damages may be awarded in cases of defamation...exemplary damages may be awarded as a punishment of the defamer with a view of satisfying the injured feelings of the plaintiff, and not so much with a view to preventing the commission of similar torts or protecting the public interest in the manner in which these considerations apply in a criminal prosecution"

There is little authority on when exemplary damages will be awarded in "*Rookes v Barnard* jurisdictions". Newspapers are often sold for profit, but this does not mean that they will normally have to pay exemplary damages. "A newspaper which reports news on daily routine and happens to make a mistake in its report is not to be mulcted in exemplary damages merely because what it does is done with a view to profit", observed Akpata JCA in Nigeria (*Dina v New Nigerian Newspapers Ltd.* (1986); the observation ultimately comes from Widgery J in *Manson v Associated Newspapers* (England 1965) p. 1041). The classic application of the "profit" basis for exemplary damages is the English case of *Broome v Cassell* (above) where the defendants knew perfectly well they were libelling the plaintiff, and went ahead in the hope of profit, to the extent of publishing a paperback of the book on the day of the libel trial! The English Court of Appeal has suggested that deliberately failing to take obvious steps to check information may be a basis for awarding these damages, which, however, should not exceed the minimum necessary to achieve the purposes of punishing the defendant, making the point that tort does not pay, and deterring others (*John v MGN* (1996)).

Actual Figures

A separate sum has historically been awarded for each libel or slander (*Sedgwick v Lepaire* (Seychelles 1967), *Kalumba v Makwaya* (Zambia 1978), *Weber v Birkett* (England 1925)). However, according to Gatley, if the causes of action are on the same libel (both the natural meaning and an innuendo, for example) one award may be directed by the judge, and presumably could be made by a judge sitting alone (para. 1462 citing *Pedley v Cambridge Newspapers* (England 1964) p. 992, *Barber v Pidgen* (England 1937); and see Carter-Ruck, 1992, pp. 169-170). (On the situation where there is defamation in the natural and innuendo sense see the Faulks Report Cmnd 5909, para. 104.)

In England it is not normal for the statement of claim to specify the amount sought by way of damages; indeed, if an amount is specified and the jury awards more, judgment for the higher amount cannot in fact be entered unless the statement of claim be amended (Gatley, para. 1085; in *Eyakuze* (above) p. 218 the judge quoted an earlier edition where Gatley said the plaintiff "should not" specify the amount claimed). It is very common, however, for amounts, often very large, to be claimed in African litigation, although the actual awards are usually much more modest.

No useful purpose would be served by listing even recent awards in the various jurisdictions; Feltoe (1992, p. 26) gives some recent Zimbabwean awards; the highest was in the *Tekere* case (1986) where $20,000 was awarded, most are more in the vicinity of $5000. In *Babigumira v Besigye* (1993) are some figures in recent Ugandan cases, including *Kibedi v FAD* (1987), where the plaintiff was awarded shs. 4.5 million, and *Mayanja v Mulengera* (1992) where the Attorney-General was awarded shs. 6 million. Courts do refer to recent awards, and may give similar amounts to those awarded in earlier cases either for similar statements or to similar plaintiffs; they will make allowance for inflation (e.g. *Zvogbo v Kingston's Ltd.* (Zimbabwe 1986)). In *Daily Times Nigeria Ltd. v Williams* (1986), the court looked at an earlier case in which another prominent legal practitioner had been awarded damages and awarded a figure of roughly the same order, taking into account inflation (but see below). In *Babigumira v Besigye* (above) the court commented on the impact of inflation on the Uganda shilling, and awarded shs 400,000, comparing the case with pre-inflation cases in which sums of shs 5000 or 8000 had been awarded (also on inflation, see *Benue Printing and Publishing Corpn. v Gwagwada* (Nigeria 1989, p. 456-7)). The court in *Kanabo v Editor of Ngabo* (Uganda 1993) referred to the "millions of shillings" cases mentioned earlier, and *Newdegger v Telecast Newspaper* (1988) where shs. 3 million were awarded, but awarded Kanabo, a successful business woman, accused of having murdered her husband, but not "ranking as high in status" (p. 99) as the other plaintiffs, a mere 75,000/-. In *Mkulichi v Central African Transport Co.* (Malaŵi 1983) where the statement was that the plaintiff was a thief and was uttered in the presence of several people, but there was an apology, the judge awarded K1000; he found one previous case where the damages had been K2500 where the words had been in public and a crowd had joined in abusing the plaintiff - *City Carbreakers Car Sales v Mobile Motors Ltd.* (1978). But the use of precedent in this area is very difficult; indeed, in *Williams v Daily Times* (above) the Supreme Court said the Court of Appeal had been wrong to take account of the award in the *Lardner* case, and that "the award in an unrelated case cannot be a useful guide". On the other hand, the gross variations between cases, such as those in the Ugandan cases, do give the appearance of some unfairness.

In some jurisdictions judges have been tempted to compare defamation damages with those in personal injury cases. Diplock LJ (in *McCarey v Associated Newspapers* (No 2) (England 1965) pp. 109-110) said damages figures for "disabling physical injury" might appropriately be borne in mind by an appeal court considering the appropriateness of a defamation jury's award of damages. But Lord Hailsham suggested that the function of damages is rather different in the two types of case: in defamation, damages are not compensation, but a vindication of the plaintiff before the public and a solatium (*Broome v Cassell & Co* (above) p. 1071). However, the English Court of Appeal recently looked at this afresh and suggested that in guiding juries there might be reference to personal injury damages (*John v MGN* (1996)). And in New South Wales the Court of Appeal held that it was acceptable for the Court of Appeal to take account of personal injury damages (but improper to instruct the jury to do so!) *(Carson v John Fairfax & Sons Ltd.* (1994)); the same year that state legislated to say that courts should "ensure there is an appropriate and rational relationship between the harm and damages", and should take into account the general range of damages for non-economic loss in personal injury awards in the state (s. 46A of the Defamation Act 1974).

Awards seem to be more restrained in Africa than they are in England. A Zambian court (*Times of Zambia v Kashita* (1982) p. 167) referred to

> ...the trend which emerges from the authorities in favour of the development of Zambian concepts and standards which generally favour more modest sums of damages than would perhaps be awarded in a similar situation in a developed country.

This may be partly attributable to traditions derived from customary law, where damages were usually small (Date-Bah, 1973a, p. 144n), and partly to the absence of a jury. However, there are signs of substantially increased damages in some countries, notably Uganda and Nigeria (see above).

Notes

1. How far such facts which may be relevant to general damages should be pleaded seems unclear. Gatley (para. 1321) suggests that they should, citing *Calvert v Tomies* (England 1963) and principle. The Supreme Court Procedure Committee (1991, Chap. X) thought otherwise, though suggesting that the Supreme Court Rules should be changed.
2. The precise source is not given but is perhaps the same book as Planiol & Ripert, *Droit Civil Francais* (see Chap. 3).
3. This element in what became the 1996 Defamation Act was dropped as the Bill went through Parliament, however.
4. For a Zambian example in which such damages were not awarded, because the case was a "storm in a teacup" see *Mkandawire v Zambia Publishing Co. Ltd.* (1979).
5. See *Ley v Hamilton* (England 1935) p. 386 - punitive damages have no analogy to punishment by fine - quoted in *Smith v Die Republiken (EDMS) BPK en'N Ander* (South West Africa 1989 p. 876. See also *Broadway Approvals v Odhams Press* (England 1965) p. 818, where Sellers LJ compared an award with fines in criminal cases; Gatley (para. 1451n) comments "*sed quaere*".
6. In that case the plaintiff had been exposed to an official inquiry into his conduct because of the libel.

20 Other Remedies

Injunction

There are very few African cases in which an injunction has been granted against the defendant restraining him from repeating the publication of a defamatory statement (one example is *Iwowo v Emelieze* (Nigeria 1977)) - slander actionable *per se*; it was refused in *Jegede v Daily Times of Nigeria Ltd.* (1980) and in *Kunene v Shabangu* (Swaziland 1978-81). This will only be done if there is reason to anticipate that the defendant will indeed repeat the words (*Proctor v Bayley* (England 1889), *Kunene v Shabangu*), and an injunction will only be granted where an action would lie - thus it will not lie where the words are spoken and not actionable *per se* unless damage is proved (*De Francesco v Barnum* (England 1889) p.172).

This reluctance to issue injunctions may be reinforced by constitutional protection of freedom of speech, as recently emphasised by the New Zealand Court of Appeal (*Auckland Area Health Board v Television New Zealand Ltd.* (1992)).

The English Court of Appeal reiterated (*Kaye v Robertson* (1990)) that the rule in *Coulson v Coulson* (England 1887) that interim injunctions, which amount to prior censorship, were to be granted only sparingly and in the clearest cases still holds. If there is any real possibility that the potential publisher will raise the defence of justification the injunction will not be granted.

> Until it is clear that an alleged libel is untrue, it is not clear that any right at all has been infringed; and the importance of leaving free speech unfettered is a strong reason in cases of libel for dealing most cautiously and warily with the granting of interim injunctions

observed Lord Coleridge CJ (*Bonnard v Perryman* (England 1891) quoted in *Nelson-Williams v Rogers-Wright* (Sierra Leone 1957-60)). Indeed it has been said, "As a general rule the plaintiff who applies for an interlocutory injunction must show the statement to be untrue" (Jessel MR in *Quartz Hill Consolidated Coal Mining Co. v Beall* (England 1882) quoted in *Roy v Bhookun* (Mauritius 1956) p. 122).

It has been said (Robertson & Nicol, 1992, p. 69):

> One important practical benefit of this rule is that journalists can approach the subject of their investigations for a response to an article in draft without fear that they will receive a pre-publication injunction instead of a quote.

The authors go on to point out that to escape the interim injunction the defendant must swear an affidavit to the effect that he intends to justify, and if he fails to proceed with this defence the damages may be substantially increased.

An injunction will not be granted if there is any doubt about whether the words were defamatory (*Liverpool Household v Smith* (England 1887)) or if the occasion was *prima facie* privileged (*Quartz Hill Consolidated Coal Mining Co. v Beall* above).

Similar observations have been made in Zimbabwe (*Schweppes (Central Africa) Ltd. v Zimbabwe Newspapers (1980) Ltd.* (1987) *Quartz Hill Consolidated Mining Co. v Beall)*. In a more recent case, however, the court did grant an interim injunction. An additional element was the defendants' threatening physical assault as well. Nonetheless, the observations of the judge: "Loss of reputation...cannot always be adequately compensated by payment of damages" perhaps indicates a difference in emphasis from that in common law systems (*Matangi v Kumbula* (1992) p. 246). An earlier case is *Philips Electrical (Pvt) Ltd. v Gwanzura* (1988). And in *Kunene v Shabangu* (above) a Swazi court said they would be more reluctant in the case of a perpetual interdict (the civil law equivalent of an injunction) than one *pendente lite*.

Correction

It is usually assumed that there is no procedure under which a court in the common law system can actually *require* a correction (though see Chapter 14 on "amends" and Chapter 19 on mitigation of damages). In a Kenyan case the plaintiff had included in his plaint a prayer for a public apology; the East African Court of Appeal said "it is a prayer that no Court that has awarded damages to a plaintiff in a defamation action would order...Damages...are a solatium for injured feeling, a plaintiff who receives this solatium cannot impose any other condition on the defendant" (*Singh v Notkin* (Kenya 1952) pp. 119-120). And in Ghana, Sowah J said "no one outside a mental hospital will suggest that our courts can enforce that remedy today" - *Odifie v Araba Panin* (1964), quoted by Date-Bah (1973a), p. 140n). The Ontario High Court has refused to grant corrective relief (*Burnett v Queen in Right of Canada* (1979)). However, a Sudanese court held that in addition to damages the court could order the defendant to give the plaintiff a written apology (*Saadani v Sassoun* (1917)); this can perhaps be put down to the flexibility offered by the "natural justice, equity and good conscience" provision. In a Nigerian case (*Omotayo v African Newspapers of Nig. Ltd* (1986)) the trial judge had ordered an apology; on appeal, however, the plaintiff lost.

The New Zealand Court of Appeal recently said it was unable to see any authority which preventing it issuing a mandatory injunction; it referred to academic authority in support of the idea (Fleming, 1978), and thought that such jurisdiction did not conflict with the New Zealand Bill of Rights. One member said (*TV3 Network Ltd. v Eveready New Zealand Ltd.* (1993) p. 447 (Gault J)),

> In defamation cases the freedom of speech and the appropriateness of a Court's direction to the press or electronic media to publish or broadcast will be of great importance...Another factor will be the lapse of time between the publication of the defamatory statement and the time for compliance with any order for retraction or correction. In many cases the gap will be such as to raise a question of whether further publication would be counter-productive. On the other hand the modern approach to the dissemination of information in fields of consumer safety, the impact on trading interests, whether malice has been proved, whether the injury is shown to be continuing and the fact that the issue of remedy arises only after it has been shown that there has been an abuse of the right of freedom of speech also may be relevant factors.

In the event the court held the exceptional requirements for such an injunction were not met in the particular case.

There is no right of reply under the common law. Qualified privilege will protect a non-malicious reply, but there is no way the aggrieved person can ensure his reply is published. In Mauritius, s. 289 of the Penal Code does provide a right of reply (based on art. 13 of the French Law of the Press of 1881), although the defendant is not obliged to comply if the reasonable person would think the reply itself defamatory (*Beejadhur v Coralie* (Mauritius 1953)).

There has been a good deal of discussion in the literature (e.g. Date-Bah, 1973a), and in law reform commissions on the short-comings of the common law in failing to provide an effective mechanism for correction. However, the Faulks Committee in England recommended against a statutory right of reply, saying "we find objectionable a principle which entitles a person, who may be without merits, to compel a newspaper to publish a statement extolling his non-existent virtues" (Cmnd 5909, para. 623). In New

Zealand the Defamation Act 1992 s. 26 provides that, at the request of the plaintiff, the court may recommend publication of a correction. In this event, no other relief is to be awarded. In Ghana, under the 1992 Constitution, there is a right of reply for those against whom statements are published in the media (art. 162(6)).

In case of settlement by means of acceptance of a payment into court it is possible for the plaintiff to make a statement in open court, designed to give him the chance to "set the record straight" and place the truth on record e.g. (Order 18 r. 2 (Bendel etc.) and Order 19 r. 2 (Lagos), Order 42 r. 2(4) (Zambia)). This would seem to be applicable to both a s. 2 Law of Libel Act defence and to an ordinary payment into court. It might seem more appropriate to the latter situation, since by definition in the former (which anyway cannot apply to *slander*) an apology will have been inserted in the press (see Chapter 14).

21 Some Procedural and Evidential Issues

While this book does not pretend to be a comprehensive treatment of matters evidential and procedural, it may be worthwhile pulling together these issues at this stage.

Joinder

It is wise to join the actions for publication of the same statement affecting the same plaintiff. This may extend to a series of related statements (as in *Ogbemudia v Uduehi* (Nigeria 1982)). Rules of Procedure will provide that some common question of law or fact should arise for such joinder.

Pleading

A Nigerian judge observed, "The present case confirms the technical nature of libel cases and how technical also is the procedure that separate rules of pleading are provided for it in our rules of court" (*Ajala v Are* (1985) p. 518).

In a case at common law the plaintiff must set out in his statement of claim the very words complained of; as Spry V-P said in the East African Court of Appeal, "This is not a mere technicality, because justice can only be done if the defendant knows exactly what words are complained of so he can prepare his defence" (*Nkalubo v Kibirige* (Uganda 1973) p. 103, citing *De Souza v Zenith Printing Works Ltd.* (Kenya 1959)). In *Amuludun v Barclays Bank* (Nigeria 1967) the judge refused to strike out the statement of claim although the precise words were not set out because the letter might be produced at the trial (and leave to amend might if necessary be sought) (citing Gatley - now para. 1073). But in *Unuakalamba v First Bank of Nigeria* (Nigeria 1979) the basic rule was applied and the case struck out because the actual words (in slander) were not pleaded.

Rules of lower courts may be less stringent; in *Ateze v Momo* (Nigeria 1958) the High Court said the substance had been set out adequately in the plaint as required by the Magistrates Court Rules. And in Roman-Dutch law it is enough to plead the "substance and effect" of the words (*Munyai v Chikasha* (Zimbabwe 1992)).

Under the common law, if the words were not in English, the language of the original must be set out in the pleading, followed by a translation (*Sowole v Erewunmi* (Nigeria 1961)). Spry V-P said that this statement in the plaintiff's pleading ought to have been struck out as not complying with this:

> That some time in September or October 1967 the defendant wrote a letter to the District Commissioner of Mubende, and some of the contents in the said letter are that the plaintiff does not allow Auditors to look at his account. And a translated copy of the letter is herewith attached as an exhibit *(loc. cit.)*.

Suppose the plaintiff is unable to find out precisely what the words were? Gatley says that this situation offers the one exception to the rule: if the action is in slander, and the plaintiff cannot find out the precise words spoken, he may file an affidavit to this effect and apply for leave to administer interrogatories to the defendant. If the defendant admits using certain words, the plaintiff may then plead them (para. 1074, citing for example, *Addison v Fosbroke* (England 1866)). Otherwise the plaintiff will have to fall back on pleading the words as best he can, hoping that he can prove a sufficient approximation to them.

The pleadings must also give the names of those to whom the words were published (*Bradbury v Cooper* (England 1883)), though not if the words were published to the public at large or to a large crowd in the case of slander (Gatley, para. 1066 citing *Wingard v Cox* (England 1876), see also *Ezeomo v Oyakhire* (Nigeria 1985), and books on pleading, e.g. Nwadialo (1990, pp. 273-4)). It is usual to use the phrase "falsely and maliciously" of the defendant, though unnecessary because the plaintiff need prove neither under the common law (e.g. *Lawson v Mahor* (Nigeria 1975, p. 156)).

As we have seen, innuendoes, true or false, alleged by either party, must be pleaded, as must the extrinsic facts in the case of a true innuendo (Chapter 9; also *Mahtani v Daswani* (Gold Coast 1941)).

In the particular context of slander it was recently pointed out that words may have a meaning in the context in which they are spoken which they might not have in other contexts. If this meaning is relied on by a party the context should be pleaded (*Bookbinder v Tebbit* (England 1989) p. 647).

In most cases damages are general, but they may be based upon certain quite specific misfortunes which the plaintiff claims followed from the defamation. But because the damages are classified as general these things do not have to be pleaded. This is unsatisfactory, as the Supreme Court Procedure Committee (1991, p. 93) observed,

> For example, the plaintiff may suddenly announce in the witness box that purely because of the libel his wife left him, he was expelled from his golf club, or that he lost his chance of promotion at work.

The mines which lie in wait for the defendant are at least as treacherous as for the plaintiff: "A defendant in a libel action must state in his defence particulars of facts on which he relies to prove such justification" (*Arnold & Butler v Bottomley* (England 1908) p. 156 quoted in *Onwuka v Utaegbulam* (Nigeria 1977) p. 375). If, however, the original statement is very specific, it will not be necessary for the defendant to do more than to plead the usual formula: "the statement is true in substance and in fact" (*Gordon Cumming v Green* (England 1891) relied on in *Denloye v Solarin* (Nigeria 1974), see also Gatley, para. 1116). But if the original statement was general (for example, "The plaintiff is a thief") evidently the defendant will have to prove and plead some specific instances of theft in order to justify (*Zierenberg v Labouchère* (England 1893) p.189, *Wootton v Sievier* (England 1913), both cited in *Denloye v Solarin*, and *Williams v Newswatch Communications Ltd.* (Nigeria 1986), *Tekere v Zimbabwe Newspapers* (1986) p. 281). The defendant is not permitted to refuse to disclose the facts on which he intends to rely just because this will reveal the names of his witnesses (which, of course, are not usually disclosed) (*Wootton v Sievier*, distinguished in *Denloye v Solarin*).

And,

> In an action for libel or slander where the defendant pleads that the defamatory statement is entitled to protection as being made on a privileged occasion particular must be given showing how and why the occasion is privileged (*Elkington v London Assoc. for the Protection of Trade* (England 1911), quoted in *Onwuka v Utaegbulam* above).

Issues arising in connection with pleading when fair comment is raised as a defence have been discussed in Chapter 15 and in connection with "falsely and maliciously" while discussing malice (Chapter 16).

Interrogatories

A party may seek to administer interrogatories to find out the source of information used by the other side. This is likely to touch on particular sensitivities if the other party is a journalist, or newspaper. Gatley's view is that neither discovery nor interrogatories will be ordered against newspapers, to require them to disclose the source of their information, even if the newspaper is relying on fair comment, and the plaintiff is arguing malice. Although the court has the theoretical power to order disclosure, it is not used (para. 1217, citing, *inter alia*, *Hennessy v Wright* (England 1888) p. 449, *Lyle-Samuel v Odhams* (England 1949)). In *Vanmali Hirji v National Bank of India* (Kenya 1932) Gamble J spoke of the newspaper situation as "settled in practice".[1] However, an interesting situation arose in a Rhodesian case in which the plaintiffs were journalists, and the defendant a member of the (illegal, Smith) Cabinet. The plaintiffs had written suggesting that the Smith regime was nearing its end, and the defendant made a speech suggesting that the plaintiffs were willing tools of the communists, or had taken bribes. When the plaintiffs sued, the defendant sought disclosure of the plaintiffs' sources of information. The plaintiffs sought to rely on public policy against disclosure of journalists' sources, but the court replied (*Serfontein v Irvine* (1979) p. 519),

> Where, as here, a journalist is himself the plaintiff complaining of a libellous attack on himself for something which he has written and published, and is claiming a very substantial sum of damages, he cannot have it both ways. If, as I have found to be the case here, it is in the interests of justice for the fair determination of damages which he should be awarded that such disclosure should be made, he has to make up his mind whether the ethical aspect is so compelling as to oblige him to withdraw or whether he should persist in his claim and make the disclosure. He is not compelled to sue.

(The court cited various cases including citing *Hennessy v Wright* above, *Plymouth Mutual Co-operative and Industrial Society Ltd. v Traders' Publishing Association Ltd.* (England 1906) pp. 416-7, *Marriott v Chamberlain* (England 1886), *White v Credit Reform Association & Credit Index Ltd.* (England 1905) p. 658, on disclosure generally and not cited specifically on the press issue.) In *Serfontein* the plaintiffs had themselves pleaded that they believed the statements they had made were true. A defendant who makes such a plea may also lay himself open to interrogatories as to the source of information (save in the case of newspapers and journalists). In Kenya the defendant was a bank which the plaintiffs claimed had made erroneous reports as to the plaintiff's credit (*Vanmali Hirji v National Bank of India*, above). The court ordered the defendants to answer (relying on *Lyle-Samuel v Odhams* and *White v Credit Reform Association*).

Evidence

In the case of libel the plaintiff is required to produce the complete document (*Plato Films v Spiedel* (England 1961)), though there may be reasons why it cannot be produced, such as being on a fixed structure or being lost, in which case normally secondary evidence may be produced (*Mortimer v M'Callan* (England 1840), *Gathercole v Miall* (England 1846) respectively, see Gatley, para. 1301). Sometimes a party may find that specific legislation prevents evidence being admissible, a problem which defeated the plaintiff in a Nigerian case in 1993, where the evidence he wished to produce was the report of a Tribunal of Inquiry (*Ogunbadejo v Owoyemi* - the legislation was the Commission of Inquiry Law Cap. 10 Laws of Ogun State s. 10).

Particularly in cases of slander the evidence may not precisely correspond to the words pleaded by the plaintiff. Is that fatal to his case? The answer is no; "proof of language substantially the same as that pleaded is admissible" (*Tournier v National Provincial Bank* (England 1924) p. 469).

Striking Out the Plaintiff's Claim

Although it is possible for the defendant to apply to have the plaintiff's case struck out on the basis that it discloses no cause of action, it is extremely rare for this to be done on the basis that the words used were incapable of a defamatory meaning. The courts have held that all that could be sought was a ruling as to whether they are *arguably* capable of such a meaning (*Morgan v Odhams Press Ltd.* (England 1971) p. 1257), and it would be most unusual for someone to sue for words of which this cannot be said. It used to be thought that there could be no trial as a preliminary issue of whether the words were actually capable of a defamatory meaning (e.g. *Morris v Sanders* (England 1954)). Neill LJ mounted a two-pronged attack on this rule: in *Keays v Murdoch Magazines Ltd.* (1991) the English Court of Appeal held that there was no rigid rule, and that such a proceeding might be appropriate where considerable costs might be saved. And the (Neill) Supreme Court Procedure Committee report (1991) proposed that this change should be institutionalised, as it was in 1994 (RSC O82 r3A introduced by SI 1975 (L10) of 1994); and the 1996 Defamation Act s. 7 provides that it is no longer possible to ask the court to rule whether the words are *arguably* capable, as opposed to capable, of a defamatory meaning. I have earlier suggested that normally it makes little sense for a judge sitting alone to distinguish between the words being capable of a defamatory meaning, and their having a defamatory meaning in the particular case (Chapter 5). However, any preliminary decision on this point would require the judge to indulge in just such an exercise - and should be done by someone other than the trial judge. In systems without jury trial, thought ought perhaps to be given to the possibility of disposing of whether the words were *actually* defamatory as a preliminary issue; certainly courts ought not to consider themselves bound by English cases premised on jury trial.

Suppose the defendant leaves it until the close of the plaintiff's case and then argues that there is no case to answer? In *Alexander v Rayson* (England 1936), quoted in *Patel v Dhanji* (Kenya 1975, p. 12), the court said, "we cannot think it right that the judge of fact should be asked to express any opinion upon the evidence until the evidence is completed". If such an application is insisted upon, the English court said that the defendant should be put to his election: if the application goes ahead he gives up his right to call evidence. As Spry Ag. P pointed out, such a procedure is undesirable anyway, since if there is then a successful appeal by the plaintiff, the proceedings will have to be remitted to the trial court - as happened in the case in which he spoke, only for it ultimately to come back to the East African Court of Appeal after the second trial, and for the plaintiff to lose (1977).

Another basis for striking out the plaintiff's claim may be that it is an abuse of process. An often voiced fear about defamation is that it may be used to block public discussion of issues. In rare cases a court may be willing to strike out a case on proof that this is the purpose of the action, and not the vindication of the reputation of the plaintiff. But the evidence will have to be very strong (*Goldsmith v Sperrings* (England 1977)). In *Ford v Law Society of Rhodesia* (1977) the court held that it was not an abuse of process for a lawyer to have instituted defamation proceedings against someone whom he reasonably believed to have lodged a complaint with the Law Society which had led to disciplinary proceedings being taken against him. This was not an attempt to stifle the complaint.

Payment into Court

Payment into court is a requirement if certain defences available only to the news media are to be invoked, as we have seen (Chapter 14). However, the original introduction of this requirement in 1843, with the creation of such special defences, involved an inroad into a pre-existing rule to the effect that payment into court *with a denial of liability* was not possible in cases of defamation. The courts held that the defendant could deny that the words had the particular defamatory meaning alleged by the plaintiff, but not that they were defamatory at all (*Davies v Billing* (England 1891)). In 1934 the English Rules of Court were changed to remove restrictions on the use of the payment-in device; and since 1948 it has not been necessary for the defendant to state whether he is denying liability (Gatley, para. 1189 n). Many African jurisdictions will have the same rule as England. However, certainly in 1970 Kenya did not, but had a rule similar to the pre-1933 English rules of court, which excluded libel and slander actions from the possibility of payment in with denial of liability (Civil Procedure (Revised) Rules 1948, Order XXVI r. 1, *Ahmedkhan Rahimkhan v Barclays Bank* (1970)).

Costs

A few special rules about costs have been mentioned earlier, involving the Slander of Women legislation (Chapter 4), certain statutory defences (Chapter 14) and nominal or contemptuous damages (Chapter 19).

Conclusion

This brief chapter touches on only a few of the issues of pleading, evidence and practice which may arise in defamation cases; it would be necessary to refer to local Rules of Court, and to texts on those topics, as well as to a work like Gatley, for a full treatment.

Note

1. I have not encountered any African examples of orders to return stolen documents, as in *X Ltd. v Morgan-Grampian (Publishers) Ltd.* (England 1991), which might be used to reveal a newspaper's sources. This case was, however, held to violate the freedom of expression provision of the European Convention on Human Rights - *Goodwin v United Kingdom* (1996) 22 EHRR 123. See Barendt *et al.* (1997) p. 71n.

22 Conclusion

This concluding chapter will make only a few, rather tentative observations about some issues which the law of defamation generates in the African context.

Who Sues and Why?

In West Africa there is a long tradition of suing for defamation, and most litigants have been indigenous; but most parties in East African cases until about the time of independence were non-indigenous people, although clearly there was much litigation in local courts, on both sides of the continent. Why so many more African litigants in the higher courts in West Africa? An important element may have been the existence of an African legal profession, which has existed in Ghana and Nigeria from the nineteenth century, but in Kenya and Tanzania only since the 1960s (Ghai, 1981, p. 149). In East Africa the lawyers were Indian and European. Their communities sued. West Africa produced lawyers partly because there was the wealth in African hands to pay for their education, and to pay for lawyers' fees. (Luckham (1976) has shown the link between cocoa prices and the growth of the legal profession in Ghana.) Such wealth was largely absent in African communities on the other side of the continent.

There is also a correlation between political activity and litigation in defamation. Political development towards independence was much slower in East and Central Africa than in West Africa, partly attributable to the lower percentage of Western educated Africans (including lawyers) in East Africa. In Kenya and Southern Rhodesia the settler population was an impediment to the development of political strategies in independence struggles. West Africans on the other hand became enthusiastic politicians, and had thriving independence movements often led by lawyers throughout the twentieth century. Indeed, the imperial experience with West African lawyers was perhaps one reason for the lack of enthusiasm on the part of the East African administrations for training lawyers (Ghai, 1981) - though until after independence most West African lawyers were trained overseas, too.

Mauritius is an extreme case in the sense that everyone is non-indigenous, so no-one had a system of customary courts to which to resort, but it has had a legal profession since the beginning of the nineteenth century (Redden, 1990, 1.7). Mauritians were litigating with vigour about defamation for some time before "English type" courts existed elsewhere. Most of the cases concerned what might be described as "public affairs" even in the absence of party politics.

One must be careful not to make too much of very limited information. The preponderance of Nigerian cases has far more to do with the size of the country and the volume of law reports than with politics, one suspects. Certainly in almost all the countries there are far more cases from after independence - but this could well be related to politics, for it was only for a few years prior to independence that there was anything like national politics. In Malaŵi where, until recently, there has been very little independent political activity, there are very few defamation cases, and these tend to arise in a business rather than a political context.

It would require a major empirical research project to identify precisely the role of the law of defamation in these jurisdictions. Others have written of the apparent dominance of politics and politicians (Muburimusoke, 1978, p. 171; Veitch, 1971). It is true that there are many such cases, and they do cast light upon some of the realities of African politics: charges of corruption, tribalism, religious favouritism, planning armed insurrection, stirring up trouble between groups of citizens and so on.

A study of the press and politics in Nigeria has shown how much of a role defamation litigation has played in the political process in that country:

> [T]he tendency was for such cases to follow the contours of party schisms, with pro-NCNC papers being taken to court by persons identified with other parties while persons identified with the NCNC or NPC took pro-AG papers to court...following fissures within parties, especially the AG and NCNC, was a spate of court cases emanating from press handling of intra-party schisms. For both this initial period and subsequent developments, however, cases brought by individuals continued to be essentially defamatory in character, and the plaintiffs tended essentially to be well-known personalities rich enough to be able to afford going to court to protect their image in the first place (Agbaje, 1992, p. 48).

On the other hand, party politics have existed in Nigeria for less than half of its independent existence. Few soldier politicians appear in these cases. There is simply less libel of public figures in the press under military rule, which is rather like a one-party state with mostly government controlled press, and there is less scope for the expression of a variety of views, including on the characters of public figures. And the military do not owe their position to public support, and have not the same need to justify themselves, put themselves in a favourable light, or court publicity through litigation. Military rulers may be more inclined to take other steps to control the press (see Chapter 1). And there have been instances of *civilian* members of military regimes suing.

Litigation may suffer a decline with that of party politics but does not disappear (though law reports do tend to fade away). Members of the elite may still find it desirable to protect their reputations, or seek the other benefits that litigation may bring. Most of the litigants do come from the elite: lawyers, natural rulers and chiefs, prominent businessmen, senior civil servants, academics, police officers, trade union leaders, "show-business" people, even religious leaders, all figure prominently.

The overwhelming majority of defendants are news media, more specifically newspapers. The major concern of the politician or public figure plaintiffs is likely to be the damage done to their reputations in the public arena. At the same time, newspapers will not be the subject to customary law - nor would litigation in customary courts provide the publicity the plaintiffs hope for. The emphasis on the news media is most striking in Zambia, but there are few unreported cases from Zambia discussed here, and political cases may be more readily reported.

Almost more interesting than "political defamation", perhaps, are the number of what seem to be ordinary middle-class people bringing actions: school teachers (especially in Uganda e.g. *Otumu v Trustees of All Saints Church, Kitgum* (1969)), doctors, (*Saraki v Soleye* (Nigeria 1972)), ordinary businessmen (*Okusanya v WAATECO* (Nigeria 1974)), the nurse (*Gyang v Iliyasu* (Nigeria 1977)), the medical assistant (*Kajima v East African Newspapers (Nation Series) Ltd.* (Kenya 1972)). The messenger at the Cameroonian Embassy in Lagos (*Visas v Daily Times of Nigeria Ltd.* (1975)) or the barmaids at the Lords Bar (*Lords Bar v The People Newspapers* (Uganda 1972)) were not even members of the professional and business classes, nor was the "small man", the motor engineer who had the temerity to sue a Sierra Leonean QC (*Yanni v Sierra Leone Daily Mail* (1967-68)). Perhaps they owed their support to the extended family.

The ostensible *causus belli* in most of these cases are not fundamentally different from those which one would find in an English court. People litigate about statements which attack their financial and general integrity, or their professional competence; or their sexual morality - though men are more likely to complain if the sexual slur impugns also their professional or political position. Some cases have a flavour which is redolent of Africa, most obviously witchcraft allegations, and some other allegations such as being "South African" (held not defamatory), or engaging in extravagant marriage rituals, and the cases about religious practices (whether they endorse polygamy (*Ezekwe v Otomewo* (Nigeria 1978)), are "paganic" (*Bandele v Daily Times* (Nigeria 1974)), or involve the granting of unorthodox titles (*Sketch v Ajagbemokeferi* (Nigeria 1989)), as well as the occasional instance of reference to genitalia. The context rather than the imputation may be specifically African: such as the argument that erupted over taking an orchestra to the funeral of a member of another Igbo age-grade (*Oforka v Anisiuba* (Nigeria 1979)).

There are very few police officers plaintiffs (among the few cases are *Adewusi v Sketch* (Nigeria 1978), *Odongkara v Astles* (Uganda 1970), *Olowo v AG* (Uganda 1972), *Marais v Haulyondjaba* (Namibia 1993) and *Smit v Windhoek Observer* (Namibia 1996) and these were hardly "ordinary" police officers). Indeed, from the litigated cases at least, it is not possible to identify strategies by groups and classes, other than politicians perhaps, such as some writers have perceived elsewhere. An English solicitor has written (Shillito, 1994):

> In the 1970s it was the headteachers; in the 1980s the hunting fraternity. Now it is the turn of the police. All these interest groups have used the libel laws to check criticism of their activities.

And of the Police Federation[1]:

> It seems to me that the Federation is not so much backing individual members genuinely concerned to protect or restore their individual reputations as using libel actions to improve its collective standing in society.

There is the factor that powerful professional, sporting and other pressure groups are less common in Africa, as in most developing countries.

Another notable absence is any significant use of defamation litigation in the literary and artistic spheres. Political novels are common but there has been no case in which an African politician has sued for what he alleges has been a representation in a novel. Such restraint may suggest that politicians have simply not identified themselves in novels; or possibly they feel that novels have little capacity to harm. On the other hand, in the UK, too, actions against book publishers are rare (Barendt *et al.*, 1997, pp. 134-5).

In the United States, "approximately one-third of all defamation claims tried to a verdict are suits brought against employers" (Shore, 1989, p. 873, citing Middleton, 1987). There are only a small number of such suits among the African cases, and as in the US they tend to be unsuccessful. Some have concerned employers who inform their employees about the disciplining or dismissal of other employees, a situation which, properly handled, is covered by qualified privilege. However, there are a number of cases of *ex*-employees suing, often successfully, for disclaimer notices intended to protect the employer but going further to suggest that the employee was dismissed for dishonesty, and some Nigerian instances of - less successful - defamation suits coupled with those for wrongful dismissal (*Osetayo v Wayne (W.A.) Ltd.* (1991)., *Akonobi v Transcomplext (Nigeria) Ltd.* (1992), *Ezaga v Embechem Ltd.* (1981), *Ishola v North Brewery Ltd.* (1973)).

The paucity of women parties to "received" litigation, compared with their prominence in at least some indigenous societies (see Chapter 2) is intriguing. It is interesting to reflect on this in the light of arguments to the effect that customary law and courts are oppressive to women (Hellum, 1993, p. 256, citing Chanock, 1985, and Rwezaura, 1985). Where women do appear as litigants in the "English" courts, it is often because their sexual role or their morality is under attack: as being of loose character, or "incapable of sexual intercourse" (see Chapter 7). There are no women in public life in these cases; there was a West African women trader (*James v Charteris* (Sierra Leone 1962), and one who was peripherally involved in a chieftaincy dispute (*Nwankwo v Okeke* (Nigeria 1980)), a Ugandan businesswoman (*Acire v Engola* (1992)) and a few women employees (all Nigerian) of whom only the Financial Controller of a parastatal held a prominent position (*Bello-Osagie v Concord Press of Nigeria Ltd.* (1986) - the other cases were*Ita v Ene* (1973) (teacher and church treasurer), *Mshellia v Barde* (1978), *Isah v Ajaokuta Steel Co. Ltd.* (1985), *Sorenson v Paterson* (1957) (expatriate teacher)). What this almost certainly reflects is the limited role of African women in politics; and the prominence of politics in the defamation litigation, whether immediately evident or not.

It is, of course, not always possible to tell what might lie behind some of these actions, what local political battles may be being fought out behind the scenes, what apparently low-profile people may be related to or acting as surrogates for public persons. The chieftaincy dispute which was as much a party battle, is an example (*Akpojaro v Bendel Newspapers Corporation* (Nigeria 1981) - it was held that the third defendant was actuated by political bias); in turn, chieftaincy issues may be concealed behind apparently simple defamatory remarks. A Cameroonian case arose out of undignified jockeying for position by two chiefs. O'Brien Quinn J (later sued in Lesotho - *Ngope v Quinn* (1987), see Chapter 12) said,

> This case is far more than just a case of defamation. Both...the 1st. appellant and...the 1st. respondent are vying with one another for popularity in the area where they both reside and the bringing of the matter before the High Court and this Court was done, not with any intention of having Justice done between them, but more with the intention of gaining a wider audience and in a vain endeavour to get the Courts to commit themselves to giving one side or the other an advantage that may be used at a later stage in the furtherance of their respective aims (*Wilson v Ntoko* (1972)).

Hayfron-Benjamin CJ, a Ghanaian sitting in Botswana, said,

> It is usual in most chieftaincy and family disputes in several parts of Africa, that the core question is never raised directly in legal proceedings. It hovers in the background while other incidental issues are litigated. The dispute gradually gets out of hand in a continuous intractable multiplicity of actions sometimes even endangering the peace of the community (*Gaborone v Gaborone*).[2]

The Judicial Record

It should not be assumed that the judges always apply the rules with no awareness of implications, and exercising no choices. In what they like to describe as their role as jurors they can decide that the words do not have a defamatory meaning. Or they can decide that in their particular society the meaning which the words have would not lower the plaintiff in the estimation of right-thinking members of society. As a broad generalisation the judges have not adopted such restrictive approaches. True they seem to have decided that they will steer clear, if at all possible, of issues of religion and ethnicity. This is true of the Ibadan Muslim titles case - "...is it not a dangerous departure from known legal procedure to make the civil Courts arbiters in matters of sin, heaven and hell?" (*Sketch v Ajagbemokeferi* (Nigeria 1979) p. 706), and the AMORC case in Nigeria (especially at the Court of Appeal level - *Awoniyi v Registered Trustees of the Rosicrucian Order* (1990)).[3] Maybe it is also true of the Kabaka/Obote case in Uganda (*Kiwanuka v Obote*), and the Nigerian case which refused to hold it defamatory to say that a person came from a particular ethnic group (*Mowoe v Aghoba* (1968)).

It is extremely difficult to put into any pattern the cases in which one is surprised to find that there has been held to be no liability. Holdings that it is not necessarily defamatory to accuse someone of tribalism (*Zambia Publishing Co. Ltd. v Kapwepwe* (1974)), or to say that a chief has been removed (*Okafor v Ikeanyi* (Nigeria 1979)), have little in common with the "tedious parsing" that held there was no reference to the plaintiff in *Onu v Agbese* (Nigeria 1985) And there are just as many cases in which the judges seem to have held in favour of the plaintiff on the "defamatory or not" question which could just as well, or better, have gone the other way.

There are a handful of cases in which judges have held qualified privilege could be claimed by a newspaper when it is unlikely that a court in England would have reached the same conclusion. It is again impossible to discern any pattern. They come from different jurisdictions, and are outnumbered by the cases in which the courts have taken the more orthodox view that merely being a matter of public interest does not support this defence, or have been really rather stringent in their interpretation of the requirements for the defence (see Chapter 14).

Overall, therefore, there is no fundamental questioning of the place of the law of defamation in modern African society. Even the occasional piece of rhetoric about the necessity for politicians to have thick skins has very little reflection in actual outcomes (see Chapter 14). On the other hand, it is very possible that in some of the cases in which the judges have made what seems a questionable decision as to whether words are defamatory or not, they have actually been striving to keep the courts out of disputes, as suggested earlier. The "estimation of right thinking members of society" principle is a useful accessory for such judicial restraint. Judges who make use of this technique are not necessarily the blinkered victims of a neo-imperialist or antiquated law, but may be using what room for manoeuvre the law allows them to steer clear of disputes into which they feel it inappropriate to venture.

Is the Law Different in Africa?

In West Africa, Nigeria especially, there has been little serious attempt by the judiciary to break away from the English model, to relate the law to local circumstances; perhaps it is more accurate to say that there is an assumption that the law is appropriate to local circumstances. To some extent this can again be traced back to the tradition and size of the legal profession in West Africa, where there were lawyers steeped in the common law.[4]

The differences are most marked in Tanzania where the argument has been made that the judiciary has applied, and even adapted, the law of defamation to accord with the socialist philosophy of the regime of Nyerere (see Mtengeti, 1985, and Goulbourne, 1976, and Chapter 11). Tanzania espoused a self-consciously new tradition into which it drew the judges.

> The concept of the judge as the neutral belonging to no party in a multi-party democracy can have no meaning here where there is one party. If he stands aloof seeming to play the apolitical role which is supposed to be his, his motives will doubtless be suspected. A new way must be found (Georges C.J. quoted by Goulbourne, 1976, p. 114).

There was also the element that the Tanzanian judges, and the colonial legal system as a whole, were under attack. Tanzanian black lawyers did not come along until independence and they came from the University (College) of East Africa. They were young and independent of spirit, and far less inclined to take on trust the doctrines of the common law. The private legal profession was small, and many lawyers, even acting for private clients, have been employed by the Tanzanian Legal Corporation. There has been a conscious rejection of the individualism of the English legal system. And the African judges themselves have been young (unless "borrowed" from West Africa), and graduates of the Dar es Salaam law school, which was more politically radical, and more concerned with the social and political context of law than faculties elsewhere in Africa (see the contributions in Shivji, 1986). We can see some impact of these factors in the cases on qualified privilege, where the courts have held that the public has an interest in matters discussed at a village meeting and published in the party press. It shows in the acceptance of reports to the ruling party (TANU) as occasions of qualified privilege (see Chapter 13). It perhaps shows in the decision on burden of proof of having committed a criminal offence, though that case seems to me to be dictated by a desire to be different rather than any other very coherent reason (*Eyakuze v Editor of Sunday News* (1974)).

Most of the cases put forward as being socialist in approach would surely have been decided in precisely the same way anywhere else. Corrupt leadership is frowned upon elsewhere as much as in Tanzania (a point also made by Goulbourne (1976, p. 103)). This is generally true of judicial protestations about "local standards"; it would be surprising if the courts did *not* take allegations of prostitution or sexual immorality seriously, and it is hard to imagine any court not doing so, even in the "West" the decline in the moral standards of which African judges have regretted (*Kunene v Shabangu* (Swaziland 1979-81)).

The nature of remedies is particularly indicative of the function of law. The English abolition of exemplary damages in defamation actions generally can be seen as a reflection of the capitalist system. The courts opted for compensation, for the price of the injured reputation, rather than for punishment, deterrence or denunciation. The refusal of Tanzania and Zambia to do the same is especially intriguing. These are among the few examples of actual differences in rules of law between the common law as applied in England and as applied in African countries. In Zambia the concern seems to be to keep the power of the press under control (*Cobbett-Tribe v Zambian Publishing Co.* (1973), approved by Supreme Court in *Times Newspapers v Kapwepwe* (1973) p. 301). In Tanzania it is much more a question of upholding public accountability (*Jonathan v Athuman Khalfan* (1980)). One might say that exemplary damages would accord poorly with the more capitalist economic system of Nigeria, which has indeed followed England in this, but that would be to fall into the fallacy of imagining that there is a simple relationship between political/economic systems and individual rules of law. While it may be true that the Tanzanian courts have made such a connection, generally the individual rules today have far more to do with tradition and inertia.

African awards of damages have generally been modest. At times there has been an emphasis upon the litigation itself as vindicating the reputation of the plaintiff which is much less apparent in English cases. It is possible that the influence of indigenous principles, and even of socialist principles, plays a part. Customary law was far more concerned with the restoration of lost discord than with punishment or financial reimbursement. Indeed, in pre-monetary economies this could not have been otherwise. Low levels of compensation survived the introduction of money (Date-Bah, 1973a, p. 144n citing *Ampong v Aboraa* (Ghana 1960), *Wankyiwaa v Wereduwaa* (1963), *Attiase v Abobbtey* and *Nkrumah v Ataa* (1972)), and have tended to be the norm in common law cases also. In Tanzania, writers have suggested that the English practice reflects its capitalist system, enabling people to make a profit out of being defamed (Goulbourne, 1976). This does not fully account for the role of the jury, which is the major explanation for the size of damages in England. Recently, however, even without the influence of juries, this emphasis in the African cases has perhaps diminished, and certainly in Nigeria there have been very substantial awards of damages. Even earlier it was suggested that in Uganda "public officers have been over-zealous in bringing suits for defamation because they are awarded a large amount of damages and they increase their popularity when they win a suit for defamation" (Muburimusoke, 1978, pp. 171-2).

Thus the ostensible rules of law hardly differ in Africa from those in the UK. None of the proposals for legislative change has reached the statute book, and even the proposed changes would have been tinkering, rather than radical. One exception to this is the proposal in Zambia that defamation of the dead be actionable; but the Faulks committee had a similar idea. The notion that Europeans are indifferent to the pain of insult, even to the ancestors, is just not tenable.

On the whole the similarities as much as the differences are striking, though this is not something particular to the law of defamation (Cottrell, 1988). An English lawyer could stray into the middle of an African (common law) defamation case and feel immediately at home. It is a testimony to the power of taught law - the legal profession is doing what it has been taught to do. It is probably also a testimony to the fact that the law suits the elite reasonably well.

The Relationship with Customary Law

Customary law principles, where they do not correspond to those of the received law, are usually excluded (subject to the occasional agonising on the part especially of Ghanaian judges - see Chapter 2). This could be said to have deprived some sections of the community of the opportunities of going to law. The absence of women and women's concerns mentioned earlier is one aspect of the issue.

The failure to give redress for insult is the most notable omission. Rattray (1929, p. 326, quoted in *Tsinagyah v Kyeiwaah* (Ghana)) said,

> The Ashanti was (and is) to our way of thinking [a European way, presumably] extremely sensitive to personal invective of every kind. To have a "good name" was well-nigh essential to his existence, to have a "bad name" rendered life, in the narrow community in which he passed his days, unbearable.

One writer suggested that "the customary law and common law rules on defamation should be brought together into a unified contemporary regime" (Date-Bah, 1973a, p. 138).

The "right thinking member of society generally" requirement inhibits the role of the common law in settling "customary disputes", for there is a risk that an allegation which would lower one in the eyes of "the narrow community in which one spends one's days" in Rattray's phrase would be held not defamatory because the larger national community would not think less of one (Chapter 7).

In the few customary law disputes which do come to the English style courts, usually as appeals from lower courts one finds tensions of life quite different from those which generate most of the high court cases. Here are insults, traded with verve and vehemence, women (e.g. *Ikuenobe v Ogbeide* (Nigeria 1980) (women *and* insults)), accusations of witchcraft, markets, village meetings, funeral ceremonies (e.g. *Osagie v Garuba* (Nigeria 1980) where an argument arose at a funeral as to the correct amount of the levy usually paid by the senior daughter of the deceased).

It is, of course, natural that Africans should feel that their law ought to reflect African values, and not simply those of, long-buried, English men. But it does seem that there is little real pressure on the courts from litigants to integrate customary principles into the received law. This may be simply because the lawyers, as gate-keepers of the legal process, imbued with the taught law, keep such cases out. It seems to me just as likely that customary courts are seen as the appropriate fora for the protection of customary values. But what we read in the judgments can reflect only what is argued in court, and the lawyer may advise his client to argue or to emphasise only those aspects of the offending statements which the lawyer believes will receive a favourable response from the court.

Who Wins and Why?

One Tanzanian writer has argued that the judges have been at times less supportive of the reputations of private individuals than of public officials (Mtengeti-Migiro, 1992, citing *Rwekanika v Binamungu* (1973) and *Novati Joseph v Sebastian Muzo* (1978) on private persons and *Eyakuze v Editor of Sunday News* (1974 in the High Court) and *Maswanya v African Buyer and Trader (Publications) Ltd.* (1981)). (To be fair to the judiciary, however, it is not clear that the judges had much room for manoeuvre in a case like *Rwekalika* - see Chapter 13.) She suggests this is hardly surprising, for courts which are "'subordinate organs' of the Party" (p. 979). How ironic where the Party Constitution, as pointed out by the same author elsewhere, provided that every member should "be willing and ready to accept criticism" (1985, p. 57). Perhaps the judges were less introducing socialist principles than protecting others in the class to which they themselves belonged!

There may be some truth in the impression that public figures fare better as plaintiffs than ordinary citizens. The many cases of public figures against the press are very often successful. The press fails to establish a general privilege, it rarely pleads justification, and very often fails in pleas of privilege - because, for example, it cannot show that reports of parliamentary proceedings were accurate - or of fair comment because it cannot show that the comments were based on facts, or were, indeed, comments at all. Want of professionalism on the part of the press has accounted for many of its defeats.

The substantive rules of law, rules of pleading, and no doubt in some cases judicial bias are other possible causes of surprising or unsatisfying outcomes. There is a depressingly large number of cases in which parties have been defeated by technicalities - depressing because some of them reveal incompetence on the part of lawyers, and some reveal lack of creativity on the part of the judiciary.

Democracy and the Press

A cynical view would be that the press in Africa is controlled by government and to a lesser extent other political interests, that journalists are not well trained or respected, but this would be very much to overstate and oversimplify. There *are* good African journalists. The desire of the public for newspapers which address the issues of the day, and of journalists to do so is evidenced by the resurgence of newspapers every time a military or one-party rule gives way, even if temporarily, to a democratic system. The rapidity with which governments crush or take over the press at the first signs of dissent (see Chapter 1) is testimony both to fear on the part of government of a free press and to the fact that the press has been critical of government.

Almost all the countries which have embraced or had thrust upon them autocratic regimes have been turning back to multi-party systems. Newspapers are burgeoning. It can be argued that the existence of the law of defamation may operate as an incentive to the press to moderate their criticism, and to endeavour to check their facts. On the other hand, the law could be said to be a threat to a vigorous press, and a threat which does not actually penalise only inaccurate reporting, but which may bankrupt a paper which cannot prove the accuracy of what it is morally certain is true. One should be careful not to overdo either argument. There is little in the literature to suggest that the civil law has been the major threat to the press (Kasoma, 1995 arguing for the importance of the media, and discussing threats to it, does not mention civil suits for defamation)[5]; although Muburimusoke (1978, p. 172n) suggested that in Uganda newspapers have gone into liquidation partly because of libel litigation, mentioning specifically the *People*. I have suggested that there is some evidence that journalistic standards are not high. But would they have been even lower if there had been no risk of libel suits?

Constitutional Challenge?

Feltoe (1993, p. 49) has written that "It is long overdue that a suitable case be taken to the Zimbabwean Supreme Court to test whether the current law on defamation infringes the freedom of expression provision in our Constitution", (see also Date-Bah, 1973b). Such cases elsewhere in Africa have been few and have met with little judicial enthusiasm.

The continent's own charter of human rights, the African Charter on Human and People's Rights, has a somewhat pusillanimous statement:

> ARTICLE 9
> 2. Every person shall have the right to express and disseminate his opinions within the law.

All these countries now have freedom of speech provisions in their constitutions (though some may be in abeyance under military rule). To take one example: the 1996 Constitution of Zambia has a very full version, although to essentially similar effect as that in several other constitutions (see Zimbabwe s. 20, Sierra Leone s. 15, Mauritius s. 12, Kenya s. 79, Gambia s. 22, Botswana s. 12, Swaziland s. 12 and Namibia, art. 21.):

> 20. (1) Except with his own consent, no person shall be hindered in the enjoyment of his freedom of expression, that is to say, freedom to hold opinions without interference, freedom to receive ideas and information without interference, freedom to impart and communicate ideas and information without interference, whether the communication be to the public generally or to any person or class of persons..
> (2) Subject to the provisions of this Constitution no law shall make any provision that derogates from freedom of the press.
> (3) Nothing contained in or done under the authority or [sc. of] any law shall be held to be inconsistent with or in contravention of this Article to the extent that it is shown that the law in question makes provision--
> ......
> (b) that is reasonably required for the purpose of protecting the reputations...of other persons...
> and except so far as that provision or, the thing done under the authority thereof as the case may be, is shown not to be reasonably justifiable in a democratic society.

The 1996 (final) South African Constitution covers "the freedom of artistic creativity" and "academic freedom and freedom of scientific research" as well as the press and other media (s. 16(1)(c), (d) and (a) respectively). Whether specific mention of the press, something of a modern trend, makes any real difference is doubtful, although there is perhaps some merit in underlining the importance of freedom of the press. In Nigeria the Constitution Drafting Committee of the 1979 Constitution rejected any special protection for the press, on the grounds that all citizens should have the same protection (Vol II para. 4.3, p. XVI, quoted by Ojo, 1976, p. 549). The 1995 Ugandan Constitution refers to press and other media - art. 29. Under the Ghana 1992 Constitution there is a special chapter on Freedom and Independence of the Media (art. 164).

Constitutions generally contain qualifications which derogate from the protection, either generally, or in relation to specific rights. In Tanzania s. 18(1) guarantees freedom of expression "without jeopardising the laws of the country", a somewhat wide exception. Many provisions allow for derogation in the interests of the rights, or more specifically the reputations of others like the Zambian Constitution (e.g. Seychelles art. 22 (2)(b), Swaziland s. 12 (2)(a)(ii)), while some specifically refer to "defamation".

The Constitution may say that the law to be protected by a derogation clause should be "reasonable" or "reasonably acceptable" or "reasonably required" or "reasonably necessary", "reasonable and necessary" or "necessary". "Reasonably necessary" is used in the European Convention on Human Rights. Two significant points emerge from the jurisprudence of the European Court: firstly that "necessary" is not, on the one hand, as restricted as "indispensable" or "absolutely necessary" or "strictly required by the exigencies of the situation", all of which expressions appear elsewhere in the Convention. Nor, on the other hand, is it merely what is "reasonable" or desirable"; it implies a "pressing social need" (*Handyside v UK*, 1976). It might be difficult to apply so stringent a test to constitutions which simply require "reasonableness". The other point is that it is not sufficient to show that the law in question is *intended* to achieve one of the legitimate objects, one of which is the protection of reputation. The means must be proportionate to that objective.[6]

A very common formulation is on the lines that law which is reasonable or reasonably necessary "in a democratic society" for the purposes mentioned, is valid; in the 1995 Uganda Constitution, "acceptable and demonstrably justifiable in a free and democratic society" (art. 43). Like some, but not all, other constitutions, this places the onus explicitly upon those who argue that a law is not justified in a democratic society. Malaŵi's 1994 Constitution introduces a new element in requiring derogatory laws to introduce only restrictions "recognised by international human rights standards", and it also provides that the derogation shall not "negate the essential content of the freedoms" (s. 44(2) and (3)).[7]

In Nigeria the High Court of Ogun State rejected the argument that the Constitution protected libel of a State Governor; Kolawole J said:

> Freedom of expression which is provided for in our Constitution is not, in my judgment, a licence to defame. There is no public duty properly so-called which entitles news media to defame holders of public offices. If such a provision were to be written into the Constitution then all public officers will have a floodgate [*sic*] of tendentious and ill-motivated accusations levelled against them without any remedy. Such a law will not be reasonably justifiable in any civilised and democratic society (*Onabanjo v Concord Press of Nigeria Ltd.* (1982, p. 92)).

And Olatawura JCA made it clear that he thought the civil and criminal law of defamation constitutional - *Nwankwo v State* (Nigeria 1985). The Zambia High Court rejected the argument that a provision (s. 69) of the Penal Code which creates a special offence of defaming the President is unconstitutional as infringing the human rights provisions: *People v Mwape* (1995, Chitengi J).

Each Constitution must be studied carefully, for differences in wording may substantially change the scope for attacking the existing law. In *Du Plessis v De Klerk* (1996) the South African Constitutional Court held that the interim Constitution did not invalidate the common law of defamation. The Constitution did not apply "horizontally" - that is to affect the rights of citizens between themselves, as opposed to as against the state.[8] The court, like the courts of Canada (*Hill v Church of Scientology of Toronto* (1995)), declined to follow the US approach. However, the final South African Constitution (s. 7) applies the fundamental rights provisions to the relationships between persons explicitly, as does the Constitution of Namibia (art. 5).

In the United States, under the first amendment to the Constitution: "Congress shall make no law abridging freedom of speech or the press", the Supreme Court held in *New York Times v Sullivan* (1976) with *Garrison v Louisiana* (1964) that criticism of a public official was privileged unless the statement was knowingly false or made recklessly - also known as "actual malice". This has effectively done away with both civil and criminal libel where public figures are the object of criticism. Subsequently the US courts have held that where a private plaintiff is suing the press he must show negligence in order to succeed (*Gertz v Robert Welch Inc* (1974)).

A Nigerian judge clearly had not had *Times v Suillivan* drawn to his attention when he said, "I am unable, from my research, to find any Constitution under any legal system which protects sedition and defamation under the guise of discharge of public and constitutional duty" (*Onabanjo v Concord Press of Nigerian Ltd.* (1982) p. 91 (Kolawole J)). It is remarkable that, presumably, counsel had not relied upon the American example, especially as the basic structure of the 1979 Nigerian Constitution was the "Washington model".[9]

In a few cases Nigerian courts have been prepared to say that the law of sedition is unconstitutional; in *Nwankwo v State* above, Olatawura JCA said,

> Let us not diminish from [*sic*] the freedom gained from our colonial masters by resorting to laws enacted by them to suit their purposes....Those in public office should not be intolerant of criticism. Where a writer exceeds the bounds there should be a resort to the law of libel where the plaintiff must of necessity put his character and reputation in issue.

(See also *State v Ivory Trumpet Publishing Co.* (1984).) One might argue that if the existence of the tortious remedies may be used to buttress assaults on much greater tools of oppression like sedition, that is a price worth paying.[10]

The assumption in the literature tends to be that the press will be criticising government, and that freedom of the press shores up democratic government. But most of the news media in Africa are government owned - or have been until recently. It may be that the right to sue for defamation may be some sort of defence against government oppression. On the other hand, one should not assume that Africa is doomed to non-democratic regimes with government owned media! Indeed, as observed elsewhere, the current trend is the reverse.

Many years ago Date-Bah wrote of Ghana, "...the encouragement of vigorous public discussion in a country such as ours is more important than the protection of the reputation of individuals" (1973b, p. 42). This does not mean that a full-fledged *Sullivan* rule is needed (Date-Bah was arguing for more protection for the press, but not going so far as to require proof of recklessness in order to succeed). If the press in Africa had been permitted to develop - instead of being stifled by government ownership or positive oppression in those 20 years - while being subject to a reasonable regime of control, maybe West Africans would not now be saying "attacks on the credible media have also encouraged the publication of rag sheets in the name of newspapers" (Arogundade (1994)).

As Feltoe observes (1993, p. 49) "It is most unlikely that Government itself would be prepared to pass legislation to correct the imbalance, because by relaxing the restrictions on the press, it would expose itself to more bold and searching scrutiny from the press". Initiative is more likely to come, therefore, from the judiciary. Courts may find ways to mitigate the potential chilling impact on political debate of the existing law by the use of constitutional principle, even if they do not take the view that radical surgery is constitutionally mandated. The South African Constitutional Court, like the Canadian Supreme Court,[11] took the view that (even under the Interim Constitution) constitutional principles should permeate the common law.[12] (The Interim Constitution s. 35(3) did require courts generally to have regard to the spirit, purport and objects of the human rights chapter, which goes further than many other African Constitutions.)

Reform?

But it is not only issues of free speech that require attention. Defamation is not an area of the law in which the most chauvinist common lawyer could feel a great deal of pride. Apart from the many technicalities which lead judges and lawyers to make expensive mistakes in the application of the common law, there is a feeling that the law does not adequately address many genuine concerns of the public, which customary law has sometimes better dealt with. At the same time the law does not really operate to clear names, for there is no remedy which genuinely tries to achieve this, except the statutory defence requiring amends and the general incentive to apologise in return for a reduced level of damages. And all lawyers know that the mere fact that a newspaper does not plead justification does not mean that the statements are not true, or that the journalist may not be quite sure of his facts. But his informants may be reluctant to testify, or the newspaper may fear enhanced damages if the plea of justification cannot be made to stick. So not only does the law fail to clear the names of those unjustly attacked, it gives remedies to those who in fact have been rightly attacked.

Proposals for change in the law have sometimes tended in the direction of making the situation of plaintiffs more difficult, thus discouraging litigation. One such suggestion is that of the majority of the Irish Commission to shift the burden of proof of falsity to the plaintiff. Again there is the appealing objection of the minority (Chapter 11), and the inconsistency of such an approach with growing concerns about privacy. An amendment to introduce such a change in the onus of proof into the UK 1996 Act was defeated (Barendt *et al.* (1997) p. 195, citing 571 HL Deb. cols. 239-43).

Other proposals have been to restrict damages, with the same objective, often coupled with suggestions for other sorts of remedies such as rights of reply or court ordered retractions (see Chaper 20). There remain, however, problems with a right to reply - on both sides. The plaintiff may well feel that the publication of an apology and correction does not totally clear his name. A Mauritian court said:

> Basile's precept "*Calomniez, calomniez, il en restera toujour quelque chose*" [Slander away! Some of the mud will always stick] is as true now as it ever was (*Hanning v Curé* (1937) p. 26.

(The reference is to Beaumarchais, *The Barber of Seville* (my (very loose) translation).) The apology serves, indeed, to remind the readership of the libel, and even to draw it to the attention of some who did not read it first time round. On the other hand, the newspaper may be compelled to publish a retraction of something which it knows to be true, and all too easily may be required to publish statements by the plaintiff which it knows to be untrue. Some have argued that a right to reply for public figures is unnecessary - that they can put their view in some other but equally public forum (e.g. Gillmor (1992, p. 154)). This argument is much less tenable in Africa where there may be no other newspaper, as we have seen.

It has even been suggested that awards of damages should be done away with, and the publication of a statement recording the outcome of litigation should suffice (proposed by the Acting Chief Justice of Zambia, see Zambia Law Development Commission 1984 p. 13, based upon a suggestion in Hodgin (1973, p. 92). This faces some of the objections raised earlier. As the law stands at present a successful action does not actually mean that the plaintiff has been vindicated; it may simply mean that the defendant cannot guarantee that he can prove the truth of what he said. If the burden of proof were shifted this objection would be removed. On the other hand, another objection would perhaps remain: that the removal of any risk of incurring liability for damages would reduce the incentive to the press to take care in its reporting. Again, this might be avoided if the plaintiff could qualify for an award of damages by proving recklessness, deliberation or negligence.

The enemies of democracy in Africa have been corruption and greed, and the cynicism on the part of the public which these engender, with the result that politics and politicians lose the support of the people, who come to believe that their salvation may lie in the hands of soldiers and dictators, only for these to disappoint in their turn. It can be argued that irresponsible and exaggerated newspaper reporting of politics exacerbates this public cynicism, and one writer suggested that rumour has a particularly unsettling effect in Africa (Veitch, 1971). The problem about such arguments - even if empirically verifiable - is that there is no logical place to stop. Justified criticism can be as destabilising as unjustified - maybe more so. So government feels it has the right to curb all press criticism in the name of stability. The argument in favour of cutting back on the present generosity of the law towards plaintiffs, even if not to the extent of the *Sullivan* position, is that the risk of public disenchantment from inaccurate reporting is outweighed by the risk of real injustice, incompetence and corruption going undetected because the press is silenced.

Finally, in the United States some have suggested that no great harm would be done by simply abolishing the common law of defamation. Summarising the arguments, Anderson (1992, pp. 43-4) says,

> A world in which reputation is not a legally protected interest is no longer inconceivable. Recent experience demonstrates that victims of defamation survive and sometimes even prosper without benefit of legal remedy. The public has learned to adjust its perceptions of the media to take into account the extremely complex relationship between truth and defamation that the present law creates; a system in which the law exerted no influence on these matters would be far easier to take into account. Political life and public discourse have adapted to the virtual abandonment of libel and would no doubt survive its actual demise.
>
> Abolishing libel law is the only step that will eliminate the chill it imposes on speech. No reform can provide a remedy for defamation that imposes no burden on speech. ...the very purpose of libel...is to chill speech. If there is no speech that deserves to be chilled, there should be no law of libel. Reasonable people can and do hold that view. Others believe damage to reputation is too elusive or evanescent to justify the chill that libel produces. Still others believe the marketplace should indeed be the only arbiter of truth.[13]

In some countries abolition would leave customary law, which could be invoked by those who have genuinely been injured in the eyes of their community. But in many countries customary law has been so emasculated, by the structure of the modern court system, or by internal conflicts laws, that it could serve no useful role even between members of the same community, while disputes between people from different communities raise other problems. And we have seen that some communities traditionally had no or very limited legal protection of reputation. Mauritians, who have litigated with such verve over the years about reputation, would be left with no law at all on the subject.

Abolition would perhaps throw out the baby of the injured private citizen with the bathwater of political defamation. Of course, the more radical of the US writers are saying there is no baby! One strain in the US literature is that a free market in ideas is required by the nature of their political system (by way of contrast, see Fish (1994, esp. Chapter 8)). Or that reputation itself is a notion inappropriate to a capitalist system (Reisman (1942) cited in Anderson, p. 43). Many of these observations are of questionable validity even in the chief home of capitalism. In the African context (where until recently capitalism has anyway not been the preferred economic system) they would be even less relevant. There is no free market in ideas where there is only one newspaper. Writers suggesting a system which aims at vindication rather than monetary compensation are coming closer to ideas of African customary law - though they are unlikely to have in mind parading offenders through the streets with a stone round their neck and preceded by a gong beater! (see beginning of Chapter 1).

Notes

1. See comments in Barendt *et al.* (1997) about the role of the Federation in the UK.
2. The parties agreed in this case to have the real issue determined, namely to which line the plaintiff belonged, depending on the nature of the union between his parents.
3. That court's strategy was held inappropriate (on procedural grounds) by the Supreme Court, which reached the same result by a different route (1994).
4. On the differences in the literature of the two sides of the continent, see Ghai (1987).
5. Where mention is made of "libel" actions leading to the closure of newspapers, it seems that this also refers to the criminal law of libel, e.g. Maja-Pearce (1990) (on The Gambia). However, one African editor has told the author recently that libel actions are something of an issue for the press in his country.
6. There have been a few cases of challenge to *criminal* law under Article 10 of the European Convention - which was the model for many early domestic human rights provisions including that in Nigeria - e.g. *Lingens v Austria* (1986), *Oberschlick v Austria* (1991), *Barford Case* (1989), see Janis & Kay (1990, p. 266).
7. The arguments concerning the possibly conflicting interests of freedom of speech and the maintenance of reputation have been well discussed elsewhere; e.g. Barendt, 1985.
8. In Canada the courts have held that the Charter of Rights and Freedoms does not affect the rights of private citizens between themselves, and does not affect

common law as opposed to statute (*Retail, Wholesale and Department Store Union v Dolphin Delivery* (1986); *Pangilian v Chaves* (1989, p. 205) and *McKinney v University of Guelph* (1990); see Fleming, 1991, p. 334).

9. See also *Jakande v Concord Press of Nigeria Ltd. (1982)* in which the learned judge decided that s. 36 gave no "mandate" to newspapers to commit libel. No US cases were cited; counsel were again G.O.K. Ajayi for the plaintiff and Gani Fawehinmi for the defendant.

   Subsequent cases have, however, shown more awareness of US authority, although not to the extent of attacking the basis of defamation. Ademola JCA said "having regard to the role we have assigned to our mass media under our Constitution" it would be more appropriate to follow an American decision giving a wider scope to privilege for newspaper reports of court cases (*Daily Times v Williams* (1986) p. 541).

   In India the provision relating to defamation under the Penal Code (s. 499) (*K.V. Ramanaiah v Special Public Prosecutor* (1961)), and the civil law of defamation have been held not to violate the Constitution (*M.B. Kanwar v State* (1963), *K.P. Narayanan v Mahendrasingh* (1956)). In the last case the court cited US decisions to the effect that there is no special privilege for the press, a statement which pre-dated the major developments in US defamation law discussed above. The courts in Singapore, where political leaders are enthusiastic defamation litigators, have reached the same view (*Jeyaratnam v Lee Kuan Yew* (1992), forcefully criticised by Hor (1992).

   The Australian example is particularly interesting since there is no Bill of Rights in the Constitution. Nonetheless, the High Court has construed from the provisions establishing a democratic polity a protection for discussion of political issues. This protects not only the press, and "political issues" are quite widely conceived. The Constitution limits common law as well as statutory rules. The onus of proof is upon a defendant wishing to gain the benefit of this new protection to show that he was not aware of the falsity of the statement, did not publish it recklessly and that publication was reasonable (*Theophanous v Herald & Weekly Times Ltd.* (1994), *Stephens v West Australian Newspapers Ltd.* (1994); Sally Walker (1995) has suggested that these cases strike a better balance than the US law).

10. Though the English Court of Appeal argued in a converse sense when they said that a local government body had no need of the right to sue in defamation since the criminal law was available! See *Derbyshire v Times* (1992).

11. But see Ross (1996) for comment that this has had little impact in the area of defamation.

12. In *Du Plessis v De Klerk*, pp. 885-6 Kentridge AJ discussed possible approaches to such an exercise, pointing to the experiences of Australia, Canada, Germany as well as the US.

13. Anderson does not share these views. The footnotes of that chapter contain a wealth of references.

Appendix: English Legislation with African Equivalents

Libel Act 1843
(Lord Campbell's Act)

1. In any action for defamation it shall be lawful for the defendant (after notice in writing of his intention so to do), duly given to the plaintiff at the time of filing or delivering the plea in such action) to give in evidence, in mitigation of damages, that he made or offered an apology to the plaintiff for such defamation before the commencement of the action, or as soon afterwards as he had an opportunity of doing so, in case the action shall have been commenced before there was an opportunity of making or offering such apology.

Kenya s. 16(1), Zambia s. 12(1), Nigeria: Abia etc. s. 17, Delta, Ogun etc. s. 8

2. In an action for a libel contained in any public newspaper or other periodical publication, it shall be competent to the defendant to plead that such libel was inserted in such newspaper or other periodical publication without actual malice, and without gross negligence, and that before the commencement of the action, or at the earliest opportunity afterwards, he inserted in such newspaper or other periodical publication a full apology for the said libel, or, if the newspaper or periodical publication in which the said libel appeared should be ordinarily published at intervals exceeding one week, had offered to publish the said apology in any newspaper or periodical publication to be selected by the plaintiff in such action; *and every such defendant shall upon filing such plea, be at liberty to pay into court a sum of money by way of amends for the injury sustained by the publication of such libel, and such payment into court shall be of the same effect and be available in the same manner and to the same extent, and be subject to the same rules and regulations as to payment of costs and the form of pleading, except so far as regards the pleading of the additional facts hereinbefore required to be pleaded by such defendant, as if actions for libel had not been excepted from the personal actions in which it is lawful to pay money into court under an Act passed in the session of Parliament held in the fourth year of his late Majesty, intituled "An Act for the further Amendment of the Law, and better advancement of justice,"* [words in italics repealed in England by Civil Procedure Acts Repeal Act 1979] and to such plea to such action it shall be competent to the plaintiff to reply generally denying the whole of such plea.

Kenya s. 12, Zambia s. 10, Nigeria: Abia etc. s. 14, Delta, Ogun etc. s. 14

Libel Act 1845

2. It shall not be competent to any defendant in such action, ... to file any such plea, without at the same time making a payment of money into court by way of amends *as provided by the said Act* [words in italics repealed], but every such plea so filed without payment of money into court shall be deemed a nullity and may be treated as such by the plaintiff in the action.

Law of Libel Amendment Act 1888

1. In the construction of this Act the word "newspaper" shall have the same meaning as in the Newspaper Libel and Registration Act 1881.

3. A fair and accurate report in any newspaper of proceedings publicly heard before any court exercising judicial authority shall, if published contemporaneously with such proceedings, be privileged: provided that nothing in this section shall authorise the publication of any blasphemous or indecent matter.

Kenya s. 6*, Sierra Leone s. 10(5)*, Zambia s. 8, Nigeria: Abia etc. s. 11(1), Delta, Ogun etc. s. 15*, Lagos s. 10,
* specifically refers to **absolute** privilege

4. A fair and accurate report published in any newspaper of the proceedings of a public meeting, or (except where neither the public nor any newspaper reporter is admitted) of any meeting of a vestry, town council, school board, board of guardians, board or local authority formed or constituted under the provisions of any Act of Parliament, or of any committee appointed by any of the above-mentioned bodies, or of any meeting of any commissioners authorised to act by letters patent, Act of Parliament, warrant under the Royal Sign Manual, or other lawful warrant or authority, select committees of either House of Parliament, justices of the peace in quarter sessions assembled for administrative or deliberative purposes, and the publication at the request of any Government office or department, officer of state, commissioner of police, or chief constable of any notice or report issued by them for the information of the public, shall be privileged, unless it shall be proved that such report or publication was published or made maliciously: Provided that nothing in this section shall authorise the publication of any blasphemous or indecent matter; Provided also, that the protection intended to be afforded by this section shall not be available as a defence in any proceedings if it shall be proved that the defendant has been requested to insert in the newspaper in which the report or other publication complained of appeared a reasonable letter or statement by way of contradiction or explanation of such report or other publication, and has refused or neglected to insert the same; Provided further, that nothing in this section contained shall be deemed or construed to limit or abridge any privilege now by law existing, or to protect the publication of any matter not of public concern and the publication of which is not for the public benefit.

For the purposes of this section "public meeting" shall mean any meeting bona fide and lawfully held for a lawful purpose, and for the furtherance or discussion of any matter of public concern, whether the admission thereto be general or restricted.

[Repealed by 1952 Act s. 18 (3)]

5. It shall be competent for a judge or the court, upon application by or on behalf of two or more defendants in actions in respect to the same, or substantially the same, libel brought by one and the same person, to make an order for the consolidation of such actions, so that they shall be tried together, and after such order has been made, and before the trial of the said actions, the defendants in any new actions instituted in respect to the same, or substantially the same, libel shall also be entitled to be joined in a common action upon a joint application being made by such new defendants and the defendants in the actions already consolidated.

In a consolidated action under this section the jury shall assess the whole amount of the damages (if any) in one sum, but a separate verdict shall be taken for or against each defendant in the same way as if the actions consolidated had been tried separately; and if the jury shall have found a verdict against the defendant or defendants in more than one of the actions so consolidated, they shall proceed to apportion the amount of damages which they shall have so found between and against the said last-mentioned defendants; and the judge at the trial, if he awards to the plaintiff the costs of the action, shall thereupon make such order as he shall deem just for the apportionment of such costs between and against such defendants.

Kenya s. 17,Sierra Leone s. 15, Zambia s. 15, Nigeria: Abia etc. s. 16, Delta, Ogun etc., s. 7, Lagos s. 14

6. *At the trial of an action for a libel contained in any newspaper the defendant shall be at liberty to give in evidence in mitigation of damages that the plaintiff has already recovered (or has brought actions for) damages or has received or agreed to receive compensation in respect of a libel or libels to the same purport or effect as the libel for which such action has been brought.*

[Replaced by s. 12 English 1952 Act - see below]

Slander of Women Act 1891

1. Words spoken and published which impute unchastity or adultery to any woman or girl shall not require special damage to render them actionable. Provided always that in any action for words spoken and made actionable by this Act, a plaintiff shall

not recover more costs than damages, unless the judge shall certify that there was reasonable ground for bringing the action.

Kenya s. 4, Sierra Leone, s. 3, Zambia s. 4, Nigeria: Abia etc., s.5, Delta, Ogun etc. s. 4, Lagos - not reproduced

Defamation Act 1952

1. *Broadcast statements* - For the purposes of the law of libel and slander, the broadcasting of words by means of wireless telegraphy shall be treated as publication in permanent form.

Kenya s. 8, Sierra Leone s. 4 , Zambia s. 18(1), Nigeria: Abia, Delta Ogun etc., Lagos s. 3

2. *Slander affecting official, professional or business reputation.*--In an action for slander in respect of words, calculated to disparage the plaintiff in any office, profession, calling, trade or business held or carried on by him at the time of the publication, it shall not be necessary to allege or prove special damage, whether or not the words are spoken of the plaintiff in the way of his office, profession, calling, trade or business.

Kenya s. 3, Sierra Leone s. 5, Zambia s. 3, Nigeria: Abia etc. s. 4, Delta , Ogun etc. Law s. 5 Lagos s. 4

3. *Slander of title, etc*--...

4. *Unintentional defamation.*--(1) A person who has published words alleged to be defamatory of another person may, if he claims that the words were published by him innocently in relation to that other person, make an offer of amends under this section; and in any such case -

(a) if the offer is accepted by the party aggrieved and is duly performed, no proceedings for libel or slander shall be taken or continued by that party against the person making the offer in respect of the publication in question (but without prejudice to any cause of action against any other person jointly responsible for that publication);

(b) if the offer is not accepted by the party aggrieved, then, except as otherwise provided by this section, it shall be a defence, in any proceedings by him for libel or slander against the person making the offer in respect of the publication in question, to prove that the words complained of were published by the defendant innocently in relation to the plaintiff and that the offer was made as soon as practicable after the defendant received notice that they were or might be defamatory of the plaintiff, and has not been withdrawn.

(2) An offer of amends under this section must be expressed to be made for the purposes of this section, and must be accompanied by an affidavit specifying the facts relied upon by the person making it to show that the words in question were published by him innocently in relation to the party aggrieved; and for the purposes of a defence under paragraph (b) of subsection (1) of this section no evidence, other than evidence of facts specified in the affidavit, shall be admissible on behalf of that person to prove that the words were so published.

(3) An offer of amends under this section shall be understood to mean an offer -

(a) in any case, to publish or join in the publication of a suitable correction of the words complained of, and a sufficient apology to the party aggrieved in respect of those words;
(b) where copies of a document or record containing the said words have been distributed by or with the knowledge of the person making the offer, to take such steps as are reasonably practicable on his part for notifying persons to whom copies have been so distributed that the words are alleged to be defamatory of the party aggrieved.

(4) Where an offer of amends under this section is accepted by the party aggrieved -

(a) any question as to the steps to be taken in fulfilment of the offer as so accepted shall in default of agreement between the parties be referred to and determined by the High Court, whose decision thereon shall be final;
(b) the power of the court to make orders as to costs in proceedings by the party aggrieved against the person making the offer in respect of the publication in question, or in proceedings in respect of the offer under paragraph (a) of this subsection, shall include power to order the payment by the person making the offer to the party aggrieved of costs on an indemnity basis and any expenses reasonably incurred or to be incurred by that party in consequence of the publication in question;

and if no such proceedings as aforesaid are taken, the High Court may, upon application made by the party aggrieved, make any such order for the payment of such costs and expenses as aforesaid as could be made in such proceedings.

(5) For the purposes of this section words shall be treated as published by one person (in this subsection referred to as the publisher) innocently in relation to another person if and only if the following conditions are satisfied, that is to say -

(a) that the publisher did not intend to publish them of and concerning that other person, and did not know of circumstances by virtue of which they might be understood to refer to him; or

(b) that the words were not defamatory on the face of them, and the publisher did not know of circumstances by virtue of which they might be understood to be defamatory of that other person;

and in either case that the publisher exercised all reasonable care in relation to the publication; and any reference in this subsection to the publisher shall be construed as including a reference to any servant or agent of his who was concerned with the contents of the publication.

(6) Paragraph (b) of subsection (l) of this section shall not apply in relation to the publication by any person of words of which he is not the author unless he proves that the words were written by the author without malice.

Kenya s. 13, Sierra Leone s. 7, Zambia s. 11, Nigeria: Abia etc. s. 7, Delta, Ogun etc. s. 10, Lagos s. 6

5. *Justification.*--In an action for libel or slander in respect of words containing two or more distinct charges against the plaintiff, a defence of justification shall not fail by reason only that the truth of every charge is not proved if the words not proved to be true do not materially injure the plaintiff's reputation having regard to the truth of the remaining charges.

Kenya s. 14, Sierra Leone s. 8, Zambia s. 6, Nigeria: Abia etc. s. 8, Delta, Ogun etc. s. 11, Lagos s. 7

6. *Fair comment.*--In an action for libel or slander in respect of words consisting partly of allegations of fact and partly of expression of opinion, a defence of fair comment shall not fail by reason only that the truth of every allegation of fact is not proved if the expression of opinion is fair comment having regard to such of the facts alleged or referred to in the words complained of as are proved.

Kenya s. 15,, Sierra Leone s. 9, Zambia s. 7, Nigeria Abia etc. s. 9, Delta, Ogun etc. s. 12, Lagos s. 8

7. *Qualified privilege of newspapers.*--(l) Subject to the provisions of this section, the publication in a newspaper of any such report or other matter as is mentioned in the Schedule to this Act shall be privileged unless the publication is proved to be made with malice.

(2) In an action for libel in respect of the publication of any such report or matter as is mentioned in Part II of the Schedule to this Act, the provisions of this section shall not be a defence if it is proved that the defendant has been requested by the plaintiff to publish in the newspaper in which the original publication was made a reasonable letter or statement by way of explanation or contradiction, and has refused or neglected to do so, or has done so in a manner not adequate or not reasonable having regard to all the circumstances.

(3) Nothing in this section shall be construed as protecting the publication of any matter the publication of which is prohibited by law, or of any matter which is not of public concern and the publication of which is not for the public benefit.

(4) Nothing in this section shall be construed as limiting or abridging any privilege subsisting (otherwise than by virtue of section four of the Law of Libel Amendment Act 1888) immediately before the commencement of this Act.

Kenya s. 7,, Sierra Leone s. 10, Zambia s. 8, Nigeria: Abia etc. s. 10, Delta, Ogun etc. s. 16, Lagos s. 9

(5) In this section the expression "newspaper" means any paper containing public news or observations thereon, or consisting wholly or mainly of advertisements, which is printed for sale and is published in the United Kingdom either periodically or in parts or numbers at intervals not exceeding thirty-six days.

Kenya s. 2,, Sierra Leone s. 10(6), Nigeria: Abia etc. s. 2, Delta, Ogun etc. s. 2, Lagos s. 9(5)

8. *Extent of Law of Libel Amendment Act 1888, s.* 3.--Section three of the Law of Libel Amendment Act 1888 (which relates to contemporary reports of proceedings before courts exercising judicial authority) shall apply and apply only to courts exercising judicial authority within the United Kingdom.

Kenya s. 6, Sierra Leone s. 10 (5), Zambia s. 8, Nigeria: Abia etc. s. 11*, Delta, Ogun etc. s. 15*, Lagos s. 10#

*refers to "Nigeria" # refers to Lagos

9. *Extension of certain defences to broadcasting.*--(1) Section three of the Parliamentary Papers Act 1840 (which confers protection in respect of proceedings for printing extracts from or abstracts of parliamentary papers) shall have effect as if the reference to printing included a reference to broadcasting by means of wireless telegraphy.

(2) Section seven of this Act and section three of the Law of Libel Amendment Act 1888 as amended by this Act shall apply in relation to reports or matters broadcast by means of wireless telegraphy as part of any programme or service provided by means of a broadcasting station within the United Kingdom, and in relation to any broadcasting by means of wireless telegraphy of any such report or matter, as they apply in relation to reports and matters published in a newspaper and to publication in a newspaper; and subsection (2) of the said section seven shall have effect, in relation to any such broadcasting, as if for the words "in the newspaper in which" there were substituted the words "in the manner in which."

Kenya s. 8(2), Sierra Leone s. 11, Zambia s. 18(2), Nigeria: Abia etc. s. 12(1), Delta, Ogun etc. s. 17(1), Lagos s. 11(1)

(3) In this section "broadcasting station" means any station in respect of which a licence granted by the Postmaster General under the enactments relating to wireless telegraphy is in force, being a licence which (by whatever form of words) authorises the use of the station for the purpose of providing broadcasting services for general reception.

Sierra Leone s. 9, Zambia s. 7, Nigeria: Abia etc. s. 12(2), Delta, Ogun etc. s. 17(2), Lagos s. 11(2)

10. *Limitation on privilege at elections.*--A defamatory statement published by or on behalf of a candidate in any election to a local government authority or to Parliament shall not be deemed to be published on a privileged occasion on the ground that it is material to a question in issue in the election, whether or not the person by whom it is published is qualified to vote at the election.

Kenya not reproduced, Sierra Leone s. 12, Zambia s. 14, Nigeria: Abia etc. s. 13, Delta, Ogun etc. s. 13, Lagos s. 12

11. *Agreements for indemnity.*--An agreement for indemnifying any person against civil liability for libel in respect of the publication of any matter shall not be unlawful unless at the time of the publication that person knows that the matter is defamatory, and does not reasonably believe there is a good defence to any action brought upon it.

Kenya s. 18,, Sierra Leone s. 13, Zambia s. 13, Nigeria: Abia etc. s. 15, Delta, Ogun etc. s. 18, Lagos s. 13

12. *Evidence of other damages recovered by plaintiff.*--In any action for libel or slander the defendant may give evidence in mitigation of damages that the plaintiff has recovered damages, or has brought actions for damages, for libel or slander in respect of the publication of words to the same effect as the words on which the action is founded, or has received or agreed to receive compensation in respect of any such publication.

Kenya s. 16(2), Sierra Leone s. 14, Zambia s. 12(2), Nigeria: Abia etc. s. 18, Delta, Ogun etc. s. 9, Lagos not reproduced

13. *Consolidation of actions for slander etc.*--Section five of the Law of Libel Amendment Act 1888 (which provides for the consolidation, on the application of defendants, of two or more actions for libel by the same plaintiff) shall apply to actions for slander...; and references in that section to the same, or substantially the same, libel, shall be construed accordingly.

Kenya s. 17(4), Sierra Leone s. 15(3), Zambia s. 15(4), Nigeria: Abia etc. s. 16(3), Delta, Ogun etc. s. 7(3), Lagos s. 14(3)

16. *Interpretation.*--(1) Any reference in this Act to words shall be construed as including a reference to pictures, visual images, gestures and other methods of signifying meaning.

Kenya s. 2, Sierra Leone s. 2(2), Zambia s. 2, Nigeria: Abia etc. s. 2(2), Delta, Ogun etc. s. 2(1), Lagos s. 2(2)

(2) The provisions of Part III of the Schedule to this Act shall have effect for the purposes of the interpretation of that Schedule.

(3) In this Act "broadcasting by means of wireless telegraphy" means publication for general reception by means of wireless telegraphy within the meaning of the Wireless Telegraphy Act 1949, and "broadcast by means of wireless telegraphy" shall be construed accordingly.

(4) Where words broadcast by means of wireless telegraphy are simultaneously transmitted by telegraph as defined by the Telegraph Act 1863, in accordance with a licence granted by the Postmaster General the provisions of this Act shall apply as if the transmission were broadcasting by means of wireless telegraphy.

18 ....(3) Sections four and six of the Law of Libel Amendment Act 1888 are hereby repealed.

SCHEDULE

Sections 7, 16

NEWSPAPER STATEMENTS HAVING QUALIFIED PRIVILEGE

[Note: all detailed provisions in the various African pieces of legislation are not noted here. The legislation must be read carefully. A common difference is between "Her Majesty's Dominions" and "Commonwealth" - the latter on the face of it embracing more countries, but other legislation may define one or both of these terms for local purposes.]

PART I

STATEMENTS PRIVILEGED WITHOUT EXPLANATION OR CONTRADICTION

1. A fair and accurate report of any proceedings in public of the legislature of any part of Her Majesty's dominions outside Great Britain.

2. A fair and accurate report of any proceedings in public of an international organisation of which the United Kingdom or Her Majesty's Government in the United Kingdom is a member or of any international conference to which that government sends a representative.

3. A fair and accurate report of any proceedings in public of an international court
Not reproduced in Kenya,

4. A fair and accurate report of any proceedings before a court exercising jurisdiction throughout any part of Her Majesty's dominions outside the United Kingdom, or of any proceedings before a court-martial held outside the United Kingdom under the Naval Discipline Act 1957, the Army Act 1955, or the Air Force Act 1955

5. A fair and accurate report of any proceedings in public of a body or person appointed to hold a public inquiry by the government or legislature of any part of Her Majesty's dominions outside the United Kingdom.
Sierra Leone: restricted to Sierra Leone

6. A fair and accurate copy of or extract from any register kept in pursuance of an Act of Parliament which is open to inspection by the public, or of any other document, which is required by the law of any part of the United Kingdom to be open to inspection by the public.

7. A notice or advertisement published by or on the authority of any court within the United Kingdom or any judge or officer of such a court.

PART II

STATEMENTS PRIVILEGED SUBJECT TO EXPLANATION OR CONTRADICTION

8. A fair and accurate report of the findings or decision of any of the following associations, or of any committee or governing body thereof, that is to say--
(a) an association formed in the United Kingdom for the purpose of promoting or encouraging the exercise of or interest in any art, science, religion or learning, and empowered by its constitution to exercise control over or adjudicate upon matters of interest or concern to the association, or the actions or conduct of any persons subject to such control or adjudication;
(b) an association formed in the United Kingdom for the purpose of promoting or safeguarding the interests of any trade, business, industry or profession, or of the persons carrying on or engaged in any trade, business, industry or profession, and empowered by its constitution to exercise control over or adjudicate upon matters

connected with the trade, business, industry or profession, or the actions or conduct of those persons;

(c) an association formed in the United Kingdom for the purpose of promoting or safeguarding the interests of any game, sport or pastime to the playing of exercise of which members of the public are invited or admitted, and empowered by its constitution to exercise control over or adjudicate upon persons connected with or taking part in the game, sport or pastime, being a finding or decision relating to a person who is a member of or is subject by virtue of any contract to the control of the association.

9. A fair and accurate report of the proceedings at any public meeting held in the United Kingdom, that is to say, a meeting bona fide and lawfully held for a lawful purpose and for the furtherance or discussion of any matter of public concern, whether the admission to the meeting is general or restricted.

10. A fair and accurate report of the proceedings at any meeting or sitting in any part of the United Kingdom of -

(a) any local authority or committee of a local authority or local authorities;

(b) any justice or justices of the peace acting otherwise than as a court exercising judicial authority;

Not reproduced in Kenya, Zambia. Sierra Leone: Magistrate

(c) any commission, tribunal, committee or person appointed for the purposes of any inquiry by Act of Parliament, by Her Majesty or by a Minister of the Crown;

(d) any person appointed by a local authority to hold a local inquiry in pursuance of any Act of Parliament;

(e) any other tribunal, board, committee or body constituted by or under, and exercising functions under, an Act of Parliament,

not being a meeting or sitting admission to which is denied to representatives of newspapers and other members of the public.

11. A fair and accurate report of the proceedings at a general meeting of any company or association constituted, registered or certified by or under any Act of Parliament or incorporated by Royal Charter, not being a private company within the meaning of the Companies Act 1948.

12. A copy or fair and accurate report or summary of any notice or other matter issued for the information of the public by or on behalf of any government department, officer of state, local authority or chief officer of police.

PART III

INTERPRETATION

....

"international court" means the International Court of Justice and any other judicial or arbitral tribunal deciding matters in dispute between states;

"legislature" in relation to any territory comprised in Her Majesty's dominions which is subject to a central and a local legislature, means either of those legislatures;

......

"part of Her Majesty's dominions" means the whole of any territory within those dominions which is subject to a separate legislature.

14. In relation to the following countries and territories, that is to say, India, the Republic of Ireland, any protectorate, protected state or trust territory within the meaning of the British Nationality Act 1948, any territory administered under the authority of a country mentioned in subsection (3) of section one of that Act [now sch. 3 British Nationality Act 1981, listing countries of the Commonwealth], the Sudan, and the New Hebrides [now Vanuatu], the provisions of this Schedule shall have effect as they have effect in relation to Her Majesty's dominions, and references therein to Her Majesty's dominions shall be construed accordingly.

[This is Part I in the Lagos Schedule]

Bibliography

Abbreviations: Ang-Am LR *Anglo-American Law Review*; Col LR *Columbia Law Review*; EALJ *East African Law Journal*; EALR *Eastern African Law Review*; ICLQ *International and Comparative Law Quarterly*; JAL *Journal of African Law*; JILI *Journal of the Indian Law Institute*; Med L & Pr *Media Law and Practice*; MLR *Modern Law Review*; NBJ *Nigerian Bar Journal*; Nigeria J Contemp L *Nigerian Journal of Contemporary Law*; NILQ *Northern Ireland Law Quarterly*; NLJ *New Law Journal*; Phil L R *Philippines Law Review*; PL *Public Law*; RADIC *Review Africain de Droit International et Comparé* [*African Review of International and Comparative Law*]; Rev G Law *Review of Ghana Law*; SALJ *South African Law Journal*; Sing L Leg St *Singapore Journal of Legal Studies*; SLJR *Sudan Law Journal and Reports*; UBCLR *University of British Columbia Law Review*; UGLJ *University of Ghana Law Journal*; Wash L R *Washington Law Review*

Abel, R. (1970), "Case Method Research in the Customary Law of Wrongs in Kenya - II" 6 EALJ 20

Achebe, C. (1963), *No Longer at Ease,* Heinemann African Writers, London

Africa Watch (1990), *Where Silence Rules: The Suppression of Dissent in Malawi,* Africa Watch, New York

Agbaje, Adigun A.B. (1990), "Freedom of the press and party politics in Nigeria: precepts, retrospect and prospects" 89 *Af. Affairs* 205

Agbaje, Adigun A.B. (1992), *The Nigerian Press, Hegemony and the Social Construction of Legitimacy 1960-1983,* Edwin Mellor Press, Lewiston, NY

Aguda, T.A. (1980a), *Practice and Procedure of the Supreme Court, Court of Appeal and High Courts of Nigeria,* Sweet and Maxwell, London

Aguda, T.A. (1980b), *Law and Practice Relating to Evidence in Nigeria,* Sweet and Maxwell, London

Allott, A. (1970), *New Essays in African Law,* Butterworths, London

Anderson, David (1992), "Is Libel Law Worth Reforming?" in Soloski and Bezanson, *Reforming Libel Law*, The Guilford Press, New York

Anon (1971), 7 EALJ 53

Anon (1988), *Amorc v Challenge: The Million Naira Judgment,* Challenge Publishers, Jos

Arogundade, Lanre (1994), "A Decade of Siege" *Liberty,* Civil Liberties Organisation Sept.-Dec.

Ashton, Hugh (1967) *The Basuto* 2nd. ed. Oxford University Press for the International African Institute, Oxford

Article 19 (1991), *Truth from Below: The Emergent Press in Africa,* London

Australia (1979), Law Reform Commission *Unfair Publication: Defamation and Privacy* (Rep. No. 11), Australian Government Publishing Service, Canberra

Barendt, E. (1985), *Freedom of Speech,* Clarendon Press, Oxford

Barendt, Eric *et al.* (1997) *Libel and the Media: The Chilling Effect*, Clarendon Press, Oxford

Bellah, Robert N. (1986), "The Meaning of Reputation in American Society" 74 Calif LR 743

Bezanson, Randall P. (1985), "Libel Law and the Reality of Libel Litigation" 71 Iowa LR 226

Bimpong-Buta, S.Y. (1973), "Customary Mores and the Sale of Photographs of a Married Woman" (1973) 5 Rev G Law 3

Boberg, P.Q.R. (1989), "Defamation South African Style - The Odessey of Animus Injuriandi" in C. Visser, *Essays in Honour of Ellison Kahn,* Juta, Cape Town

Bogdan, Michael (1989),*The Law of Mauritius and Seychelles: A Study of Two Small Mixed Jurisdictions,* Luristforlaget i Lund, Lund

Bohannan, P.J. (1957), *Justice and Judgment among the Tiv,* Oxford University Press, London

Brazier M. (1976), "Judicial Immunity and the Independence of the Judiciary" PL 397

Brietzke, P. (1972), "Witchcraft and Law in Malawi" 8 EALJ 1

Brown, B.J. (1992), "Latent Effects of Law: The Defamation Experience" Sing J Leg Studies 315

Burchell, Jonathan M. (1974), "The Criteria of Defamation" 91 SALJ 178

Burchell, Jonathan M. (1985), *The Law of Defamation in South Africa,* Juta, Capetown

Carter-Ruck, Peter F. *et al.* (1992), *Carter-Ruck on Libel and Slander* (4th. ed.), Butterworth, London

Chanock, M. (1985), *Law, Custom and Social Order: The Colonial Experience in Malawi and Zimbabwe,* Cambridge University Press, Cambridge

Chloros, A.G. (1977), *Codification in a Mixed Jurisdiction: The Civil and Commercial Law of Seychelles*, North-Holland, Amsterdam

Clerk & Lindsell (1995), *Clerk & Lindsell on Torts* (17th ed., Gen. editor Margaret Brazier) Sweet & Maxwell, London

Cmnd 5909 (1975) *Report of the Committee on Defamation* (Faulks Report)

Cotran, E. (1970), in A.N. Allott, *Juridical and Legal Systems in Africa* (2nd. ed.), London

Cottrell, J. (1988), "The Role of the Law of Torts in Africa" 31 JAL 161

Crabb (1956), "Statements respecting race" 46 ALR 1287

Dalloz, *Hebdomadaire de Jurisprudence* 1939 [precedents weekly]

Daniels, Janet (1973), "Protecting the Chastity of a Modern Modest Matron" 5 Rev G Law 27

Danquah, J.B. (1938), *Cases in Akan Law: Decisions Delivered by the Honourable Sir Ofori Atta KBE*, Routledge, London

Date-Bah, S.K. (1973a), "Reflections on the Law of Defamation in Ghana" 10 Rev G Law 129

Date-Bah, S.K. (1973b), "The Right to Publish the Truth and the Plea of Justification: A Reappraisal" 10 UGLJ 36

Date-Bah, S.K. (1973c), "Unauthorised Use of a Unmarried Woman's Picture: Defamation or Unlawful Invasion of Privacy?" 5 Rev G Law 17

Date-Bah, S.K. (1977), "Defamation, the Right to Privacy and Unauthorised Commercial Use of Photographs: *Kate Anthony v University of Cape Coast* Revisited" 14 UGLJ 101

Deng, Francis (1965), "The Family and the Law of Torts in African Customary Law" SLJR 535

Devlin, P. (1956), *Trial by Jury,* Stevens, London

Driver, Christopher (1996), "Odyssey of the new Nigeria", obituary for Nnamdi Azikiwe, *Guardian* (UK) May 14

Edgeworth B. & M. Newcity, (1992), "Politicians, Defamation Law and the 'Public Figure' Defence" 10 *Law in Context* 39

Ewelukwa, D. (1977), "The Independence of the Judiciary" 14 NBJ 38

Fawehinmi, G. (1992), *Courts' System in Nigeria: A Guide,* Nig. Law Publishers Ltd., Lagos

Fawehinmi, G. (1988), *The Murder of 'Dele Giwa - The Right of a Private Prosecutor* Nigerian Law Publishers, Lagos

Feltoe, G. (1976), "Private Lives and Public Sins" 16 Rho. LJ 21

Feltoe, G. (1992), "Damages for Defamation" 4 (4) *Legal Forum*

Feltoe, G. (1993), "The Press and the Law of Defamation: Achieving a Better Balance" 5 (2) *Legal Forum* 43

Fish, Stanley (1994), *There's No Such Thing as Free Speech: And It's a Good Thing, Too,* Oxford UP, New York.

Fleming, J. (1978), "Retraction and Reply: Alternative Remedies for Defamation" 12 UBCLR 15

Fleming, J. (1992), *The Law of Torts,* (8th. ed.) Law Book Co., Sydney

Fleming, J. (1991), "Libel and Constitutional Free Speech" in P. Cane and J. Stapleton eds., *Essays for Patrick Atiyah,* Clarendon Press, Oxford

Ghai, Yash (1987), "Law, Development and African Scholarship" 50 MLR 750

Ghai, Yash (1981), "Law and Lawyers in Kenya and Tanzania" in Dias, *et al.*, eds., *Lawyers in the Third World: Comparative and Developmental Perspectives,* Scandinavian Institute of African Studies, Uppsala

Ghartey, Joe (1994), "Right to Freedom of Expression" *Liberty* Sept-Dec. 25

Gillmor, D.M. (1992), *Power, Publicity and the Abuse of Libel Law,* Oxford, New York

Gluckman, M. (1963), "Gossip and Scandal" 4 *Current Anthropology* 307

Goldin B. & M. Gelfand (1975), *African Law and Custom in Rhodesia,* Juta, Capetown

Goulbourne, S. (1976), "Recent Trends in the Tanzanian Tort of Defamation and their Reflection of Tanzanian Socialism" 9 EALR 99

Green, M.M. (1964), *Ibo Village Affairs* (2nd. ed.) Praeger, New York

Harris, Matthew (1996), "Sharing the Privilege: Parliamentarians, Defamation and Bills of Rights" Auckland ULR 45

Hellum, A. (1993), "Gender and Legal Change in Zimbabwe: Childless Women and Divorce from a Socio-Cultural and Historical Perspective" in Adelman, S. and Paliwala, A., *Law and Crisis in the Third World*, Hans Zell, London

Helmholz, R.H. (1985), *Select Cases on Defamation to 1600*, Selden Society (Vol. 101) London

Hodgin, R.W. (1973), "Defamation in East Africa" 17 JAL 66

Holdsworth, W.S. (1941), "A Chapter of Accidents in the Law of Libel" 57 LQR 71

Hor, M. (1992), "The Freedom of Speech and Defamation" Sing J Leg Studies 542

Hudson, A.H. (1987), "Dictation: Libel or Slander?" 131 SJ 1236

Hudson, A.H. (1990) "Defamatory Allegations of Insolvency" 41 NILQ 267

Hunt, P.M.A. (1970), *South African Criminal Law and Procedure*, Juta, Capetown

Ireland, (1991), Law Reform Commission, *Civil Law of Defamation*, Dublin

Janis, Mark W. & Richard S. Kay (1990), *European Human Rights Law*, Univ. of Connecticut Law School Foundation Press, Hartford

Kanyoke, S.E. (1973), "Problems of Choice of Law" 5 Rev G L 31

Karikari, Kwame (1993), "Africa: the press and democracy" 34 (3) *Race and Class* 55

Kasoma, Francis P. (1995), "The Role of the Independent Media in Africa's Change to Democracy" 17 *Media, Culture and Society* 537

Kleyn, D. and Viljoen, F. (1995), *Beginners' Guide for Law Students*, Juta, Capetown

Kodilinye, Gilbert (1982) *Nigerian Law of Tort*, Sweet & Maxwell, London

Konde, Hadji S. (1984), *Press Freedom in Tanzania*, Eastern Africa Pubs. Ltd., Arusha

Kwikima, M.H.A. (1966), "Defamation in Nyamwezi Law and Custom" 1 J of Denning Law Soc 39

Lawson, Amos & Walton, (1967), *Introduction to French Law* (3rd. ed.), Clarendon Press, Oxford

Lee, R.W. and Honoré, Tony (1979), *The South African Law of Obligations* (2nd. ed. by Newman and McQuoid-Mason) Butterworths, Durban

Lidsky, Larissa B. (1996), "Defamation, Reputation and the Myth of Community" 71 Wash LR 1

Liebesny, H.J. (1975), *The Law of the Near and Middle East*, State Univ. of NY, Albany

Lippman, Matthew *et al.*, (1988), *Islamic Criminal Law and Procedure: An Introduction*, Praeger, New York

Littleton, Richard (1991), "The Libel Belt" *Punch* 21-27 August 22

Luckham, R. (1976), "The Economic Base for Private Law Practice" in Davies & Woodman, *Essays in Ghanaian Law,* Faculty of Law, University of Ghana, Legon

Mair, Lucy (1977), *African Kingdoms,* Clarendon Press, Oxford

Maja-Pearce, A. (1990), "The Press in West Africa" 6/19 *Index on Censorship*

Maja-Pearce, A. (1991), *Who's Afraid of Wole Soyinka? Essays on Censorship,* Heinemann, Oxford

Majzoub, A.E. (1985), "Some Comparative Aspects of Islamic and English Law of Defamation" SLJR 3

Makec, J.W. (1988), *The Customary Law of the Dinka People of Sudan,* Afroworld, London

Markesinis, B.S. and Deakin S.F. (1994), *Tort Law,* Clarendon Press, Oxford

McCullough, J.W. (1971), "Defamation among the Luo of Kenyan" 7 EALJ 191

McGonagle, Marie (1990), 12 *Dublin University LJ* 138

McGregor, Harvey (1988) *McGregor on Damages,* (15th. ed.) Sweet & Maxwell, London

Mendoza, Vincente V. (1987), "The Supreme Court and the Supreme Law: An Annual Survey 1988-89" 62 Phil LJ 407

Middleton, (1987), "Employers Face Upsurge in Suits Over Defamation" National LJ 1, May 4, 1987

Molotsi, S.M. (1984), "The Law of Defamation: Suggested Reforms" App. III of Zambia Law Development Commission Working Paper on Law of Defamation, Lusaka

Moreau, R.F. (1944), "Joking Relationships in Tanganyika" XIV *Africa* 386

Morris, H.F. and Read, James S. (1972), *Indirect Rule and the Search for Justice,* Clarendon Press, Oxford

Mtengeti, R.A. (1985), "Trends in the Tort of Defamation in Tanzania" 6 J Media L & Pr 47

Mtengeti-Migiro, R. (1992), "Freedom of Expression, the Press and Defamation: The Case of Tanzania" 4 RADIC 972

Muburimusoke, C. (1978), "Application of the Received Law of Torts in East Africa and the Problem of Transplanting Legal Norms" in T.W. Bechtler, ed., *Law in a Social Context: Liber Amicorum Honouring Professor Lon L. Fuller,* Kluwer, Deventer

Mukale, J. (1986), "My 28 days in captivity" *Index on Censorship* No. 8 of 1986, p. 26

Mustapha, Z. (1971), *The Common Law in the Sudan,* Clarendon Press, Oxford

Mustill & Boyd (1981), *Law and Practice of Commercial Arbitration,* Butterworths, London

Mytton, Graham (1983), *Mass Communication in Africa,* Edward Arnold, London

Narebor, Dorubo (1993), *Customary Courts: Their Relevance Today,* Jodah, Benin

New Zealand (1977) *Recommendations on the Law of Defamation: Report of the Committee on Defamation*

Nigeria, Law Reform Commission 1987 *Report of the Review of Pre-1900 English Statutes in Force in Nigeria,* Federal Government Printer, Lagos

Nigeria, Constitution Drafting Committee (1976) *The Draft Constitution,* Lagos: Federal Ministry of Information

Nketia, J.H. Kwabena (1963), *Drumming in Akan Communities in Ghana,* T. Nelson for the University of Ghana, Edinburgh

Nsugbe, Phillip O. (1974), *Ohaffia: A Matrilieal Ibo People,* Clarendon, Oxford

Nzunda C.M.S. (1981), "The Controversy over the Statutes of General Application in Malawi" 25 JAL 115

Obi, S.N.C. (1977), *Customary Law Manual - for Anambra and Imo,* Government Printer, Enugu

Ochieng, Philip (1992), *I Accuse the Press: An Insider's View of the Media and Politics in Africa*, Initiatives Publishers & ACTS Press, Nairobi

Ogunniran, Hakeem (1992), "Awarding Exemplary Damages in Tort Cases: The Dilemma of Nigerian Courts" 36 JAL 111

Ojo, J.D. (1976), "Freedom of the Press in Nigeria Since 1960: A Comparative Analysis" 18 JILI 529

Ojwang, J.B. (1992), "Civil and Customary Law in Tandem: A Kenyan Case Study in Legal Pluralism" *The Advocate* (Law Society of Kenya) Vol. II No. 1, 26

Olowofoyeku, Abimbola A. (1992), *Law of Judicial Immunities in Nigeria,* Spectrum Law Publishing, Ibadan

Olowofoyeku, Abimbola A. (1993), *Suing Judges: A Study of Judicial Immunity,* Clarendon Press, Oxford

Osei, E.A. (1970), "The Criminal in the Civil Court" 7 Rev G Law 84

Othlogile, B. (1991), "Defamation by a Judge: A Note on *Idah Ngope v James Aiden O'Brien Quinn*" 7 Lesotho LJ 107

Otieno-Abuodha, J.N. (1992), "Aids and the Tort of Defamation" 2 *The Advocate* (Law Society of Kenya) 23

Patfield, F. (1993), "Defamation, Freedom of Speech and Corporations" Jur Rev 294

Penwill, P.J. (1951), *Kamba Customary Law,* East African Literature Bureau, Nairobi

Perrott, D.L. (1965), *Index of Sudanese Cases on Personal Property, Tort and Workmen's Compensation 1898-1964* (Khartoum) (reprinted from [1965] SLJR)

Planiol, Marcel and Ripert, Georges (1952), *Droit Civil Francais Tome VI: Obligations* [French Civil Law, Vol. VI Obligations], Librairie generale de droit et de jurisprudence, Paris

Post, Robert C. (1986), "The Social Foundations of Defamation Law: Reputation and the Constitution" 74 Calif LR 691

Poulter, Sebastian (1970), *The Roman-Dutch and Sesotho Law of Delict*, Sijthoff, Leiden

Radcliffe-Brown, A.R. (1952), "On Joking Relationships" in *Structure and Function in Primitive Society,* Cohen & West, London

Raphael, Adam (1993), *Grotesque Libels,* Corgi, London

Rattray, R.A. (1929), *Ashanti Law and Constitution,* Basel Mission Book Depot, OUP, Kumasi & London

Redden, K.R. (1990), *International Cyclopedia Vol. 6, Mauritius,* Hein, Buffalo, New York

Reisman, David (1942), "Democracy and Defamation: Control of Group Libel" 42 Col LR 727

Roberts, S. (1979), *Order and Dispute: An Introduction to Legal Anthropology,* Penguin, Harmondsworth

Robertson, G. & Nicol, A. (1992), *Media Law* (3rd. ed.), Penguin, Harmondsworth

Rogers, (1981), "Some Problems of Fair Comment and the Press" 10 Ang-Am LR 225

Ross, June (1996), "The Common Law of Defamation Fails to Enter the Age of the Charter" XXXV Alberta LR 117

Rwezaura, B. (1985), *Traditional Family Law and Social Change in Tanzania,* Institut für Internationale Angelengenheiten der Universität Hamburg, Baden-Baden

Sarbah, J.M. (1904a), *Fanti Law Reports of Decided Cases on Fanti Customary Law* (2nd. selection) William Clowes & Son Ltd., London

Sarbah, J.M. (1904b), *Fanti Customary Law* (2nd ed.), William Clowes & Son Ltd., London

Savatier, René, (1951)*Traité de la Responsabilite Civile en droit francais civil, administratif, professionel, procedural* Ed. 2 Vol. 1, *Les sources de la responsabilite civile*, [Treatise on civil responsibility in French civil, administrative, professional and procedural law, Vol. 2 The sources of civil responsibility] Librairie generale de droit et de jurisprudence, Paris

Scotton, J.F. (1970), "Judicial Independence and Political Expression in East Africa - Two Colonial Legacies" 6 EALJ 1

Sharland, Andrew and Loveland, Ian (1997), "The Defamation Act 1996 and Political Libels" PL 113

Shillito, R. (1994), "Police Libel Actions" 144 NLJ 194

Shivji, I. ed., (1986), *The Limits of Legal Radicalism,* Faculty of Law, University of Dar es Salaam

Shore, L. (1989), "Comment: Defamation and Employment Relationships: the New Meaning of Private Speech, Publication and Privilege" 38 Emory LJ 871

Singer, (1985), "The Subtlety of Legal Change: a lesson from Northern Zambia", A.N. Allott & G. Woodman, *People's Law and State Law,* Foris, Dordrecht

Sogbesan, A. (1971), "*Coker v. Daily Times of Nigeria*: A tedious or sagacious exercise in timorous justice?" 2 Nig J Contemp L 36

Spiller, P.R. (1989), "The Making of the Law of Delict: A Melange of Sources" in D.P. Visser, *Essays on the History of Law,* Juta, Cape Town

Spry, John (1976), *Law of Defamation in East Africa,* East African Literature Bureau, Nairobi

Stafford & Franklin, (1950), *The Principles of Native Law and the Natal Code*

Supreme Court Procedure Committee 1991, *Report on Practice and Procedure in Defamation,* London

Sutherland, D. (1992), "Fair Comment by the House of Lords?" 55 MLR 278

T.H.B. (1936), Note 10 Tulane LJ 647

Todd, Stephen M.D. *et al.*, (1991), *The Law of Torts in New Zealand,* Law Book Co., 1991

Tunc, André (1965), "The Twentieth Century Development and Function of the Law of Torts in France" 14 ICLQ 1089

Tunc, André (nd), Chapter 1 (Introduction) of *Torts* Vol XI of *International Encyclopedia of Comparative Law,* Mohr, Tübingen

Uchendu, V. (1965), *The Igbo of South-Eastern Nigeria,* Holt, Rinehart & Winston, New York

Veeder, Van Vechter (1903-4),"The History of the Law of Defamation", originally published in two parts (1903-4) 3 Col. LR 546, and 4 Col. LR 33, the first part revised and reproduced in *Select Essays in Anglo- American Legal History* (1909 Little Brown, reprinted by Oceana 1968) Vol. III, 446

Veitch, E. (1971), "Civil Defamation in Uganda 1960-70" 7 EALJ 39

Vidal, John (1997), *McLibel: Burger Culture on Trial*, Macmillan, London

Voet, Johannes (1698), *Commentarius ad Pandectus* translated by Percival Gane J (1955-8) as *The Selective Voet*, Butterworths, Durban

Walker, Sally (1995), "The Impact of the High Court's Free Speech Cases on Defamation Law" 17 Sydney LR 43

Wambali, M.K.B. (1989), "The Court of Appeal of Tanzania and the Development of the Law of Torts" 16 EALR 213

Weill, Alex and Terré, Francois (1983), *Droit Civil: Les personnes,* (5th. Ed.) Dalloz, Paris

Wilcox, Dennis L. (1982), "Black African States" in Curry, Jane Leftwich & Dassin, Joan R., eds., *Press Control around the World,* Praeger, New York

Williams, G. (1951), "The Aims of the Law of Tort" 4 CLP 137

Wilson, G.M. (1967), "Homicide and Suicide Among the Joluo of Kenya" in Bohannan, *African Homicide and Suicide,* Atheneum, New York

Zambian Law Development Commission (1984) Working Paper on Law of Defamation, Lusaka

Ziegler, D. & Asante, M.K. (1992) *Thunder and Silence: Mass Media in Africa,* African World Press Inc., Trenton NJ

Index